"Luke O'Neil is not on st[...]

"Unbelievable." – Ben Sha[...]

"The Left's new low." – Tucker Carlson

"Too many journalists are failing the American public by desperately clinging to the rules of the old world, before the Trump Nuclear Bomb hit us all. Luke O'Neil is one of the few writers who faces our grim reality the way it is, and not the way we wish it was. Compiling *Hell World* is a sin-eater's task, and we are indebted to him for doing it." – Dan Ozzi, co-author of *Tranny*

"A widely read, offbeat newsletter..." – Mike Isaac, *The New York Times*

"Luke is convinced he lives in a nightmare. Truth is, he's one of the last few people on the outside of it. *Welcome to Hell World* is a distress call from a place where hope still exists, dispatched by a man who clearly sees the insanity of life in America and believes it doesn't have to be this way. It's adorable." – Keith Buckley of Every Time I Die, author of *Watch*

"The defining feeling of being alive at this awful stupid moment in time, for me at least, is that of being locked inside myself and my perspective, looking out helplessly as various horrible things happen and keep happening and while various crimes are committed right in front of my face. It's a very specific sort of horror and a very difficult thing to write about, and I don't think anyone writes about it with more anger and more empathy or with more insight than Luke does. How he somehow makes it all enjoyable to read is something I haven't quite figured out yet, but it's a pretty remarkable achievement. Hellworld is hellworld, and this is a bad time, but Luke sees it clearly and writes about it with his whole heart, and that, to me, is good." – David Roth, Deadspin

"You're such a great writer and a handsome boy but you know I can't read that type of stuff." – Maryann O'Neil

"I don't know if there's another writer working who better channels the dread of the age than Luke O'Neil, and I know few that are his equal in terms of wit, style, and pure coruscating honesty when it comes to apprasing what happens to the self, and the soul, in a severely dysfunctional society." – Joe Keohane, author and longtime Luke editor

"One of my favorite things I read all year..." – Frida Garza, Jezebel's The Best Political Writing 2018

"Luke O'Neil's writing reverberates the pulse of our modern dissolve in ways that inspire, provoke and engage. The stories shared in Welcome to Hell World and the analysis O'Neil brings inspire self-reflection and pause in an otherwise chaotic era." – Jared Holt, Right Wing Watch

"*Welcome to Hell World* relentlessly examines the human toll of American government and society. O'Neil brings to this examination a complete lack of fear—of what people will think of him, or where logic will take him—but also an abiding sympathy for people who've been wronged. And, deploying considerable writing skill, he somehow covers these serious issues in a personal style that would make Welcome to Hell World a compelling read even if it were a series of dispatches about a restaurant's mediocre soup, instead of America's moral collapse." – Matthew Segal, civil rights lawyer

"Luke O'Neil is like no other journalist working today, fusing original reporting with memoir and frequently-profane observational humor to create what feels like a new type of truth-telling: precise, fucked-up, infuriating, and, somehow, beautiful. O'Neil's *Hell World* is bleak but humane; awful but hopeful; despairing but hilarious. In leading his willing readers to confront the daily horrors of this bizarre time, he honors the subjugated while taking a long, warm piss in the powerful's salmon tartare. This is what it looks like when a gifted writer finds his voice." – Hamish McKenzie, author and co-founder of Substack

"There's nothing out there like *Welcome to Hell World*; it's sui generis, with a sparse, Hemingwayesque writing style that smuggles in its insights to your mind. O'Neil is always landing punches, but they're always aimed upward, with surgical precision, at the people who've so meticulously crafted the Hell World we live in. O'Neil harnesses the dual forces of social transformation—anger, and white-hot empathy—with relentless skill." – Talia Lavin, author of *Culture Warlords*

"For a certain type of journalist, digging into the deep, dark secrets of modern life and laying it out there for the world to see is the only work worth pursuing. At *Hell World*, Luke is doing just that—and you can tell that he's loving the work, even when it hurts. This collection better be just the first of many." – Eoin Higgins, Common Dreams

"Luke is a beautiful and brilliant writer. His unapologetic commentary is deeply satisfying. The best part is how he invites you in like you're in your dorm with your best friends, but his words get lodged in your brain and haunt you." – Shaleen Title, Massachusetts drug policy activist

❤

WELCOME TO HELL WORLD

WELCOME TO HELL WORLD

DISPATCHES FROM THE
AMERICAN DYSTOPIA

LUKE O'NEIL

OR Books

New York · London

All rights information: rights@orbooks.com
Visit our website at www.orbooks.com
First printing 2019

Scary bunny illustrations by Nicole Barr.

Many of these essays appeared, sometimes in different form, in Luke O'Neil's Substack newsletter "Welcome to Hell World."

Library of Congress Cataloging-in-Publication Data: A catalog record for this book is available from the Library of Congress.

Typeset by Lapiz Digital.

Eagle cover: paperback ISBN 978-1-68219-211-5 • ebook ISBN 978-1-68219-215-3
Cliff cover: paperback ISBN 978-1-68219-219-1 • ebook ISBN 978-1-68219-218-4

To be caught happy in a world of misery was for an honest man the most despicable of crimes.
– Virginia Woolf, To the Lighthouse

If you wonder what I need, I will tell you just what I need.
But I gotta hear your wondering sound.
– Family Band, "Moonbeams"

You can't stay angry forever, or so I'm told.
– Pianos Become the Teeth, "Hiding"

CONTENTS

I DON'T KNOW WHAT THIS BOOK IS

Some guy from New Zealand named Hamish wanted to meet me for drinks to talk about newsletters in the summer of 2018. He said he wanted me to write a newsletter because he was starting a newsletter company and I said I don't know mate that seems like a lot of work. People from New Zealand love it when you call them mate because it makes them feel at home and you seem worldly. Fine I said then the day came when he was here in Boston and I said I was too hungover to go out on account of the recently acquired alcoholism I was cultivating but he guilted me into it and then I went and we had some drinks and then I wasn't hungover anymore which is called punting your problems into tomorrow.

As luck would have it I happened to be at one of the lowest points of my writing career and my life lol and quickly running out of money. I had been writing for a lot of fancy publications for years and that was pretty cool because when you say you write for a place people have heard of they think you are smart and good except it wasn't making me happy it had been making me miserable for a long time to be a part of the content generation cycle and besides that the industry was crumbling around me and still is. What if you could write about whatever you want Hamish said. I don't know if he actually said that but it's better for the story if I attribute it to him. Fuck it I said I'll write the stupid newsletter I said and I am glad I did because now the newsletter is a book and once you have a book out everyone thinks you're smart and good so thank you for that mate.

One thing people say about Hell World a lot now when they talk to me is that it's really good to see someone *finding their voice* and I say thank you that's very nice of you to say but the truth is I didn't have to find it I knew where it was the whole time I just needed someone to let me use it and that person was you and the people who subscribed to the newsletter so thank you for that also.

Here's the thing about whatever this all is. Starting Hell World was as much about the things I didn't want to do anymore as the things I could. I was sick of having to ask for permission to write about stories that interested me. I was sick of convincing an editor that a story would scale or do traffic. I was sick of waiting for something to be published based on marketing whims or business concerns I was not privy to. I didn't want to have a timely news peg. I didn't want to fit into the 800-1000 word count that is the norm for web writing. I didn't want someone to edit out my jokes or worse add new ones in you'd be very surprised how often that happens! I didn't want a billionaire to see me saying pee pee poo poo to human rights violators and decide my article was not deferential enough to the powerful and delete it which also recently happened as you may or may not have heard.

More than anything I didn't want to start a podcast.

I also didn't want to write a story from the neutered and dispassionate center that most mainstream publications require. I didn't want to hear from a person suffering and then give space to the person causing that suffering to explain themselves. Something I wrote in one of the first newsletters I sent out was that my only promise to the readers is that I will never hear both sides and I think I kept that one.

So thank you for buying this weird book or subscribing to the newsletter. Thank you to everyone who ever mistreated me or underpaid me at any of the publications I've written for over the years for sucking massive shit. Thank you to anyone who has ever fired me which is pretty much everyone I've ever worked for and wait hold on maybe I'm the asshole here?

Hmm no it's everyone else.

Thank you most of all to Michelle for being the only good person in the world and also to everyone who has shared my work online and thank you to the chat boys for listening to my bullshit every day and thank you to my bunny who haunts me in my backyard wait why I am writing this like an Oscar acceptance speech I'm going to make like $500 off this thing.

I don't know buddy. What an absolute luxury it is to be able to have anyone pay attention to your pain I guess is what I want to say. If you're lucky you get to smuggle your sadness into something that tricks other people into paying attention to it like a book or a song and then they go and tell you how good you are for making it and sometimes even pay you money for it. It's the perfect crime. It doesn't make the pain go away but it's still better than nothing. Most people don't have that option. Most people suffer in anonymity unless they happen to be suffering in a sufficiently newsworthy fashion in which case we all glance at them briefly and say holy shit but mostly we're just glad it's not us that it's happening to until some day it is.

– *Watertown, MA.*
June 2019

I WOULD WANT TO DRINK THEIR BLOOD

GOD WILL PUNISH THEM

There's a girl I never want to let myself forget. Her name is Samar Hassan and we killed her family.

In January of 2005 in the northern Iraqi town of Tal Afar, Samar who was five years old at the time was riding in the backseat of her parents' car as they returned from bringing her young brother to the hospital. It was getting dark and nearing curfew and her father likely aware of this was driving faster than normal. Fearing that the driver was a suicide bomber an army patrol in the area that evening was given permission to open fire and so they did because that is what army patrols do.

As Specialist Brad Hammond would tell it years later he and multiple other soldiers fired at least 20 rounds each into the oncoming car. When it finally came to a stop Samar and her siblings spilled out of the back with their parents now slumped over in the front seat dead from the torrent of gunfire.

"I was like, 'Oh my god. What did we do? What did we do?'" Hammond said in the film *Hondros* a 2017 documentary about the life of the late acclaimed conflict photographer Chris Hondros who was on hand at the shooting.

Hammond still smells what he smelled that night.

"Blood, brains. You ever smelled . . ." he says in the film inhaling deeply.

Hondros was embedded with Hammond's Apache company at the time. He quickly snapped a series of pictures of the family we destroyed including one which became one of the most searing and defining images of the war. He'd soon be banished from traveling with the company after disregarding military command's request not to publish the photos.

Samar's parents were but two deaths in the conservative estimate of 500,000 or more that came as a direct result of combat or its aftermath in the collapse of Iraqi infrastructure and the subsequent takeover of parts of the country by the Islamic State but the photographs Hondros captured of Samar and her siblings—traumatized, bloodied, devastated—did something that reading an abstract number like that can't ever do. It brought the dead—the distant, unknowable, easily ignorable Iraqi dead—to life.

Look at her face in the photo now. I can't print it here but you should put this book into the trash or the toilet and go find it and stare at it for a couple hours and you'll understand my general thesis.

Are you looking? What can she be thinking? Did she have any idea why her parents were murdered? By who?

A subsequent military inquiry determined that the attack on the car was "reasonable in intensity, duration, magnitude."

Samar's brother Rakan who was badly injured in the shooting as well was brought to Boston the next year for treatment for his injuries. It was aid he was afforded in no small part by the widespread attention the photos had garnered and the advocacy of an American aid worker named Marla Ruzicka. Three years later the boy was murdered in an attack by insurgents. Their uncle who was taking care of the two children at the time suspects his home was targeted specifically because the boy had traveled to the United States.

Ruzicka would also be killed in a car bombing in Baghdad not long after.

Hondros would die himself from wounds sustained in a mortar attack while covering the Libyan Civil War in 2011.

But Samar. I was trying to remember her name in September of 2018 as the weeklong destination wedding-ass funeral and round-the-clock 24/7 corpse-watch for John McCain continued its interminable slog on cable news. I worried for a while I wouldn't be able to bring something Samar said in an interview last year back to memory. I felt guilty for having let the specificity of her anguish slip from my mind.

The documentary makers behind *Hondros* tracked Samar down for the film. Eighteen by then they had come to see her in part to bring her an apology from Hammond. He appears in the film himself now as a broken man unable to emotionally process the extent of what he did. Hammond still has nightmares every night he says in the film over shots of an overflowing bag of medication. Anxiety pills and so on. He still sees Rakan walking down the street when he goes to sleep.

He asked the documentarians to please tell Samar if they could find her that he is sorry.

She did not accept the apology.

"Everybody knows my story and saw my picture," she tells the filmmakers in between the pauses as a translator relays her words leaving ample time for them to spread out and fill the space of the room.

"But it's not going to help me with anything."

She remembers that night. It's never gone from her thoughts.

"I hear them screaming in my head and the sound of shooting."

"What would sorry do?" she asks. "They're gone. Is sorry going to bring them back? No, it won't. That's it. It's done."

That weekend I saw a tweet that got 100,000 retweets in the first twenty-four hours it was posted. It was a video taken from John McCain's funeral at the National Cathedral in which Michelle Obama can be seen taking a piece of candy from George W. Bush.

Another tweet that weekend from the *New Yorker*'s Susan Glaser captured the sepia-tinted nostalgia theme that abounded across social media: "Hillary Clinton and Dick Cheney next to each other at John McCain's funeral . . . seems so much how Washington used to be, and is no longer. When America hears these stirring patriotic songs today, do they even hear the same words?"

As Glasser would later write in a piece in which she inducted Bush into the #resistance—a sentiment hundreds of Beltway lanyard-fuckers echoed on Twitter and elsewhere—McCain's funeral was not just a beautiful tribute to a heroic man but more importantly a stirring rebuke to Donald Trump. Obama, Bush, and Meghan McCain's eulogies were pointed shots across the bow at the nasty Trump who is the first bad president and a man whom they not-so-subtly attempted to contrast with the honorable war hero.

Needless to say the occasion of McCain's death drove the white-collar pundit class absolutely fucking insane in all manner of ways.

"The angels were crying. Here at CNN—just a few blocks away—no rain. Just there," CNN's Dana Bash tweeted.

But this rehabilitation of kindly old grandpas Bush and McCain and the other architects of the Iraq War into a throwback to the good old days of politics when we all had our disagreements sure but everyone lined up and shook hands then hit the showers together after a sporting debate is a fucking bridge too far. Imagine seeing Dick Fucking Cheney anywhere outside of an iron maiden in Hell and finding something to be nostalgic about?

Here's what Meghan McCain said about her father to resounding applause at the funeral:

"The America of John McCain is generous and welcoming and bold. She is resourceful and confident and secure. She meets her responsibilities. She speaks quietly because she is strong. America does not boast because she has no need. The America of John McCain has no need to be made great again because America was always great."

I don't know if any of the smooth-brained dullards in the media eulogizing John McCain—whose own theater of bravery lest we forget led to at least a million and a half deaths including an estimated 600,000 civilians—remember much from the Bush era or just how ravenously horny for invading Iraq or any other country he thought had it coming McCain was at the time. Distance does have a way of sanding off the edges. But here's something that came from Bush and McCain's war I'd like more people to hear. It's one of the last things Samar says in the documentary about the men—Bush and McCain's men, our men—who killed her family for nothing.

What would she say to them if they were to tell her they were sorry?

"I will never forgive them. I will just leave it to God. God will punish them," she says, her voice rising in anger.

"If they were in front of me, I would want to drink their blood," she says.

"Even then I wouldn't be satisfied."

❧

EVERYWHERE IS THE SAME PLACE WHEN YOU'RE DRINKING IT'S THE PLACE WHERE THE DRINKING IS

I REMEMBER THE FIRST TIME I WAS EVER SCARED IN MY LIFE

My sister who doesn't drink anymore wrote a story a few years back about our grandmother all of which was true. Shirley Madden had grown up vacationing in a little lobster town called Round Pond, Maine, and she and my grandfather bought a cottage there after they were married. My grandfather died relatively young like most everyone who came before me so I don't have too many memories of him but when I try to think about him I remember a day when I was sick as a boy. He'd gotten me a can of ginger ale to settle my stomach and I fell asleep on the couch in their old sprawling farmhouse near the fireplace where the crows flew in. I woke to take a sip and the can was filled with ants. It took me a minute to realize what was happening and I spit out as many as I could but it was too late for some of them they were inside me now.

I think my grandfather was the second man she ever loved. She would tell us about the first guy that she didn't marry sometimes until she was like 80 and she died on a hospital bed in our house near where she'd spent the past decade drinking gin. I think she wondered her whole life how things might have been different. I don't have a picture of my grandfather on me but I have one of my grandmother and her old boyfriend right here in a little frame she sent me which feels like a sort of betrayal so sorry about that. They're both holding ukuleles and she's got a flower in her hair. I don't think she ever got the chance to travel much but I think she went to California one time and maybe this was it. That was how far she made it.

On the back of the frame there's a piece of paper attached that she must have cut from *Reader's Digest* or something and it reads "Life is not a journey to the grave with the intention of arriving safely in a pretty and well preserved body, but rather to skid in broadside, totally worn out and proclaiming: Wow, what a ride!"

She always sent me horse shit like that, positive affirmation magical thinking type stuff and I never paid attention to it because I never appreciate anyone in my life until they're gone.

Sometimes I talk to people who've lived to a ripe old age the same way you would when someone has just finished a marathon or climbed a mountain. Oh wow that sounds like a lot of work. And then they tell you how hard but rewarding it is and you say how you think you're going to handle it the same way someday but you know probably you won't but you say it anyway.

We'd visit Maine in the summers when we were young and I'd go there throughout most of the rest of my life. I haven't been in years though and my mother and aunt tell me every time I see them how my wife and I simply must go it's so different now and I say we will but we don't and I don't have a particularly good reason for that.

One year they filmed a movie there called *Message In a Bottle* starring Kevin Costner which was very exciting for them you can imagine because they had no stoplights in town and now they had a guy who knew Julia Roberts. My grandmother would encourage my sister for years after that to try writing a message in a bottle with her own kids like they did in the movie but she never did because no one listens to their grandparents until they're gone.

I remember the first time I was ever scared in my life and it would have been around the time I was drinking the ants. I was at my other grandmother's house and my cousins and I decided to watch the movie *Poltergeist* and I remember the sense of dread of everything inside the house coming alive and trying to drag you down into the graveyard below. It was the most horrifying thing I could imagine. Also the doll. The fucking doll.

I ran outside in a panic afterwards and the door slammed somehow on my foot and gashed it open and left a scar that may or may not be there right now I haven't even thought to look at it in years it's so much a part of my body now. That grandmother died relatively young from smoking I think and her husband was dead before I knew any better but apparently he was a real piece of shit so not my problem. Well it is but you know what I mean. Three of her children including my father all died around age 60 from drinking and drugs and the various shit that accumulates after a life like that. One of her children the successful one we were all proud of died in his pool though so it's not inevitable this shit will get you there's also the possibility you could die in a tragic swimming accident. On my stepfather's side of the family everyone tends to live into their 90s but a lot of them seem to get leukemia so sort of a mixed bag in terms of options were I offered the chance to choose my genes.

Sometimes I talk to my friends and family who've had cancer the same way you would when someone has just gotten back from someplace terrible and you don't ask them too much about it because you're not sure you want to know. Oh wow what was Hell like?

I have gotten to travel to a handful of countries around the world for writing jobs and the appeal of it in theory is that it breaks you out of your routine. You get to see beautiful new places and experience different cultures and visit museums and geological marvels and all the other things the travel sites advertise and that is true to an extent but mostly in my experience it's been a series of chances to drink things I might not normally drink in slightly more exciting settings than I would have otherwise. Maybe that's because I spent so many years writing about booze and trying to explain to readers what it tastes like and how it makes you feel but you already know. Everywhere is the same place when you're drinking it's the place where the drinking is.

Another thing I'd do whenever I'd travel is find a way to keep exercising compulsively no matter what I was missing out on. If I'm not careful I'm going to end up permanently hurting myself I said and then not too long after that I did ruin my back and abdominals to the point where I can't really do anything but swim now. One thing that's great for pain is drinking I can tell you that. You feel the ache in your body and you pour a pint of whiskey on it and it goes away until tomorrow.

When my grandmother died we went to Round Pond to spread her ashes out into the water that she loved along the craggy coast. My sister and her kids finally wrote the letter she was waiting for and tossed it into the ocean. Five years later on the anniversary of her death the bottle washed up about 200 miles away in Scituate, Massachusetts, where she had lived the rest of her life. Some dude found it and called my sister and we were all like what the fuck and things like that. A few years later on November 9 the same day they found the bottle we discovered an older sister we never knew we had that my grandmother had made my mother give away 40 years earlier. She was too young to have a child because she was a child. She likes to drink just like me and our parents it turns out. It finds you.

I used to think that drinking and doing drugs was taking me somewhere else. Not in the tripping sense I never did like those sorts of drugs but in the way that it summoned some part of me that lived inside and sent it out into the world to handle the logistics for me. A sort of publicist or travel agent that brought me places I wouldn't have typically gone and handled the schmoozing. But that doesn't last for long and eventually it does the exact opposite which is it sits you in your place. I drink on my back porch at night now alone mostly and my wife sits inside and sometimes she drinks there on the couch and my mother sits in her room watching TV and drinking and my step father sits in the other room drinking and none of us goes anywhere.

People love to talk about the plans they have to try something new. My comedian friends often talk about how many people tell them they've been thinking about trying standup some time. Music fans are fascinated about life on the road and want to know what it's like playing shows. People have long told me that they're going to start going to the gym or they've been thinking about getting a tattoo when they see one of mine. Do it I say. Stop thinking about it and do it. In a nicer way than that but still. But people don't do it. They're afraid of what they might find out about themselves if they travel from the exact same place where they're standing right now.

What's it like over there literally anywhere but here I want to know from anyone who's ever done anything and maybe I'll like it or maybe I won't but as someone who's written about traveling so many times I know that hearing about it from someone else doesn't do it justice it's not real until you've gone yourself.

Sometimes I talk to my friends who are sober the same way you would when someone has just gotten back from a vacation to somewhere cool you've always wanted to go. Oh wow what was Japan like? And they tell you how great it is and you say you definitely are going to go someday but you know you probably won't but you say it anyway.

THE WIND SOMETIMES FEELS IN ERROR

EACH YEAR THE BALLOON STRAINED AND STRAINED AGAINST ITS CORDS

Just outside the gates of the Hofburg Palace the massive baroque seat of power for the Habsburg kings and emperors of the Holy Roman Empire and in the shadow of the 13th century cathedral the Michaelerskirche with its elaborate series of subterranean crypts there's an open-air museum in the center of the popular Michaelerplatz. Amidst the tourist bustle and high-end retail shopping and cafés with blankets strewn over chair backs and the omnipresent wall-mounted cigarette vending machines the excavation looks like a narrow scar carved into the earth that opens a window into Vindobona which is a Roman military outpost that is believed to be where Marcus Aurelius died in the year 180.

Aurelius's *Meditations* were something like the first self-help book albeit one that set the course for Christianity and Western civilization. In short it was a set of guidelines for being a good man written by himself to himself. Everything happens for a reason he'd say. "The universe is change; our life is what our thoughts make it." Sorry but since I've been rewatching *True Detective* season one it's almost impossible not to hear shit like that in Matthew McConaughey's voice.

"Time is like a river made up of the events which happen, and a violent stream; for as soon as a thing has been seen, it is carried away, and another comes in its place, and this will be carried away too."

We build on top of ourselves burying the past I thought. We live on top of the dead I thought while staring down into the ruins there snapping photos of the ancient culture's bones on my phone so I could remember them some day in the future. Eventually you accumulate too many memories on your phone so you have to decide which ones to delete. You have to go through and be like do I absolutely need to remember this hamburger?

The past is very easy for me to imagine because it has already happened. Either I was there for it or someone else was there for it and they wrote it down and so now we know. The present is also easy to imagine because well I don't think I need to explain that one. I have never been very good about thinking about the future though and I don't think any of us are. We make plans sure and if you were to ask us what we might be doing a year from now or five years from now or twenty years from now we could probably spackle together a plausible approximation of what it might look like but the future isn't real because no one has written it down for us yet.

I saw a story where scientists said the pitch at which whales near the Antarctic sing has been getting progressively lower over the past couple decades. Blue whales sometimes sing at a pitch so low that it's beyond the grasp of human ears which sounds magical doesn't it that there are massive creatures communicating in a manner that we would never be able to hear if we didn't amplify it with technology. Maybe they just don't want us eavesdropping. Maybe they're talking about us behind our backs.

One of the reasons they've had to change the way they sing is because they have to compete with the sound of icebergs cracking and falling apart.

I read another story which is the same story but this time in the *Washington Post* called "Everything is not going to be ok" and the writer spoke with a woman named Nikki Cooley who grew up on Diné Nation lands in Arizona and now manages a climate and tribes program there "acting as an emissary between her ancestral world and the modern one that upended it."

"In Arizona, in the summer, the pinyon pines don't smell like they used to," she said, "and the wind sometimes feels in error, like it's blowing the wrong way, at the wrong time of year."

Everything we do today comes at the expense of the future. That can be little things like how last night I basically ate an entire loaf of bread. You know the kind that sticks out of your shopping bag and you go like haha look at me I'm a French guy over here ayy forgetaboutit. Or it can be taking pleasure or comfort in all the things you know you shouldn't do but nonetheless feel good right now in this moment and tomorrow is not your problem. Someone else is going to have to deal with it and even if that person is actually you it's still you tomorrow and you don't know that guy so let him figure it out.

It was about two years ago and there was a sadness inside of me I had been hoping to run away from and by chance an alcohol company offered to send me to Europe to go drink their specific type of alcohol there so I went and did that. Turns out though that for better or worse and no matter what this dude Marcus Aurelius might have said to the contrary sadness travels well across borders. Unlike hand lotion you can smuggle grief onto the plane and no one will know it. Pain doesn't show up on the x-ray scanner at all it's the perfect crime.

"No difference between here and there: the city that you live in is the world," Aurelius said. I don't know what he meant by that exactly but I take it to mean it doesn't matter where you are it's still you that has to be there.

You can see all those old castles and cathedrals and shit from the rooftop bar of the circus-themed hotel I stayed in. It was appointed with retro pommel horses and medicine balls and gymnastics rings and what have you like they went into a haunted circus and gentrified it. "We are all mad here" the sign on the facade outside and on the walls inside say which makes it sound like getting hotel-nude in a room you can't figure out how to charge your phone in is slipping through the looking glass and I guess it kind of is.

I went running along the Danube when I got there because I could still run at the time and I also could not sleep. I'd trudge down the streets ignoring the cute Viennese crosswalk signals that show a little green woman leading a man by the hand and bluster into traffic like a galumphing American dumbass because to be an American and specifically a white American man is to understand intuitively that you can do whatever you want.

I would have been reading *A Little Life* by Hanya Yanagihara that trip so now I am going to go ahead and remember it in front of you. It's a sprawling bildungsroman about loss, self-loathing, self-harm, suicide and . . . friendship(?)

We all have friends or people we love who exist in all three tenses: past present and future. And we all have friends and loved ones who exist only in the past. You can't have a friend who exists exclusively in the past and the present however, it doesn't work that way, although I guess you can now that I think of it you just can't be aware of it at the time. Maybe they're going to die or leave you in an hour or two and then the future them you had always assumed would be around is taken out of the equation for you. People can do that. They can disappear. They don't even have to consult with you although it's generally considered a courtesy to do so.

You probably have someone in your life who you have always worried there won't be a future for regardless of if you're involved in it or not. They're still there until they are not and you spend a lot of time preparing yourself for their absence which is arriving any day now presently here it comes ah not yet ok here it comes.

Anyway that was the character of Jude in the book.

I had the sense that he was in a hot-air balloon, one that was staked to the earth with a long twisted rope, but each year the balloon strained and strained against its cords, tugging itself away, trying to drift into the skies. And down below, there was a knot of us trying to pull the balloon back to the ground, back to safety. And so I was always frightened for him, and I was always frightened of him, as well.

Can you have a real relationship with someone you are frightened of? Of course you can. But he still scared me, because he was the powerful one and I was not: if he killed himself, if he took himself away from me, I knew I would survive, but I knew as well that survival would be a chore; I knew that forever after I would be hunting for explanations, sifting through the past to examine my mistakes. And of course I knew how badly I would miss him, because although there had been trial runs for his eventual departure, I had never been able to get any better at dealing with them, and I was never able to get used to them.

One of the themes of *A Little Life* is how there are some people for whom the past is always the present and always the future. Some people have terrible things happen to them when they are young and it stays with them forever and they end up growing older but they aren't really older they're still who they were when it happened and that can be too much to overcome sometimes.

I haven't read any J. D. Salinger in a long time. Someone said I write like him in here and man that would have been a big compliment back when I was younger during the time when not much terrible was happening to me. I guess we're not supposed to like him anymore when we're adults in part because whoops turns out he was a pervert or something I forget what that was about but also because the things we liked when we were younger are supposed to seem unserious now. Like imagine you met a guy now and he said his favorite writer was J. D. Salinger you'd be like what and then you'd look around to see if anyone else was hearing this shit.

I went back and read "A Perfect Day for Bananafish" just now and I had forgotten almost all of it except for the end which is also how a lot of memories of friendships and romances go. Seymour Glass is on the beach with a young girl named Sybil who is jealous that he'd spent time with another young girl the night before.

"'Ah, Sharon Lipschutz,' said the young man. 'How that name comes up. Mixing memory and desire.'"

That last bit is a reference to the first part of T. S. Eliot's *The Waste Land* "The Burial of the Dead." I definitely remembered all of this by heart just to be clear. I only went to Wikipedia just now to see if anyone else remembered it as well and as good as I did.

April is the cruelest month, breeding
Lilacs out of the dead land, mixing
Memory and desire, stirring
Dull roots with spring rain.

Eliot also begins that part with a quote from the Satyricon which would've been written around one hundred years before our man Marcus Aurelius was born.

"For once I saw with my own eyes the Cumaean Sibyl hanging in a jar, and when the boys asked her, 'Sibyl, what do you want?' she answered, 'I want to die.'"

In Greek mythology Cumaean Sibyl was a prophet who among other things guided Aeneas through Hades. Getting in was very easy she told him but finding your way out was another thing altogether.

Trojan, Anchises' son, the descent of Avernus is easy.
All night long, all day, the doors of Hades stand open.
But to retrace the path, to come up to the sweet air of heaven,
That is labour indeed.

Welcome to Hell World in other words.

Sibyl was mortal but she lived for almost a thousand years according to the myths after she made a bargain with Apollo. In exchange for her virginity she asked to live for as many years as there were grains in the pile of sand in her hand and Apollo said whatever sure ok but then she later spurned his advances so he was like welp you didn't look at the fine print bitch and she was cursed to live that long while growing older and more decrepit every year until she withered away smaller and smaller and smaller until she could fit inside a jar and then she got so small that all that was left was her voice.

I drank a lot those few days in Europe because that was what I was being paid to do. I went to a speakeasy in Vienna which was set up like a living room for example. You were supposed to take your shoes off when you came in and I was like uh I don't know buddy. I forget if I did or not but that's probably not germane to the vibe I'm going for here. You probably didn't imagine what type of shoes anyone I mentioned in here so far was wearing. This isn't the type of book where you know about what shoes people have on.

The bartender there didn't like listing what was in the drinks before he served them.

"If you know before what's in the drink you taste it differently," he said. "You focus on the spirit."

Some people like that sort of thing and some people don't. Most people do not want to change who they are and they do not want to change what they drink which is a part of who they are. You've got to surprise them by letting them surprise themselves.

Here's a surprise. Did you know that the cream and chocolate filling ganache was actually a mistaken invention? A chocolatier's assistant told me that the next day as she was spreading and chopping and spreading and chopping a mesmerizing blob of viscous green liquid on a steel table in a kitchen to cool it. I don't remember what she looked like but I remember the big green blob on the table because I see a very high number of women on a regular basis but a comparatively smaller number of sugary green blobs.

Around 1850 a confectioner's assistant in a Parisian pâtisserie accidentally spilled hot milk over chocolate making his boss furious as the story goes. Ganche! he yelled which apparently means donkey in French. But the dude's fuck-up paid off and who's the donkey now hmmm? Then again they're both dead so they probably aren't worried about getting credit for the chocolate anymore unless ghosts are real which they aren't because I just read a piece in *Mother Jones* about how airport workers threatening to strike didn't have anything to do with the end of the government shutdown it was actually all Nancy Pelosi's leadership and do we really want workers to have that sort of power anyway the guy wrote? The fact that Mother Jones herself isn't currently haunting the offices of that magazine with a blood-curdling wail after a take that bad is proof that ghosts don't exist.

If you've ever wondered what it's like to see a group of adults set free to have their way in a chocolate shop it's pretty much exactly like the saying about kids in a candy shop only with a thicker undercurrent of shame. Imagine Willy Wonka but everyone already knew what their specific vice was.

I don't think this has anything to do with anything but I just took a break a minute ago and made some coffee and went out on my porch to smoke and the views from my porch aren't quite as nice as any of the ones in Vienna I'm sorry to report. I usually sit there and see the young boy playing Wiffle ball or street hockey with his dad and he always hits the ball over the shrubs into our yard and has to sneak through a little hole in the fence to come and get it and I wonder if he thinks about the future. Probably not due to kids are generally too stupid to be melancholy.

"If you have an infant daughter, she is expected to live 81.1 years, and so she will be here for 2100, a year that is no longer mythical," the *Washington Post* story I mentioned earlier where they talked about the wind being wrong said. "She may see the world's largest naval base, in Norfolk, swamped by rising seas. If she lives in Phoenix, she may feel nearly double the number of 100-degree days. During her lifetime, the oceans will acidify at a rate not seen in 66 million years."

I wonder if they'll get to dig a hole into the earth and look through the wound at what we were someday and if someone will write a meandering essay about it that is supposed to be a metaphor about why he's sad for mistakes and losses he's had in his life. A society can live a thousand years and then some crying baby gets to make it about him.

The thing about the whales and the Roman shit reminded me just now to go back and read a poem I liked a lot when I was younger called "The Fall of Rome" by Auden which is about a lot of things but also about going about our petty business in the looming shadow of inevitable decay and societal collapse. It ends with some lines I think about a lot.

> Unendowed with wealth or pity,
> Little birds with scarlet legs,
> Sitting on their speckled eggs,
> Eye each flu-infected city.
> Altogether elsewhere, vast
> Herds of reindeer move across
> Miles and miles of golden moss,
> Silently and very fast.

The other people I look at on my porch weren't there just now. There's the old man with more past than future left who is always yelling at his tiny dog to get the fuck in the house and the old woman who yells at him about yelling at the dog. There's a giant tree a little further back that Michelle said someone saw some kind of big hawk in recently. Must have been a pretty cool hawk for us to all know about it.

I asked the chocolatier what he thought about America and specifically what he thought about how much we love to go around shooting everyone all the time with our guns over here.

In Austria he said you have to have a license for hunting to own a rifle. To own a shotgun you have to have a good reason to apply for one like maybe you run a jewelry shop for example. No one is carrying guns out in the street. Even if you're part of a shooting club you're not allowed to carry a loaded weapon or even transport a gun and bullets together at the same time he told me. You have to make two separate trips.

"Nobody questions this rule," he said. "You hear about the massacre in Las Vegas, everybody here says 'Come on. Stop this.' This guy had 30 weapons. It's impossible here. There are a lot of weapons, but if you get caught, you go to jail."

Then again in an election held that same week the far right nationalist strongly anti-immigration and anti-Islam Freedom Party landed its best results in Austria in decades. I'm not an expert in Austrian politics but that seems bad.

Not my problem in any case because after that I went and ate some pounded fried veal and then went to another bar where they presented me with a statue-like vessel with an angelic figure on top that pissed alcohol into my mouth out of its little tiny angel dick.

If you ever get the chance to go you will take so many pictures in Prague. You'll wander around in a stupor marveling at the dreamlike logic of the concentric centuries of gothic renaissance and baroque architecture piled on top of one another and try to smuggle the beauty of the Prague Castle and the Charles Bridge and Old Town Square into the frame of your phone camera and it will not work. You will be disappointed because you want to share what you're experiencing with your friends to make it seem real. I tried anyway climbing the steep steps toward the gardens around the castle with a panoramic view of the city. I climbed by the heavily armed guards and the tourists eating sugar and walnut pastries rolled around a stick and the busker singing "Knockin' on Heaven's Door" in a thick accent. This will all look amazing on Instagram I thought but it did not it just looked like some roofs and a guy with a guitar.

People tell me it's strange to spend what little time you have while traveling exercising but when I could still do it the solitude of a run through an unfamiliar place always allowed it to reveal itself to me in a way that a guided tour or merely walking around with a phone in your face never did. And so I ran while I was there dodging the surprisingly dangerous traffic exploding through the narrow streets up and down distressingly steep hills getting lost. I arrived at the Kafka Museum just too late in the evening to be permitted entry which seemed a little on the nose so instead I went down to the Vltava River to spend some time with the swans there due to they are very famous swans more famous than that hawk that was in a tree near my house that one time. Dozens of them tussled with one another over scraps of bread and their feathers were brown from the muck of the river bank making them appear a lot less less majestic than their reputation would lead you to believe. I thought of "The Hunger Artist" panther fat from its indulgence.

Later on in the bowels of a reconstructed twelfth century building I found a subterranean bar that once stood at ground level but like many of the structures around here it was covered over during an outbreak of the plague in the early 1700s. When people get that sick you have to pour mountains of dirt on top of it to make it all go away. Amid the lowlight I contemplated the now useless windows looking out over nothing. A window to dirt. Still later on that night I got into a shouting match with a Czech bartender about our differences over the niceties of hospitality at a Harley themed bar complete with a Jack Daniel's Confederate flag on the wall while "Smells Like Teen Spirit" played and I thought I'm glad Kurt Cobain isn't alive to see this all because he'd probably kill himself.

A couple days later I went to Berlin where I was awoken in the morning by the mournful howls of the monkey cage just below my window at a hotel overlooking the Zoological Garden. I took a tour of Kreuzberg which was formerly one of the poorest most migrant-heavy neighborhoods of West Berlin. Bordering the Spree River and Checkpoint Charlie it is now renowned as a center of iconoclastic counterculture. The wind blew heavily as we crossed from East to West Berlin as our guide pointed out some of the looming wall-sized pieces of street art that define the neighborhood's aesthetic. Aside from this bridge she said your only hope of crossing at the time was to jump the wall and swim the river and pray that a sniper wouldn't shoot you which is more or less what getting to school in America is like now.

Berlin as a city doesn't have the resources to keep up with the Sisyphean task of removing the graffiti all over the place anymore so once one piece of street art is removed another takes its place. All along the river corporations and land speculators have been transforming the area with high-rises and luxury condos but Kreuzberg remains a redoubt for gentrification or at least it was trying to at the time who knows what has happened since then I bet the tides of capitalism have reversed somehow. Maybe if I don't look it up I can maintain that fantasy.

Just kidding capitalism has a way of always winning out in the end and many of the buildings that have been painted by international street artists there have since been turned into points of attraction for the landlords hoping to raise rents. Rather than let their statement of defiance be turned into a marketing point some of the artists here will go and sabotage their own work painting over it as a way of saying fuck you.

You cannot escape the clouds of smoke in Berlin I have been meaning to mention which is sort of a blessing and a curse if you smoke like me. Being given too much of what you desire is never all its cracked up to be. There should be a parable about that.

I spoke with a bartender in the backroom of a restaurant called Schneeweiß which means Snow White I think and he asked me why it is we like what we like. Because someone told us to he said. Because that's just how we've always done things. He gave me all manner of shit to try without explaining what it was and asked me to name what it was I thought I was experiencing. To name it specifically in order to know it better.

"Taste only happens when you find a word for it," he said. "It's like driving around lost without any street signs."

"If you don't find words for it it never happened," he said.

Another person I see when I sit on my porch is a bunny and I think it's always the same one because although my town is overrun with them this particular little one sits in the same spot under the hedge and stares up at me sometimes and sometimes even lays itself out on the dying winter grass in this languorous pose like it's trying to seduce me. Is this rabbit trying to fuck me lol I think but it's not because that would be weird.

Sometimes my bunny is not there for a while and I wonder what she's doing and if she's staying safe. Sometimes I throw vegetables out there into the yard because I worry she's not eating well enough. She never says anything back to me when I say hello.

I never gave the bunny a name because it seems crazy to name something that you're not sure is going to be around that long. When someone is gone you can hear their name once and it makes them exist all over again with their past and their future all coalescing right in your present. They won't know it but you do and then it's your problem to figure out what to do with the burden. Later on years from now if someone carved an opening into your chest they might be able to make out the faintest outlines of where a long forgotten people once lived but they would never really understand it from that vantage point because the only people who were there for it don't exist anymore and the language they spoke can't be translated.

WE'VE ALREADY ESTABLISHED THAT NOW WE'RE JUST HAGGLING OVER THE PRICE

IF KIDS DON'T EAT IN PEACE, YOU DON'T EAT IN PEACE

In June of last summer Homeland Security secretary Kirstjen Nielsen who has been and will forever be the pinched public face of Trump's cruel ethnic cleansing policy was confronted at a Mexican restaurant near the White House. In a video protestors can be seen approaching her table clapping and chanting. "No borders! No walls! Sanctuary for all!" they shouted. "If kids don't eat in peace, you don't eat in peace" they said to her and other shit like that. After about ten minutes she left escorted by her guards having had her table-side guacamole completely ruined which is another kind of tragedy in its own right.

For a lot of people being chased out of a restaurant by people who hate your fucking guts would be the worst thing to happen to them for a long time. Maybe their entire life. Most people would probably remember that for a while. It would hurt. Why is this happening to me they'd say. I'm not a monster they'd say.

Nielsen's attempt to have a casual dinner in public on any other day would've been justifiable grounds for disruption but this was the day that the shit tornado over her enforcement of the separation of children from their parents at the border reached a crescendo. News was circulating widely about the existence of baby jails which we literally have now and have just sort of gotten used to. It was a mind-boggling show of hubris for her to show her face in public anywhere only further adding insult to injury that the incident occurred at a Mexican restaurant. You might wonder if she appreciated the irony but I don't think that sort of self awareness has been kept particularly well stocked in this administration. Self awareness? Ah let me go check out back they'd say when you walked in looking for some. Sorry I don't think we carry that anymore.

It was reported in April of 2019 that Nielsen was finally resigning from her post or had been fired by Trump which is the same thing in any case.

"Its been an honor of a lifetime to serve with the brave men and women of @DHSgov," she tweeted. "I could not be prouder of and more humbled by their service, dedication, and commitment to keep our country safe from all threats and hazards."

And now presumably much like everyone who has come and gone from the Trump administration she will embark on the next chapter of her life which will be taking a high-paying lobbying or consulting job and she will expect to be welcomed back into polite society appearing on the Sunday morning shows and such and the thing is she probably will be and all the careerists with Beltway bipolar disorder will thank her for coming on. Thank you for coming on they'll say. Thanks for having me she'll say and she'll hope that we all forget why we know about her in the first place but I'm not going to and I don't think history will either although in fairness history is pretty fucking forgetful.

Ideally decades from now kids in school if we still have kids and we still have schools will have to memorize Nielsen's name as the answer on a history test and they'll get a B- on it and be proud of themselves because generation Z5000 are all lazy and spoiled as anyone will tell you. These kids with their fancy oxygen masks are too coddled to even canoe to school anymore we'll say.

What's your favorite Beatles song or Prince song or whoever else it is with a lengthy catalogue? It's hard to say right? You have a half dozen you could rattle off easily but it would be hard to fully commit to just one because as soon as you said it you'd remember another one and be like wait wait hold on. That's how I feel thinking about Nielsen's racism discography. There was for example the time she said "We do not have a policy of separating families at the border. Period." That certainly has to go on the Mount Rushmore of lies I think we can all safely agree.

As it turns out despite being ordered to stop separating families at the border by a judge Nielsen and the boys kept doing it and hundreds were ripped apart in the months following. Business was too good.

Another tune I can't get out of my head was the time a couple days before her chicken mole went cold on her when she was asked on CNN whether the separation policy amounted to child abuse and she said no it doesn't count as child abuse because they have a TV there for the kids to watch in their kid prisons.

"We have high standards. We give them meals and we give them education and we give them medical care. There are videos, there are TVs," she said.

Another thing she said on CNN the same day which is a line Trump has trotted out frequently was that these weren't even authentic families in the first place. It's all a con she said. These people are trying to game the system. Their pain isn't even real they just want to come and take your shit.

Those are all good lies but if you asked me to pick a favorite I would go with the time she pretended not to know about the demographics in Norway. In a Senate hearing in January of 2018 she was asked to respond to recent reported statements that Trump had made about "shit hole" countries like Haiti and other places black people live and how he preferred immigrants from Norway.

"I don't dispute that the president was using tough language" she admitted but she attempted to explain the obvious racism away by saying Trump was hoping to move to a merit-based system for immigration. Whether it's immigration or hiring for a job or accepting students to schools a merit-based system is what we call it when we conspire to ensure that certain groups of people suffer under terrible enough living conditions that it would be nearly impossible for them to rise to the level of merit in question. They would have to be superlatively exceptional to cross the merit bar and then we would reluctantly let a few of them through as tokens to be like see we are not basing this on race.

"Being from Norway is not a skill," Pat Leahy responded to Nielsen in the hearing which is a hilarious line on its face but also not entirely true. Being white looks absolutely stellar on a resume or school application it's maybe the biggest skill a person can have.

"What does he mean when he says he wants more immigrants from Norway?" Leahy asked and Nielsen tried to pass it off as a testament to the hardworking Norwegian character which we all know about and then Leahy said Norway is a predominately white country right and she stammered.

"I . . . um . . . ah . . . eee," she starts and you can actually pause the video and see the moment when she realizes she's got to risk it all with one last shot.

"I . . . ehh . . . I actually do not know that sir . . . but I imagine that is the case."

Norway is one of the whitest countries in the world I probably don't need to say.

"White House officials" tried to launder her reputation in anonymously sourced pieces from the access-addled civility reporters after she stepped down saying that she pushed back against some of the president's harsher policies all along and advised him when actions he's proposed such as shutting down the border entirely aren't how do you say . . . *legal* and I am sure a lot of people are going to fall for that but not you and me due to we are the smart ones aren't we.

The bastard of the thing is she wanted to position herself as being the relatively compassionate one compared to Trump due to she was fired for failing to rise to his impossibly high standards of cruel racism all the while remaining the overseer of one of the single worst human rights disasters in recent American history. If there is any justice in the world which there is not she will never be able to appear in public again without being asked to get the fuck out.

I'm not saying Trump and Nielsen are Nazis because that's not fair they're only *aspiring* Nazis who didn't complete all of the prerequisite coursework as of yet but I was reminded of these documents I came across which is a trove of unclassified interviews with and conversations among Nazis conducted in American POW prisons in 1944 compiled by the CIA.

It's striking to see the casual discussion of the war from the people who carried it out. It's like when you go out on one with your buddies and you text each other the next day like woh what the fuck was that.

A lot of them are like ah I'm starting to get the impression we fucked up here mate. Some of them are like well at least we are still the master race we still have that after all and his buddy will be like shut the fuck up.

Ok read this next part below on your own while I go have a cigarette because I don't want to read it again. It's from Colson Whitehead's novel *The Underground Railroad* which is about a runaway slave named Cora and it's . . . not easy reading. This scene is set after another runaway slave has been captured and brought back to the plantation in Georgia he is imprisoned on by a slave owner named

Terrance Randall. Randall is particularly cruel even grading on the unfathomable sliding curve of horror perpetrated by people like him. It's fiction but it's not.

> Big Anthony was whipped for the duration of their meal, and they ate slow. The newspaperman scribbled on paper between bites. Dessert came and the revelers moved inside to be free of the mosquitoes while Big Anthony's punishment continued.

> On the third day, just after lunch, the hands were recalled from the fields, the washwomen and cooks and stable hands interrupted from their tasks, the house staff diverted from its maintenance. They gathered on the front lawn. Randall's visitors sipped spiced rum as Big Anthony was doused with oil and roasted. The witnesses were spared his screams, as his manhood had been cut off on the first day, stuffed in his mouth, and sewn in. The stocks smoked, charred, and burned, the figures in the wood twisting in the flames as if alive.

> . . . When Terrance got to Cora, he slipped his hand into her shift and cupped her breast. He squeezed. She did not move. No one had moved since the beginning of his address, not even to pinch their noses to keep out the smell of Big Anthony's roasting flesh.

I started reading the book in April after I learned it appeared on the 10th grade MCAS which is the standardized tests students take in Massachusetts. That doesn't sound so bad until you learn that the essay prompt was to read a passage from the book about Cora being reluctantly helped by a blatantly racist woman named Ethel who is the wife of a man trying to help her escape and who later betrays the slaves.

Here's how the question went:

"Based on The Underground Railroad, imagine how the story might have been told differently if it were written from the point of view of Ethel. Create a journal entry written by Ethel reflecting on the events that happened in the passage. Your journal entry should provide insight into Ethel's thoughts and feelings, as well as her relationship with Cora. Be sure to use what you know about the characters, setting, and events from the passage to develop your journal entry."

After the test a number of groups including the MTA, the Boston Teachers Union, the American Federation of Teachers Massachusetts, the Massachusetts Education Justice Alliance and the New England Area Conference of the NAACP all called for the test results to be nullified saying the question was widely inappropriate and had traumatized students.

"They had to jump in the shoes of a character who harbored racist notions toward the enslaved character in the book," MTA president Merrie Najimy said. "It was traumatic for them, so this group of educators had to conduct counseling in their classrooms as a way of helping their students cope."

"Whoever came up with the question has done a great disservice to these kids, and everyone who signed off on it should be ashamed," Whitehead himself said in a statement about his book being used in such a teaching opportunity.

Ultimately the state decided the question wouldn't be graded and that students taking a makeup test the following week would be instructed to ignore it but the fact that it got that far is nonetheless telling.

I don't know if the crimes we are currently committing against migrants are comparable to what was done by the Nazis or the slave owners in America—and in fact right now as I'm editing this the

biggest controversy on the news is whether or not it's rude to call concentration camps concentration camps—but what do you call wrench-
ing families apart, losing track of children, giving them away, allowing
private companies to profit off the entire ordeal, tear-gassing impov-
erished asylum seekers on the border, dragging toddlers in front of
tribunals, letting children die in our care, forcing raped young women
to give birth, fostering a climate conducive to sexual assault by ICE
agents and DHS prison guards, subjugating people to inhumane living
conditions and housing them in cages like dogs sometimes leading to
suicides of despair, and sending many back to the countries they fled
to meet what will likely be certain death amid the violence they hoped
to escape?

What would you call it when the people enacting these heinous
crimes do so proudly and in fact make it the cornerstone of their entire
administration? And on top of all of that characterize the people trying
to come here as vermin and an infestation and rapists and criminals
who will slit the throats of decent white women everywhere the first
chance they get? Maybe those things aren't as bad as the other stuff but
it's not exactly a weird comparison to make is it?

There's an old joke that's been attributed apocryphally to dozens
of people over the years and admittedly is not quite up to current sensibilities but it goes roughly like this:

Would you sleep with me for $1 million?

Yes of course.

How about for $1?

No! What kind of person do you think I am?

We've already established that now we're just haggling over the
price.

So here's a thought experiment. Maybe the Massachusetts test has
a point. Maybe we should try to put ourselves in the shoes of people

like the racist old lady in the Whitehead novel or some of the captured Nazis or Kristjen Nielsen or Donald Trump. How does it feel to be that type of person? What does it look like inside a brain like that? Do you feel as if you should hang yourself in shame from a doorknob right now and if not why not?

I FINALLY ERASED IT BECAUSE I FELT IT WAS TIME

THEY'RE ALSO BOXES WE CARRY AROUND THAT STORE OUR CONVERSATIONS WITH GHOSTS

I don't remember the final conversation I had with my father. Toward the end of his life he was hard to understand on the phone as years of substance abuse and failing health had garbled his voice. He'd call at inopportune times from a rehab center or hospital on Cape Cod or the home of a friend in Florida he had somehow charmed his way into and I'd hurry to get off the phone. Sometimes I'd find myself annoyed by his attempts to reconnect and let the call go to voicemail. It had been more than fifteen years since we'd had anything resembling a normal relationship and more than thirty since he and my mother had. Even in my frustration it was hard not to think of his looming existential deadline. *I may never get the chance to talk to him again* I'd say to myself but I always did until of course I didn't.

On good days he'd tell me about his latest living situation calling from a flip phone with a number that changed as frequently as a drug dealer's. He'd ask about my writing and where I'd traveled to lately seemingly in awe of all the opportunities I had that he didn't. Even approaching 40 I'd revert to the role of a young boy eager to make his father proud despite having received plenty of love from my mother and stepdad. He'd lobby me to put in a good word with my sisters on his behalf a message I would relay. *Just call the old bastard back* I'd tell them. *You'll regret it someday if you don't.*

I do remember the exact day and time of our final few text exchanges though because they're still on my phone and at least as long as the cloud exists and I stay current on my bill they'll live there forever. There's a photo I sent him from December 2015 just after I'd had a chance to interview Tom Brady. What Massachusetts dad wouldn't want to see that? It kind of breaks my heart to read his reply again now: "im so proud of u my son i cant wait to show everyone tomorrow i cant express my joy dad go get the big fish son agAIN IM TO PROUD FOR WORDS LOVE YOU DAD."

Reading other texts from around that time makes me laugh: "i feel like such lo gool o gohurrf horp," he wrote. ",,ro jlpw up pi f." I still have no idea what he was talking about. And then in February 2016 the last message I'd ever receive came: "hello my son how you doing today i have been in the hospital for two weeks now but I'm getting better TALK TO you Soon love Dad."

I was thinking about those texts during a family dinner at my mother's not long after he died. Someone had asked about a wall of photos that functions as an ad hoc memorial to assorted ancestors on my mother's and stepfather's sides. *The Wall of the Dead* we joked of the missing people all mustachioed and bonneted and stoic. But it occurred to me that the pictures were different from my father's text messages much like the letters I have stashed away from my beloved grandmother stuffed with newspaper clippings she thought I'd like and uncashed $5 checks for "pizza." My wife just found one in which my grandmother tried to persuade her to get me to give up on writing and find a real job which I found insulting at the time but man is that good advice. Those artifacts are moments frozen in time and part of my distant past.

Our phones on the other hand are tools we live with every day. I could respond to my dead father's final text right now and add to the running conversation. Our devices are where we carry out the business of living our lives and are increasingly our primary means of communicating with the people in them. Should they also be where we lug around our memories of the deceased? Do the digital ghosts the dead leave behind make it harder to let them go at all?

The idea that the dead can speak to us feels like something from a horror or sci-fi movie. Yet the reverse where we're talking to them from the here and now whether it be through prayer or quiet reflection or even speaking out loud doesn't seem strange at all. Keeping our loved ones stored in our smartphones often not deleting their contacts for a long time after they're gone has made this even easier to do. We ask our devices for directions home or to bring us food or to broadcast our entire selves to the world. Now they're also boxes we carry around that store our conversations with ghosts.

A friend of mine named Megan Summers is the perfect example. She told me she has voicemails from two deceased friends that she can't listen to now but she needs to know they're with her just in case. "It's almost as though I am saving them for the future," she says. "They just really need to be in the world to me. If I lost them, I'd be devastated."

Shortly before Selene Angier lost her mother she received a voice message of her mom singing "Happy Birthday." It was before she knew how bad her mother's cancer was and now years later the song serves as a time capsule of happier days. Angier listens to the recording on her cell on her birthday every year. She's even backed it up just in case she loses the phone or something unexpected happens. "I cherish that voicemail, and a few other random ones I have not deleted yet, even the super-boring stuff like 'I'm running late, be there soon!'" she says. "It's a great comfort to still hear her voice, more so on the day she brought me into this world." When we spoke her father was also dying of cancer and she was preparing his digital memorial saving everything. "I asked him to leave me a voicemail singing 'Happy Birthday' to me, so I'd have his, too. He mistimed the recording, and all that's there is '. . . to you!' followed by a minute of silence." He's since passed away.

Lindsay Mace lost a close friend in 2011 and saved his contact in her phone for four years. For the first year and a half she regularly dialed the number. "The saddest part was calling and not hearing his voicemail anymore but a disconnected line. I left one message for him after he passed. I just wanted to hear his voice and get some reassurance he wasn't really gone." Calling was a means of staving off some of the more overwhelming emotions that she couldn't deal with all at once: "I finally erased it because I felt it was time. Long after the number had been shut off. Sort of like, *I don't need this anymore.* I feel like I know he's still here."

Texts and voicemails are just two of the ways in today's digital world that we can stay connected to those who've passed away. But when it comes to online memories cherished or not they're hardly the only ones.

By some estimates, 8,000 to 10,000 Facebook users die every day. What survives is a trove of digital footprints. So where does it all go? Turns out you can name an account executor who is presumably a close friend or family member to come in and tidy up your social media belongings in the event of your death although that person will not be given access to your private chat logs. Immediate family members can also select the option to memorialize the account by turning off certain features such as birthday reminders which many users report are exceptionally painful to see.

Gmail has a tool called the Inactive Account Manager that lets you tell Google what to do with your account after you have stopped using it for a certain amount of time. Before the deadline Google will reach out to see if you're still there sort of checking your digital vital signs.

If you don't respond it will contact your preselected trusted contacts with a message you've written. "Hey man I'm dead lol. Don't look at my nudes, please," or something to that effect. And Twitter has the option to remove the account of a deceased family member but only if you submit official proof of death which is not exactly a breezy task when you're grieving.

As technology advances it promises to change the very nature of how we mourn our loved ones. In a *Wired* piece in 2017 James Vlahos documented his final few months with his father during which he tried to capture the idiosyncrasies of his dad's voice and upload it into an artificial intelligence chat software he called the Dadbot. It was an attempt to effect a sort of immortality which is a concept many are working on around the world and one sure to be improved upon. One company recently made headlines by promising to preserve your brain and upload it to the cloud which sounds like a cool idea except they have to kill you to do it.

For the forward thinkers among us there are options to plan our communiqués from the other side. Moran Zur is the founder of a service called SafeBeyond which he explained to me as a sort of "emotional life insurance policy." It was inspired by the deaths of his wife and his father. His wife had been suffering from cancer for years and he wanted her to leave behind messages for their children that they could receive at various milestones in their lives as they got older. "These are future conversations they will never have the chance to have, but now even if it's going to be one-sided, she's recorded them for them in advance," he said. "It's not just leaving money behind; it's leaving words of wisdom, being there for them at significant moments of their life."

Being able to hear from their mother will likely be a salve to their children but it's worth asking how we can ever move on in this brave new digital era if the dead are never truly gone?

It's been a couple of months now since I first reopened the texts from my father and I've been looking at them again swimming in the absurd melancholy of it. I could do the same with others who've died but it would take an extra step of rummaging around in old photo albums and digging through letter boxes in the back of the closet. Now in the time it takes to look up a movie schedule or restaurant menu I can call up the history of my relationship with my dad.

Right now we don't know much about the impact of our devices on mourning academically speaking. There just haven't been many studies of it Elsa Ronningstam an associate professor at Harvard Medical School and clinical psychologist at McLean Hospital told me. I suspect that when it is studied we'll find that phones have vastly complicated and perhaps even forestalled our ability to grieve in a natural fashion.

Our digital mourning isn't nearly as separated from our everyday lives as the experience of visiting a graveyard or holding a physical letter or photo. Such a ritual "is an act that has space and takes its time," Ronningstam said. "That has been part of our human lives for many, many years." The ease with which we can access memories of lost loved ones on our phones or social media accounts on the other hand may end up trapping us in our grief. "Say you're in a romance, and the romance breaks up and you've got that person's voice on your telephone," Donnah Canavan, an associate professor of psychology at Boston College told me. "I think to the extent that you use listening to the person's voice to keep you connected to that relationship, it's bad for you."

Allowing yourself to remember is part of the mourning process added Michael Grodin who is a professor of psychiatry at the Boston University School of Medicine that works with trauma patients from around the world. "You can't get rid of the memories, but you don't want to constantly be in the moment." In his estimation there's nothing abnormal or unhealthy about returning to digital artifacts; it's no different from cherishing an old blanket or wearing a loved one's T-shirt. It's just a matter of monitoring the extent of it. "If it's interfering with relationships, everyday functioning, your ability to work and carry on with life, then it's worth seeking professional help," Grodin said.

Even after all of these interviews and the hours I've spent thinking about my father's texts it's not entirely clear what they mean to me or if they even mean anything at all. Contending with the digital endpoint of a relationship with a person who was a constant and loving part of your life for a long time is a lot different from when it is a reminder of someone who was absent. I can no longer call my father on the phone but that was true for most of my life anyway. Perhaps I should have done so more often. Perhaps he should have. Every text I have now is a glaring reminder that neither of us bothered to. I feel guilty about that. In part that's because he had the foresight to die before my loving step-father thereby hogging all of my weepy "my dad died" writing before the man who actually raised me could get the chance. I wonder if he was capable of thinking about any of this stuff in the last week or two he spent in a medically induced coma at the hospital as his children and exes reemerged to say goodbye one final time. It was like a dress rehearsal. We were talking to him, but he couldn't talk back. I guess I'm doing the same thing now.

Although we still cannot speak directly to the dead these days they can call back out to us. And what they say whether it's in a voicemail or a text or a tweet is the most important message any of us will ever be able to convey: I was here. I am gone now but I was here.

I just went back and looked at one of my last text messages to my father sent shortly before he stopped responding. "Hi dad was planning on calling soon," I wrote. "Glad to hear you're well." I wonder how long he saved that one from me? Probably right up until the end.

♥

SO THAT NOTHING IS WASTED IN NATURE

EVERY DAY I THINK ABOUT UNTWISTING AND UNTANGLING THESE STRINGS I'M IN

Ah fuck I gotta write this thing I guess so here goes. I was gonna start with a story about two New York City detectives and what they did to an eighteen year old woman and I kept thinking about it and not wanting to write it but maybe I'll start and see what happens no promises ok? That's how these stories work right they're so upsetting that most of us look away and pretend it's not happening.

It was September of 2017 and a young woman and two of her friends were hanging out in a car near Coney Island when the cops slithered out of the midnight inky ocean or however it is cops arrive places. They were plainclothes narcotics officers and I'm not sure what happened to get them inside of the car but we can probably fill in the blanks in the timeline with an interstitial title card that says COP STUFF and in any case they found a bit of pot and some Klonopin on the girl or woman I can't decide what to call an eighteen year old in a story like this and they arrested her and brought her into their unmarked van where she says they raped her while driving around the city. She said she remembered the route they took because she saw things she recognized out of the window like the Verrazzano-Narrows Bridge and her grandmother's apartment.

After they were done with her they let her go and she went to the hospital where she told a nurse what had happened and other police arrived and they listened to her story and eventually arrested Richard

Hall and Edward Martins who have maintained their innocence all along by saying the sex with the girl woman teenager they had arrested had been consensual and who knows maybe it was maybe a young woman out with her friends all of a sudden confronted by cops and nervous about the prospect of getting in trouble for drugs decided she wanted to have sex with two older men while handcuffed in a van driving around Brooklyn of her own volition or maybe it was the much more obvious thing that happened who knows.

A year and a half later prosecutors decided to drop most of the charges against the cops due to they think the woman wasn't entirely truthful in her testimony in front of a grand jury and they say that she had changed some of the details in her story a couple of times such as what she was wearing at the time and what the inside of the van in question looked like. I'm fairly certain that sort of confusion about specificity of detail can arise during a traumatic experience like that but I am not an expert on this matter or anything else.

As of March 2019 the two cops were only facing a series of less serious charges including official misconduct and bribery of services according to the *New York Times* and they still might get seven years in jail for that although I wouldn't necessarily count on it because you can murder a guy and not go to jail. Nonetheless that's a lot better than the twenty five years they had been looking at as far as they are concerned and as an added bonus they get to talk about how the girl is a liar now at trial probably which is one of the classic defenses when it comes to sexual assault. You point out how the woman has lied about one thing and then it's only natural to start to wonder what else she might be lying about. So much of human communication whether it's in trials like this one or discussions online or political disagreement comes down to finding an inconsistency in what someone has said or done before and then using that as a means to cast doubt on everything they are saying currently and that's the one move it's the only thing humans have devised in terms of dialogue after all this time bitching at each other. You would think we would have come up with a second rhetorical maneuver by now.

While that story is bad enough on its own the particulars of it aren't even what stand out here for me because did you know that back in the day many years ago all the way back in 2017 when this was happening that it wasn't even illegal as of yet for police officers to have sex with people in their custody in New York? What the fuck? It was indeed a crime for a prison guard to have sex with an inmate but not this type of thing where the person was still relatively free where it was only the *idea* of prison that hovered over the entire proceedings. Then it was sort of a gray area under the law and you could get away with it and cops often did and may still.

New York has since closed that loophole in their state laws but as of last year according to the ACLU New York was one of thirty five states where consent could be used as a defense when a police officer is accused of raping someone they have arrested.

Writing on the story last year Buzzfeed reported that "of at least 158 law enforcement officers charged since 2006 with sexual assault, sexual battery, or unlawful sexual contact with somebody under their control, at least 26 have been acquitted or had charges dropped based on the consent defense, according to a review of a *Buffalo News* database of more than 700 law enforcement officers accused of sexual misconduct."

Police sexual misconduct is pretty common you might not be surprised to hear.

"According to a 2010 Cato Institute review, sexual misconduct is the second-most-frequently reported form of police misconduct, after excessive force," according to the Associated Press.

Sometimes they even get in trouble for it.

In 2015 the Associated Press counted almost one thousand officers between 2009 and 2014 "who lost their badges in a six-year period for rape, sodomy and other sexual assault; sex crimes that included possession of child pornography; or sexual misconduct such as propositioning citizens or having consensual but prohibited on-duty intercourse."

That number was likely to be a vast understatement they said because it only counted officers who actually lost their jobs and many states including California and New York where there are quite a fair few number of cops didn't have records about such things because why would they. In some states where they reported no firings for sexual misconduct they found cases through news reports or court records that it had actually happened so those states were lying or negligent or both.

"It's happening probably in every law enforcement agency across the country," Chief Bernadette DiPino of the Sarasota Police Department in Florida who studied the issue told the AP. "It's so under-reported and people are scared that if they call and complain about a police officer, they think every other police officer is going to be then out to get them."

What's more a significant percentage of these incidents involve particularly vulnerable people like minors or women of color or sex workers or addicts or in other words people who the police perceive as having even less power than the average person and are therefore less likely to make a whole thing about it.

As the *Washington Post* reported last year a study from the National Institute of Justice looked at over 6,700 officer arrests throughout the country over a seven year period and found half of the arrests were for sexual misconduct involving minors.

This part is even worse than all of that which is that cops often prey on women who are victims of domestic violence who call the police for protection.

"As one officer quoted in an investigative report by the Philadelphia Inquirer said, 'I would see women that were vulnerable where I could appear as a knight in shining armor,'" the *Post* reported.

"He explained, 'I'm going to help this woman who's being abused by her boyfriend, and then I'll ask for sexual favors.' Another bragged that getting dates with such victims was like 'shooting fish in a barrel.'"

It was Ash Wednesday the other day which if you're not familiar is the one day every year a couple of people show up at your work with dirt on their face and you're like what the hell and then you remember it's Jesus dirt. For Christians the day of repentance marks the beginning of Lent which is the forty-day period leading up to uh I'm struggling to remember all this shit uh Good Friday which is the day Jesus was crucified and then Easter which is the day he was born again or as it was otherwise known when I was an altar boy a real fucking emotional whirlwind.

I was thinking about it yesterday not because I saw anyone with dirt on their face due to I barely left the house but because I remembered what they used to say to us before they blessed us with the ashes which was remember that you are dust, and to dust you shall return, which is a pretty fucked up thing to say to a LEGO-playing nerd who can barely do division.

The prayer is based on a quote from Genesis which goes like this:

"By the sweat of your brow you will eat your food until you return to the ground, since from it you were taken; for dust you are and to dust you will return."

While I was writing this song by Oneohtrix Point Never with Iggy Pop came on and it set the tone perfectly. Here's how that song goes:

The pure always act from love
The damned always act from love
The truth is an act of love
Some day, I swear, we're gonna go to a place where we can do everything we want to
And we can pet the crocodiles

I was thinking this morning when I woke up way too early from too vivid dreams that when someone dies which is to say when they begin their journey back to ash that we typically can still look at them for a while. Their body is still there and after some hard work by a mortician remember that show *Six Feet Under* that was really good wasn't it you can see them and remember them how they were. Maybe they have their favorite dress or a necklace they loved on maybe it was one you gave them many years ago. But they can't speak and they can't smile anymore and so the process has begun of stripping away the parts of them that made the person real to you and isn't that also what happens when someone who is still alive is removed from your life. You can remember how they looked but after a while you start to forget what their laugh sounded like or what it looked like when they walked across a room and so piece by piece it's stripped from you and then someday it's all gone and it's dirt now.

We think there's another part that's coming later still though don't we. We don't believe it but we think it. Maybe it's heaven or just later on down the road years from now and we get to pet the crocodiles together.

Another song I like is one called "Headache" by Grouper and it starts like this: "My mother once told me she walked into the ocean.

Didn't want to die, just couldn't tell where the horizon was. Wanted to have a closer look. Why is this costume weighing me down?"

Here's the part I actually wanted to get to this whole time and it's about a woman named Laura Gilpin. Gilpin wanted to be a poet and she went to Sarah Lawrence College and got an MFA from Columbia University and then she was a poet not because of the degrees but because she wrote poems which is what a poet does. I wanted to be a poet once and I went to school to be a poet and I wrote some poems but I'm not a poet anymore because I do something else now.

Gilpin's first book *The Hocus-Pocus of the Universe* was a marvel and people knew it at the time which is such an unlikely thing to happen. Imagine writing some poems and then people liked them and gave you money for them? What a world.

She won the Walt Whitman Award for it in 1976 which is a prestigious award for first time poets and I just looked on Amazon and you can buy a used hardcover copy of the book today for $1,099 which seems a bit steep even considering how good it is.

Here's one of the most memorable pieces from it:

"The Two-Headed Calf"

Tomorrow when the farm boys find this
freak of nature, they will wrap his body
in newspaper and carry him to the museum.

But tonight he is alive and in the north
field with his mother. It is a perfect
summer evening: the moon rising over
the orchard, the wind in the grass. And
as he stares into the sky, there are
twice as many stars as usual.

After that book was published Gilpin decided maybe she didn't want to be a poet anymore or at least didn't want to have that on her business cards because of course you never stop being a poet or do you but the thing she went and did was become a nurse and an advocate for better standards in patient care.

"Laura became a registered nurse and one of the first staff members of Planetree, an organization dedicated to developing and implementing a patient-centered model of care in hospitals," her obituary reads. "This became Laura's life work, and for over 20 years she wrote and spoke tirelessly and traveled the world to promote this vision."

Then Gilpin died at the age of fifty seven from brain cancer but not before she published one more book of poems and that bracketing makes a perfectly sad sort of sense to me because I've always said poetry is best written by and best appreciated by the young and the old because it's meant to be a manual of sorts that teaches us how to live and how to die with grace.

Michelle had never seen the Sopranos and I hadn't watched it since it was first on so we started watching it this spring and naturally Tony's ducks have resonated with me since I'm always crying about the goddamn bunny in my backyard. This part from episode three stuck with me.

TONY: Somebody called me a Frankenstein today.

MELFI: Really?

TONY: This Hasid I'm doin' business with. These Hasids, they're out there, but they got their beliefs, you know. They're not afraid of death. At least this one guy wasn't.

MELFI: Maybe they have the belief because they are afraid.

TONY: I'm not afraid of death. Not if it's for something. You know, a war, something like that. A reason. But Jackie, to see this, this strong, beautiful man just wither away to nothing. And you can't do nothing about it. And you, you can't fight it.

MELFI: Do you envy the Hasids and their beliefs?

TONY: All this shit's for nothing. And if all this shit's for nothing, why do I gotta think about it?

MELFI: That's the mystery, isn't it? The mystery of god, or whatever you want to call it, of why we're given the questionable gift of knowing we're gonna die. Do you feel like Frankenstein? A thing lacking humanity, lacking human feelings?

I sometimes think it's a rip off to be the type of person who is obsessed with mortality and riddled with existential dread because it doesn't make a difference in the end. The blissfully unbothered and the curdled nighttime cowards all end up in the same place it's just the latter have to spend the trip there in a panic.

About a year ago Michelle was teaching a unit on crayfish to her third-graders and so she went to the fish store or whatever the fuck it is and bought some and got the thing to put them in and set it up in the classroom and they were supposed to take care of them for the rest of the year. One of them came without any hands though so the rest of the crayfish turned on him I think it's a him and they bullied him to the point that she had to take it out and put it into its own space. At the end of the year the rest of the piece of shit crayfish either died or were sent home with students I forget that part but now the one crayfish nerd lives at our house and it sits in a little aquarium where it has a fancy stone pineapple it hides in. After a while it grew its little pincher hands back. We dumped food into the water and it turned that food into new hands.

I just went to dump a few pellets of food into the water and he's hiding in there and when he sees you coming he'll scuttle backwards so fast it almost looks like he teleports from one spot to the next. Sometimes he sheds his entire skin and then we both go and look like wow what the shit and then we come back and it's gone because he ate his whole ass other body. We call him Survivor and he's very lonely although we talk to him sometimes and I have existential panic attacks some nights when we can hear him scraping against the walls of his prison and I hope very much that its tiny fucking brain is too small to understand the concept of hell because if not he might think he's in it.

YOU HAVE ETERNITY TO BE DEAD SO JUST WAIT

I DON'T PARTICULARLY CARE WHAT HAPPENS TO THEM

The electrician found the body that morning but I guess it took a little while for the news to spread. It had been waiting there for three days but we didn't know that yet we just knew all of a sudden that a person was a body now and that was that. It would have been early evening when I found out about it. April. My football coach broke the news to me in a football coach voice because that was how you found out about things back then. You'd walk around not knowing some shit until someone would tell you and then you had to wait to bump into someone else and go ahead and tell them. I don't remember exactly what he said but it was something like *ay your boyfriend Kurt Cobain killed himself.* Football coaches don't like it when you care about anything other than football such as music for example which is for homosexuals. Kurt was twenty-seven years old which everyone remembers as the famous age to be dead at. I remember my coach mispronounced his name as *Co-burn* which is something a football coach would do on purpose to fuck with you and then we had to go and lift weights. I don't remember if we listened to Nirvana while we lifted the weights but I hope we did not.

Like fifteen years later a friend of mine was at the state fair in New Hampshire and he took a video of an Army guy at a recruiting tent doing pushups while "Smells Like Teen Spirit" was blasting out of his truck speakers and I sometimes wish he hadn't shown me that shit.

My football coach would have been around thirty-three back then which is insane to me because that is how old a little tiny baby is. I'm gonna picture him in my mind right now. He's got a blue shirt on and it's really tight and he's got really big arms and they're folded across his chest and he's yelling about some football business that isn't my problem anymore except for sometimes when I dream about it and I never can find my helmet in the dream and everyone is pissed off at me vis-à-vis the helmet's whereabouts. The only reason I know how old he was by the way is I just saw his name in a police report. He's a teacher at a different school now and the police charged him with indecently touching a child under fourteen and then touching her again when she was over fourteen and that is very surprising to me because he was a hard ass but I wouldn't have thought he would go and do something like that. I asked a lot of my friends from high school and some who worked with him as teachers later on and they said they weren't that surprised about it to be honest and they would know better than me because I am awful at remembering things.

They found Mac Miller's body on a Friday in September and pronounced him dead at 3:51. He was twenty-six years old. At 4:25 I saw it on TMZ and I tweeted about it and Twitter says 67,000 people saw the tweet so that was how a lot of people found out about Mac Miller being dead I guess. Someone said he was out watching football the night before he died. He was from Pittsburgh and he liked the Steelers a lot. I liked his music a lot too. The first song of his I ever heard was called "Donald Trump" and it was really good and it was from 2011 which might as well be 5,000 years ago if I try to think about what was going on in 2011 right now. I was thirty-three then which is how old a tiny baby is.

Miller struggled with addiction and depression throughout much of his young life and it was something he talked about openly. When you hear about someone who struggles with depression and addiction and talks about it openly it's surprising when they die young but not *that* surprising. When you struggle with depression and addiction you think about being dead a lot which is something I can attest to because I'm addicted to everything. Also my best friend is an addict and depressed and tells me he wants to be dead a lot and I have tried a lot of different things to get him to stop thinking that but sometimes I think I'm maybe not the best person to present the case because I tell him things like *Yes, bitch, I want to be dead too but you can't do it. You have eternity to be dead so just wait like everyone else there is no point in rushing to be dead.*

I wonder what the little girl who my football coach allegedly touched like they said in the newspaper is going to be addicted to.

Some of the things they think lead to a propensity for addiction in life are sustained stress in childhood like physical or sexual abuse or chronic pain like Kurt had in his stomach and I have also in my back and stomach. Some people think brain trauma from playing football at a young age can lead to depression and subsequently addiction later in life and I wrote about that one time which maybe I'll go ahead and throw that one in here in the book too not sure yet I'm not sure if it's weird or not to be mixing *Hell World* pieces with the stuff I write with my normal brain at my job at the writing store.

All of that is depressing but here's something more depressing: Richard Sackler, whose family owns the multibillion-dollar Purdue Pharma, was granted a patent for a new form of buprenorphine, an opioid that can be used to ease withdrawal symptoms for people addicted to painkillers. That sounds like a good thing except for the fact that Purdue Pharma is also the company that is responsible for getting everyone in America addicted to OxyContin in the first place. The *New Yorker* called the Sacklers "The Family That Built an Empire of Pain" in a stunning piece last year, which would be a great song title if I felt like making a joke about it right now which I don't really feel like doing. The company has been sued thousands of times and now numerous states are suing them as well: New York, Massachusetts, even the bad ones, like Texas and Florida whose politicians you might think don't mind so much what happens to their citizens. Colorado is the latest to sue, as the *Washington Post* reports:

> The lawsuit states that Purdue Pharma "downplayed the risk of addiction associated with opioids," "exaggerated the benefits" and "advised health care professionals that they were violating their Hippocratic Oath and failing their patients unless they treated pain symptoms with opioids," according to the statement from the Colorado attorney general's office.

Sometimes people ask me what *Hell World* is and I guess a massive pharmaceutical corporation getting everyone addicted to fancy heroin then patenting a medication that will help everyone stop being addicted to the fancy heroin is a pretty succinct definition.

It's weird to me that people who do shit like that never seem to want to kill themselves.

Here are some of the things I have been addicted to in my life or at least abused pretty significantly for a while: cigarettes, cocaine, alcohol, exercise, food, laxatives, gambling, sex and love, sleeping pills, social media, and I forget what else but that's a pretty decent catalog of shit I think. You would not be laughed out of a meeting with that resume I don't think. Sometimes I just stopped wanting to do one of them or sometimes one of them replaced the other and I didn't need it anymore because now I had the new thing to focus on. A new addiction is like a new relationship in that it's thrilling at first but then you both start to get sick of each other and so something has to change.

My therapist printed out a quote for me once that was something like "Change happens when the pain of staying the same is greater than the pain of change," and I always liked that but I just looked it up right now to double-check what the quote was and I guess it was Tony Robbins that said that shit and he's a big fucking phony so now I don't know who to trust.

One thing I have never been addicted to is heroin or opioids of any kind. I tried heroin once at a gross heroin house in my twenties because I was in a band and that is what gross band guys do in their twenties and also there was a woman there at that particular party who used to date Kurt Cobain now that I'm thinking of it and she wrote some songs about him which were good and sad. I think maybe she also dated Elliott Smith and I have to be honest both of those things are exceptionally cool to me. I don't think the gross heroin house heroin worked on me that time due to I only snorted a little but the point is I never wanted to get addicted to that sort of thing or even fuck around with it just in case. We had a lot of Oxy in our house for a couple years after Michelle had surgery and I never even opened the bottle once to look at them because you just know once you do it's going to be a whole fucking thing. We don't have them here anymore don't come and rob my house please they're in the toilet somewhere wherever the toilet brings things.

Someone did some weird sexual shit to me when I was a teenager. It was at Disney World which is pretty funny but I'm not going to talk about it right now because I have to ask my friends who were there with me and who were also on the football team what I said about it back then as they would know better than me because I am awful at remembering things which I may have mentioned earlier.

I guess the only things I am addicted to right now are cigarettes and alcohol and social media which is pretty good all things considered. Weirdly I was never anything even remotely approaching an alcoholic until about three years ago now I guess when some bad things happened and some other bad things I did came back to haunt me and I wanted to die most days off of all of that. Drinking is a really good way of making yourself not want to die in the moment but also sort of a bad coping strategy I'm told by people who would know about that sort of thing. People who wanted to die for a long time then didn't anymore.

There's a Morrissey lyric I think about a lot but not as much lately because I had to stop thinking about Morrissey as much as I normally might have due to all of the racism he was doing. But here's how it goes: "When I'm lying in my bed, I think about life and I think about death. And neither one particularly appeals to me."

I don't want to die anymore just to be clear. I don't want my best friend to die. I don't want anyone to die really except for people like the Sacklers. I don't particularly care what happens to them.

IN THE WATER MOST OF THE DIFFERENCES GO AWAY

WE'RE ALL SUBMERGED AND YOU CAN'T REALLY TELL WHAT ALL IS GOING ON UNDERNEATH

A while back I was at the Pain Center which sounds like a much more metal place than it actually is. It's really just a place where they send you when your real doctor takes a look at your whole deal and is like eh not my problem. A nurse was taking my blood pressure and the machine malfunctioned somehow so she wheeled it out of there sort of embarrassed and then never came back and I never saw her again.

Eventually a doctor turned up and I was telling him about my back pain. I had a bottle of water with me and he knocked it over accidentally then we both sort of watched it spill out onto the floor. When you have back pain the world becomes very small. Literally, because you don't want to go anywhere and also figuratively because it's hard to care about anything else.

I had had back pain before but on this particular visit it was one of the worst in my life aside from the time I snapped myself in half on the squat rack at a gym somewhere in Arlington, Virginia, when I was working as a White House intern during college which really just meant printing out articles to read and jacking off in the bathroom near where Al Gore worked. That type of back pain is bad it's where you don't want to leave the house type of pain and you have to do physics equations and shit when you're trying to sit down type of pain.

The doctor spent thirty seconds examining me and he was nice and sympathetic but he could only tell me what I figured he would which is that I have to stretch so essentially he told me nothing. He said there was a type of shot they can give me to relax the muscles but it wouldn't be for three weeks and not because they're too busy or anything the process itself takes minutes but because it takes weeks for the insurance company to say it's ok to do. Three weeks doesn't seem like too long but when you've got back pain every second is forever and any task encompasses summoning the entirety of the world.

He recommended acupuncture which I do now but it's so expensive he said and I agreed it is and he wished insurance would cover it and I agreed with the doctor on that also. They cover fentanyl patches but not acupuncture he said which makes no sense he said. So he gave me a script for muscle relaxers and then went and found some weird coupon for a patch you put on the muscle that got me twenty dollars off so thank you for that. There were some leftover Oxys in our closet at home at the time and I could feel them in there like they had a voice that would pulsate out to me sometimes but I never took them because that's the last shit I need at this point. When the bottle of water spilled the doctor didn't do anything for a minute then realized he probably should so he bent down to move it back upright and that was it and he walked out and I got dressed and the puddle of water was still there on the floor when I left.

On top of the acupuncture the other thing I do now which I may have mentioned before is swim every day and it somehow loosens my back up but I hate it so much now it fucking sucks it sucks so bad going there and getting in there and I hate it. Ok hold on now I'm in the locker room at the pool for this next part.

We speak so many languages in here. Some of us are half dressed and some of us are fully dressed in the locker room I'm compelled to go to but we're all either on the way toward or just coming back from being naked and exposed which is a necessary step before getting into the water. We speak Russian and Mandarin and Japanese and Spanish and we're so old some of us older than you would think a person could be or so young or somewhere in between like me which is an age defined by its distance from either of those unimaginable poles. Think about what you think of when you think about what Boston looks like and the locker room is the opposite of that.

We are strong in here or frail or full of confidence or hesitant and ashamed of the sin of our bodies. Sometimes I glance at the powerful ones and imagine what it would be like to live inside of there and sometimes I glance at the decaying ones and imagine what it would be like to live inside of there and sometimes I glance at my own and imagine what it would be like to not live inside of there anymore. Sometimes I don't think much of anything at all I just sleepwalk through it all letting the numbing routine of it carry me along to where I was always going to end up which is in the water.

There's a steam room too and I go in there before swimming and one time a guy was in there on his phone watching trailer after trailer for the Nathan Fillion series *The Rookie*, Tuesdays on ABC in the opaque humidity and I was like what the fuck but I didn't ask him what his deal was because it's not my business.

In the water most of the differences in age and appearance go away because we're all submerged and you can't really tell what all is going on with someone's whole thing underneath. The ways we get into the pool vary though. The unbothered squealing children bomb into the water and the older people lower themselves in hesitantly. I do a sort of half jump half fall like a reluctant skydiver and then I sink to the bottom for a minute where it's quiet and no one can see me.

When you think about people running which is something I can't do anymore due to I broke myself you might typically imagine a young fit person running along so fast and an older person plodding through but that's not what it's like in the water it depends on how much time you've spent in there over the years. An older person might skitter with practiced finesse like a pond bug and a strong young oaf might sputter along so much slower than the effortlessness he's used to in every other aspect of his life thinking Jesus Christ this sucks and things of that nature. Sometimes I swim so fast I feel like a leviathan displacing tidal waves with every stroke and sometimes I can't remember how to breathe right or do anything besides not drown and I swallow gallons of piss and snot which the pool is filled with something I know because I put my own piss and snot in there too.

In the water the things you take for granted everywhere else such as not being on the precipice of dying any second go away and you have to make a conscious effort to think about every stroke forward and ideally it just becomes another part of who you are after enough practice but I'm not there yet I still have to try really hard which is probably good for me because I don't like to let my mind have a moment of stillness. So I look at the blue line painted on the pool floor that they put there so you know when you've just about gone too far and have to turn around before you smash your head on the wall something I've done more times than I care to confess or else I turn over on my back and there are flags suspended in the air that serve the same purpose. Time to slow down they say. Someone told me you can get an iPod that goes underwater now so you can listen to podcasts and such when you're trying not to drown but I'm not gonna listen to a podcast life is too short.

The YMCA was founded in 1844 which is so much older than I would have guessed before I looked it up. It was founded by a guy named Sir George Williams in London and its general operating premise was something called Muscular Christianity which sounds like an extremely specific fetish for religious perverts which it is but not in the way that it sounds. Basically it meant teaching young men not to be such pieces of shit and if we're being honest that has traditionally been a pretty tall order throughout the entirety of human history. It also meant getting them to practice teamwork and discipline and so on through athletics. They talked about "the expulsion of all that is effeminate, un-English, and excessively intellectual," but I'm pretty sure that part isn't mentioned too much at the YMCAs around the world anymore and certainly not at the one I go to which goes to great lengths to promote its inclusivity.

Originally they were organized as a way to provide housing for rural laborers coming into the city around the onset of industrialization and as an added bonus they gave the young men a more wholesome outlet besides things like gambling and fucking and drinking. Of course they also wanted the big boys to do Bible study. The motto they agreed upon in 1855 was taken from the Book of John. "That they all may be one."

Another thing they set up not long after was public pools which is pretty ingenious I have to admit because it is not particularly easy to gamble or fuck or get wasted while you're swimming laps. I went to see a painting I really like at the ICA in Boston a few years back called *Swimming, Smoking, Crying* by an artist named Dana Schutz and I would have called it a big mood but no one had said that particular phrase yet. There's a photo I have in my phone from that night of Michelle posing in front of some fucking painting that I don't remember in my mind but I remember how cool she looks like too cool for me to be there with.

Eventually the YMCA went on to give the world a whole bunch of really cool shit like basketball which was invented in 1891 at a YMCA in

Springfield, Massachusetts, and volleyball which was invented in 1895 at a YMCA in Holyoke Massachusetts and the song "YMCA" which was invented in 1978 by the Village People in New York City. "YMCA" was my grandmother's favorite song and when we were young my sister and I would choreograph dance routines to that and the *Grease* soundtrack for her and have her play them over and over again. I am not entirely sure she knew what was going on with the Village People and their deal. Another thing she really liked to do a lot was to drink a whole bunch of gin and she got pretty good at that before she died.

In Massachusetts where I grew up there is roughly one week a year where the water isn't frigid but it never matters I will always get into the ocean and swim and float and let the waves slap into me because that is what I've always been compelled to do against my better judgment. In Maine I'd climb down the slick rocks tearing my feet on the barnacles and jump in not listening to my grandmother who constantly warned me about the riptides because no one listens to their grandparents until they're dead then you listen to them all the time which I may have mentioned earlier. One time on the western coast of Mexico I waded into the voracious undercurrent of the desolate beautiful beach next to our hotel where no one was swimming because it was too dangerous and I got in anyway because I needed to feel what it was like to almost be carried away and guess what those people who were not swimming there were geniuses because that shit was very stupid of me to do in retrospect. Another time in Vermont Michelle and I pulled over under a picture-perfect covered bridge and I jumped into the freezing river and felt a current so strong I felt like it could break me in half. Another time at the very tip of Scotland I waded out into the water of a desolate bay that felt like the end of the world and swam alone out to an island that I had no business swimming to then I went back to the hotel and drank whisky until I didn't have to think anymore.

There's a difference between swimming for leisure and swimming out of necessity which is what I do now since I broke my body. You feel alive in the open water. It's the most natural thing in the world. It's a return to where we came from. The pool that I'm compelled to go to now is claustrophobic and lonelier than you would expect despite the fact that I'm surrounded by people all forcing themselves through the same steps I am. I've been a very strong swimmer my entire life I just never really learned how to do it the right way. They say getting help from other people works and I take lessons from a nice young woman sometimes.

The rest of that quote from the Bible goes like this: ". . . that they may all be one. As you, Father, are in me and I am in you, may they also be in us, so that the world may believe that you have sent me."

Around the time they were taking my older sister away from the hospital fucking up my mother for the rest of her life my father was doing things such as burning down part of my grandmother's house where we all lived and going to jail for that. My father never learned how to live very well and now doesn't live at all but he was very prolific at bringing others to life. Another thing he was good at was drinking a lot although I just realized now I have no idea what it was he actually liked drinking which is sort of like knowing your father was a talented baseball player but not having any idea what position he played. We all went to watch him die years later after he'd learned how to live a little better and I would go to the hospital and look at his once powerful and now ruined body and imagine what it would be like to live inside of there but it wasn't all that hard to do because it feels like I already do.

Y

WE ALWAYS THOUGHT MY SEXUAL ASSAULT WAS THE FUNNIEST THING

I AM TRYING VERY HARD TO REMEMBER WHAT HAPPENED AFTER THAT BUT I DON'T REMEMBER

The hot tub was warm I remember that and the man in the warm tub said had I ever thought about being a model. I had thought about that to be honest because I had just done a fashion show at the mall with my friend whose mother worked at the hair salon there and so we walked on a runway with our bouncing nineties hair and felt pretty cool about that at the time as you can probably imagine.

The tub in question was at the Grand Floridian Hotel at Disney World which I remember seeming like the fanciest place in the world owing to the fact that I was seventeen and I'd probably visited three states in my life at that point. We'd driven all the way there from Massachusetts in my friend's parents' van and I was just ecstatic to be anywhere besides the mall where I had done that modeling gig I mentioned before. They don't have many stores at the mall anymore it's mostly bowling alleys and such and I saw recently that Soul Asylum was playing at the bowling alley there which made me pretty sad to think about. When you're in a band you're supposed to say things like a gig is a gig but I never believed that type of horse shit which is probably why none of my bands ever made it very far. One time I saw a guy who was on *Baywatch* there going to the movies and he was the most in-shape guy I've ever seen in my life.

A couple years before that I had sex for the first time at the same haircut friend's house. It was at a party and I didn't want to do it but she was older and I was fifteen and it was the first time someone had ever seemed like they really wanted me and that is what you do when someone wants you you let them have you. I don't remember her name anymore but I remember worrying for a while after that I had gotten AIDS from it because I was a child and children are fucking stupid when it comes to knowing about things like sex and AIDS.

I don't know how well regarded the Grand Floridian is today vis-à-vis hotels at Disney World or anything about Disney World. My high school friends go there all the time with their children but I don't have any children and as a result of that no real pressing need to get back to Disney World in any sort of hurry. Another time I went there with my own family when I was around thirteen and I had an *Appetite for Destruction* T-shirt on in the pictures I don't have access to anymore but that comprise the bulk of my memory regarding that particular trip which I remember feeling pretty cool about at the time. In my memory I'm a fat little mess.

One of the main jobs you can get in modeling as everyone knows is when you have to pose in your underwear so we had better go get a look at you in your underwear inside there in the bathroom the man told me which seemed to make sense so we got out of the tub and went to go take care of that one last formality before my modeling career was about to take off. I don't remember what the man looked like but I remember the layout of the bathroom vividly. I could probably draw a blueprint of the bathroom if I had a big drafting table and one of those visors that architects wear in movies when they're doing architecture stuff in the role of like Jennifer Aniston's boyfriend the handsome architect.

There's a song that I would have been listening to a lot back then that used to make me cry and it's about a young addict who is being abused by her boyfriend and she says something like she's never been in love she don't know what it is she only knows if someone wants her and I just looked up the lyrics and the next line is "I want 'em if they want me" but I've spent the last twenty five years thinking it was "I wonder if they want me?" which seems a lot sadder and is also a question I think every time I meet someone. I've only really ever been any good at two things in my life which are writing and making people want me because when someone wants you that is how you know you are good.

The song is just two chords over and over incidentally. G A G A G A G and it just goes back and forth like that forever.

One other modeling insider tip I can share with you is that a lot of times the guys when they pose in their underwear in the magazines and such they need to have a bit of a bulge going on down there and one way to do that is to rub yourself a little bit so it shows off better so why don't we do that and see what happens.

I am trying very hard to remember what happened after that but I don't remember. I do not remember. I don't really remember a single other thing that happened on that trip besides one thing which is what my friend the big time modeling agent told me and that is that I had potential but I would have to work on tightening up my abs a little bit and there are two reasons I remember that because it is something I have thought about every minute of my life since then, how I need to tighten up my abs a little bit, and also because it became a funny little joke among me and my friends who I was there with at Disney World because we didn't know how to talk about what had happened to me in any other way besides joking because young men are fucking stupid when it comes to knowing about things like sexual assault. I guess adult men are stupid about that too because I still don't really know if this counts as sexual assault. What is it called when an adult brings a teenager into a bathroom and convinces them to touch themselves in front of them and maybe touches them a little bit too but you don't remember because you blacked out?

In any case we decided to all treat it like a joke because we didn't know what else to do or how to talk about anything due to having the brain damage of being young men.

I asked my two friends who were there and our other friend who we would talk about everything with back then what they remember about that night.

"I remember you started the story by saying, 'Something really weird happened . . .'" my friend Mike told me the other day.

"I believe when you first told us it happened, you just said the guy asked to see you naked. It was late '90s, right? So I think we were all still in the mode where it was silly that gay men asked to see your stuff," my friend Nick said. "It was basically another chapter in a book you were writing that had life experiences the rest of us, in this clique, would never imagine happening to us. I actually never thought of you as a victim at all, until the last few weeks."

If I had to guess what my friends back then thought about me it would be something like that. I was somewhat more advanced in terms of life experiences because when people want you you get all sorts of opportunities that other people don't such as modeling contracts.

"I remember you talking about it pretty nonchalantly," my friend Chris said. "I think that's why I took it as a goof of sorts. You also were one of my friends who it seemed like weird, odd, funny things happened to way more than me so I chalked it up to 'Luke being Luke.' I couldn't imagine being in that situation, but I could see Luke having it happen to him."

"We definitely thought it was funny, and every remembrance of it in the last twenty years was framed in humor," Nick said. He mentioned once that he had assumed I had liked it owing to me being the type of person who liked getting attention.

"I don't know if I thought you liked it, but at the time I definitely thought, 'Nobody would do that if they didn't want to do that.' I think a key thing is that I believe it was years later that you admitted someone touched you . . . or did he? My memory tells me you told us he asked to touch it, but you didn't want to and just showed it to him. But am I remembering right now that he actually touched you?" I don't remember.

"I know from day one I thought it was all fucked up. Every piece of it was odd, and strange, and crazy, but it didn't surprise me that you were in that situation," Nick said. "To this day, I cannot imagine how that situation evolved. Having spent more time in Disney World than any other person I actually know, I can say with 100 percent certainty that nothing remotely like that has happened to me, and I would wager in my nearly fifty trips to Disney World, probably forty-five or so since that event happened, I think about it every time I'm there. I always find this situation fucked up, but I don't know if I ever knew, or actually know now, the whole truth about what happened."

"We would definitely bring it up as a joke, but it also seemed more odd and inappropriate than funny," Mike said. "I don't think we ever conceived of it as a violation, which it clearly was. Maybe it's outrageousness made us laugh."

Chris said he had wondered sometimes if I'd just made it up as a funny story.

"I don't know if I fully believed you made it up, but more it was my own defense mechanism of it couldn't have really happened. Especially at Disney World. I may have thought you might have embellished for the story afterwards, like it happened, but maybe you were more of a willing participant going back to how you would strip and be naked for laughs with us."

Being naked among your guy friends out of nowhere is a very reliable form of comedy when you are young and don't really know what else to do.

"Did we assume men couldn't get assaulted in that way?" Mike asked. "No way we would have the same reaction if you were a girl."

I kind of wish I hadn't brought this up all of a sudden but I guess it's too late now. I feel like my experience pales in comparison to what other people have gone through, especially women, and that maybe it doesn't even count? Earlier I wrote about how my high school football coach had been charged with molesting a thirteen-year-old girl in his class and I just read in the news that the school knew about it for three months and didn't report it to police and they sent the girl back into class with him and he ended up touching her again during that time.

I was a big strapping teenager after all I probably could have fought the guy off if I wanted to and besides he wasn't forcing me to do anything so maybe I was sexually assaulting myself and there just happened to be someone there to watch? Now that I think of it it was in June which means I had probably just turned eighteen a couple of weeks before. That's the sort of thing they make a whole production out of in porn when the girl has just turned eighteen because it's supposed to be exciting that you would go to jail for having sex with her a few days before but now you won't. And then once she's there in porn there are two types of roles they make her play which is one where she really wants to have sex with the guy a lot more than you might expect her to due to the guy is always a lot older and then there is the kind where she doesn't want to and he has to sort of convince her and eventually she gives in.

One thing my therapist told me the other day is that when young people are taken advantage of they might experience a particularly insidious type of shame because sometimes while knowing instinctively that what is happening is wrong they also inadvertently can get pleasure out of it in some cases and that really fucks them up pretty bad.

I wrote last year about a thing I have in my brain called exercise bulimia which means I compulsively exercise to the point of self harm so I won't get fat and I wrote at the time if I didn't get it under control I would probably end up doing some permanent damage to my body which happened not too long after the piece came out as it turns out haha. But everyone told me I was good and brave for writing it and tons of people wrote to me saying it's important for people to talk about stuff like this and thank you for doing it Luke you are good and making a difference which is nice to hear but also probably a bunch of bullshit. I'm writing a piece where I have had to talk to about ten young men about their experiences being body shamed when they were young and all the fucked up things that has done to them throughout their lives in terms of hating themselves and having depression and anorexia and sometimes I worry that I'm not the right person to be talking about all this shit publicly because I have not gotten better and no amount of talking about it has helped me make any changes in my life like I write about in all the articles people tell me I'm good for doing. I'm certainly no role model. I've done my share of disreputable shit in the pursuit of being wanted such as being reckless and promiscuous and unfaithful at times in my life.

The past year I haven't been able to run or lift weights because my back and the entire right side of my abdominals went to shit and I worry that that means no one is ever going to want me ever again. Instead I started swimming every day to try to get back into shape and every day after I get out of the pool I go and stand there naked in the locker room and stare at myself in the mirror for a few minutes while people are trying to get shit out of their lockers and dry themselves off and putting their bathing suits in that little bathing suit machine that sucks all the water out of it and sounds like a lawn mower and I think sometimes I look ok and sometimes I think I am disgusting but one thing I think every single time is that I'd be a lot better off if I could just tighten up my abs a little bit.

WHO EATS THE SIN-EATER'S SINS?

MOST PEOPLE DO NOT ATTEND HOURLY TO THE SINS OF THE WORLD

In 2010 a fundraiser was held to repair the grave of a man named Richard Munslow. In the century since Munslow had been buried in the town of Ratlinghope about an hour outside of Birmingham the stone that marked his life had fallen into disrepair. After a few months the £1,000 needed to hire a local stonemason was raised and the work was done.

"This grave at Ratlinghope is now in an excellent state of repair," the Reverend Norman Morris, the town's vicar, told the BBC at the time. "But I have no desire to reinstate the ritual that went with it."

The ritual in question was known as sin-eating, the art of which Munslow is believed to have been the last practitioner. In the eighteenth and nineteenth centuries in the surrounding area and up through Scotland and Wales sin-eaters would have been a familiar sight if not one exactly sanctioned by the church. Having a monopoly on the redemption of souls they would have seen such a practice as muscling in on their corner.

The essence of Munslow's duties was to perform a sort of shamanistic ritual in which a piece of bread and a bowl of ale were passed over the remains of the recently deceased. The sins of the deceased were *as any idiot will obviously understand* thereby subsumed into the meal and the sad bastard would dine on them taking the sins on as his own and ensuring that the dead would pass unmolested through the gates of Heaven.

Sin-eaters were commonly itinerant and destitute types traveling here and there until they were called upon in haste. Who but the most desperate would agree to such a one-sided metaphysical bargain in the first place? They were paid very little for the gruesome task and furthermore shunned as foul pariahs for their trouble when it was done. Each bite of bread and each sip of ale further curdled their own load-bearing souls.

Munslow was unique however in that he was said to be a well-established farmer in his time before getting into sin-eating. It was the loss of his four children that drove him to the practice it's been written. Perhaps it was out of grief or perhaps it was an attempt to ensure their safe passage into the next life. You almost have to respect it. Unlike the other gig economy sin-eaters our man did it for the love of the game. All of a sudden the world's collective goth girlfriends look like hacks in comparison.

Here are some things that happened in August of 2018.

On a Tuesday a woman being held in jail in Texas killed herself. She couldn't afford the $1,500 she would need for bail. Meanwhile a GoFundMe for Peter Strzok a very well-off cop who lost his job for being rude to the president had raised almost $450,000 in less than a week.

On a Friday dozens of Yemeni children were bombed to their deaths by a missile fired by the Saudi-led and U.S.-supported coalition. It hit their school bus. As CNN reported the "500-pound laser-guided MK 82 bomb" was made by Lockheed Martin. A BBC reporter posted a picture of what was left of their belongings to Twitter and the image is an array of bright blue UNICEF backpacks strewn along the ground splattered with blood.

On a Wednesday a man named Joel Arrona-Lara was seized by ICE while stopped at a gas station in San Bernadino. He was in the process of bringing his pregnant wife to the hospital to give birth.

The agents left her to fend for herself and the aftermath was caught on the security camera of the gas station. She's crying and distraught and very very pregnant standing there next to the Doritos and shit. "Mom forced to deliver without dad" the chyron on CBS LA read.

That same week a Houston doctor was sentenced to ten years' probation after being convicted of raping a sedated patient in her hospital bed who was there after experiencing a severe asthma attack. Shafeeq Sheikh lost his medical license but would serve no time.

"Testifying in Spanish through an interpreter, the former patient said in the early morning of Nov. 2, 2013, she awoke to find a man at her bedside in a white doctor's coat saying he needed to examine her. He pushed up her gown and touched her breasts in an 'ugly way,' and she pushed the call button repeatedly, she said. Witnesses testified that it had been unplugged from the wall," the *Houston Chronicle* reported.

Sheikh testified that the sex had been consensual saying that she was the instigator and then his lawyer showed the jury images from Laura's Instagram where she had posted a number of "sexy" photos as part of her job promoting a clothing boutique which is the universal signal that we all understand which means it's ok to rape someone.

"He made a mistake, but he didn't sexually assault her," his attorney Lisa Andrews argued. "Here we have this Latina woman with her fake boobs that came onto that little nerdy middle-aged guy, and he lost his mind."

Every so often a poll will come out that says something like 3 percent of respondents had "little to no awareness of Donald Trump" and we tend to scoff in amusement at that sort of thing like lol must be nice. But I wonder sometimes about those people—those beautiful, smooth-brained and innocent children of god—whether or not they're on to something the rest of us aren't.

Most people do not attend hourly to the sins of the world in its perpetual cycle of grief and misery on Twitter. Most people have better things to do with their lives than read 10,000 posts. Presumably if you are reading this you trend toward the heavier news diet than most if not quite on the *Clockwork Orange* eyeball torture feed I subsist on.

I wonder if there's a better way to live without abstaining from the feed entirely?

What exactly is it we're doing those of us who scroll through our newsfeed endlessly like an addict lifelessly pulling the lever on a slot machine waiting for information and sadness to spill out?

Certainly there are ways to effect change in the world—taking to the streets, protesting, boycotts, pressuring your representatives, helping register people to vote—but those of us on the barricades of the news cycle I think sometimes delude and flatter ourselves that by paying vigilant witness we're performing some necessary function.

Sometimes I think like the destitute sin-eaters that I behold the grief of the world without respite because I have no other choice. Each sin I consume I can turn into a living. Much like them it's a paltry one to be sure and we're not much respected either. Other times I think a lot of us and this includes myself tend to be more like ol' Bobby Munslow. We've been driven mad with grief and we know nothing else but to continue to compound it in a gluttonous feast. We gorge ourselves on the sins of others until it sickens us hoping without any sort of reliable proof that in the end it might help someone but knowing nonetheless that it won't.

Y

EXTENDING THE AREA OF FREEDOM

TO BE CAUGHT HAPPY IN A WORLD OF MISERY WAS FOR AN HONEST MAN THE MOST DESPICABLE OF CRIMES

Around 12:30 on a Tuesday at Westside Middle School just outside of Jonesboro, Arkansas the fire alarm went off. Andrew Golden an eleven year old student who had pulled the alarm raced outside into a field near the school where he found his friend thirteen year old Mitchell Johnson. Johnson was waiting there with nine weapons and thousands of rounds of ammunition they had stolen from their families.

There had been construction going on near the school at the time so when the loud noises started many of the students and faculty who had dutifully marched outside were slow to realize what was going on. Why would they have any idea? When people started falling to the ground they still didn't immediately put it together survivors have since explained.

It was twenty one years ago and while it wasn't the first school shooting bullet-riddled children's bodies weren't a perpetual specter in the national consciousness as of yet. It wasn't the grim ambient horror we take for granted today. That wouldn't happen until Columbine which was a little over a year later. The school shooting when everything changed and then nothing much changed.

On the anniversary of the Columbine shooting in 2018 millions of people in hundreds of cities around the world gathered for the March For Our Lives a student-led demonstration in support of gun violence prevention. The march was inspired by a different school shooting which happened the month before in Parkland, Florida in which seventeen people were killed and seventeen more injured. The school shooting when everything changed and then nothing much changed.

And thus the shooting at Westside felt like it was being overshadowed once again by a larger one as some of the survivors said last year according to NPR.

People often say after attacks like this and the shooting at two mosques in New Zealand in March of 2019 that we're not supposed to publicize the killers' names. That's what they want people say and that may be true but there are so many of them now who could ever keep track? Have I used that line already in this book? I think so but there are so many stories like this we have to write after shootings who can keep track of our clichés? Try to name as many shootings as you can. Wrong there were way more than that. How many shootings like this can any one person be expected to hold inside of them forever? Unless you were there of course in which case you likely never forget a second of it.

"It has bothered me ever since, and I'm sure it will haunt me the rest of my life," Dale Haas told the *Arkansas Democrat Gazette* last year. Haas was the county sheriff at the time of the Jonesboro shooting. He's retired now and he homeschools his fourteen year old son but his wife still goes to work every day as a teacher in Jonesboro.

"It just kind of makes you sick at the pit of your stomach that it keeps happening," Haas said. "I don't see it stopping anytime soon. I think the moral compass of the country needs to be reset."

By the time the little boys in Arkansas were done massacring everyone five people were dead at Westside including four students and a teacher named Shannon Wright who people later said stepped in front of a child to shield her with her own body. Ten others were injured.

Golden and Johnson attempted to flee to a van they had parked nearby with ample supplies but were soon caught by police. They were found guilty and sentenced to prison until their twenty-first birthdays due to the fact that Arkansas law at the time did not yet allow for juveniles to be sentenced to life.

During the trial both boys attempted to show a type of remorse. "My thoughts and prayers are with those people who were killed, or shot, and their families," Johnson said, which is nice of him because in that apology as the killer he inadvertently wrote the script for politicians when these types of shootings happen. Thoughts and prayers. "I am really sad inside about everything," he said. "My thoughts and prayers are with those kids that I go to school with."

Both were released at twenty-one. Johnson went on to have more trouble with the law and Golden largely disappeared but what's curious about that is that they actually lived. The familiar beats we all know about how this type of story is supposed to go hadn't yet been established. They're supposed to kill themselves shortly after the attack right? It's like going back to the early days of a now familiar genre of story and seeing that the reliable structure hadn't been solidified.

We know what happens now after the killing though which is nothing much. Not in America anyway.

There have been at least fifteen fatal shootings at houses of worship since 2012 including a shooting at the Tree of Life Congregation synagogue in Pittsburgh in October of 2018 in which eleven were killed and six were wounded.

There were at least 103 incidents of gunfire on school grounds in America in 2018 according to Everytown For Gun Safety. That meant 60 deaths and 88 injuries — numbers that have been steadily rising since they started keeping track in 2013. That was shortly after the shooting in Newtown, Connecticut when a couple dozen babies were shot to death. That was the one that was well you know how it goes.

Many of the survivors of attacks like these go on to struggle with one important question which is the question that all of us ask anytime there's a mass shooting: Why?

Bobby McDaniel was the lawyer for the Jonesboro families and he helped secure a civil verdict against Johnson and Golden in 2017. The families were awarded $150 million which is money they knew going into it they would likely never see but was nonetheless a symbolic gesture. Symbolic gestures are always in ample supply because nothing else is ever available. Not in America anyway.

"This effort was never about any money for us," Pam Herring whose child was killed told the *Jonesboro Sun.* "We had to honor our loved ones and tell the court how much it hurt to have them taken from us, even all these years later."

"We also hope something can be learned from their depositions which may help prevent a similar situation in the future."

"The real important aspect of this case is the why was it done, what did we learn from it, and how can we implement what we've learned?" McDaniel said.

So what have we learned? Nothing much.

Two days after fifty were killed in New Zealand prime minister Jacinda Ardern addressed the country and the world. "There will be changes to our gun laws," she said. Changes in gun laws including a likely ban on semi-automatic weapons which came six days later.

"I absolutely believe there will be a common view amongst New Zealanders, those who use guns for legitimate purposes, and those who have never touched one, that the time for the mass and easy availability of these weapons must end. And today they will," she said.

She also said that the country would be putting together a generous buyback program for citizens who already own such weapons in an effort that will cost between $100-200 million and doesn't all of that sound so reasonable it's almost hard to believe it's possible? Australia did something similar after a mass shooting in 1996 buying back around 650,000 guns and then something super surprising happened once there were fewer guns around in that suicide and homicide rates plummeted.

"The average firearm suicide rate in Australia in the seven years after the bill declined by 57 percent compared with the seven years prior. The average firearm homicide rate went down by about 42 percent," according to Vox.

Here's another crazy and true thing. The opposition leader in New Zealand Simon Bridges who is the head of their center-right National Party there agreed immediately with Ardern that this was the right and just thing to do.

"We agree that the public doesn't need access to military-style semi-automatic weapons. National supports them being banned along with assault rifles," he said.

What the fuck.

Unsurprisingly among the people to point out the rot at the heart of this deeply shameful country and our love affair with playing big strong army man who everyone wants to hug and kiss was Alexandria Ocasio-Cortez who tweeted in part that "Sandy Hook happened six years ago and we can't even get the Senate to hold a vote on universal background checks," and that is very true and a good point and all but did you realize Sandy Hook was only six years ago because to me it feels like it was a lot longer than that. It feels like it's a story that we were born with. It's like the thing about how Romulus and Remus were raised by wolves and then went onto found Rome but in our case it's about how a guy with a gun massacred a school full of tiny little babies hundreds of years ago and we decided to build a country on the very spot to mark the occasion and weave its inevitability into our patriotic mythology. If we ever end up redesigning the American flag it should probably be a third grader with a bullet hole in her face and then you could have an eagle or something in the background so everyone still thinks we're tough.

Sometimes I get up and say ok I'm gonna go write the fucking newsletter now and I close my eyes and open my computer and wake up an hour or three later and it's there written like I blacked out and sometimes I sit here all day saying fuck fuck fuck and nothing happens. Today I tried to electrify my brain worms by paging through To the Lighthouse and it made me depressed because how could anyone ever hope to write something that beautiful. I have a really old dusty copy of it on the bookshelf and there are two different sets of notes scrawled in the margins one in a woman's hand but I have no idea who I don't remember and one in someone else's hand that I guess is mine but I don't recognize it or remember doing it so maybe those were written by someone else I no longer recognize as well. I stopped on this part which me or someone else like me had highlighted.

. . . as if to be caught happy in a world of misery was for an honest man the most despicable of crimes...

I don't remember all the details but I'm pretty sure Ramsey is a big time shit head in the book so maybe I don't want to identity too much with him but that's what it feels like sometimes when I am not thinking about how bad everything is and then something will come along and snap me back into reality.

One thing I think about a lot is how insane it is that writing things and talking to people and reading is my job when I watch Michelle come home at 5:30 after leaving at 7 a.m. to go teach kids all day how to be a person. A lot of people tell themselves they worked hard for the nice jobs they have and sometimes people tell me I'm a hard worker and it's really embarrassing because it's not true or maybe it is I don't know it's like how you can't ever see your own eye ball. I stole that line just now which is one of the things a writer can do to become successful quicker than normal and then lose their job quicker than normal once you get caught. Or at least you used to people don't seem to get all that red-assed about plagiarism anymore at least not when it's someone powerful doing it.

Here's where I stole it from:

Most people don't have to think about what their faces mean the way I do. Your face in the mirror, reflected back at you, most people don't even know what it looks like anymore. That thing on the front of your head, you'll never see it, like you'll never see your own eyeball with your own eyeball, like you'll never smell what you smell like, but me, I know what my face looks like. I know what it means. My eyes droop like I'm fucked up, like I'm high, and my mouth hangs open all the time. There's too much space between each of the parts of my face—eyes, nose, mouth, spread out like a drunk slapped it on reaching for another drink. People look at me then look away when they see I see them see me. That's the Drome too. My power and curse. The Drome is my mom and why she drank, it's the way history lands on a face, and all the ways I made it so far despite how it has fucked with me since the day I found it there on the TV, staring back at me like a fucking villain.

It's from this book I read called *There There* by Tommy Orange which everyone seems to have lost their shit off of. I usually am pretty skeptical when everyone loses their shit off of a book but boy were people right in this particular case because I was hooked at the epigraph.

In the dark times
Will there also be singing?
Yes, there will also be singing.
About the dark times. — Bertolt Brecht
And it goes on like this . . .

Some of us grew up with stories about massacres. Stories about what happened to our people not so long ago. How we came out of it. At Sand Creek, we heard it said that they mowed us down with their howitzers. Volunteer militia under Colonel John Chivington came to kill us—we were mostly women, children, and elders. The men were away to hunt. They'd told us to fly the American flag. We flew that and a white flag too. Surrender, the white flag waved. We stood under both flags as they came at us. They did more than kill us. They tore us up. Mutilated us. Broke our fingers to take our rings, cut off our ears to take our silver, scalped us for our hair . . . .

Oh right. I guess we do actually have a specific violent mythology about the founding of America now that I think of it. We don't need to update it to the Sandy Hook thing we already have blood in our bones.

They didn't call them mass shootings back then though they called it manifest destiny. Andrew Jackson called it "extending the area of freedom." Some other stuff he said around the time of the Indian Removal Act were things like "What good man would prefer a country covered with forests and ranged by a few thousand savages to our extensive Republic, studded with cities, towns, and prosperous farms embellished with all the improvements which art can devise or industry execute,

occupied by more than 12,000,000 happy people, and filled with all the blessings of liberty, civilization and religion?"

One of the things Michelle has to do at her job that is an actual job is to prepare the tiny little children whose brains she is responsible for to know what to do in case a guy comes along and wants to extend the area of freedom which is a reality that teachers everywhere have been forced to contend with.

In January during active shooter drills at an elementary school in Indiana what the police there did is they rounded up the teachers and brought them into a room in groups of four and staged mock executions.

"The incident, acknowledged in testimony this week before state lawmakers, was confirmed by two elementary school teachers in Monticello, who described an exercise in which teachers were asked by local law enforcement to kneel down against a classroom wall before being sprayed across their backs with plastic pellets without warning," according to the *Indianapolis Star*.

"They told us, 'This is what happens if you just cower and do nothing,'" said one of teachers. "They shot all of us across our backs. I was hit four times.

"It hurt so bad."

"It's a soft, round projectile," White County Sheriff Bill Brooks whose department was pretending to shoot the teachers said. "The key here is 'soft.'"

So stop being such fucking babies I guess is what he meant.

"They all knew they could be [shot]," he said. "It's a shooting exercise."

Does something about the term "active shooter" bother you because it has always bothered me and I don't know why. You hear it on the news whenever someone is going around extending the area of freedom and it always seems like an unnecessary qualifier to me.

What would the opposite of an active shooter be you might ask and it never really occurred to me until now that it would be a passive shooter which sounds like something that couldn't exist but that's technically the term reserved for when police kill somebody.

I wrote somewhere in here what a terrible idea it is to call the police on someone going through a mental health crisis because surprisingly they show up and after about thirty seconds of standing around playing with their dicks they usually end up pissing their pants and shooting the guy to death. Well it's not the police who shoot them it's some nebulous unknowable causality that transpires whereby the bullets located in the cops' guns teleport into a new form inside of the victim's body. A local news report about a man in Pennsylvania this year demonstrated how this magic works.

"A man is dead after a shooting this afternoon," one of the anchors said by way of introduction. "Police aren't saying much else only that officers became involved in a shooting that left a man dead," the second added.

He was black just so we're clear. I know you were already thinking it but wanted to make sure we were on the same page.

Or try another report on the same shooting from a different local station.

"One person is dead following a shooting," the anchor said before throwing to a reporter on the scene. "One person has died after an officer involved shooting," she said and then the police chief came on to call it an officer involved shooting which the reporter dutifully repeated once again.

I'm not sure if this is related to any of that stuff above but for the second day in a row schools in Charlottesville, Virginia were closed in March after someone made a racist death threat.

Someone "claiming to be a student at Charlottesville High School, one of the region's largest schools, warned white students to stay at home so they could shoot dead non-white students in an act of 'ethnic cleansing,'" Reuters reported.

What do you want to do when you see something like that? You want to find the person and grab them by the neck and scream in their face that we don't do this sort of thing here. This sort of thing does not happen and we will not allow it you'd say but somewhere inside you'd know you were lying because it always has and we always do.

I WAS THINKING ABOUT MURDERING BABOONS

PEOPLE ALWAYS TURN THE THINGS THEY WANT TO KILL INTO PESTS

It's early morning in the hills of South Africa and the fog has yet to burn off and the men are breathing heavily in their camouflage and Indiana Jones costumes. A black man in hunter green and a bright red hat seems to know his way around and he's pointing into the distance saying look over there and that sort of thing. About six hundred yards away a group of baboons is running along a cliff side and there seems to be a lot of them which is very exciting news for the hunters as you can probably imagine. As the camera zooms in from over their shoulders you can just make out the shapes of the scrambling baboons but the image isn't very high quality so they look like poorly animated blurry pixels. Y'all better shoot 'em one guy says, they're gonna move. You shoot the one on the right I'll shoot the one on the left let's go. At first they miss and there's an explosion of activity as the baboons run for cover. There's one on the horizon Rob you see him, one guy says to Rob, big one coming down, there he is, he says, then Rob shoots and the baboon tumbles off the side of the cliff like King Kong falling off a building which is an image that occurred to me because they have it written in the video intro and in the title and in the description on YouTube three different times. Highlight of a predawn mountain climb & hunt was a baboon falling off a cliff like King Kong it says.

I watched another baboon get assassinated just now on a video. This one was in South Africa too. There's a family of boars foraging around in the foreground and the baboon rolls up into the frame look-ing left and right to make sure the coast is clear and he climbs on up this fallen tree and sits down and crosses his arms and legs sitting there with great posture like you would when you're in the little place they put you before you're about to go into a job interview. The group who posted the video run package hunting tours where they'll take you out on trips like this one so you can respect animals and they've got all the costs broken down for you in a handy chart that tells you how much it is for a hunter guide and a ride from the airport and for them to go collect the giraffe you shot and turn it into a trophy. Children under five are free to come along but ages five to fifteen are $150 a day they say. So whether you eat or drink or whatever you do, do it all for the glory of God their website says.

The baboon is sitting there and they've put some dramatic soft-listening piano music on the video like you'd hear in a life insur-ance commercial about how you're a deadbeat if you don't plan for your kids' college tuition before you have a stroke and the gun goes off and it sounds like a weird distorted snake hiss or snare drum with too much reverb and the baboon falls over and its mouth opens in a scream like what the fuck and the boars start running like shit they're about to do it out here and the voices off camera all laugh and slap each other on the back saying things such as nice one mate then the camera pans back and back and back and back and there's a guy 850 yards away laying on his stomach looking through the scope of a rifle. Eight hundred fifty yards is so far away. You would have no way of knowing there was a baboon or anything else 850 yards away if you didn't have a tool to show you.

I have to admit it never really occurred to me that hunting pri-mates was a thing people did. I guess I assumed there was some sort of unspoken agreement we had with other primates about shooting them to death like how in baseball they have unwritten rules where you don't bunt when there's a no-hitter in play due to sportsmanship. But they say baboons are pests and they need to be culled in a lot of places in Africa because they fuck with people's crops and such. I don't know if that is true or not because people always turn the things they want to kill into pests in their minds to make it easier to do. Some scientists said a couple years ago that 300 types of mammals including 126 primates were in danger of being hunted to extinction if we didn't stop fucking around. I guess one of the things that got them to thinking about that was how lions were starving because they didn't have enough other species around to hunt for themselves. Sometimes baboons will eat other primates too is something I learned.

I was thinking about murdering baboons because I just read a news story where an Idaho Fish and Game Commissioner named Blake Fischer was catching a bunch of shit about doing it. Some other hunting officials in the state were suggesting he step down not necessarily because he went to Africa and killed a family of baboons, which he did, but because he took photos of it and shared them with a bunch of people and that sort of thing makes responsible hunters look bad they seem to think which is correct.

He and his wife went to Namibia and they killed enough animals to get a good start on Noah's Ark or at least a moderate-sized zoo that you would bring your kids to and get depressed about the whole thing when they got disinterested and made you buy them chicken fingers. It was his wife's first trip to Africa and his third and she wanted to see him hunt he wrote in an email boasting about the trip according to the *Idaho Statesman*.

"So I shot a whole family of baboons," he wrote under a photo of the pile of primate corpses he attached. "I think she got the idea quick."

Steve Alder of Idaho for Wildlife told the *Idaho Statesman* the photos troubled him due to they are the equivalent of doing a bat flip in baseball I gather or celebrating too much after you score a touchdown.

"The biggest thing is the baboon thing. I was really troubled. That's my biggest issue. He killed the whole baboon family and you've got little junior laying there in mom's lap. You just don't do that," he said.

"I hate wolves as much as anyone, but I'm not going to take a wolf family and put it on display and show the baby wolf," he said, which makes me wonder what wolves did to him but he didn't specify.

About three years ago something tore inside of me and I don't know what it is and I can't make it go away. I was running and then the next thing I knew I was on the ground and it felt like my entire upper right abdominal had detached from my musculature. I walked back the rest of the way once it died down. It would come and go sometimes over the next few months like one time when I went to see Michelle getting her hair cut at a time when we both wanted to disappear and I asked to use the tiny bathroom in the tiny salon she was in and pushing to take a shit made me keel over in agony paralyzed and embarrassed and I was worried they were going to have to come carry me out of there to the hospital and my dirty ass and balls would be hanging out and it would probably leave a bad impression with her hair stylist which is an important relationship for a woman to maintain. I decided a little thing like that wasn't going to stop me from running or lifting weights for another year after that so I kept doing that until it started to hurt every day and I had to stop doing anything but sit here and sit here and sit here.

That doesn't have anything to do with shooting monkeys I don't think but I was lying there earlier thinking about it on the table at this guy's regular ass suburban house with needles sticking into my legs and back pumping electricity into my muscles to motivate my body's own healing abilities like when you have to get a jumpstart for your fucked up Camry in the parking lot of a sad mall. He's a nice Chinese fella and his house always smells like fried meat and his wife asked me not to park in front of the neighbor's driveway one time because I'm guessing they had gotten rip shit about it in the past. Sometimes other people come in when I'm lying there and I can hear him bending their spines and they do a little whimper that breaks your heart.

I just saw a tweet from Fox News and here is the tweet:

Antifa attacks again—swords and vandalism at New York GOP office

The far left Antifa strikes again the reporter said in the piece. The guy in the video they showed waving a sword around is Gavin McInnes the leader of the Proud Boys who were the ones any Antifa types would have been there to stand up to. Got to think Fox could've spotted him since he's been on there so many times but maybe they just made an honest mistake.

Some other stuff that happened that night were dozens of Proud Boys jumped some people and kicked the shit out of them yelling things like faggot and so on. McInnes was in New York to speak at the Metropolitan Republican Club which is a gathering spot for respectable conservatives which just means you believe all the same things the extreme right like the Proud Boys do but you are more polite about it. One of the gags he was performing there was the recreation of a Japanese socialist leader being assassinated with a sword.

I saw a video someone posted of the attack. They swarmed around the guy who probably had no idea they were coming and next thing he was on the ground. Then they posed for pictures proud of what they'd done.

Donald Trump likes to drop references to Antifa into his speeches. In an August 2018 meeting with a group of Christian leaders he warned them about the violence that would be forthcoming if Republicans lost the midterms which they did pretty badly it turned out.

"You're one election away from losing everything you've got," he said. "They will overturn everything that we've done and they'll do it quickly and violently. And violently. There's violence. When you look at Antifa, and you look at some of these groups, these are violent people," the president told the religious people.

It echoes the type of rhetoric used regularly by the NRA.

"They use their media to assassinate real news," Dana Loesch says in one video I watched at the time. "They use their schools to teach children that their president is another Hitler. They use their movie stars and singers and comedy shows and award shows to repeat their narrative over and over again. And then they use their ex-president to endorse 'the resistance.'"

"All to make them march. Make them protest. Make them scream racism and sexism and xenophobia and homophobia. To smash windows, burn cars, shut down interstates and airports, bully and terrorize the law-abiding—until the only option left is for the police to do their jobs and stop the madness."

People like Fox News and the NRA and the president say Antifa and the left are a menace and a threat and need to be stopped before it's too late because they fuck with people's property and freedoms and such. I know that isn't true but people always turn the things they want to kill into pests in their minds to make it easier to do.

Three people were arrested in relation to the fights and eventually they got in some trouble on account of the fascism they had gotten up to and last thing I saw was that everyone was ostracizing McInnes and his wife in the fancy neighborhood they live in and he was getting pretty red-assed about that and was threatening to sue the Southern Poverty Law Center for calling him a racist or whatever but that's not my problem.

Fischer, the Idaho Fish and Game Commissioner, stepped down from his post not too much later after being asked by the governor to resign. "I recently made some poor judgments that resulted in sharing photos of a hunt in which I did not display an appropriate level of sportsmanship and respect for the animals I harvested," he said.

THE ONLY GERMAN WORD I KNOW IS WELTSCHMERZ

MAYBE IT WAS THE WISH OF MY THOUGHTS

If it hasn't happened already it's likely that each of us will be the mark of an attempted online scam of one kind or another. You may imagine some shadowy cabal of Nigerian gangsters targeting naïve senior citizens unschooled in internet security or Anonymous-style hackers trolling for credit card information and you probably wouldn't be too far off.

But what does it mean when the face on the other end of the scam looks a bit more familiar? What if it's your own?

That's a question I was confronted with when I was contacted out of the blue by a recently divorced German woman on Facebook claiming to have been involved in a months-long burgeoning romance with a man she had never met. That man was me sort of. Her broken English only served to heighten the sense of disconnect from reality as she explained the details of her affair:

> normally it is not my way to contact an absolut strange man at
> facebook, but it might be, that this i want you to tell is a little
> bit interresting for you. first sorry, because of my bad english,
> but i am a german and not otfen using english words. so, now
> the little story i want you to tell. you are not really a stranger
> for me, okay only your fotos are not strange, because a few
> month ago i got a friendship request from a man at facebook.

i was a little bit curious to know more about this man, he sent
me some fotos, fotos from you. now, four month later i found
out the real identity of the man showing at this fotos are you
and i found out that the man, who uses your fotos is an nigerian scammer.

My initial reaction to reading this was one of bemusement.
Naturally someone would use a photo of me in a situation like this I
thought. Aren't I the handsome fellow?

But after going back and forth with the woman over Facebook it
occurred to me that maybe I was actually the mark of a meta-scam
wherein the real scammer is falsely claiming to have been scammed
by someone claiming to look like me in order to get the type of sympathy that these sorts of romance scams rely on. Although none of the
internet security experts I asked had ever heard of that approach in
particular there was a perverted sort of logic to it. The role of the scammer in these ploys is to engender sympathy from the victim in order
to convince them to send money. What better way to inspire sympathy than through personal guilt? After all wasn't it my fault in a way
for making this woman fall in love? This poor heartbroken woman
had convinced herself she was in love with a man who looked exactly
like me.

Did that implicate me in her predicament? It's vanity after all that
makes any of us susceptible to these crimes in the first place. What else
besides that and loneliness would compel us to believe that someone
across the world we'd never met would fall head over heels in love with
us over email?

Romance gambits are one of the fastest-growing and sadly most
effective scams on the internet. Twenty-one thousand people were
victims of romance scams in 2018 the Federal Trade Commission

reported losing $143 million in the process. And those are just the ones that report it. The ensuing shame that can result from realizing you were a victim of such a crime or the stubbornly romantic nature of the broken-hearted dupes ensures that many more instances go unreported.

The nature of scams like these is to prey on the loneliness of online singles many of whom are over forty and divorced or widowed in order to lure them into a complicated scheme that begins with declarations of love but soon shifts to requests for money to overcome financial emergencies.

It's an offshoot of the classic Nigerian prince gambit where many of these schemes are believed to originate from. Even the least inter-net savvy among us are wise to that unrealistic con by this point but love—that greatest con of them all—seems to be too hard to resist. That's what makes them particularly sinister. A 2012 University of Leicester study on the psychology of online romance scams points out "victims of the romance scam receive a 'double hit' from this crime: the loss of money as well as the loss of a relationship."

One of the easiest ways to affect this sort of scam has been through Facebook where despite constant reminders to the contrary many of us still operate on an all-are-welcome approach when it comes to who we let into our social circles. Facebook issued a report in early 2018 noting it had disabled a combined 1.3 billion fake accounts in the previous two quarters and the company has estimated that up to 4 percent of its monthly users are fake.

That's where my convoluted brush with this scam began in a vertigo-inducing online fake-identity existential crisis. In my case it wasn't my information or identity that were being stolen in the traditional sense of the crime but rather being used to try to steal others' identities and money.

Here I was confronted with evidence of my vanity at work. I was the equivalent of one of those bikini babes you see on fake Facebook profiles used to lure horny dudes to accept their friend requests. Then again a really savvy criminal probably wouldn't want to use the image of someone too good-looking so wait does that mean I'm only average-looking after all? You can see how this has played havoc with my sense of self. Not anywhere near as much as it did for her.

At least I think.

I mentioned the story as a curiosity to my friends many of whom reacted with a laugh and cautioned me against taking the woman at face value especially considering I never actually saw her face. Something about her story convinced me nonetheless that what she said was true even as she subtly massaged my ego and dropped references to my writing and conspired with me in a "isn't this whole thing funny" in-joke.

Was she, in fact, scamming me? I asked her. She replied:

> sorry sir, I am not looking for a new relationship, but maybe it is a good idea to think about a new career, perhaps as a scammer. no, i enjoy my life like it is and what shall i take from you? an insider information where i can get the best drinks in boston? this i can read in one of your books, lol. i am not looking for revenge or profit. as i'd found out, that my black eyed loverboy using the fotos from an american writer, i couldn't stop laughing. and if i had seen, that these are fotos from a boring person i would had never tried to get in contact with you.

She explained how the scammer in her story moved the communication over to email—the traditional next step in the process—where he sent her romantic poems and declarations of undying love. Next they moved to online chat and finally to the telephone. She admitted, "I must say, he has really a soft and smooth voice. I still like the sound of his voice."

That last bit there almost broke my heart. Despite her protestations to the contrary I had been picturing a lonely woman who was actually beginning to fall in love with a man she had never met even though she didn't want to believe it.

To no one's surprise the scammer explained that he was a successful contractor and that he had to fly to Nigeria where he would have to pay the salaries of his new staff and a certain unexpected tax. He didn't have the funds necessary as it turned out. Textbook stuff. She said she told him she would send the money but told me that she never had any intention of doing so. Her suspicions led her to an online scam forum where she did a reverse search of the image of me she had been looking at which revealed my true identity. Or the man in the picture's true identity whoever that guy is.

I continued trading messages with her in a sort of perverse mirroring of her ordeal. She'd apologize for her poor English as we talked back and forth over a couple weeks but she seemed sarcastic and likable.

"I'm sure my English is better than your German," she joked. That's an understatement I said. The only German word I really know is "weltschmerz."

Eventually she confronted her Nigerian lover with accusations of being a fraud, saying she had found verbatim texts of the notes he had sent to her in collections of common romance scam forums. He protested of course and grew angry all while still insisting on his need for the money.

"You are doing this to yourself," he wrote. "You don't know when true love is in the air. You don't know when people really mean something. When people really feel real love. Maybe it's because you have been hurt too many times. Don't let the internet mess with your head."

That seemed like a particularly cruel twist of the knife.

And yet for some reason she maintained the illusion even after all that. What did she want from him? He obviously wasn't real. It had become like a game to her this assumption of identities but I could still detect sadness in her resignation.

I knew this romance was fake and he knew it and she seemed to know it at that point but I still couldn't help but feeling somewhat upset. Not for this fraudulent love in particular although I did sympathize with her. Rather for the idea of love itself. This was a hyper-contemporary update on the metaphor of love and our motivations for seeking out companionship and of persevering in the face of hardship and of the lies that we tell ourselves to accept the failures of the relationships that we have. In real-world love it's often hard to tell where our own identities end and our lovers' begin. How often do people ask themselves if the love they're feeling for someone is real or if it's just a game?

"Maybe it was the wish of my thoughts," she wrote when I asked what kept her pushing for something that wasn't real.

The University of Leicester study found denial to be a common emotion experienced by victims of these crimes: "Victims found it difficult to visualize the real criminal even after being told they were scammed." Many described the experience as akin to being mentally raped.

"I started to live somewhere between reality and illusions, but my mind had ever warned me to believe in the truth," she wrote me, "but he always was been here, when I needed anybody to talk about my problems, he made me believe that I can trust him. Where are the borders between truth and fake, sometimes closer than you think, sometimes without borders?"

Meanwhile I was waiting for the other shoe to drop which would be the hook that would pull me further into this scam than I already was. A request for money that she had given him perhaps or moving the conversation to email. It never came.

So why bother involving me in the first place, I wondered.

i just wanted to tell you, that these pictures are abused to cheat people . . . You wanted to know more about this story and i have nothing to hide, you are a part of this story, or better, your face is a part of it. this is the reason, why i have contacted you. and the reason why i still have the contact to this scammer is, that i want to find answers. i always want to find answers for things, where other people need any answer. Perhaps i am searching for answers of my own way of life, really, i don't know. *Sometimes something inside my mind* force me to do this and it's confusing. And maybe i want to get an answer how he looks like, how he really looks like.

In short she wanted to interact with someone who was real. The man she had imagined didn't exist so perhaps I was the next best thing. Those are motivations that cross the boundaries of both geography and language. Motivations of identity and how who we love so often informs how we see ourselves.

"Oh, there is something else i want to tell you, i think you know more than only this german word," she had written to me after I'd confessed my linguistic ignorance, "i think you know it, without to know it, kindergarten. And isn't the whole world sometimes like a kindergarten?"

It really is because none of us have any idea who we are and we're all desperate for attention.

It was comments like that that made me enjoy talking to this woman whether she was actually real or not. At this point I will probably never find out for certain. After initially accepting her Facebook friend request I quickly reversed course and thought better of it. In the real world love and friendship may be worth taking a chance on but online it's just too risky. You never know who anybody really is.

SHE'S A WOMAN NOT A SPIDER

THE WATER SMELLED UNNATURAL SHE SAID

It was a Sunday night in September and the rains of Hurricane Florence had finally subsided so Dazia Lee decided it would be safe to strap her one-year-old boy Kaiden into the car seat of her 2010 Hyundai Elantra and travel from Charlotte about an hour away to visit her grandmother. The roads seemed fine to her she told the *Virginia-Pilot* and there were other cars about so she figured the worst of the storm was over. Before long she came across some orange barrels that were positioned on the road but didn't seem to be blocking it off entirely as other cars were coming the other way. Lee is twenty and had Kaiden when she was still in high school but wanted to keep him so she raised him on her own with the help of her parents while working jobs at Dunkin' Donuts and an Amazon warehouse where she was likely paid very well and treated kindly if we know anything about those sorts of jobs.

It was dark now and the car began to hydroplane and the next thing she knew water was rushing into the car so fast and what a shock it is to see water engulfing the inside of your car it's not something you can prepare yourself for even though it happens on TV a lot and they almost always get out and you think oh yeah that's how you do that I am proficient in this now. She grabbed her son from the backseat and made it out of the window of the car where she fell to the ground in the quickly rising waters. She had her son held to her chest tightly and of course she would never let him go but then she didn't have hold of him anymore and he was gone off into the water.

The water smelled unnatural she said.

"I did everything I could," she told a reporter from the *Pilot* later. "From the moment I was pregnant until the moment I lost him. I did everything I could to save and protect him."

It would be hard to imagine a crueler punishment for a lapse in judgment like that. You would think there would be no worse fate for a young mother than to lose her baby like that. God can be cruel you might think but god has nothing on the criminal justice system because Lee was soon charged with involuntary manslaughter in the death of her boy the sentence for which can be up to twenty years and no less than thirteen months.

Monroe County sheriff Eddie Cathey said in a statement that he felt bad about the circumstance but you know how it is the jails aren't going to fill themselves.

"The tragic death of this child and the circumstances surrounding this case are heartbreaking. We continue to pray for all those suffering as a result of this child's death. However, after a very thorough investigation and taking all facts into consideration and applying the law, we feel that these charges are appropriate."

"If you look and watch the news report when they were interviewing her. She didn't even act like a grieving mother," one person commented on the police's press release on Facebook. "She made a choice to drive through a barricaded road. Her choice cost a life," wrote another human being. "I'm sure she's suffering but she had a choice and now she can face the consequences. Do I feel sorry for her, NO! Just as I don't feel sorry for the officers who did the same things that cost 2 lives......"

There are a lot more like that and some sympathetic ones too but I'm not going to read them because I don't need to look at any more of that type of thing today.

Judy Buenoano was executed by the state of Florida in 1998 for the murder of her husband and son and the attempted murder of a fiancé over the course of a few years in the early '80s. She had poisoned her husband with arsenic they said and drowned her paralyzed son they said and tried to fire bomb the other guy to get insurance money. She was the first woman executed in the state in 150 years. The one before that was a freed slave who had killed her former master.

"Throughout Sunday, she had been talkative and upbeat, a corrections spokesman said," as the *Orlando Sentinel* wrote at the time.

But when she entered the death chamber shortly after 7 a.m. Buenoano held tightly to the hands of two male guards who helped her walk. She was pale and terrified. But she seemed determined to face her death with a kind of stoic dignity.

Asked whether she had a last statement Buenoano said "No, sir" in a barely audible voice. Moments later as the current flowed her fists clenched. She seemed almost dwarfed in the seventy-five-year-old oak chair the reports said. Smoke rose from the electrode attached to her right leg.

Some people who opposed the death penalty were protesting there and they held signs that said she was "a woman not a spider" due to they had been calling her the Black Widow in the news and such. One witness to the execution was a guy named Wayne Manning who brought his seven-year-old grandson to see the show.

"He needs to learn what is going on in this world," he told the *Sentinel*. "Maybe he won't get into a situation like this, himself, if he is exposed to it now."

One thing I also know about Buenoano's execution is what her final meal was because that is a thing that people want to know about for some reason whenever someone is executed and in her case it was broccoli and asparagus and strawberries. It's something I was reminded of because a restaurant in Japan recently had a death penalty-themed menu pop-up which people seemed to be pretty excited about. One of the other dishes they were offering was John Wayne Gacy's final meal of a dozen fried shrimp and a bucket of KFC chicken with fries and a pound of strawberries. One hundred percent of the people I just wrote about wanted strawberries right before they died and I don't have a metaphor or anything to make out of that.

There are around fifty countries in the world that still use capital punishment including—you guessed it—this fucking one you're probably reading this in. Every European country besides Belarus has abolished it but other countries like Taiwan, Singapore, Japan, Saudi Arabia, Vietnam, Indonesia, India, Nigeria, Iran, and Jamaica still kill their own citizens for shit they did and other shit they often didn't do.

Hours after the shooting at the Pittsburgh synagogue in October 2018 in which eleven people were killed the president went to a campaign rally and said we have to bring back the death penalty. We still have it but he probably meant we have to use it more frequently.

"And when you have crimes like this, whether it's this one or another one on another group, we have to bring back the death penalty. They have to pay the ultimate price," he said. "They have to pay the ultimate price. They can't do this. They can't do this to our country. We must draw a line in the sand and say very strongly: never again."

You probably remember that Trump had called for the death penalty in the Central Park Five case after a group of black and Hispanic teens were convicted of a sexual assault in New York City in 1989. Trisha Meili a twenty-eight-year-old jogger was left in a coma for two weeks after she was attacked one night. Trump took out advertisements in four newspapers demanding as much.

Years later when the group of young men were released from prison and awarded a $41 million settlement from the city for being wrongly imprisoned Trump didn't back down calling it "a disgrace," and "the heist of the century" and now today he's saying poor migrants fleeing violence are hardened fighters coming to kill us so we gotta send the troops down there to scare them off with helicopters and tanks and such.

In November of 1999 I had just moved to New York City for the first time. I had graduated from college that May and had been commuting for a few months from the home of my girlfriend's parents in Fairfield and after we broke up I never got to thank them for that and I always felt badly about that so thank you. I would drive my shitty Chevy Celebrity from their beautiful home every day to the Metro North and sit there for an hour and a half or so and I'm guessing read a book because people didn't look at their phones all the time back then because there wasn't much on them to see in the first place. A lot of times the car would break down on the way to the train station and I'd be pretty embarrassed about that because that's a very nice area and at any rate I finally found an apartment on the Upper East Side where I lived with two other guys one of whom was paying $600 to sleep on the couch and I was paying $800 to have a lofted bed in basically a closet and we thought that was expensive back then.

I was working at Condé Nast for their fledgling internet concern and we'd make quizzes and all manner of awful nothingness for a few of the magazines and most of the time I'd leave for a while and go to the gym nearby where I'd bring them all the magazines we had lying around for a discount on my membership or else take all of the books that would be sent to the office and return them to Barnes & Noble which is a scam you could still do back then so I could afford to eat like a panini with roasted red peppers on it which is a vegetable everyone was very excited about at the time.

When I've told this story in the past I say it was my first day actually living in the city but I'm not sure if I made that part up to sound more dramatic but either way it was early on and I was on Madison Ave and 42nd or so and there was a loud thwack like someone had just socked a home run to the moon and then there was a woman on the ground and the blood from her head was spreading so fast it was like when you knock an entire bottle of merlot over but instead of tipping it upright you just leave it there to spill until it's empty. Goddamnit you say. And you can't get the stain out but you Google how to do it anyway and give it a try. Fuck fuck fuck fuckuufucukc you say.

A man had run up behind her and smashed her in the head with a brick people said and I don't remember anymore if I saw the man do it or I filled in the details later because even eye witnesses are exceptionally unreliable but I do remember the blood everywhere and there were so many people rushing to help her right away and a police officer was right nearby trying to help her so the rest of us a few people back just stood there and watched a woman probably dying like hypnotized audience members at a magic show who aren't convinced if what they just saw was real or not. If I had a smart phone at the time I probably would've made a video of it and then some dipshit on the news would have asked me for permission to broadcast it across all mediums until infinity but like I said earlier we didn't do much with our phones back then.

The woman was named Nicole Barrett and she was twenty eight and from Texas and the man they said did it was a homeless fella named Paris Drake who was thirty-six and he had called her a rich white bitch when he caved her head in is what they said he had said. Surprisingly she lived and he got 25 years which means he's still in prison now. They wrote stories about what happened to her in the *New York Times* the following year about how she was determined to get on with her life and especially to be able to ride a horse again. Her father had died earlier that year from cancer and Nicole said at the time: "All of a sudden one day, he told Mom, 'I think it's time to go.'" He'd written a manual for his wife for how to do all manner of things around the house that he had usually done after he was gone so they would be able to take care of things which is a very dad thing to do worrying about the lawn getting mowed and so on even after you're dead.

Drake's lawyer said during the trial it was a case of mistaken identity and that authorities were desperate to find someone. The attorney general said they had other homeless and criminal informants who said Drake had talked about what he had done so that was that and they got him for it but like I said I was right there and I have no idea what the guy actually looked like. He looked like a brick arcing through the air to me.

Rudy Giuliani was mayor at the time and he was trying to reassure people that New York City was safe which is crazy to think about now that he's one of the worst liars alive and shouldn't be doing anything besides working as the racism sommelier at a haunted mansion. Crimes like this create an "undue amount of fear" he said. And it's true that "conditions of life in all parts of the world and America carry with it a certain degree of danger you are never going to eliminate all of it completely" as he said and that is one true thing he has said in his life so you have to give him credit for having done that.

I suppose that woman's head spilling out onto the sidewalk is the worst thing I've ever seen in my life in person. One time I helped pull a woman out from under a city bus in Harvard Square and her leg was . . . not good and she had a head wrap on I remember and still had her earbuds in although I'm not sure what music she was listening to when the bus drove over her because she was crying a lot and it broke my heart in a way that little else ever has. One time when we were kids I saw a friend trying to climb a fence fall and get his arm caught on the top of the fucking thing there and it ripped his entire bicep off and he was walking around oddly calm with a flapping bicep barely attached like an unseasoned chicken breast. All things considered that's not such a bad list compared to what a lot of people have to look at or have happen to them. I am pretty sure there will be worse things to come though for me and for everyone and probably pretty soon.

We're not people we are spiders I think sometimes. Spiders spend most of their days waiting and waiting and waiting and then something big happens in their world and they run over and act like a spider.

HE IS NOTHING LESS THAN A TRAITOR, A MONSTER

HOW COULD SOCIETY NOT HAVE AN ABSOLUTE RIGHT OVER HIM?

In the age of sovereign rule any crime committed was considered a crime directly against the king. As Foucault writes in his 1975 book *Discipline and Punish,* the crime was in effect a declaration of war against the sovereign, and the criminal, now an enemy combatant, must therefor be retaliated against in kind. This retribution often took the form of public torture in which the body of the criminal was ritually and publicly violated in order to balance out the offense against the king who embodied and symbolized the totality of the law.

Over time as power began to shift and the rights of citizens gained primacy the victim of any crime began to be understood as society itself. A crime was now an affront against all of us.

Thus as Foucault wrote, "a formidable right to punish is established, since the offender becomes the common enemy. Indeed, he is worse than an enemy, for it is from within society that he delivers his blows—he is nothing less than a traitor, a 'monster.' How could society not have an absolute right over him?"

Previously the crimes that were typically punished were the most serious in nature: murders and violent attacks and so on. The rise of prison as the preferred form of punishment followed the increasing desire to focus on more minor crimes. Not those against people's bodies but crimes against property. It would have been inefficient both financially and politically to torture every petty criminal and it often had the opposite effect of engendering sympathy for the punished. So prisons provided a means to punish vast numbers of us out of sight of the public with little hope of inspiring public revolt.

The shift led directly to the establishment of the carceral state and enlisted each of us into its disciplinary ranks!

At least thirteen people were dead in the water as Hurricane Florence devastated the coast and nearly a million remained without power. Also a dollar store may have lost some merchandise.

The Wilmington, North Carolina police sent out a tweet during the emergency in September of 2018. In the wake of record floods and devastation striking the area a large enough number of people in the area witnessed the "looting" of a store that the police felt compelled to say *please stop snitching to us we already know.*

"We are aware of the looting occurring at the Family Dollar Store at 13th & Greenfield Sts," the Wilmington Police tweeted, "unfortunately management has asked not to intervene at this time.

Unfortunately.

According to the police the store had decided not to press the issue figuring perhaps in a rare bit of corporate humanity that much of their merchandise would likely be written off as a loss in the destruction of the storm anyway and that some people in a crisis availing themselves of needed goods was not at the top of their list of concerns at the moment. Perhaps the police had other pressing issues they could be occupied with?

A response to the tweet came in from a local TV news reporter. It was typical among many.

"EXCLUSIVE: This is video I shot outside a Family Dollar in Wilmington. @WilmingtonPD say they are aware of the looting and were told not to intervene by store management. #HurricaneFlorence has turned #wilmingtonNC into chaos," tweeted Hannah Brewer of WFMY.

"Management needs to be fired. The looters need to be arrested," replied another person on Twitter.

"You have sworn an oath to serve and protect the public not respond to management of any store. Do your job!" added another critic.

"But you are supposed to honor the law? What are we teaching people? The insurance carrier will not be happy with management," wrote a third. "This is why the 2nd amendment exists my dudes. Blast them," said a fourth.

Living as a citizen of the carceral state not only incentivizes such behavior it insists upon it. A case of water taken from a large corporation isn't just a crime committed against the store itself after all it's a crime committed directly against the millions of petty tyrants operating in the coordinated implementation of punitive fascism.

Before the storm hit South Carolina governor Henry McMaster issued a mandatory evacuation along the coast. "We do not want to risk one South Carolina life in this hurricane," he said. Multiple prisons in the area declined to evacuate the prisoners in their care.

"In the past, it's been safer to leave them there," Dexter Lee, a South Carolina Department of Corrections spokesperson said.

Safer for the rest for us he means. Not the prisoners.

A source in one of the local prisons told the *New Yorker* that they were not being allowed to hold onto extra water as the storm approached.

Extrapolating on Bentham's architectural design of the Panopticon Foucault described the next step in discipline and punishment known as Panopticism.

"Panopticism is the general principle of a new 'political anatomy' whose object and end are not the relations of sovereignty but the relations of discipline," he wrote.

The result is a society in which people are always aware that they are being watched at all times and not just by an unseen guard as in

Bentham's design but by everyone everywhere. We're no longer worried about the police or the king or any other authority catching us violating the law but of our neighbors. The threat of discipline has become universal.

In a book last year called *Citizen Spies: The Long Rise of America's Surveillance Society*, Joshua Reeves traced the evolution of this universalization of fascism from WANTED reward posters in the American frontier to the rise of Neighborhood Watches, *America's Most Wanted*, the prevalence of "See Something Say Something" in a post-9/11 country, and the enlistment of citizen snitches by police departments' use of social media.

In our nation of snitches, informing on our fellow citizens he writes isn't just an unfortunate responsibility of our daily lives, it's been elevated to a patriotic and moral duty. Why else would so many of us call the police when we see a black person occupying a space we assume they don't belong in? Why would so many of us be willing to subject people with Hispanic surnames to torture and imprisonment by informing on their whereabouts to ICE? We may not all be like George Zimmerman capable of murdering a young black man in order to fulfill our allegiance to fascism but those of us who are willing to snitch are comfortable all the same seeing someone else perform violent discipline on our behalf.

When the waters of Hurricane Katrina began to rise many of the deputies guarding the inmates in Orleans Parish Prison abandoned their posts. Not before, according to prisoner testimonies obtained and published by the ACLU, taking extra cautionary steps like handcuffing the prison cells shut to make sure no one could get out in the event of the doors opening.

"As the locked cells began to flood, prisoners hung signs out of the broken windows for help, and others jumped into the water below," the

ACLU wrote. "According to the testimonials, deputies and members of the Special Investigation Division shot at some of the prisoners who were attempting to escape the rising water inside the jail, and several prisoners report that they witnessed fellow prisoners getting shot in the back.

"When the prisoners were finally evacuated from the jail, many were forced to wade through toxic, waste-filled water to the Broad Street overpass on Interstate 10. Prisoners reported that the armed guards at the overpass had K-9 dogs, which were used to threaten them and that they were maced and beaten. Female prisoners also report that deputies directed degrading and sexually offensive comments at them."

They compiled hundreds of testimonies from prisoners who were abandoned as the waters rose.

In the preface to a 1972 book called *Anti-Oedipus*, a book of ethics by Gilles Deleuze and Felix Guattar, Foucault cautioned against our surrender to fascism.

"And not only historical fascism," he wrote, "the fascism of Hitler and Mussolini—which was able to mobilize and use the desire of the masses so effectively—but also the fascism in us all, in our heads and in our everyday behavior, the fascism that causes us to love power, to desire the very thing that dominates and exploits us."

There are roughly 2.3 million people incarcerated in the United States at the moment. With a little over 4 percent of the world's population we house around 22 percent of its prisoners.

During Florence there was a report from local news station WECT. "Hey guys, you know you're looting, right? You know you're stealing," the reporter lectured a group outside the store. "You know you're looting and that's illegal?" she said to a man carrying out a case of water.

What fate is it exactly that reporters like this and the people demanding the North Carolina police "do their job" that weekend think they are sending the alleged criminals to? Do they picture something like what the prisoners during Katrina suffered through? Would that make them even more thrilled?

Who is the victim of the crime here? It's supposed to be you. Do you feel victimized?

SOMETIMES I CANNOT CONTROL MY LIFE

I THINK THE GUESTS ARE CONFUSED

Qing Wei sleeps with her phone nearby in case the call ever comes. Not the bad one not the call you might typically think of when you hear about someone sleeping with their phone nearby *just in case* but a good call. She's hoping she'll get a shift at work. The way things work now is that she often might not know about a shift until an hour or two beforehand and she can't afford to miss the opportunity to go clean up your shit at the hotel. It's too expensive to live in the Boston area already she says and she has a kid in college she says. One missed call could mean she can't pay her bills that month she says.

Wei is fifty years old and has worked at the Sheraton Boston for thirteen years as a housekeeper. She gets paid $30 an hour on a typical day cleaning about fifteen rooms a shift (the average is around $21 an hour). In the summer during the busy season when the tourists tromp through the city in search of history and fried fish she'll mostly reach forty hours but in the dead of winter when the streets and the hotels are empty that number declines significantly. If there's no mess to clean up then she's not getting paid.

"The company never gives me a schedule," she says. "I have a different schedule, always. Sometimes they don't put me on the schedule. Sometimes I cannot control my life."

Losing hours means more than losing pay. If she doesn't reach the 80 hours a month threshold she'll also be ineligible for her insurance plan.

In 2017 *Fortune Magazine* placed Marriott International, which owns the Sheraton Boston, at #33 on their "100 Best Companies to Work For" list.

"Employees feel that 'at Marriott, we are family'—even when there are 136,000-plus of them," they reported. "They say they feel 'treated as individuals and not one large machine' and embrace the company's commitment to diversity."

Marriott is the largest hotel chain in the world and they run over 6,500 properties in 127 countries. They had $22.9 billion in revenue in 2017. Following the Trump tax cuts in 2018 Marriott was among a number of high profile companies that pledged they would be giving back to their employees. The $140 million they pledged would amount to a one-time $5-to-$1 match of up to $1,000 into their retirement funds.

Arne M. Sorenson, chief executive of Marriott International, talked about the tax cuts on a call with his board this year.

"If you wave a wand and say tax reform is done, and our . . . taxes decline by a certain amount, I don't think that, by itself, is going to change our capital availability," he said.

The savings he admitted would "likely to go back to shareholders."

Through August of 2018 the company had repurchased 14.1 million of their own shares for $1.9 billion. Weird.

Wei's mother is seventy-one years old and she also works for Marriott as a housecleaner. Wei says her mother can't retire yet because she can't afford the insurance she would have to pay for if she did so she cleans the rooms with her seventy-one-year-old hands and back. She pushes the cart into your room and knocks on the door and hopes you'll want her to clean up your shit. The rooms go for

$500–600 a night but if they clean one they get an extra $10 in the pocket Wei says.

"It's hard for her. A lot of my coworkers are sixty-seven, sixty-eight and pushing their bodies to work fifteen-hour days."

The alternative is worse because if they aren't given the opportunity to push their bodies they might not be able to afford to live. John Willard Bill Marriott is 86 and the top executive of Marriott. He's worth $2.8 billion and I wonder if he pushes his body very often these days.

Wei told me she and her fellow members of UNITE HERE Local 26 hotel workers were ready to go on strike if something didn't change. In September 2018 the union authorized the bargaining committee to call for a strike at eight Boston Marriott hotels, which followed similar actions in cities around the country from Boston, San Francisco, Detroit, Seattle, San Jose, San Diego, Oakland, Honolulu and Maui.

"Workers are demanding the chance to live in Boston, support a family, and retire with dignity by working one job," the union wrote in a statement. "In addition, workers are demanding greater job and safety protections, including advanced notice on technological advances, and progressive changes to the company's confusing 'Your choice' / 'Make a Green Choice' program that offers guests points while keeping housekeepers out of work or in pain."

"If there is a hotel strike in Boston, it will be Marriott's failing," UNITE HERE Local 26 president Brian Lang says. "Marriott is the richest hotel company on the face of the earth. It's about time corporate executives respect the work we put in every day that makes Marriott billions. Our demand is simple: one job should be enough."

"If they don't figure out this key issue then we're going to go on strike," Wei says. She's talking about the Green Choice program, the type of ostensibly environment-friendly program many hotels like Marriott have put in place over the past decade or so. The idea is that by giving guests the option to refuse room cleaning services, they are reducing waste and energy resources. Many hotels will even bribe guests into refusing service, offering up a Starbucks gift card or hotel points and the like. It's all wrapped up in a feel-good bow of conscientiousness and do-gooding and it's ruining people like Wei's lives. She doesn't know if most people are aware of that and now that you're reading this I suppose you are.

"I think they think about us," she says of guests, as if we think we're taking a load off their backs by refusing to have our rooms cleaned. "But a lot of the guests they don't know the Green Choice, I think the guests are confused. They don't have it explained to them, the rest of the guests think it's good for us, because the job is easier or something."

Here's a question you can ask yourself and think about on your own time because I'm not a scientist and I don't know whether or not programs like Green Choice that are meant to benefit the environment will actually do anything in the long run—companies like Marriott certainly suggest they are effective and maybe they are and that is very nice and good. But when a massive company sees an opportunity to reduce the hours and benefits they have to pay out to their thousands of employees they are going to take it. If they can sell that back to their customers as charity with a positive PR spin they will do that also because the nature of a massive company is to steal as much money from everyone they can—their customers, their employees—and filter that back up to the top of their corporate board and investors all while convincing us they're the good guys.

"It's taken a good, full-time, predictable job and turned into an on-call job, and it creates havoc in people's lives as a result," Lang says of the Green Choice movement. "It's a brilliant marketing program, but it's done at the expense of, largely, immigrant women."

All of the signage used for employees at the Marriott hotels in Boston are printed in four languages, Spanish, Chinese, English, and Haitian Creole.

What's funny is that workers have been saying this for years.

Juan Medina thinks environmental initiatives are great. A houseman for eleven years at the Westin Boston Waterfront, he certainly understands that doing things to reduce water waste and the use of chemicals in hotels and such are things companies should be trying to do.

"They have it set up in the rooms where they're saving water from the toilet, the sink and all that. They can have recycling in the room and regular trash, there are other steps without this program," he says.

The motherfucker of it all is that while Green Choice reduces the number of hours he and coworkers like Wei get, it also makes the hours they do have even harder. It usually takes about fifteen minutes to clean an occupied room, he says, thirty minutes to clean a check-out room. Guests who opt to let their mess build up for a couple days at a time naturally increase the amount of time it takes to clean. It could be forty-five minutes to an hour or more now. And they say the amount of chemicals they have to use to clean a multiple-stay day room is actually more than they would have if they did it every day. People make a hell of a mess in their hotel rooms. They don't exactly come out and say we're all disgusting pigs but I would not entirely blame them if they said that because it would be true.

Hotel companies could do all their nice and good environmental stuff while still giving people like Medina an actual full-time job. The two things are not mutually exclusive. It might cost shareholders and executives a little bit of money but we do not care about them because they are vampire pigs who can spare the fucking change and do you ever wonder sometimes how hard it would be to build a guillotine anyway.

"When the guests choose to have the Green Choice program they don't get service for three days, so when they leave the room is a mess. It's harder for the room attendant to clean the rooms, and it's harder for us as the housemen when we have to help them. They're thinking it's helping us but what it's doing is hurting us," Medina says.

"A lot of people aren't getting hours. It's harder for people to pay our bills, to have health insurance. We expect to get 40 hours. Due to the Green Choice it's affecting us really bad. Marriott is one of the world's richest hotels."

Most of the people he works with can't afford to live in Boston. He lives in Weymouth, not too far away, but others come from as far as New Hampshire, Providence, or Fall River, commuting hours to clean up your jizz towels.

"We're hoping with the negotiation we'll come to some kind of agreement with the union and the company," Medina says. "But we need to get our voices heard because it's really affecting everybody. Nobody is getting hours and the people getting hours they're giving them too much work. We work when it's busy and the slow season after Thanksgiving they don't give people with lower seniority the hours. What happens is you don't have insurance. I'm a diabetic, I can't afford to lose my insurance. I need my medications. I'm fighting for insurance year-round. This is a rich company, when it's slow we should still be able to have our insurance, retirement."

Last April Medina was blocked out of his insurance benefits because he didn't have enough hours in the preceding three months to qualify.

"I work with women with kids, their families are in their insurance. I know ladies here that have husbands that are sick and they worry about their insurance, they can't get medications, they can't get seen."

Back in 2008 Bill Marriott, son of Marriott founder John Willard Marriott, gave a speech inducting his father into the Labor Hall of Fame at the U.S. Department of Labor in Washington D.C.

"Dad was a hard worker and our employees emulated that same work ethic," he said. "He also believed the key to a successful business was to, first and foremost, take care of your employees because he always said, 'If you take care of them, they'll take care of your customers and the customers will keep coming back again and again.'"

Not long after I spoke to the workers they would vote to go on strike. Forty-six days later Marriott finally gave in.

"This victory is a testament to our members' strength and tenacity," Lang said. "Hotel workers stood strong for more than six weeks in the wind, the rain, and the snow, up against the largest hotel company in the world. It was a hard-fought victory, but in the end, Marriott showed leadership and listened to our members' concerns. From Day 1, we've encouraged Marriott to use their leadership in the hotel industry to make jobs in their hotels enough to live on, and today's settlement goes a long way for Boston workers. Now we expect the rest of the hotel industry to follow that leadership and settle new agreements for the thousands of hotel workers with expired contracts across Boston and Cambridge."

THEY WERE PROBABLY JUST GUILTY ANYWAY

DUE PROCESS ONLY APPLIES TO THE POWERFUL

You hear a lot about due process lately from the right. Fresh off a series of sudden epiphanies about the capriciousness of justice when it comes to men like Brett Kavanaugh, Paul Manafort, and men accused of sexual assault, one might be heartened to see such a renewed attention to the concept of innocent until proven guilty. You would be stupid to have believed in the sincerity of any of that though because it was all concern trolling and lies. If it weren't we might have heard a single word from any of them about the latest development in one of the most sprawling and egregious miscarriages of justice in the history of the criminal justice system in Massachusetts.

The news came on a Thursday in October of 2018 when the Supreme Judicial Court here ordered the dismissal of additional thousands of drug cases worked on by chemist Sonja Farak at a lab in Amherst, Massachusetts. More than 11,000 had previously been dismissed when it was found that Farak had herself been high at work for years using the very drugs she had been tasked with testing. Farak pled guilty in 2014 and was sentenced to eighteen months in prison.

But now the court has found that all of the cases worked on at the lab in question between 2009–2013, not just those Farak dealt with herself, must be dismissed. And following the finding that two former prosecutors withheld crucial evidence about the extent of her misconduct—efforts that resulted in numerous people either remaining in prison, being sent back to prison, or having their tainted convictions needlessly upheld—the court has imposed penalties on the attorney general's office in a rare instance of misconduct having actual consequences.

You might be thinking that all of this sounds vaguely familiar but you're probably just remembering the other corrupt drug lab chemist Annie Dookhan who served three years in prison back in 2013 and had over 20,000 of the drug cases she worked on dismissed after being found guilty of falsification of records and obstructing of justice.

This all seems a little confusing and overwhelming to understand but in short two separate drug lab chemists in Massachusetts went to jail in the past few years—one for being fucked up on the shit she was testing all the time and one for just inventing shit because she wanted to put more addicts in prison—and as a result tens of thousands of drug cases have been dismissed. In a way it's a victory but a late-arriving one. We shouldn't have ever gotten to this point in the first place.

I spoke with Matthew Segal, legal director of the ACLU of Massachusetts, who has been leading the charge on the Farak case, about what these new dismissals mean and how the two scandals differed, and what happened with the misconduct from state prosecutors.

HOW DO THE NEW DEVELOPMENTS FROM LAST WEEK DIFFER FROM WHAT WE'VE KNOWN ABOUT THE DRUG TESTING SCANDALS IN MASSACHUSETTS FOR A WHILE NOW?

What's different about the Amherst lab scandal is that after Farak was arrested there were two Assistant Attorneys General that had engaged in a cover-up of the extent of what Farak did. They hid evidence about the duration of her misconduct, and one of them even wrote an intentionally deceptive letter to a judge saying all the evidence they had had been turned over. Not only was that not true, she later testified that she had reviewed none of the files. That was bad! It was the most remarkable testimony I'd ever seen outside of watching *A Few Good Men*. She took to the witness stand and confessed to deceiving a judge.

AND THE DECISION LAST WEEK ADDRESSED THAT MISCONDUCT?

What was left to be decided in the Amherst lab scandal was if there should be more dismissals and what to do about the prosecutorial misconduct. What the court decided last week was: Yes there needs to be a more significant remedy for the Amherst scandal than for the Dookhan scandal. Partly because of the prosecutorial misconduct and partly because of what Farak did. The court said we're going to order the dismissal of all the cases where Farak was assigned as the chemist, all of the meth cases during her tenure, because she was messing with the meth standard, and all of the cases that went through the Amherst lab from 2009–2013, a decent chunk of her tenure.

We already knew the courts were dismissing between 9,000–11,000 drug charges with cases tied to Farak. Thursday means there will be some additional number of dismissals. It's probably going to be in the thousands.

WHAT WERE THE DETAILS OF THE COVER-UP?

Farak was arrested in January of 2013, and a search of her car was conducted. She was prosecuted by the same assistant attorney general who prosecuted Dookhan. Some of this is accounted in Thursday's opinion, but basically a state trooper in 2013, within about a month of when Farak was arrested, sent an email to the prosecutor with the subject "Farak Admissions," and attached were these worksheets where Farak had been keeping track of her drug use. One of them was very obviously from 2011. It was the attorney general's position, for a good chunk of time after she was arrested, that Farak had only been using drugs for a few months. Based on that people were denied release from prison, people had to serve out their sentences, and at least one person was sent back to prison on the theory that his case was before Farak had started using drugs.

THAT'S DISGUSTING.

An attorney named Luke Ryan led the charge of defense attorneys who didn't take the word of the attorney general at face value. He said show us what you've got on Farak, and the attorney general's office did not turn over these worksheets. That went on for a while. Ryan submitted a subpoena to the attorney general's office for the files, they moved to quash it with all these excuses, and the judge said can I see what you're claiming you don't have to turn over? That's when a different assistant attorney general, the one assigned to defend this decision to withhold the documents, wrote this letter to the judge and said actually I went back and looked and turns out there's nothing for you to see. She later testified she did that without even looking at anything.

WAIT, FARAK WAS DOCUMENTING THE FACT SHE WAS HIGH AT WORK ALL ALONG?

Farak was using a company to get drug counseling. It's a company called ServiceNet that helps people deal with problems relating to addiction. She was using one of their diary notes to track her cravings, to track when she used, including at work. It's a person who was struggling with addiction, and this was one way she was trying to overcome it.

WHAT IS THE MOTIVATION OF THE ATTORNEY GENERAL HERE BEING WILLING TO KEEP PEOPLE IN JAIL? JUST SO THEY DIDN'T LOOK BAD?

I really can't look inside their heads to understand why they made the decisions they made. One possibility, although I don't know, was a strong desire for the Farak scandal to not be as big as the Dookhan scandal. The first thing that happened after Farak was arrested was then attorney general Martha Coakley went out and did press saying this is a very small scandal.

HOW WAS FARAK'S MISCONDUCT DIFFERENT FROM DOOKHAN'S?

Dookhan was not using the drugs, she was basically cutting corners at work. She wanted to be very productive and she also, according to emails, wanted to get defendants off the streets. She was like a war on drugs drug warrior according to her emails. So she was inventing the test results, she wasn't actually doing the testing required to confirm something is cocaine or heroin or whatever. She also forged people's signatures and all sorts of other things. She was cheating at her job committing forgeries, they call that dry-labbing, when you just eyeball the substance and say what it is.

Farak was herself addicted to drugs, and was basically tampering with the drugs in order to use them. Also, presumably, she was high every day when she was performing these tests. And that's one of the reasons why it's been difficult to pin down when she was doing what. It's like pulling someone over if they've been driving drunk and asking them how fast were you going. So even assuming she wanted to tell the truth it's not clear she could.

ARE EITHER OF THEM STILL IN PRISON?

They're both out.

WHY HASN'T THIS ALL BEEN A BIGGER NATIONAL STORY?

I've been surprised about how it's been covered. Honestly if you've seen how criminal justice stories somehow get covered, sometimes there's . . . I guess I'll just say the magnitude of the coverage has not really matched the magnitude of the story. It's not really just a story about this massive misconduct, it's showing that the substantial part of the entire war on drugs in Massachusetts is basically this house of cards. One person who was causing people to be convicted of drug crimes making stuff up and cutting corners that would never be cut when it comes to white collar defendants. Imagine a forensic accountant who does white collar crimes and convicts a bunch of people and it turns out whoops she was just making it up? That would be a very big story.

"They were probably just guilty anyway" is something I heard a lot. But this kind of corner-cutting and due process violations would never be tolerated if the defendants had more power and less pigmentation.

DO YOU HAVE A SENSE OF THE DEMOGRAPHICS OF THE PEOPLE CONVICTED HERE?

In a scandal that affects thousands it's going to be a cross-section of the defendant population, and we don't have race and data for these defendants. I don't know specifically but we do know based on broader data sets that the war on drugs in Massachusetts, as in so many other places, harms people of color and tends to affect poor folks. In the Dookhan case we had data analysts look at the list. What we saw was that in over 60 percent of cases the drug crimes were solely for possession. In 90 percent of the Dookhan cases they were prosecuted in District Court, as opposed to Superior Court, where the more serious cases are brought. So in 90 percent of these Dookhan cases the District Attorney had already decided it wasn't a particularly serious case.

WERE PEOPLE SENT TO PRISON IN MANY OF THESE CASES OR WERE THEY LARGELY PROBATIONARY?

A lot of them were sentenced to incarceration we think. One of the horrible consequences is that a lot of folks had served their time before the scandals were uncovered or while they were being covered up. A decision in October 2018 for cases prosecuted in 2004 doesn't help much to a lot of folks who already served their time. We do know some folks are still incarcerated. I heard of at least one person who walked out of prison this week because of last week's decisions. I know about people who have been deported. Then there are all the collateral consequences of people who can't get jobs and housing. One of the really awful consequences of the scandal is that information about them, and therefore the remedies, are coming too late for a lot of folks.

YOU HEAR A LOT ABOUT DUE PROCESS FROM THE RIGHT LATELY, HAVE MANY OF THEM COMMENTED ON THIS?

It's pretty obvious that Trump and many of the politicians supporting him don't believe a word of what they're saying about due process. What they really mean is powerful people should be protected from any consequences. Although we have had some folks on the right sincerely interested in due process and fairness who have been helpful. The Cato Institute filed an amicus brief in support of some of the remedies we sought in the Amherst lab scandal. There are conservative voices out there who take due process and prosecutorial misconduct seriously. But what we're seeing from Trump and his allies is something completely different. It's a bad faith effort to try to use the rhetoric they've heard from progressives, but they don't believe a word of it, and especially not for poor folks or people of color.

THE TWO WOMEN SERVED A COUPLE OF YEARS FOR THIS I THINK. NOT THAT I'M AN ADVOCATE FOR LONG PRISON SENTENCES, BUT TO HAVE WRONGFULLY IMPACTED SO MANY OTHER PEOPLE'S LIVES, SENDING THEM TO PRISON . . .

It's a weird situation for the ACLU. Similarly, we don't really think the answer to most problems is to throw someone in jail. But I would say that one reason why people get wrongfully convicted is because it's so rare to see any consequences for the misconduct. What happened here was there was a cover-up by the attorney general's office, then a change in administration, with a new attorney general now. Then there was this testimony, which I said was a pretty remarkable one for the two Assistant Attorneys General saying I wrote this letter to a judge to deceive him. Even after that testimony the attorney general's office said these were merely unintentional mistakes, not prosecutorial misconduct. A Superior Court judge said, No this is egregious, and that started the train toward the remedy we got on Thursday. In addition to the dismissals they say they want to change the criminal rules in Massachusetts to say there is more of a duty on behalf of prosecutors to disclose evidence. They also want the attorney general's office to pay for notifying the defendants as a monetary sanction. Letters and other notices need to go out saying you were wrongfully convicted and so on, and we have to find the people and send them these notices. The attorney general's office has been ordered to pay for that, for what its former employees did. That's not sending anyone to prison but it's very rare to see even that level of accountability for prosecutorial misconduct.

IT'S INSANE THEY DON'T FACE ANY SORT OF PENALTIES FOR SCREWING UP SO BADLY. ON PURPOSE IT SEEMS.

That is one reason why we have so many instances of wrongful conviction in this country. Basically the justice system operates on the principles that punishment deters wrongdoing by poor people and people of color, but does not for powerful people and therefore there's no reason to even punish powerful people. That was basically the attorney general's argument in the case that was decided. They said Well, there was already a strongly worded opinion and negative press attention and that was punishment for them enough they argued. That is decidedly not the argument when a poor person messes up. I don't think defense attorneys have much luck when they say Your Honor, it's already been published that my client was arrested . . .

WHERE ARE THE TWO ASSISTANT ATTORNEYS GENERAL INVOLVED IN THE COVER-UP NOW?

The person who received the email with Farak's mental health work-sheets and didn't turn it over is Anne Kaczmarek. The one who was tasked with trying to quash the subpoenas is Kris Foster. There's a pending bar complaint against them from the Innocence Project in New York that has been pending for over a year with no results. Kaczmarek is presently a clerk magistrate in Suffolk County. Foster is the general counsel for a government agency.

LOL. ARE YOU HAPPY? HAS JUSTICE BEEN DONE HERE?

A lot of justice has been done. We represent two people who've moved on with their lives and are recovering after this now. For them and thousands of other people we really do think this is a substantial victory. It's going to help them move on, get jobs and houses because of this opinion. But we hope that these scandals will start to turn the tide in favor of a public health approach with the problem of addiction in Massachusetts and all over the place and lead to a new way of dealing with wrongful conviction which says the default should be to dismiss them and prosecutors should have the burden of dealing with them. We think that shifting the burden can make everyone think twice about the war on drugs. The easiest way not to have wrongful conviction is not have a conviction in the first place. We've seen officials in Massachusetts say they want a public health approach to drugs but we hope these decisions in these scandals cause them to actually do that.

✶

PEOPLE VERY MUCH WANT TO BELONG

NEITHER OF US ARE GOING TO COME OUT OF THIS

The president is on TV in Montana and he's still very excited about this fact even now. He takes a moment to point out the row of cameras in the back of the room with a jape about how unhappy they all are with him and no one really knows what he means specifically but they get it all the same because the pink crowd is delighted and laughing and the proceedings have shifted into that fever dream sitcom where we elected Rodney Dangerfield in *Natural Born Killers* president. There they are he says gesturing broadly as if he's grounding himself. When you wake up from a nightmare you're not sure has finished and it's dark and quiet but the light from the moon creeps in through the blinds just so and you can make out the faded shapes of your bedroom furniture and calm yourself down. Like that sort of thing. Ah yes here I am.

He goes on to praise Montana rep. Greg Gianforte who assaulted a reporter from the *Guardian* last year a place I write for sometimes. "Never wrestle him, you understand that?" he says mimicking a body slamming motion. "Any guy who can do a body slam is my kind of guy," he says.

This is all as he refuses to condemn the Saudi government for the obvious and apparent torture and murder of *Washington Post* writer Jamal Khashoggi a place I write for sometimes. If we're being honest we're probably only a couple weeks away from Trump pantomiming his death at a rally as well. Bone saw! They said they brought a bone saw he'll say looking around for someone behind him off camera. I don't know do we like the bone saw he'll say pretending to saw his own arm off and the crowd will roar. Nasty business but we love it don't we.

I was sitting in a mobile home and it was 2010 and we were riding out to Coney Island for a fashion shoot for *Black Book* magazine and I remember wanting Gavin McInnes to like me very much. I was interviewing him about his *Street Boners* book that had just come out and we all thought that was just about the funniest shit in the world at the time even though we should have known better. I wasn't even particularly young but I don't know what to tell you about that. There was still some plausible deniability left in the whole scam if you wanted a reason to ignore it I guess for example if you were a white male hipster who never had anything bad happen to you in your life. When you are convinced of your own self-evident goodness saying transgressive shit becomes the joke itself because you're obviously a good person right and you don't really believe that sort of thing right so it goes all the way back around and is funny now. I remember thinking everyone involved in the shoot was the coolest person alive and there were like a dozen models both men and women there and I thought about how exciting it must be to be a hipster model in New York City skateboarding to parties and dying from cocaine overdoses and such but in retrospect they were probably getting paid shit like I was getting paid shit and I wonder if any of them ever went on to have a real career in fashion or if it was just something they did when they were young for a little while before moving back to the Phoenix suburbs and dying from cocaine overdoses there.

I just went back and read the piece for the first time in years. I was clearly very excited about the shoot the freak metaphor that I built it around, the boardwalk carnival game that I thought said something about the whole Dos & Don'ts shtick Gavin was famous for back then.

Reading it now there are a lot of red flags that I probably should've picked up on but there's also enough genuinely funny stuff that reminds me why many of us liked him in the first place.

> Before getting in a cab to come to the shoot, McInnes tells me, he popped an Adderall and drained a cup of coffee. Not a good idea before his morning shit, it seems. He vividly recalls feeling like a pregnant lady in the movies, breathing heavily, hoping the driver doesn't hit any big bumps. Retelling the story gives him an idea for a bit where the cabby gets out to help perform an emergency delivery but instead gets sprayed in the face with diarrhea. What follows is a discussion about the best ways to rig the fake shit and what angle to shoot it from so it looks most believable.

> McInnes seems like he's constantly workshopping bits. Twitter and the comments section of Street Boners are his favorite place for trying out new ones, although he does get a little annoyed with some of the meaner comments on Street Boners. "It bums me out when people talk about the girl's bone structure or something. Your beef is with god, not her. But the internet is all horny fourteen-year-olds. So you're fourteen and you can't get anyone to fuck you, and now you're mad at chicks."

That last bit seems like an eerily prescient description of his latest venture the Proud Boys who earlier in 2018 had gang-stomped some people in New York City after Gavin's appearance at a fancy Republican Club.

"There's this assumption that if you antagonize people they're just going to take it," Gavin says at one point in a video put together after the incident by video comedian Vic Berger. Richard Spencer the famous Nazi is standing next to him and they all seem to be having a great time. "I think those days are done now."

Fuck me? No, fuck *you* is a powerful drug you see. Trump often talks about how he fights back and people like that very much. They line up for hours to hoot and holler amid a sea of sunburned car dealership guys and boat owners and let the fuck *you* come over them. You can get people hooked on fuck *you* and they'll do almost anything you tell them to.

One of the things they say about Mohammad Bin Salman Al Saud the crown prince of Saudi Arabia who likely authorized the plan to torture and murder Khashoggi is that he's a reformer taking steps to modernize the country such as finally allowing women to drive cars. Another thing that is reportedly happening in Saudi Arabia is they are arresting a lot more women there now which is a big step for equality I think we can all agree. Many of them are being arrested and detained for speech crimes as Adam Coogle a Middle East researcher for Human Rights Watch told *The Young Turks*.

"This is a new kind of deal. Typically in Saudi Arabia jailing of women was something that's pretty taboo. It wasn't really done," he said.

The boom in jailing women has led the country to seek out aid from the U.S. in training people to run the prisons, a program for which the State Department is reportedly seeking contractors to bid on. Fair play to them because if there is anything we know how to do better than almost any other country it's run prisons.

"People are often held in these facilities pre-trial and put in solitary confinement and are mistreated with a view towards coercing confessions that are later used in court to convict the person. We have lots of accounts of that," Coogle said.

At least 300 people were killed and 2,000 injured in 2018 in violence carried out by the police forces under the control of Nicaraguan president Daniel Ortega according to an Amnesty International investigation. The violence came after protests against social security reforms erupted around the country. Earlier in the summer a twenty-five-year-old woman named Dania Valeska Alemán Sandoval shared a video to Facebook live of herself and fellow protesters under attack by government forces that soon went viral.

In her video Sandoval can be seen crying and asking her mother for forgiveness if she is killed. *Perdoname* she says. She and some 200 other students had taken cover in a church in Managua. Two of her friends were killed that day she later told the *Daily Beast* a place I write for sometimes. Although she survived she was arrested and tortured and forced to give a false confession that the government then used as propaganda against the protesters to say they were paid and fakes and that sort of thing which is what a fascist says to convince everyone he is actually good and it must work because they keep doing that shit over and over.

"They said that they were going to kill me and my family," Sandoval said in an interview later on. "Later they brought one of my *compañeros* and put him on his knees and put an AK-47 to his head. They told me if I didn't cooperate and read what they would give me they were going to show the execution of my *compañero*, and then there would be another and another. There was nothing else I could do but read the script that they had ready for me."

Amnesty International say such false testimonies have become common and that the death toll may be a lot higher than they estimate because people are scared to even report anything owing to fear of reprisal by the government. The violence has led to tens of thousands of Nicaraguans being displaced and applying for asylum mainly in neighboring Costa Rica because that is what happens when the government is killing its own people the people try to migrate away from there and go someplace they suspect they will be safer.

Another thing Trump said in Montana is that people are being paid to migrate in a caravan passing through Guatemala en route to the States.

"A lot of money's been passing through people to come up and try to get to the border by Election Day because they think that's a negative for us," he said. "They wanted that caravan and there are those that say that caravan didn't just happen. It didn't just happen," he said. He later shared a video that Rep. Matt Gaetz of Florida had also shared on Twitter that they said showed people being paid to join the caravan and "storm the border at election time" because they think that their followers will believe made up shit like that which is true they will believe it because they will believe anything.

In August I talked to a young man who had migrated from El Salvador to here because his father was being threatened by gangs. "I didn't want to come over here," he said. "To go to another country. You know you have to walk, cross the river, sleep over in the woods in the night. You don't even know what's going to happen. But you got two choices, go over there, or stay here and let's see what happens to you. You die."

I don't think he probably knew what a Democrat or a Republican was when he did the whole fleeing for his life from gangs in his country thing but who knows maybe his plan was to come here all along and vote for Maxine Waters fifty times who can ever really say.

Sometimes I get emails from people who say things such as fuck *you* and they will kick my ass in and things of that nature and I usually don't worry about them too much because it is something so common for journalists that if you got scared every time you were threatened you wouldn't really have much time to do anything else. Here's one I just got after I'd written a piece about how a writer for Stephen Colbert had gotten everyone on the right pissed off at her for an obvious joke about Brett Kavanaugh's life being "ruined." It's not particularly bad but it's the most recent one so there you go.

> Oh sure tough guy it was a joke you know how many people lost their jobs because they made a joke about Obama you live in a one-sided dim-witted world. Really you're going to hide behind it was a joke and call Fox News Watchers stupid. You're the typical hypocrite you can dish it out but you can't take it you walk around with that tough look on your face buddy if you ever going to be near Virginia send me a shout I wipe that smile off your f****** face.

I don't know buddy.

The last time I talked to Gavin he had written me an email whining about how I called out a piece on Street Carnage his post-Vice site. I had written for it a while prior to that but had stopped by then due to all the racism and also that he refused to pay me any money. Mostly I had written my typical lefty horse shit but also some things that I probably wrote just to try to seem edgy and ironic because when someone is charismatic and funny and saying that sort of shit all the time you want to impress them which is embarrassing to say but it also happens to be true.

"Sad to see this once-hilarious site finally follow in the footsteps of its founder into complete reactionary right wing racist apologist mode with this piece 'Seven Cliches About Racism,'" I wrote.

Why don't I refute it with evidence, he asked, instead of just crying out racism which is the type of shit people like that always want you to do but is always a trap and no matter what evidence you offer back it won't work. The point is to just frustrate you.

I still stupidly thought it was just a phase for him. I didn't want to believe a guy I had looked up to as being so funny and cool really believed the type of stuff he was saying. Surely it must have been an edgelord con of some kind. I was fucking stupid and it's shameful to admit that now but that is how it was so I don't know what else to say on that account.

"I really hope you get past this stuff some day," I told him. "You're a hilarious writer, and much smarter than this type of paranoid fear-mongering scared conservative pussy routine. It bums me, and a huge majority of your fans, I'd imagine, out to see you turn into a doddering old racist."

Then it went on and on back and forth with all manner of shit that I'm sure you can picture but by the end I had finally talked myself into an epiphany I guess.

"Neither of us are going to come out of this having convinced one another of anything are we?" I wrote. "I think my deep-rooted biases for equality are probably too steadfast for you to open my eyes. I'm a lost cause for conversion to the dark side."

I sometimes wonder if any of the people falling for the nationalist and nativist stuff that's going on around the world and in our country in particular right now will look back on it someday and think to themselves *Ah, what the fuck was that*? I hope a lot of them do but I'm not overly optimistic. People very much want to belong to any group that will have them.

We have a bunch of old magnets on our fridge and a lot of them are cute little things my grandmother who is dead and who loved us very much made for my wife such as some hats and magnets that say things like I am fairly certain that given a cape and a nice tiara I could save the world! and The secret to life is girlfriends and a good martini! We also have a bunch of old wedding invite magnets which I guess was a trend there for a while and a lot of them are faded now like the idea of the marriage itself washed away over time which it literally did in some cases because the couple got divorced pretty quickly. Half of the magnets on there are for couples who have gotten divorced actually but we keep them up there anyway and I'm not sure why. I was thinking about that this morning and I thought it was the saddest thing I could think of but I don't think it's all that sad anymore relatively speaking at this particular moment. I don't really know all that much about what happened in any of those marriages but I know at some point someone got fed up and decided they didn't have to live like that anymore. They could just leave and not look back.

WE NEED TO MAKE SURE THAT YOU BELONG HERE

THE BANAL EVERYDAY INDIGNITIES

On Monday in May of 2018 Lolade Siyonbola a black graduate student at Yale University posted a video of her encounter with the police. Siyonbola's offense was falling asleep in a common area of her own dorm. Two videos she posted to Facebook including a confrontation with the woman who reported her, a fellow grad student, and a second of her interaction with the police soon went viral with a combined 2.5 million views that week. Despite showing the officers her school ID and room key they continued to investigate the incident as if a serious crime had occurred.

"We need to make sure that you belong here," one of the officers in the video can be heard telling her.

In late April a similar interaction with police played out in Rialto, California, when four African American artists were questioned by police after exiting an Airbnb. A neighbor had called suspecting a burglary was underway. One of the renters named Donisha Prendergast who is a filmmaker posted to Instagram from the scene in a video that pulled in tens of thousands of views and soon spread widely. Also that month a video taken of two black men being arrested in a Philadelphia Starbucks for not purchasing anything fast enough exploded across the internet gaining millions of views.

See? many of the millions of people who shared each video would say online. *We've been trying to tell you.*

In each case none of the stories would have garnered much national attention if the people in question or a concerned bystander hadn't been on hand to document it in video form. It's one thing to read a story about a person of color being fucked with by the police particularly for people whose white privilege often shields them from these sorts of hassles. It's another entirely to witness the reality of it as it happens.

We've seen a shift in recent years as the ubiquity of cellphone cameras has started to change the way we talk about police violence in America from Eric Garner to a Miami police officer who was charged with assault in 2018 for kicking a man in handcuffs in the face. But these sorts of encounters differ in a way. It's no surprise that something as shocking as police murdering or brutalizing citizens would attract widespread attention. What is happening now is a less sensational sort of harassment. The banal everyday indignities people of color are often forced to deal with—things white people like myself rarely have to think about—are being shared widely. Consider the group of black women who had the police called on them on a Pennsylvania golf course for not golfing fast enough or the Native American brothers who were removed from a campus tour at Colorado State University because their presence made a parent nervous or Darren Martin who had six police officers arrive to detain and question him while he was moving into his apartment in New York City or the woman in Oakland who called the police on a group of black people for "grilling illegally."

When it comes to police violence it's become common to ask ourselves and others: *Can you imagine how often these things happened and how little we heard about them before cameras?* We could just as easily ask the same question about the types of encounters Siyonbola and Prendergast and others have posted about. These encounters happen across America every day. The mere act of existing in the world—taking a nap, barbecuing, moving into an apartment, shopping—is seen as de facto inappropriate when it's being done while black.

Of course this is not news. This has not just started happening. What is different is that people have become wise to the fact that sometimes going viral is their only recourse so we are seeing more videos of it posted. And on the plus side many more people do seem to be paying attention to it. Had white Americans listened to people of color talking about their own lived reality for decades they might have understood that this happens all the time. But America at large doesn't tend to do that. Even with the rise of the Black Lives Matter movement there will remain a steadfast and indignant percentage of people—even when given clear evidence of actual crimes, even cold-blooded murder being carried out by police—insisting on seeing all the evidence or those who wonder what the obviously guilty black man must have done to provoke the righteous police into killing him. *They always have it coming.*

For those people I doubt there is any hope whatsoever. But for people inclined to stand in solidarity but not necessarily always fully invested—because, of course, it won't happen to "us"—there's one critical takeaway: do not call the police every time you are made marginally uncomfortable by a situation. As the Native American writer Kelly Hayes explained on Twitter in the wake of these stories: "Police don't enforce laws. They enforce social norms. Gentrifiers who chronically call police aren't concerned with safety. They want to dictate social norms and conditions. They want control. And they know what it could mean to call. They are simply prioritizing their own power."

In the video in which Darren Martin is being detained by police while trying to move in he asks what prompted them to suspect he was breaking into his own apartment. One of the cops has the dispatcher read out the call they'd received. Someone "was trying to break into the door," she says, "possibly a weapon. A large tool."

Now you know why we're here, the officer says.

"I know why y'all are here," Martin says.

Then one of them jokes about how many likes he's getting on the video he's live-streaming.

These sorts of videos are now thankfully going as viral as the more sensational ones which can be an opportunity for outside observers to practice the empathy they'd like to think they have. What would it be like to be hassled by the police for simply taking a nap or renting an Airbnb or golfing? To be told that an investigation had to be launched on *whether or not you belonged here*? After a while you might start to question whether or not you do.

MY UNDERSTANDING IS THAT EVENTUALLY YOU WILL BE UNIFIED

DO THE CHILDREN HAVE ANY SENSE OF WHAT'S HAPPENING TO THEM?

On a Sunday in June of 2018 U.S. Senator Jeff Merkley of Oregon tried to visit a detention facility for migrant children in Brownsville, Texas. It did not go well. In a video streamed to Facebook which has since been viewed millions of times Merkley detailed his frustrated efforts to gain access to the building which was a repurposed Walmart after being denied access multiple times by staff.

The senator had two simple questions: What was going on inside the building and where were the children?

That same weekend Merkley made another trip to a similar facility called the McAllen Border Patrol Processing Center where he said he saw children being kept in cages much like in a series of photos from 2014 that had recently spread across the internet.

None of us had any idea at the time how much worse things would get.

"They have big cages made out of fencing and wire and nets stretched across the top of them so people can't climb out of them," Merkley said. "Every time I probed yesterday on the circumstances, the response was just basically a generic, 'That is what's required for security, this is what is required for control.'"

The trip came after an exceptionally draconian new set of policies were put into place by Jeff Sessions and the Trump administration in which children were being purposefully separated from their parents at the border as a means of deterring others who might try to cross over.

"If you don't want your child separated, then don't bring them across the border illegally," Sessions said in May when the new zero-tolerance policy for any adult trying to cross the border was announced.

The facility in Brownsville Merkley tried to enter is run by a company called Southwest Key which has dozens of facilities across the country that bring in tens of millions of dollars in federal grants to operate every year by subcontracting for the Office of Refugee Resettlement under the Department of Health and Human Services. Although they're a nonprofit the leaders of the company are paid an exorbitant salary. Then-president and CEO Juan Sanchez received $770,860 in compensation in 2015 which was a nice bump from the year prior so good for Juan. Nonetheless they insist their efforts are all aimed at the best interests of the children.

"At Southwest Key Programs, we share Senator Merkley's concern for children, and we appreciate that he took time to travel to the border," the company said in a statement. "For more than 20 years, Southwest Key has acted as a humanitarian first responder, caring for immigrant children arriving in this country without a parent or guardian. We provide round-the-clock services including: food, shelter, medical and mental health care, clothing, educational support, supervision, and reunification support."

That may be the case who's to say. The problem was as Merkley's visit showed very few people outside of the company had been able to gain access to what goes on inside. Of the dozen immigration aid and legal groups I contacted that summer most indicated they had never been allowed into one of these detention centers. In a statement a spokesperson for the HHS Administration for Children and Families said Merkley "attempted to enter an unaccompanied alien children's shelter unannounced and broadcast live via social media last night in Texas. Thankfully for the safety, security and dignity of the children being cared for there, they were denied access. The Department of Health and Human Services takes the legal mandate to care for these children seriously. No one who arrives unannounced at one of our shelters demanding access to the children in our care will be permitted, even those claiming to be U.S. senators."

One person who had been inside places like this albeit not the Brownsville location is Rochelle Garza an immigration attorney in the area who represented the seventeen-year-old known as Jane Doe last year in a high-profile case where the government refused to allow her to leave her detention facility to have an abortion. She was eventually allowed to do so although the Supreme Court ultimately threw out the precedent in question.

I spoke with Garza about the frustrations of trying to represent children who have been taken from their parents at the border and why she thinks the new policies under the Trump administration are only making things worse.

WHAT HAS TRADITIONALLY BEEN DONE WITH UNACCOMPANIED MIGRANT CHILDREN?

First, some context: the Trafficking Victims Protection Reauthorization Act of 2013 and the Flores Settlement Agreement are the two pieces of law that control the treatment of unaccompanied minor children. These are children typically from Central America's northern triangle. Any child that presents themselves or is found in the U.S. without a parent is an unaccompanied minor. You don't usually see Mexican children, as they're usually returned back to Mexico, unlike Central American children. Those are the ones in facilities like this one, a lot of times fleeing violence in Honduras or El Salvador, coming here and trying to find a parent or someone else here.

MUCH OF THIS HAS BEEN GOING ON FOR A WHILE, INCLUDING UNDER OBAMA. WHAT IS DIFFERENT NOW?

The family separation issue is new. Children are being taken from their parents and being made into an unaccompanied minor. That is under the new policy Jeff Sessions announced in May. It's a crisis of sorts and it's self-imposed. We're separating parents from kids and the kids are flooding the Office of Refugee Resettlement. The parents are being persecuted and funneled through the immigration system. That's the context we're talking about.

The Brownsville facility has a capacity for 1,200 to 1,500 people. The last I heard there were 1,200 in that facility alone. At one point there were about 20 facilities in the Rio Grande Valley here in south Texas.

WHAT ARE THE FACILITIES LIKE INSIDE?

It depends on which facility you go into; I've been to several of them. They have classrooms, some of them are in old schools, some of them are in new buildings. This one is an old Walmart. There are rooms with bunk beds. There are classrooms where children are given English classes and basic education courses.

DO THE CHILDREN HAVE ANY SENSE OF WHAT'S HAPPENING TO THEM?

That's part of the big picture. When a child comes into the Office of Refugee Resettlement, they're provided with a know your rights presentation. There are legal service providers located anywhere there's a facility. They explain to them they're in removal proceedings and what their rights are. They explain a little of the court system and what to expect. But no child is expected to understand. They're children and they're explaining things in another language to them. We have to contextualize this all that way. They're given a legal screening and evaluated for immigration legal release, it could be asylum, a juvenile visa or visas for victims of trafficking. There are some services, giving them some information about what they're doing there. My sense is the kids understand kind of what's happening but don't really understand. They're kids.

DO THE PARENTS HAVE ANY IDEA WHERE THEIR CHILDREN ARE, TYPICALLY?

Right now what's happening is no, the parents that are being separated from their kids are not being provided information as to the location of their children. If you go into federal court where they're being criminally prosecuted, the parents will ask: "Where is my child? Will I be deported with my child?" The federal judges are just like, "I don't know." They'll say something like, "My understanding is that eventually you will be unified." We don't know the veracity of those statements. Right now we're at this point where we really don't know what's happening. We know parents are being separated from their kids, and that there's an influx. These kids are not traditionally unaccompanied minors [until the government makes them so].

HOW WARRANTED IS THE RECENT BURST OF OUTRAGE HERE, AS EVIDENCED BY THE VIRAL NATURE OF SOME OF THE STORIES ON THIS STUFF?

What's happening is atrocious. It's really unbelievable to separate a child from their parents, children as young as five. The parents don't know where their child ends up. They're being pushed through the criminal system and immigration system without any knowledge of where their children are and their children don't know where their parents are. That's against the whole point of the unaccompanied minor reunification process. The whole thing is garbage right now. The kids are not being sent to any parent. It doesn't make any sense.

HAVE YOU EVER BEEN DENIED ACCESS TO ONE OF THESE FACILITIES?

I have been denied access to a client—at one of these facilities—a child. It's outrageous. There is no respect for the attorney-client relationship. There was another Jane Doe case I handled [a second young woman who wanted to get an abortion] and they were just like, "You can try talking to the Department of Justice." The Office of Refugee Resettlement is hell-bent on denying access to reproductive health care for these young women. It's an agenda of theirs. It didn't surprise me that it happened to the senator.

WHAT CAN THE AVERAGE PERSON DO WHO'S SEEING THIS HAPPEN?

I think call your representative and ask them to look into this issue. Tell your representative: We do not support family separation, this kind of abuse of the American system and American ideals. We're here to welcome people: *Give me your tired, your poor, your hungry . . .* That's absolutely not what's happening here.

GIVE US THE MONEY OR WE'LL KILL YOUR SON

I TOOK A BUS FROM MY CITY AND WE CROSSED MY COUNTRY

When the news about children being held in immigration facilities along the southern border began to emerge I started to search for people who had been held in one of the centers run by Southwest Key—the most trusted name in Baby Jails!—to see what it was like to actually spend time in one. I came across a young man named Elmer who was running a Facebook page for people who had been held there so they could commiserate and share their experiences.

He agreed to tell me his story about leaving El Salvador at the age of 17 in 2014. Conditions for immigrants were much better then as he explained but still exceptionally arduous and dangerous. He left his country he told me because gangs were extorting his father who was a shoemaker. Pay us or your sons die they said. What choice would a man have but to pack off his children and place them in the hands of coyotes who'd smuggle them to America? What would you do?

WHAT WAS IS THAT BROUGHT YOU TO THE UNITED STATES?

I'm from El Salvador, I don't know if you've seen all this news. The reason why I come from there to here I was scared to die, all these gangsters, MS-13. We used to have a business, so they try to get some money from you. They were trying to do that with my dad. My dad, he was a shoemaker in San Miguel.

SAN MIGUEL IS ONE OF THE MOST VIOLENT PLACES, RIGHT?

Yeah. It was like a small city, the neighborhood, everybody knows each other, so they were aware of what my dad was doing. There was a gang MS-13 in the neighborhood right there, and let's say you gotta cross the river to the other neighborhood there was another gang, they're called 18, Vatos Locos or something like that. They left a piece of paper in the door with our name, this amount of money, saying *We're gonna kill your son. We know what school they're going to, what way they take to come home*, me and my brother. My dad, he decided, yeah, to do something.

HOW OLD WERE YOU? WHEN DID YOU DECIDE TO LEAVE?

I'm 21 now, my brother is 22. Nothing happened yet, so we moved to my grandfather's house close to the beach, living in the country, like a small town. And we were there about a year. We started over at a new school, new people. Then it kept going again. There was a decision with my dad, he was like, *No, you gotta go, if you guys stay over here you could die or something could happen to us.*

I didn't want to come over here. To go to another country. You know you have to walk, cross the river, sleep over in the woods in the night. You don't even know what's going to happen. But you got two choices, go over there, or stay here and let's see what happens to you. You die.

ARE YOU GIVEN THE CHOICE TO JOIN THE GANG?

Yeah, they give you the option to join to the gang. But ours was kind of different, they were asking for money. If you don't give us the money we're gonna kill all your sons. I wasn't the kind of guy, I wasn't going out with friends to the mall or to play soccer. I was just like from the house to the school, from the school to the house. I was like away from all this kind of stuff to join to the gang. But yeah some people they give you the choice to join the gangsters, or they're gonna kill you. So, you gotta join, because if you don't they're gonna kill you or someone in your family. And the first thing you gotta do when you join the gangsters is you gotta kill somebody.

AND YOU OBVIOUSLY DIDN'T WANT TO DO THAT.

Exactly. It's like, let's say you want to play for this soccer team, but oh yeah, to join the team you gotta kill that man over there. It's hard.

SO HOW DID YOU GET FROM EL SALVADOR TO THE STATES?

It was a long way. I took a bus from my city, and we crossed my country. We went to the border of El Salvador and Guatemala. You know, that was easy to cross, because . . . you know. Then we slept over in some houses. When we crossed from Guatemala to Mexico we had to walk. Immigration to Mexico was kind of hard. They need like a visa, all your information if you want to cross legal. Then it was a long way. You have to take buses, cars, trucks, and sometimes you got to walk. There was a lot of soldiers in the street they were checking the buses and checking cars, so we would walk.

WERE YOU SCARED?

I was like, I don't know what's gonna happen. I don't want to say I was scared, because in Guatemala I was like, This is weird, this is another country and they don't have the same culture, so I was like, ok, that's Guatemala. Then we crossed to Mexico, you think about all these gangsters, narcos and shit. These gangsters called Zetas. They know all these people they were crossing the border to go to America, so they would just take them and kill them, or take them, and then call your family and ask for money. I was . . . at that time you don't know what's gonna happen.

HOW DID YOU CROSS THE U.S. BORDER? DID YOU PAY SOMEONE?

My brother he came first, in 2013. This guy took my brother, so my dad, he paid to this man to take my brother. A year later he took me. Well my brother was like about $5,000. American dollars. In El Salvador we use dollars. For me it was like half the price.

WERE YOU HIDDEN IN A TRUCK OR GO ACROSS THE RIVER?

We crossed the river, we were just walking. Rio Bravo! It was people who were healthy enough to cross the river. A lot of kids, mostly kids, ten, twelve, [a] 6-year-old kid, sixteen, fourteen, crossing the river. Do you have a daughter? Just imagine you have a daughter sixteen years old crossing the river with people like that.

DO YOU MEAN THE YOUNG GIRLS WERE BEING TAKEN ADVANTAGE OF?

No, no, I'm just saying, it was just like kids.

DID THE COYOTES TREAT YOU WELL?

There's a big system of people, you start from El Salvador and Guatemala, you got a bunch of people, coyotes. So, some people they were nice. Some people they were assholes.

WHAT HAPPENED AFTER YOU CROSSED THE RIVER DID YOU GET CAUGHT?

Yeah! I got pulled over by immigration, in Texas. I forget the name of the city. After we crossed the river, the coyote was like, *Ok, go, you gotta walk. You got a long way to go.* They said there's a black van, they're gonna pick you up. We were just walking, walking, then we got pulled over. Immigration, to be honest, that was my first time so I didn't . . . it was like, to be in school. They were like: make a line, get all your ID's and information ready. We were put into cars. They were regular, they weren't that mean. We're talking like four years ago, so now it's different.

WHERE DID THEY TAKE YOU FROM THERE, TO SOUTHWEST KEY?

Nah! That was a long way! They called it *hielera*, like, the cooler. A jail, but they keep it really cold. We were in line a lot of people. They would call each name, then we got to go to the room. It was like about three days. That was terrible. Imagine, it was like inside a small house living room, and like a hundred people in the same room. The bathroom was like open, so you can see whoever going to the bathroom.

DID YOU THINK YOU WERE GOING TO BE SENT BACK?

I didn't know what was going to happen. I was scared to go back. Then they took us to another jail exactly like that for two days. After that they take you to a plane to the airport. It was like an Air Force plane, like an army plane. We went all the way to Phoenix, Arizona. We went to this place, another jail. I was there for a week. There, yeah, I was excited to come back. I was like in hell.

They would treat you like an animal, like a dog. They would give the food, three times a day, but they would give you a burrito, like every day the same kind of food. We were cold, there was aluminum foil blankets. Every time you ask for one they would be like, Do you want one? And we would say Yes yes! And they would throw them, like boom boom. And they were just laughing. I was like, what kind of people are this? It was a lot of kids.

I don't know why they were treating us like animals. Every time you'd ask for water, they would drop it on the floor, like go ahead. You can imagine all these kids trying to get the water. Like if you drop a piece of candy on the floor.

WHAT HAPPENED NEXT?

After seven days, they call my name. We took the bus, they take us to the airport again and we flew to Houston. Houston was where they took us to the Southwest Key center.

WHAT WAS IT LIKE THERE?

Hey! It was amazing. Oh my god. They give you a shower. You can see a bed. There was like a big TV, Playstation, they got food.

COMPARED TO THE OTHER PLACES IT SEEMED GREAT?

The other places I never in my life seen anything like it. It felt like being in jail, treating you like animals. It was kind of hard to see all these kids, four years old, thirsty, asking for food. Oh man, I was crying. I was seventeen at the time. I was like, that's it, I'm done, I want to come back.

YOU MAKE IT SOUND NOT THAT BAD AT THESE CENTERS, BUT WE SEE ON THE NEWS ALL THE TIME HOW BAD THEY ARE. DO YOU THINK IT GOT WORSE?

Oh yeah. Now it's more harder. Now they're shooting people at the border. I was in the Southwest Key center two months. My uncle couldn't take me, so we had to find other people to take me. Somebody had to sponsor me, I have a family member here. My aunt, from [redacted], she says she's gonna take care of me. Put me in school.

BECAUSE YOUR AUNT SAID SHE'D TAKE YOU IN THEY LET YOU GO TO HER?

Yeah. [The] policy was like that in that year. She's a resident.

NOW THAT THEY'RE NOT LETTING PEOPLE DO THAT ANYMORE WHAT DO YOU THINK ABOUT HOW IT'S CHANGED?

People are just trying to survive. It's hard, man. It's hard to see your son and know they can get killed where you live. And they're just trying to save his life. That's why you send your son to another country. You can't protect them. Now it's different. You send them to hell. Now it's different.

WHAT DID YOU THINK OF THE U.S. BEFORE YOU CAME HERE?

Well, a bunch of things. They tell you the job opportunities, the schools, the security. So everything, they would tell a lot of good things. Now everything has changed. My two little brothers they are in the same way.

Now, my dad he can't decide to send them to America because he fears they'd be killed at the border. He can't say he's gonna send my children to the United States because they can't protect them. I don't want to say they're gonna kill them, but, they're not for sure what's going to happen, they're going to be in jail or they're just gonna send you back.

YOU LIVE HERE NOW, WHAT DO YOU THINK ABOUT DONALD TRUMP?

Donald Trump, like almost everybody else around the world, everything is about money. Donald Trump he's just trying to help people with money, they don't care about me, or you, or a poor family. Donald Trump is stopping people who are just trying to get a dream, or just survive something that's happening in your country. It's not only my country, it's happening around the world. Syria they got wars, bunch of people in other countries they got gangsters. America is really famous because everybody thinks America is a country that's going to take care of you, and make you secure. It is! It is for sure. But it's been changing.

ARE YOU IN SCHOOL NOW OR YOU HAVE A JOB?

Yeah I graduated high school last year so now I'm working.

JUST SO YOU KNOW, AS FAR AS I'M CONCERNED YOU'RE WELCOME HERE.

Oh, and one more thing, I got my green card!

Y

IF YOU WONDER WHERE I AM I WILL TELL YOU JUST WHERE I AM

I GOTTA HEAR YOUR WONDERING SOUND

The house was burning rapidly because it was firebombed and they were also shooting into the house from outside. Vernon I believe they got us this time, Ellie Dahmer said to her husband. The threats had been coming for a while now and it was just a matter of waiting for the worst to come true. It was a Sunday night in January of 1966 in Hattiesberg, Mississippi. The area there had been populated by the Choctaw tribe for hundreds of years but we got them to cede the land through a treaty in 1805 and then forcibly removed most of the rest of them when Andrew Jackson signed the Indian Removal Act of 1830 and you could make a case he was our cruelest most racist president but who knows anymore.

She knew they had to get out she said years later. Betty, their young daughter, was burning she said. *She had got burned and was burning.* Betty just rolled over in the grass out there, she was hurting so, she said. Her husband was hurting badly also and he went into the barn because it was darker there and he was worried if they came back they would be able to see him in the light of his burning house and then they would finish him off.

She said all of this in an oral history she gave to the University of Southern Mississippi which is bittersweet or ironic or fucked up depending on how you look at it because for years Vernon's friend and fellow NAACP activist Clyde Kennard had been trying to enroll in that very school which went by a different name at the time. After *Brown v. Board of Education* they couldn't legally deny him the chance to do that but they still didn't like it all that much you can probably imagine so the officials would lose his application on purpose and fuck with him in a variety of ways. At one point the police planted whiskey in his car and arrested him for it and in 1960 they framed him real good by saying he hired someone to steal $25 worth of chicken feed. An all white jury deliberated for ten minutes and sentenced Kennard to seven years in prison for the thing he didn't do and then he died a couple years later from cancer after being denied medial treatment in the prison he didn't belong in. Medgar Evers called the trial a mockery of judicial justice and so they put him in jail for thirty days for that because it was contempt of court is what they said he had done there.

There's a photo of four of the Dahmers' sons examining the wreckage of their family home the next morning and they're all in their military uniforms because they were enlisted at the time serving their country which is the term we use for that particular job.

Vernon Dahmer was a fierce proponent of voting and dedicated much of his life to helping other African Americans exercise that right. After the Voting Rights Act of 1965 was passed which was a law that forced us to let black people actually do the voting they were already supposed to be able to do he would keep a voting registration book in his store to make it easier for people to register. He went on the local radio station one night to say that he would personally pay the poll tax for anyone who couldn't afford it and as it turns out that's the night the KKK killed him.

"I've been active in trying to get people to register to vote. People who don't vote are deadbeats on the state," he told a reporter after the fire and before the severity of his injuries had set in. "I figure a man needs to do his own thinking. What happened to us last night can happen to anyone, white or black. At one time I didn't think so, but I have changed my mind."

I'm so tired and sick all the time and maybe it's because at night I typically drink too much because I don't like the sounds my brain is making and then in the day I will sometimes take a pill to make my stomach injury stop hurting and that makes me drowsy and I really have nowhere to be or no responsibilities anyway so I could just lie here doing nothing if I wanted to on any given day and no one would notice which is sort of a blessing and a curse if I'm being honest.

Who would you rather run over with a car a baby or an old person? Researchers from the MIT Media Lab published a study in 2018 that asked people as much in an attempt to jumpstart the thinking on the types of ethical dilemmas that will likely one day go into the programming of self-driving cars.

"The study is basically trying to understand the kinds of moral decisions that driverless cars might have to resort to," Edmond Awad the paper's lead author said. "We don't know yet how they should do that."

Over two million participants from 200 countries around the world took part in a survey they designed which was a sort of update on the Trolley Problem. By and large there were many consistencies in how people answered the questions throughout the world—spare the lives of humans over animals they said and drive into fewer people instead of large groups when possible and so on. One interesting difference was that in Asian cultures where they tend to revere older people rather than despise them like we do here there was less of a tendency to automatically choose to save the lives of young people.

I'd be pretty alarmed by the whole thing but I don't really think driverless cars are ever going to be real. There won't be time.

I just read a story in the *Boston Globe* about a young woman who died from an asthma attack while waiting outside of the emergency room at a hospital near where I live. It was early in the morning and the doors were locked and she couldn't find her way in so she called 911 saying she was at the hospital what the fuck let me in etc. The dispatcher eventually alerted the hospital that she was out there but a nurse poked her head out and didn't see her sitting on a bench dying and so she lost all the oxygen to her brain and they had to make the decision to give her organs away pretty soon after that.

Her husband wrote the article and it's probably the most heartbreaking thing you'll read in a long time and I'd like to tell you more about what happened in this perfect storm of systemic breakdown and institutional failure but I had to stop reading it because I didn't want to think about it anymore. I remember one line from it that the husband wrote about his wife that shouldn't be dead and it was that she was exceptionally active and fit despite her asthma and that she could bench-press more than her body weight which is something a good number of men can't do and very few women. She had packed a gym bag full of clothes to bring with her on the way to the hospital because she probably figured she'd be in and out and since she was up she might as well get a workout in anyway but that didn't end up happening.

One time I saw a movie or read a book where the apocalypse had come or was coming up soon in any case and the main characters came across an old man in his house who was helpful to them somehow if I remember it correctly. His wife had recently died due to the bad thing that was happening which I don't remember the nature of and he didn't have much use for the world anymore after that fact so he curled up next to her in bed and sent himself off to sleep forever holding her there and that is what that story made me think of.

Vernon Dahmer died the next day as a result of the fire that the white people had set. It was the smoke that killed him his wife said.

"The smoke that the doctor said he swallowed," is how she described it.

It all seems like the distant past but both of my own parents were alive then and probably yours were too. I was only negative ten years old.

Fourteen men were indicted for the attack. Only four of them were convicted and they spent a few short years in prison. Former Ku Klux Klan Imperial Wizard Sam Bowers who was likely behind it all was tried four times and each one ended in a mistrial because he kept invoking his Fifth Amendment rights which were guaranteed to him under the Constitution. Twenty-five years later the state reopened the case and after a trial that lasted seven years he was sentenced to life in prison. He died there but he got to see fifty more years of progress than Dahmer did.

"If you don't vote, you don't count" was a thing Dahmer would often say.

I just saw on the TV that they asked the president what proof he had that people were trying to vote illegally.

"All you have to do is go around and take a look at what's happened over the years and you will see," he said.

"There are a lot people, in my opinion and based on proof, that try and get in illegally and actually vote illegally," the president said on the TV. "So we just want to let them know there will be prosecutions at the highest level."

There's a song that hurts my heart and it's about the most romantic song I've ever heard. In the video two skeletons break out of their prison in the dirt and spend a night together doing all the things they used to do. And when the night is over they go back into their tomb to wait for their chance to do it again. Maybe it's not an ongoing thing actually maybe it was the last time they would ever get to do it. That is probably the sadder reading so I'll go with that.

"This book is two pages deep," it goes. "There are no pictures, no screens. Don't you leave this one up to me. I will write it too honestly. If you wonder where I am, I will tell you just where I am. But I gotta hear your wondering sound."

WE HAVE TO HAMMER ON THE ABUSERS IN EVERY WAY POSSIBLE

THEY ARE THE CULPRITS AND THE PROBLEM. THEY ARE RECKLESS CRIMINALS

How much money would you need to go and kill someone? You wouldn't even have to be there for it or pull a trigger or do anything else to get your hands dirty you would just collect the money and somewhere out there someone you have never met would die. Not just die though they'd die most likely after a period of terrific pain and addiction and withdrawal and perhaps spend months or years before their death resorting to all manner of desperate measures to acquire the one thing in life that brings them relief. Maybe they'd hurt some people along the way too. What can I put you down for that? What's it gonna take for me to see you walking out of here today the proud owner of a body?

Between 2008 and 2016 the Sacklers, the billionaire family behind Purdue Pharma, extracted $4 billion in profits from the company in large part due to sales of OxyContin the highly addictive pain medication they buried the country under. During that time around 235,000 people died from overdoses from the drug so if we do a little back of the napkin math here that breaks down to about $18,000 a head. Would that do the trick for you? Or maybe you'd need to move a little weight to make it worth the heavy conscience. I'm not saying you would be comfortable killing 250,000 people that would be crazy. What about twenty people to the tune of about $360,000? You could get a pretty decent house in most markets for that kind of money. Not in Boston of course but somewhere they have to still have houses for that little.

The rot at the heart of America's worst family has been known for some time now but newly un-redacted documents in the state of Massachusetts' lawsuit against the family show their direct involvement in a push to aggressively increase sales of the drug and downplay the risks of addiction.

In 1996 the Sacklers and Purdue had a launch party for OxyContin which is a pretty funny thing to have a party for in retrospect. It would be like having a launch party for a new type of cancer. There would be passed hors d'oeuvres and even though it's an open bar the line would be kind of long and someone would be like this fucking line at the bar is too long at the cancer launch party let's get out of here.

But around the debut of the Oxy thing one thing Dr. Richard Sackler said at the time was this which was that it would be "followed by a blizzard of prescriptions that will bury the competition." And he's right there if by competition he means sick patients a lot of them were certainly buried.

Not his problem though because years later after the harmful effects of the drug started to become more widely discussed Sackler devised a way to shift the blame.

"We have to hammer on the abusers in every way possible," he wrote in an email in 2001. "They are the culprits and the problem. They are reckless criminals."

Imagine if there was a family and a company that patented and marketed the massively popular concept of dying in a fiery car accident. We'd probably go ahead and stop them right. You would hope we would stop that. We wouldn't because I just remembered the concept of the gun lobby but still you would hope that we would.

Around 2009 the Sackler family contracted the services of McKinsey the consulting firm of choice for rich sociopaths around the world. Among the ideas they came up with according to documents filed in the lawsuit was a slide presentation that said prescriptions could be increased by getting doctors to think opioids would offer "freedom" and "peace of mind" and give people suffering "the best possible chance to live a full and active life."

As ProPublica reported, "In a meeting with Purdue executives, McKinsey planned how to 'counter the emotional messages from mothers with teenagers that overdosed in [sic] OxyContin' by recruiting pain patients to talk about the need for the drugs."

Another bit of advice the consultants had was to focus on the doctors who already seemed willing to prescribe the drug prolifically which is just sound economic theory in my opinion. Seeing that "prescription rates rose in tandem with visits from sales reps to doctors," McKinsey "recommended increasing each salesperson's quota from 1,400 visits a year to closer to 1,700."

In 2009 one Purdue sales manager started to grow a conscience of sorts and wrote to a company official that they seemed to be pushing the drugs to a particularly unethical illegal pill mill.

"I feel very certain this is an organized drug ring," they wrote in an email. "Shouldn't the DEA be contacted about this?"

The DEA was not contacted about this.

None of which is to say the Sacklers are all bad. For example at one point they looked into developing medications that would help those addicted to their product. Dr. Kathe Sackler participated in talks about such a thing in 2014 with a team the court documents suggest.

"It is an attractive market," they outlined in a presentation. "Large unmet need for vulnerable, underserved and stigmatized patient population suffering from substance abuse, dependence and addiction," they said. Wouldn't it be beneficial for the company to transition into an "end-to-end pain provider"?

They also considered dipping their toes into the booming Narcan market, the reverse-overdose agent, and due to they are marketing geniuses they thought the best way to do that would be to push Narcan on the same doctors who prescribed the most Oxy which would be like pushing diarrhea medicine to restaurants that sold the most tacos.

They didn't end up going ahead with those plans in the end but good news though because Richard Sackler did receive approval on a patent for a medication meant to help people suffering opioid addiction recently. Here's a paragraph from the patent:

> One of the fundamental problems of illicit drug abuse by drug addicts ("junkies") who are dependent on the constant intake of illegal drugs such as heroin is the drug-related criminal activities resorted to by such addicts in order to raise enough money to fund their addiction. The constant pressures upon addicts to procure money for buying drugs and the concomitant criminal activities have been increasingly recognized as a major factor that counteracts efficient and long-lasting withdrawal and abstinence from drugs.

Speaking of addicts another email explained in the court filings came in 2010 after a period of slower than usual profits for the Sacklers. The expected quarterly payout to the family of $320 million was starting to look more like $260 million which is fucking nothing get $260 million out of my face that is an insult.

Mortimer D. A. Sackler, son of one of the company founders also named Mortimer, was particularly red-assed about this. "Why are you BOTH reducing the amount of the distribution and delaying it and splitting it in two?" he wrote in an email. "Just a few weeks ago you agreed to distribute the full 320 in November."

The name Mortimer and I just looked this up although I already suspected it comes from the French and it means dead sea or dead pond or stagnant lake.

The Sacklers aren't the only people getting rich off of a corrupt narco empire of course, another one is John Kapoor the billionaire founder of Insys Pharmaceuticals makers of a fetanyl spray. Insys executives are also being sued in Boston as we speak and Kapoor himself was arrested in 2017 for a number of charges related to an alleged practice of bribing doctors with cash and other gifts so they would prescribe more of their product Subsys. Insys reportedly made more than 18,000 payments to doctors in 2016 alone amounting to over $2 million and to be honest that doesn't seem like that much you would hope that buying off a doctor so he'd give out more of your addictive death spray for cancer patients' families to abuse would cost more than that but maybe not. Nine hundred people have died from Subsys since 2012 by the way.

Most doctors don't want to prescribe dangerous drugs unless absolutely necessary you would think and Insys knew this so one clever little trick they engaged in according to the lawsuit which is something that is very common in pharmaceutical sales is they made sure to hire hot young women to work as sales reps and "encouraged them to stroke doctors' hands while 'begging' them to write the prescriptions as *Mother Jones* has reported. One particular detail that has the news all riled up as the court case is ongoing was an alleged incident in which an Illinois doctor named Paul Madison who ran a pain clinic there got a lap dance from an Insys rep who used to be a stripper. There's nothing wrong with being a stripper mind you but how do you go home and tell your parents what you do for a living is sell fetanyl to dirty doctors?

People who work in medical sales have told me that it's an almost universal practice to hire young attractive sales reps to travel around from doctor's office to doctor's office pushing drugs on them and I will tell you it had never occurred to me that there was a direct and causal chain of events that begins with a doctor getting horny one time off a low-cut blouse and someone going ahead and dying from an overdose on pain medication but that probably happens a lot more than you would think. Ah fuck my doctor had a particularly urgent boner two years ago and now I'm dead.

The Sacklers' name is attached to dozens of the world's most revered museums and some of the best hospitals in the country and part of me thinks that's an effort on their behalf to launder their blood money because maybe somewhere inside they feel guilty for being drug dealing sociopaths but it's probably just vanity. When you don't actually do any work but have hoarded a disgusting amount of wealth you need to put your name on a museum or whatever because that gives you something to do. You get to go the museum there and look at it and think about how you made that possible. All the beauty inside there and it's all thanks to you. You're a good person. You've changed the world.

I'm not a particularly vengeful person and the rate at which we imprison people in this country for crimes far less serious than those committed by billionaire death profiteers is an affront to decency but I'm conflicted on what I think the Sacklers and people like them deserve. There was a time in my life where I might have said let them taste the fruits of their own machinations. Let them become dependent on opioids and thrust them each into a cycle of dependency and desperation. How does it feel I'd say.

But no that is not a healthy way to think. I don't want to think things like that. I don't know if they are going to end up facing any consequences for what they've done we don't tend to punish billionaires particularly frequently these days but at the very least I think we can all agree to remember their name for what it is. They love having their names attached to big impressive things so let us call the opioid crisis by what it is let us make sure to say the name Sackler every time we mention it. The Sackler opioid crisis. That way they can be remembered on throughout history like they always wanted.

My father was an addict just like his father was an addict just like I am an addict and I've been thinking about him today writing about opioid addiction because that was one of the things he had gone and developed over the course of his relatively short ass life and also because I just read a pretty stunning piece in the *Guardian* by a writer named Joel Golby called "'You will behave weirdly': what I learned from becoming an orphan at 25" which I encourage you to go and read now as well or maybe later once this is over. A couple of parts resonated with me in particular like this part about the awkwardness of spreading a loved one's ashes around.

> . . . passing around the big ice-cream tub that had Dad in it, sprinkling that, and so of course he went everywhere, big billowing clouds of Dad all around us, sticking to boots and trousers, clots of grey Dad on the ground.

And then when he writes of doing it all over again after his mother dies. "Then you have to get the old band together again, i.e. get all the family to one chosen place to reverently pour dust on the ground."

In any case it reminded me of a piece I wrote when my father died a couple of years ago so I thought I'd share it here because you probably didn't read it back then. It's about a family member dying of course but also about how awkward it is to announce that to the world now via social media.

The fifth time I went to watch my father die was the one that finally took.

He'd been in and out of hospitals, and hospice, and nursing homes for so many years. He'd clawed his way out of so many comas. We all assumed up until the final moments that this time would be no different. In fact, I still half-expect to get a phone call from him today, his tobacco-ravaged voice asking me to call him back, like so many of the voicemails he left me over the past year or two. He was only 61, but a lifetime of dogged, determined substance abuse and enough related ailments had finally conspired to finish the job he had started at a young age.

When I found out he had finally passed, I was driving, on my way from Boston to Foxwoods. We had been at his bedside all day, back and forth to the hospital all week. My siblings and I—a cabal of half-, step-, and adopted-then-re-found sisters that you'd need one of those charts in the back of a Russian novel to understand—had made the life-changing decision to kill him. At least, that's how it felt.

Of course, as the doctors at Mass General Hospital explained, we weren't actively doing anything to end his life. We were simply allowing nature to take its course, to remove him from the H. R. Gigerian exoskeleton of machines and tubes that allowed him to breathe, lowered his critical blood pressure, and provided him with the barest of sustenance, a thin gruel of intravenous sugar water.

How do you explain that to a Facebook friend?

Earlier this year, Facebook rolled out a new feature called "Reactions." While the long-speculated "Dislike" button didn't make it in with "Like," "Love," "Haha," "Wow," "Sad," and "Angry"—a sort of Kübler-Ross model of casual impulse emotion—one of the prime motivations for the additions, it seems, was to include a way for users to "sympathize" with one another. The limited, emotional-homogenizing parameters of the "Like" button are something most of us have come across when a friend shares news of a breakup, a lost job, or any other number of Significant Life Events. The death of a loved one, for instance.

My wife and I had planned an overnight to the casino resort in Connecticut several months back, and were informed there was no telling how long it might take for my dad to go. It could be hours, it could be days. In truth, the thought of watching his last rasping gasps was too horrible for me to consider. The resort was an appropriately absurd place to be, given the circumstances: the oppressive, relentless din of the slot machines, the haggard demeanor of the assorted walking dead that populate most casinos, the artificial feel of every detail, down to the light quality and the elevated oxygen levels. If a casino is a place where the living go to deaden themselves with indulgence, what better place for the living to figure how to feel about the dead?

To be sure, that's not something I was in any shape to discern then, or even now, a couple of weeks later.

My father did not raise me.

That job was undertaken by an amazing man, my stepfather, and my loving mother. My father was not a significant part of most of my adult life, until recently, when we'd started to reconnect. Much of that, I suspect, was because he was fearful about reaching the end without a relationship with his various children from three different wives. He was, like many fathers before him, and many surely to come, abusive to my mother, something that, once I learned about it as a young man, caused me to cut him out of my life for a long time, and something that is near impossible for me to forgive even now.

But there's something about death and dying that lets us overlook past sins, and he was always good to my sisters and I when we visited as children and teenagers. He seems to have been a good father to my half sister, some 17 years younger than me. I would never have forgiven myself if I didn't get to know him at least a little bit once again before he was gone.

I'd been expecting him to die for so many years, that at some point the thought of how to openly talk about his death overtook my thoughts of his actual departure from this earth. Perhaps that's the writerly instinct kicking in. Even in the midst of the most harrowing of life events, you can't help but pause to notice a detail and think where it would fit in the story.

As a group of us watched him slip away, we poked and prodded at his tattoos, still just-visible on his arms, enlarged and bloated from so many tubes, now bruised and blood-red. There was my mother's name, long since covered up by a black panther; his most recent ex-wife's name; a naked Porky Pig, dick and balls and all; a devil with its tongue sticking out, straddled by a naked woman; and other assorted tattoos one apparently picks up along the way in various motorcycle gangs and clubs.

They say tattoos tell the story of someone's life, and in staring at his, we actually began to tell it to each other, this assembled group of family and friends. It was cathartic in the way speaking of the dead can be, although macabre at the same time, as he wasn't even dead yet. I couldn't help but be taken aback by the existential horror of being vaguely conscious, unable to move or talk, while everyone you know is standing around your body crying. *Ah shit*, you'd probably think. *I must be really fucked this time*.

Still, I found comfort in hearing stories from the parts of his life I wasn't there for, many of which you might rightfully consider sad. But given the bastard's charisma, they now took on a softened edge in the transubstantiation of an addict's antics into black comedy.

How do you translate that into a status update?

Should you?

For much of those first 24 hours after he died, I wrestled with that question. It was something I'd thought I had been prepared for for years. But faced with the prospect, I found myself shrinking from the pressure. As someone who pours most of the details of his life out online, both as a writer and as a social media addict, I found myself torn by two opposing motivations.

On one hand, everything we do has become grist for the content mill, and people seem to think nothing of posting the most intimate details of their lives, successes, losses, and failures on Facebook, Twitter, Instagram, and elsewhere. But the idea of inserting the passing of a man's life—especially one as messy as his—felt somehow diminishing.

There goes the news of a man's death, sandwiched between a deluge of memes, cranky political rants, and hyperventilating over the latest trending topic from the celebrity industrial complex. And yet, not saying something seemed like a violation as well. There's a reason why we still run obituaries in newspapers, for even the most average among us, because to note the ending of a life is to remind us all of the most important thing that binds us together as people, as communities, as a civilization. To point out that someone died is to point out that they lived at all.

And so I posted the fucking thing on Facebook.

It felt somehow both celebratory and an immediate failure, as if this most private of emotions was Hoovered out of me by the unquenchable hunger of the marrow-sucking content beast. Post something for the likes. Test out that new reaction feature.

I wrote:

Like a lot of people, I had a complicated relationship with my father. He didn't raise me in the traditional sense, but I spent a lot of formative time with him when I was younger, and he is very much a part of the person I turned into. We'd been out of touch for a while, for reasons I don't fully understand, and now never will, but we had started to become closer again in the past couple years. I am grateful that I got to see him a few times this year and hear more about him as a man. He wasn't perfect, but which of us is? And in recent years he raised a fine young woman, and was a good father to her. I'm not sharing this here because I want sympathy from any of you, in fact I'd rather those of you I don't know very well don't say anything. I am simply writing to announce the passing of a life, the life of Edward Grenham. He will not soon be forgotten. He was always proud of me, in whatever minor successes I have had along the way, and that made me happy to have been able to do that for him. Among other things, I owe him my good looks, and, unfortunately, my hairline. I would often grumble about how often he would call on the phone so much of late, but I would love to hear his voice again. Thank you for recognizing his life in whatever way you see fit.

The post pulled in 362 reactions: 323 likes and 39 hearts. It got shared two times, by my sisters. There were 75 comments. Not bad in terms of engagement, right? That's how we measure everything important these days, right?

Dutifully, friends and near-friends and who-the-hell-are-yous commented to show their sympathy, despite my specifically asking people not to. I had pictured myself becoming enraged at the mealy mouthed, half-hearted "our thoughts are with you" and "thinking of you" posts—the same empty dreck you get on your timeline every year on your birthday from people who you haven't heard from since your last birthday. But to my surprise, their sympathy, earnest or not, was a sort of salve that hit its mark. There also were genuinely heartfelt notes from people. Why did I expect that notion to be the exception to the rule?

"What they really want is the ability to express empathy; not every moment is a good moment," Mark Zuckerberg said last year.

Empathy and sympathy are two different things of course, although it's not surprising that Zuckerberg would mistake the two. No one will ever fully understand how you feel when someone dies, but sympathy isn't supposed to be understanding. When you sympathize, you're not feeling another's feelings as your own—that's empathy. You're simply recognizing that their feelings exist.

What more could you expect of a Facebook friend?

Facebook is an undeniable ill for many reasons, and a boon for countless others, but it's also an extremely efficient tool for the doling out of such sympathy. Without Facebook, a few hundred people would never have known of the passing, or the life, of a man, regardless of how flawed that man was.

If getting people to stop for a moment, to reflect—even in the brief time span that it takes to toggle between "Like" and "Sad" and "Love"—on a human life is the end result, I'll take it.

It's not much, but most of our lives aren't either. In spite of everything, we're trying to connect with those who have hurt us. We're trying to make sense of it, and the tools aren't perfect, but we're trying.

Y

GO VIRAL OR DIE TRYING

I HAVE TO GET MY STORY OUT AND MY FACE OUT WHEN I CAN

In late February 2017 Senator Tom Cotton stood before his constituents at a town hall meeting at Springdale High School in northwest Arkansas and attempted to explain why the free market won't necessarily kill them. The capacity crowd bristled with energy and frustration in the type of scene that became common throughout the country at the time when angry voters demanded answers from their representatives about what a long-promised plan to repeal and replace the Affordable Care Act would actually look like. Many Republicans like Utah's Jason Chaffetz the House Oversight Committee chairman dismissed the crowds as disingenuous paid protesters. In truth they represented what has become an all-too-typical strain of worry which is people frightened about what will happen to them if they get sick or as in the case of Kati McFarland a constituent of Cotton's at the meeting what will happen if coverage for a pre-existing life-threatening condition is eroded.

McFarland who was a twenty five year-old photographer and student at the University of Arkansas waited for her turn at the microphone to confront Cotton. Suffering from a genetic disorder called Ehlers-Danlos Syndrome she has trouble walking or standing without severe pain and sometimes blacks out but she summoned her strength to ask the senator point blank: Did he intend to leave her behind? She was nervous because of the size of the crowd she told me a few weeks later but also because Cotton "is a Republican, Tea Party senator and I am like this liberal Episcopalian borderline socialist person."

"Without the coverage for pre-existing conditions, I will die," she told him. "That is not hyperbole. Without the protections against lifetime coverage caps, I will die. So my question is, will you commit today to replacement protections for those Arkansans, like me, who will die or lose their quality of life, or otherwise be unable to be participating citizens trying to get their part of the American dream? Will you commit to replacements in the same way you've committed to repeal?"

Cotton thanked McFarland for her question then moved on as the crowd erupted in boos. "Do your job!" they chanted. Momentarily abashed he made a half-hearted stab at addressing the question assuring her that he wanted to make sure all Americans have access—*access*—to affordable care.

McFarland's stance garnered immediate and widespread attention with coverage across cable news. On MSNBC the next day she explained her thinking. "If they're going to do this, if it's going to possibly kill me in the next couple years without health care, I have to get my story out and my face out when I can. Maybe if I put a human face and voice on it, give them something they can really recognize, like their daughter, or their niece, then maybe it would change their heart. Or at least change other Americans' hearts."

Like many Americans who suffer from rare and expensive diseases or those who simply cannot afford the associated and unexpected costs that accrue from the most mundane ones MacFarland had set up a fundraising page on YouCaring. It's one of many crowdfunding services focused entirely on helping Americans defray the costs of their health care by appealing to the kindness of strangers. In a post from November 2017 she said she was excited to receive $265. It was a small amount but enough to cover a motel for her next trip to Dallas to see a specialist unavailable in her state. A few days before the town hall she posted a more alarming message.

"Hi y'all — unfortunately a dire update. Here's the situation: if this fundraiser doesn't do better I could soon be homeless, lose electricity/internet/heating to my house, or lose my health insurance . . . My benefits won't cover all bills and premiums, and I've had to spend so much savings on medical bills that I have none left from my dad's estate . . ."

The TV hits were a boon for McFarland. Shortly after the town hall her fundraiser had grown from $1,500 to $24,000. She watched in shock as it continued to grow refreshing the page continually.

Around the same time as Cotton's town hall three men were shot in a Kansas bar in an apparent hate crime leading to the death of Indian American engineer Srinivas Kuchibhotla, and the injuries of his friend Alok Madasani and bystander Ian Grillot. Four separate fundraisers were launched in the immediate aftermath of the attack which eventually combined to bring in more than a million dollars to cover medical expenses and recovery costs and memorial services for the victims. That was thanks in no small part to the sensational horrific story becoming international news.

After trying their hardest Republicans weren't quite able to dismantle the AFA which is some small solace but not exactly a cause for celebration if only because a broken system wasn't made worse. Regardless of what transpires with health care down the line, at a time when more than half of the country has less than $1,000 in savings in case of an emergency it seems guaranteed that more and more people will turn to the aid of their Facebook network for health care.

For a steadily increasing number of Americans including millions who now regularly use sites like YouCaring and GoFundMe health care has in fact become about competition. No not the kind Republicans usually talk about but a competition for individuals in the marketplace of virality.

"I won't lie, a lot of [the money I raised] is because I shoehorned the link to my fundraiser into my appearances on TV," McFarland told me. "I feel bad about that, but when you're in dire straits like I am, with no savings left, no family, I was going to lose my home, you do what you have to do."

The advice for best practices most of these sites share are to tell a good story and spin a narrative and appeal to people's interests which becomes almost absurdly macabre when the subject is human lives. McFarland is a unique case in that she proved an especially effective advocate for herself: She's young and photogenic and internet-savvy and has a heartbreaking story having lost both her parents at a young age. Many others are much less fortunate.

On top of managing your health and your expenses now you have to make sure you present your malady with authenticity. Think of your cancer as the origin story a tech startup tells about itself on the About section of its website. And then start hoping a celebrity takes an interest in your plight online. It might be a shorter wait for that than a doctor anyway.

While smaller forms of crowdfunding as we now know it stretch back at least to the turn of the millennium—initiated most notably by artists and musicians hoping to raise cash for creative projects—it wasn't until rewards-based crowdfunding sites like Indiegogo in 2008 and Kickstarter in 2009 began in earnest that the concept became a regular part of life online.

Around that time the idea of raising funds for those experiencing life-changing events—often medical—began to take root. GiveForward which specializes in medical causes was among the first major crowd-funding sites in 2008 and has since raised hundreds of millions. GoFundMe followed in 2010 then YouCaring in 2011. Indiegogo has since launched a medical and personal-issues spinoff called Generosity.

From its inception GiveForward realized there was a space for this type of charitable giving CEO Josh Chapman said. Today around 70 percent of the company's fundraisers fall under the medical category. Its first successful fundraiser in 2009 focused on two sisters one of which required a kidney transplant. Since one of them had had another organ transplant earlier in life her life-insurance policy had been maxed out. The younger sister was a match but there was no way they could pay for the procedure out of pocket. They turned to GiveForward and raised $30,000 to make it possible.

The platform has managed a number of high-profile efforts in the years since including one for Jessica Kensky and Patrick Downes who were victims of the Boston Marathon bombings who lost limbs. A fundraiser for the couple who were portrayed in the *Patriots Day* film pulled in almost $900,000. Another successful fundraiser collected money for Billy Ray Harris a homeless Kansas City man who returned a diamond engagement ring to a woman who'd accidentally lost it when putting money in his cup. Onlookers who saw the story in the media came together to donate almost $200,000 to Harris.

YouCaring has also seen steady growth in the medical category according to Jesse Boland the company's director of online marketing. YouCaring now raises around $200 million a year; 40 percent of that is for medical-based needs he said.

"Medical fundraisers typically do better than a fundraiser for a pet or a mission trip because the need is very clear, and it's a dire situation, Boland said. "They're typically more viral and the ask is very clear, so people typically give more." Among the most common fundraisers on YouCaring are for people suffering from cancer including pediatric cancer and leukemia and and lymphoma as well as ALS and Parkinson's disease and birth defects and traumatic injuries such as car accidents.

The industry leader by far is GoFundMe. Over the past five years the platform has raised more than five billion for various causes according to CEO Rob Solomon. It's an amount that's increased exponentially year by year with medical remaining in the top three categories.

"Medical is a very interesting category, it's really what helped define and put GoFundMe on the map," Solomon said. "A lot of people perceive it as a place for just medical bills, but in reality there's a lot of nuance. Traveling to get treatment when family come to town is a big part. We see a lot of fundraising for foundations and charities. People are living a lot longer, so we're seeing elderly people try to raise money for their care."

But while everyone I spoke to in the crowdfunding industry is proud to be able to provide aid to users it's also not an easy job. "It will break your heart to see some of the things people are going through," Boland said.

It's that heartbreak that's one of the major factors in the seeming ubiquity of medical-based crowdfunding in our social media feeds. The large number of fundraisers as observers of the industry say has become a self-fulfilling growth engine. The more people see others doing it the easier it is to realize they can ask for help themselves.

"There is a little bit of an avalanche effect: One person does it, it works, another does, it works better, and a platform develops around it," Anupam B. Jena, a professor at Harvard Medical School and a practicing physician at Massachusetts General Hospital in Boston told me. "The first time it was probably a strange thing, now it wouldn't be uncommon to hear about a young family with a child with cancer who is trying to crowdsource funds for treatment." The money for the people in need is important Jena said but it's the interaction with the community that can often be the real emotional or spiritual uplifting salve.

Dennis Disbot remembers his last beer. It was in August of 2016 a year and a half after he'd been diagnosed with testicular cancer. Then he found out it had recurred in his liver. He called a friend and they went to the Barrelhead a local brewery in San Francisco where he lives with his wife and young son and decided he needed one last hurrah. "It was a very symbolic gesture," he said. "OK, now it's time to get down to business."

When we spoke a couple years ago Disbot had just wrapped up seventeen days of treatment at UCSF medical center where he was undergoing another round of chemotherapy and cell transplants. His aggressive cancer had recurred twice within a two-year period after Disbot had first been diagnosed in February of 2015 which was the same week his son was born.

While Disbot and his wife both had health insurance at the time of his diagnosis they began accruing large expenses almost immediately draining their savings accounts. Child care and rent and lost wages began to add up quickly. They tried raising funds on a smaller level by soliciting friends on Facebook and hosting events and so on but in November they realized they needed a boost and started a YouCaring page. He's since raised $46,000 of his $75,000 goal.

The biggest hurdle Disbot told me was is the inherent reluctance many people have to reach out. "It's challenging to stand up and keep your head high and say, 'Hey, we need help. I am maxed out.' It's amazing, because people in our community, nine out of ten times they'll say, 'Let me know how I can help.' Being as specific as possible allows one to align their needs and feel heard and seen." Seeing people from so many networks and times of his life from kindergarten to college coming together has been exceptionally moving, he said.

"The secret prize for people who raise money on the site is they find out how much people care about them,' YouCaring's Boland said. "The money is the primary ask but they end up being better off for having connected to their community, so they get a sense of peace and belonging."

For Glenn O'Neill who lives in Columbia, South Carolina that community has proven larger than he ever could have imagined. His daughter Eliza was diagnosed at three years old with Sanfilippo Syndrome which is a rare terminal and rapidly degenerative disease sometimes referred to as Childhood Alzheimer's. The family crowd-funded almost $2.1 million to establish a non-profit 501c3 called Cure Sanfilippo Foundation which has been busy funding clinical studies. The work has already given the O'Neill family hope that their daughter and others like her may find some relief. But they couldn't get there without solid production value.

Both O'Neill and his wife Cara who is a pediatrician for special-needs children had quality health care but even the best of plans don't prepare you for rare diseases with no known cure or treatment. "Since it's a rare disorder, people don't just give millions to these types of things," he said.

"Government grants are difficult to get, the lead time is years. We knew we had to act fast."

After six months they had raised $200,000 on their own which was still a relative drop in the bucket so they turned to GoFundMe. They posted a video of Eliza at the end of 2013 which brought in another $40,000 but "it wasn't going viral," O'Neill said.

He began researching how to make things stand out online. Eventually he came across a photographer named Benjamin Von Wong who said he wanted to help. He came to the O'Neills' home with a crew and spent a week shooting forty hours of footage then emerged a few days later with a professional video that sits atop the fundraising page today. Within fifteen days the family had raised $500,000. By the end of 2014 they had $2 million which they spent funding pre-clinical work for clinical trials.

"GoFundMe was everything to us," he said. "That link [to our fundraiser] was in every media story about our effort. Every parent deserves the same chance we got and that other kids will get."

O'Neill doesn't understand why 35,000 people around the world felt touched enough by Eliza's story to donate but he remains heartened by everyone who did like the people who comment saying they are out of work but wanted to give $10 to the cause.

"I knew people were good, the majority of people, but I never knew how good until what's come into our lives," he said. "They were strangers to us before the diagnosis, but come into our lives and say they just want to help. I'm always taken aback by that. I have a stake in this, my daughter has it, but why would you be doing this?"

The O'Neills like others who've had success with crowdfunding realized that successful crowdfunding is about storytelling. Having a sick child in and of itself isn't enough to galvanize people—we collectively ignore the plight of millions of sick children every day. But it's when the specific story of one individual can be harnessed that we feel moved to take action. One sickness is a tragedy. A million is merely a statistic.

"It's about allowing donors to be part of something bigger and I think that's what these campaigns do," O'Neill said.

I often joke lately that I used to think I've wasted my life on Twitter but it might actually come in handy when I inevitably need to crowdfund an operation. You have to hustle. You have to market. You have to build your brand.

"There's a lot of people who believe you just post a fundraiser and donations are going to immediately come in, and that's not the way it works," Chapman said. "We have thousands of pages posted every week on our site. The big thing is spreading the word. Once you get that momentum going the key becomes providing updates, what the money is going towards."

"A picture is worth 1,000 words, a video is worth maybe a million," GoFundMe's Solomon said. "It's really a storytelling platform, the more interesting and compelling the story the better these will do."

In essence, crowdfunding is all about becoming your own agent and publicist and advocacy group all rolled into one whether you're raising money for a social media robot dog or trying to stave off your impending demise.

"You capture the heart and the mind will follow," Andrew Dix the CEO of trade site Crowdfund Insider told me. "I think presenting a good narrative that shows a pressing need, and a challenging situation can compel people to contribute to somebody they really don't know, they don't have a relationship with."

Specificity is important he said as is appearing credible. "The last time I contributed to one, I noticed the person had gone to the same university I went to. I read the story, did a little fact-checking, and I said I want to help this person because they're trying to do what's right."

"I think a lot of people have story fatigue Amy O'Leary the editorial director of Upworthy a site that often featured crowdfunding campaigns said. "At this point in human history, we see more stories every day than any generation ever before, so I think it's a real challenge. There's compassion fatigue, especially when seeing the same kind of stories over and over again. Sort of the same principles for really great story telling apply to how you get people to care about an issue: vivid details, and a character that's relatable that you can come to care about through story."

While it's undeniable that crowdfunding has saved many lives it's hard not to wonder how we got here and whether this new piecemeal health care workaround brings other types of ingrained biases. Two recent studies have found that race plays a role in the success of crowdfunding projects although those focused on the more entrepreneurial and equity side of services like Kickstarter.

"I think it's unfortunate we have a healthcare system where people need to do this," Harvard's Jena said. But he added that even in countries with socialized medicine people still need extra money for health care. "If you're in the U.K., which has a national health service there may not be access to certain treatments that are too expensive to be provided by the federal government, so people may crowdsource funds to come to the U.S."

Among reporters who have covered campaigns like these for years, the entire operation can seem especially perverse. Hudson Hongo an editor at Gizmodo at the time who covered the phenomenon of viral stories said the decision about whether to feature a crowdfunding story often hinges on the individual's social capital. "Local indie legend needs transplant, or whatever," he said.

In the absence of another viable alternative Hongo was often sucked into the piecemeal health care lottery game as much as the rest of us governed by our own whims and biases. "Last week I gave to an acquaintance from back home for a medical recovery crowdfunding thing because I like him. But it's not like assholes deserve to not be ruined by medical problems."

Stephen Bramucci who was an editor at Uproxx said he hopes he applies a different standard to life or death stories. If he were considering covering a story about someone crowdfunding to travel the world which is something he sees a lot of as a food and travel editor he'd ask if there is a good hook? Do they have a strong sense of their brand? Are there good photos? Will they give a good soundbite?

"With travel the concern is always the same: They get funded super-quick when it's a really hot couple we can relate to in some degree and we want to see them posting pictures on Instagram of each other's butts. If you're holding people's health to that standard it's really fucking scary."

"What if it's some [old sick] guy who doesn't have a daughter who's a good writer?" Bramucci said. "I'm an editor and I get pulled in because it's someone who can tell a story. That means this guy doesn't get funded? It's a fucking minefield."

And what happens to the people too shy or attention averse to share the intimate photos of their physical suffering? Upworthy's O'Leary was reminded of a hugely popular story her site covered a few years ago about a young man who'd had lap-band surgery, but now lived with excessive loose skin. "What was remarkable about it was he took pictures of himself and showed everybody what it was," she said. "Once he saw his story was picking up viral steam there was a crowd-fund that started. He was so open and vulnerable by sharing those photos I think people were moved."

Abby Ohlheiser who covers digital culture for the *Washington Post* said that she tends to write about campaigns that have already gone viral or have a large potential audience looking for them because they're already part of a larger news story. "I do see these campaigns shared into my own various social media feeds at a sobering pace," she said. "And when I see a celebrity retweet or share one of these campaigns, it makes me wonder how many equally deserving requests for a signal boost like that were missed."

Chapman and the other sites' representatives agree that ideally they wouldn't have to exist but say that even with a health-care system that covered everything people will never stop needing funding in times of poor health. Nonetheless it's tempting to see the pawning off of caring for citizens onto others' charitable impulses as keeping with Republicans' gutting services for the poor and needy while justifying it by saying they also give at church.

"Given the current political environment, we've definitely seen a lot of apprehension and fear of what is going to happen in the coming months and years," Boland said. "There are a lot of treatments that aren't covered by insurance, a lot of experimental treatments that people want to try so only crowdfunding can help them. But we are definitely seeing people who are a little apprehensive."

Both times she appeared on television Kati McFarland explained her thoughts on the Affordable Care Act. It isn't perfect she said but it saved her life by keeping her coverage despite her condition. But she's uncertain about what's going to happen down the line: even with the ACA's provisions remaining in place, her costs of coverage are almost insurmountable.

"It's so sad I have to come on these things and spend time talking about the issue saying 'go to my fundraiser' because that's what we have to do in this country, and that's abhorrent to me," she said. "I know people think socialized medicine, that's a nasty word, but if that was the case we wouldn't have to do this. If they spent a fraction of what they spend on the military on the ACA—not even socialized medicine—then the premiums wouldn't be high, it wouldn't be the mess it is now."

She read a funny joke on Tumblr the other day. "It was something like, 'What if we put in a GoFundMe for everyone's health care all at once, and everybody in the country paid for it, and the money it raised went to help everyone?'"

❌

THIS IS NOT WORTH DYING FOR

WE'VE GOT TO BE THE LIGHT

It was a Wednesday afternoon in the nation's capital and Grace McKinnon was heading back to her office when she saw the man crying out for help. The police officer was pointing his gun at Anthony and the police said *he's got a knife.* Anthony was in clear distress and unsure what to do and didn't immediately comply with the officer's instructions and we've seen this exact scenario happen enough times to know what comes next so Grace pulled her car over in the middle of the street and exercised the defiant and liberating act of compassion.

She captured the encounter on video which she later posted to Twitter.

"I literally think I just saved someone's life . . . I'm shaking y'all . . ." she posted.

"You see him trying to shoot me, I ain't done nothing to nobody," Anthony tells her while the officer is holding his gun on him yelling. Sirens are wailing in the background to come assist the officer with the kind man who has done nothing.

"You saw me sleeping right?" Anthony asks her, near tears. "I had that knife in my possession, but I'm *out here,*" he says by which he means he's sleeping on the streets.

The officer tells Grace to get back but she asserts her right to observe. Anthony becomes agitated as another officer arrives yelling that he doesn't have any other weapon on him. "Get on the ground," Grace pleads with him. "This is not worth dying for." Over and over again she says it. "This is not worth dying for. They're killing us out here." And then, when he does get on the ground she reaches out and touches him kindly.

Anthony sleeps in Union Station in D.C. and was the subject of an interview by the Invisible People project in March of 2018 in which he talked about his dreams of one day opening an orphanage if he got on his feet again. His mother had recently died of cancer and since her passing he hadn't had a place to stay.

What's your future like? the interviewer asked him.

"Hopefully once I get myself together I want to build an orphanage, to house orphans," he says. "Free, open house, kids, adults, whoever. People that don't have nowhere to go or who've been neglected. I also want to build a feeding program for homeless youths and feed kids. Also, if I have the money, or have people to help me, build a recreation program for after-school kids that need help with work, studying, searching for jobs things like that."

If he had three wishes what would they be?

"Have a house that's over my head," he says. "Be able to give back to others, and a nice job. That's it."

I called Grace to ask her about what compelled her to intervene in what could have been a dangerous situation. She's a twenty-four-year-old social worker with a master's degree who spent ten years herself off and on being homeless and lost her brother to suicide a couple of years ago. Since then she's been trying to help erase some of the stigmas about suicide through her effort Roses4MyBrother, and following this encounter started a GoFundMe for Anthony which eventually raised $25,000.

IN YOUR VIDEO WE SEE THE CONFRONTATION ONCE IT'S ALREADY UNDERWAY. WHAT DID YOU SEE BEFOREHAND?

I was coming back from a hospital visit, I'm a social worker at Community Connections in D.C. I was on my way back from the hospital and in the middle of the street I see the man in the video, Anthony, really crying out for help. I see the police officer with his gun pointed. At that moment I knew I had to stop. Any compassionate, sensitive human being would. It's something that pulls at your heart. I had to stop. So I put my car in park in the middle of the street, pulled out my phone—us millennials, we're good for that—and I started recording. I was trying to engage with Anthony to get his attention. I just went into an automatic, for me, thinking . . . how can I help this man. I don't want him to get killed. Sadly that's the reality so often these days.

WHAT DID YOU SAY TO HIM?

In the video you see me talking to him, encouraging him, imploring him to please get on the ground. You hear me saying it's not worth dying for. I could tell he was homeless, you can see the pain in his eyes, the fear in his eyes. I've been homeless before so I know what that looks like, the clothes and presentation.

He said, You know miss I wasn't doing anything, I was trying to sleep. The police tried to get me to move back but I told the police I'm not going to move back it's my right to record. He finally got on the ground and threw his hands up and started crying. I was trying to hold it together in the moment because we both couldn't be crying. After that was kind of a blur. I almost saw someone die. To be able to be in that space at that time. I'm deeply thankful I was there to help and intervene. I'm thankful he's alive and I'm alive. I'm still trying to figure out a way to get into contact with him.

I'VE REACHED OUT TO THE CAPITAL POLICE TO SEE IF THEY ARRESTED HIM AND ON WHAT CHARGES AND I WILL LET YOU KNOW WHEN I HEAR BACK. [IT WAS ASSAULT ON A POLICE OFFICER WHILE ARMED AND CARRYING A DANGEROUS WEAPON]

Thank you for that. The interview with Anthony really touched me. You can see him saying all these things he wants to do like start an orphanage, help kids after school. That's the fabric that social workers are made out of. I've been crying for the past few days so full of emotion and gratitude.

I've been homeless and I know what it feels like to not have somewhere to stay and to be so young. His mother just died. It's just so much. He's so kind and compassionate, even in the video you see the compassion in his eyes. How could I just drive by and not help? Compassion is the most important thing to me.

YOU ALSO WORK ON A PROJECT FOR SUICIDE AWARENESS?

My brother Matthew died by suicide on October 25th, 2016. I just started it recently, it's pretty much a support network for people contemplating suicide or who have a loved one who died by suicide . . . and the focus is education and awareness through storytelling and compassion. Telling my story, that's what I'm passionate about. I think suicide is something we need to break the stigma around. Life is a precious gift, if you can stop and say hello to someone or speak to a person, ask them how their day is going, who knows maybe my brother would be alive today.

WAS YOUR BROTHER LIVING ROUGH AT THE TIME?

There are a lot of causes of suicide, it's a complex issue. A lot of trauma, and lack of perceived support. Sometimes people may not think they have support when they really do have people around them willing to help. Sometimes we're isolated and don't want people to help us and we don't allow people in. When you're having a tough month or year those problems get compounded. My brother was super smart, he could tell you a million stats about fast cars and animals, he just needed more support and motivation. If you put someone in a dark hole and they can't see the light you can't just tell them there's light on the other side, they won't believe it. We've got to be that light. It feels so good to be kind to others. I know my brother is with me and I know he's proud of me.

I'M SURE HE IS. DO YOU THINK MORE PEOPLE SHOULD DO WHAT YOU DID? IT SEEMED LIKE A GREAT HELP HERE BUT OTHER PEOPLE, PARTICULARLY AFRICAN AMERICANS OF COURSE, COULD BE PUTTING THEMSELVES IN DANGER BY TRYING TO INTERVENE.

That's a good question. Every situation is different and everybody is different. I think it depends on you in the moment. If you feel comfortable you do what you can. That might be stopping and recording, whatever you can do to help someone else and also preserve your own well-being. I'm a social worker so this is what I do, I help people. I'm also a member of Delta Sigma Theta Sorority, Inc. and our primary objective is service. That's ingrained in me. I love people and I think life is the most important thing. Some people told me that what I did was stupid, but I wasn't thinking about myself. If I say I believe in compassion—in Latin "compassion" means to suffer with somebody. If I say I am suffering with somebody I'm not thinking about myself. I didn't even think about the fact I could've lost my life. All the comments online people saying you could've died too. I started crying I was like wow I didn't think about that.

YOU SAID YOU WERE HOMELESS, HOW LONG WAS THAT FOR?

I was homeless in eighth grade. My family was living with my grandma's family at the time and they kicked us out. After that it was a cycle of homelessness from 2008 up until about—even in college—about ten years living with friends. I've never had a room of my own. I still don't. That's something I'm working on. I'm hoping that the universe brings me goodness. I'm passionate about people that are homeless. I'm a social worker—we use person-first language, by the way. Saying "homeless people" devalues people. You say "people that are homeless." I used to take showers at community college, get up at 4 a.m. in high school and fall asleep in my classes. I took five AP classes in high school, I had a 4.5 GPA. But sometimes pressure makes you work harder. I finished my master's program in December 2017. I finished, praises up, and I'm a licensed graduate social worker.

I know now that if I can use my experience to help others my brother's life will not be in vain.

I JUST WANT TO THANK YOU FOR WHAT YOU DID. I'M PROUD OF YOU.

Thank you and thank you for sharing my story.

IT FEELS LIKE COMING OUT AS A CRAZY PERSON

THOSE MOMENTS HAVE INFLUENCED EVERY DAY OF MY LIFE

The view from atop the pyramids is breathtaking. From the ruins of Monte Albán with the verdant valleys of Oaxaca spread out at your feet it's hard not to imagine what the Zapotec people saw when they built these structures almost three thousand years ago. Around the great plaza at the center of the ancient city runs a series of tunnels to tombs and altars and courts for playing ball games. Throughout you'll find cave paintings and carved stones including the Danzantes or "dancers" believed to depict mutilated sacrificial victims whose bodies were destroyed so the culture could thrive. I can picture it all now. I just wish I had been there to see it in person.

I had to ask my wife what it was like to visit because at the time I was making a pilgrimage to Gimnasio Calipso Centro Histórico which is one of about a dozen fitness centers in Oaxaca City. The views from that site which I scouted out weeks before our trip weren't quite as remarkable as from Monte Albán. It was a shambling two-story structure painted aqua blue. It looked like a gym. But when you have an eating disorder like mine no view is beautiful enough to override your compulsion to purge.

After my workout I went for a nice run in the afternoon rain along the cobblestone streets of the Plaza de la Constitución. Oaxaca is an outstanding culinary destination and so the night before we had eaten a huge meal of Oaxcan cheese and tlayuda and chapulines and mescal so I had to earn the next day's meal. In retrospect the steps of the pyramids would have been a pretty good spot for running stair sprints.

I often tell this story when my wife and I get into conversations about traveling. I relate the anecdote as if it were a quirky character detail like *haha yes, it's a bit weird but that's me.* There was the time I found myself lifting weights alone in the fitness room of a middle school in the Scottish Highlands looking like a deranged bench-press pervert in lieu of a whisky tasting at a distillery. Later I went running through the gorgeous sheep-filled hills until my phone battery died and I got lost. Or the time I must have spent $300 on cab rides and guest pass fees to get to Reykjavík's sprawling fitness center with an Olympic-sized outdoor heated pool doing laps among the universally fit and attractive Icelanders who may all go to hell in my opinion. Back home when the subject of the gym comes up I tell friends that I go around 360 days a year. Sometimes Christmas gets in the way.

You wouldn't know it by looking at me. I am six feet tall and between 180 and 190 pounds depending on the month. I am by no means the picture of health or even particularly muscular-looking certainly not for someone who exercises this much and definitely not compared to most of the men I see at my gym.

Or maybe I am? That's the problem: what I see when I look in the mirror doesn't correspond with reality. I see a fat piece of shit and then I think to myself that it's time to punish my body for letting me down. Scarcely a half hour of my day goes by when I'm not thinking about when and how I'm going to exercise next or what food I can and cannot allow myself to eat. Of course I'm not getting bigger because the body needs rest to build muscle which is something I won't give it. And of course I don't get thin enough because when you starve yourself all day it's too easy to binge on crap later on.

I used to think that my fitness regimen was admirable but I've come to recognize it as an eating disorder called exercise bulimia. The *Diagnostic and Statistical Manual of Mental Disorders* doesn't specify exercise bulimia as its own illness but it is categorized as a subset of bulimia nervosa. The difference is instead of vomiting or abusing laxatives a person will use compulsive exercise as a form of purging. Exercise bulimia manifests itself in different ways—from excessive exercise to compensate for calories consumed to starving oneself but continuing to exercise to an all-consuming obsession with exercise to the point of serious self-harm as in my case at the moment. In all cases the results can be debilitating both mentally via emotional distress when you're unable to exercise sufficiently and physical problems like bone density loss from lack of nutrition and joint pain and constant muscle soreness or recurring injuries and persistent fatigue.

Today I will run and lift weights despite instructions from my doctors to take it easy this year as I deal with a back injury. I will run until my knees ache and my back stiffens and I will manage the ensuing pain with too much Advil. Being skinny even with back pain feels a lot better than being chubby. And then once I feel I have earned it I will eat a large meal thereby resetting the cycle of guilt and begin the process all over again tomorrow. It's a problem as destructive as any other type of addiction which if we're being forthcoming I also have plenty of experience with.

Studies have found a correlation between people who suffer from substance-abuse issues and eating disorders, as Eric Strother et al write in "Eating Disorders in Men: Underdiagnosed, Underrated, and Misunderstood." But too often it is the substance abuse itself and not its relationship to the eating disorder that is prioritized in treatment. That's particularly true when it comes to men. Or so the thinking goes because there isn't an overwhelming consensus on much of this stuff.

The problem is that unlike early research on substance abuse which was long considered a male-centric issue eating disorders have been studied through a primarily female lens. It wasn't until the 1960s that men were even considered in any such studies and research on the effects and causes of eating disorders in men are still rare. Things have improved according to Arnold Andersen who is one of the preeminent researchers in the field but there's a long way to go.

Andersen and others point to a shift when the rise of "peak" male form in the action films of the 1980s and 1990s and on the covers of magazines altered our cultural expectations of how men are supposed to look. Men stopped wanting to be like Burt Reynolds and Paul Newman and instead idealized Arnold Schwarzenegger and Sylvester Stallone. Batman and Superman stopped looking like average schlubs and started being portrayed as muscular behemoths or lithe athletes. Brad Pitt happened. As women have known for much longer that sort of thing can fuck you up particularly in your teens and early twenties which is when men are most commonly diagnosed with eating disorders. There's another story my wife tells about her first memory of me long before we started dating when I came over to hang out with her brother. I was standing in her parents' kitchen looking at my own reflection in the stove. "Am I too broad?" I asked of no one in particular. I was fifteen years old.

While numbers vary on how many men suffer from eating disorders—in part because of the gender bias in studying it—a widely cited study from 2007 found 25 percent of anorexia and bulimia cases occur among men. Another study found 20 million women and 10 million men in the United States will suffer from an eating disorder at some point in their life. (There are no widely agreed upon numbers on exercise bulimia.) But those statistics get complicated by the many men who don't present themselves for treatment, or who don't even realize that they have a problem at all says Andrew Walen a spokesman for the National Eating Disorders Association.

"The general cultural understanding is that to speak up about an eating disorder is to feel like you have an un-masculine disease," Walen told me.

He's right. As someone who has no problem sharing all manner of personal information about himself online every day and who certainly doesn't consider himself one to conform to outdated gender stereotypes writing this feels embarrassing in a way I am unfamiliar with. It feels like coming out as a crazy person and admitting I have lost control of myself. People will assure you they do not lose respect for others suffering from issues like this but it's a hard bias to overcome.

"People might think, 'I'm a man and I struggle with these insecurities and self-esteem and self-worth issues and I put a lot of onus on my body to give me that self-esteem, so does that make me a narcissist or an egomaniac?'" Walen said. "No, it makes you someone who has a brain disease that is actually a lot more common than most people are willing to admit. I think it's harder for guys to say we have a feminine-normalized issue, just from our culture saying *man up*."

Eating disorders show a strong correlation with anxiety, depression, and other mental health issues. So bingeing whether in the traditional sense or through exercise can be a way to distract yourself from other problems or to try to exert control over things that seem out of hand. I don't know much about what's going to happen in the world today but I do know what my routine at the gym will be.

"The sense I get is that it's on the rise," Jennifer Rollin, a psychotherapist and eating disorder specialist based in Maryland told me of exercise bulimia and other subsets of eating disorders like orthorexia which an unhealthy fixation on healthy eating and wellness and muscle dysmorphia in which male weightlifters obsess over feeling too small and inadequate. Movements in recent years to push for physical activity and health are great Rollin said "but if somebody has the underlying genetics or temperament that predispose them to eating disorders or compulsive exercise, that message can turn dangerous."

Signs of compulsive exercising may be hard to spot because they overlap with what we generally consider markers of healthy living but there's a point when things tip. Indicators include following rigid routines and getting anxiety about breaking them. "Often because of that anxiety, people who struggle with compulsive exercise may find social relationships suffering, or they may go to extreme lengths—exercising when ill or injured, or despite physical comfort," Rollin said.

They may refuse to go on certain amazing trips, for example, because there's no gym in the rainforest or the Scottish Highlands. They may regularly hold up family dinners on holidays because they have to go for another couple laps around the block to "top it off," as I laughingly call it. They might resort to doubling their exercise routine to reach the "high" they're seeking, or suffer from severe depressive symptoms if they're forced to go without exercise.

I often joke when I'm talking about my issues—drinking too much, smoking cigarettes, spending way too much time online—that at least I'm *also* addicted to the gym. And most people agree. "Man, I wish I could have that sort of motivation to work out," they'll say. I tried to explain the issue to a recovering alcoholic friend of mine the other night and it didn't seem to register. *Alcohol can ruin lives* he seemed to be thinking. *How can the gym?*

"People don't get it, that's what's sad," Rollin said. "[Compulsives] are driven by a mental illness. It's not something to admire. Men are often praised for spending more time at the gym, but you would never praise an alcoholic for sitting at the bar."

The first step to dealing with exercise bulimia is recognizing that it is a problem then reaching out to a mental health professional who specializes in eating disorders. Setting behavioral goals is important as well which you'd think would be easy for someone who puts so much effort into setting workout goals. Instead of planning out your workout making plans to de-escalate and sticking to them is a good start Rollins told me. So is intuitive exercise: "Work to find more flexibility in your routine, maybe try new forms of movement. And listen to your body. If you're really tired, maybe take a walk instead of a run. And on days when you have a lot of energy then you can go harder," she says.

Or you could try to seek out other forms of engendering well-being. (No, not drinking whisky.) If you're craving the feeling you get from a run, try meeting that need through another activity, Rollins said.

If you have a friend you suspect is teetering on the edge you should listen to them and take the problem seriously particularly if it's a guy friend who may find it hard to talk about. "The first job is normalization," Walen said. "If we feel normal, we think, 'okay, I'm part of this bigger tribe, and that's where I find my strength.' Men find that in work teams, athletic teams, military units. That's what guys respond to. If we're feeling alone, we're going to shy away, and eating disorders are a disease that thrives on isolation."

And as much as our generations-long assumptions about how men are supposed to behave and feel have changed, it's still out of the ordinary for a dude to turn to his buddy and say, "I'm sad because I feel fat today."

So, for what it's worth, here is me speaking up. I recognize the symptoms in myself. You may recognize some of them in yourself. I don't know that I can offer any real help but I can say this: You're not alone and it's okay to talk about. You're not going to die from the embarrassment. Your eating disorder on the other hand might do the trick if you let it.

Ah fuck I didn't take my own advice. That was from a piece I wrote in *Esquire* in 2017 and after that I kept right on doing exactly what I was doing until my back and my abdominals tore themselves apart and after that I kept on doing it still guzzling painkillers because I was afraid if I stopped I'd get fat which it turns out I eventually did due to I literally could not run or lift weights anymore and instead what I went ahead and did was become an alcoholic to deal with that and some other mental health crises lol whoops.

So I tried giving it another shot writing about it the next year but this time from some younger men's perspective and it went a little something like this. Ah one ah two ah three:

The locker room at my gym is an anthropological world of wonders. Inside you'll find every type of body imaginable on display in its full glory. There are older sagging bodies and young and toned ones and everything in between.

In the adult world men's bodies go largely unremarked upon what with age and maturity having given most of us a certain comfort level with the skin we inhabit and an understanding of the boundaries of personal space. But in high school and college locker rooms there's no flaw or irregularity that can't be exaggerated into a joke or a put-down. The weak bodies are called out and the less developed muscles are laughed at and for the most part boys and young men all go along with it. It's just how things are. It was the case when I was young and based on my interviews with several young men it's no less true now.

Colin Ashby, twenty four, from Texas, remembers his earliest experiences with body shaming around age fifteen when a growth spurt made him look even skinnier than he already was. "People called me an 'anorexic giraffe' and constantly told me I looked weird, odd, and 'just not right'" while changing in the locker room for the swim or cross-country teams, he said.

It's something he hasn't gotten over. "I don't like to go to public swimming pools," Ashby said. "I don't like taking pictures that show my full body. I constantly wear baggy clothes to hide it. I hate it."

It's been just over two years since the phrase "locker room talk" exploded into the discourse being used as a casual dismissal of the way men like the president talk about women when they don't think there are any around. But the other locker room talk is the way boys and young men talk about each other. For some of us like me the nitpicking never goes away. Although it's been more than twenty years and I don't remember what my school locker room looked like I still remember the bodies inside. The ones I wanted desperately to have for my own and the ones I worried I actually did.

The fact that this sort of locker room commentary starts around the onset of puberty makes it particularly impactful.

Research suggests that being teased about weight predicts issues like weight gain and binge eating and extreme weight-control measures. About twenty nine percent of teenage boys report that they're trying to lose weight and twenty eight percent are on diets and fifty one percent say they exercise to prevent weight gain according to the National Center on Addiction and Substance Abuse.

Over the past several decades the concept of size and strength has also changed. Athletes have become larger and more powerful than in the past. A quick scan of NFL or NBA team rosters today compared to a few decades ago will confirm this.

Though there's a lack of research on the rates of body shaming among boys according to Roberto Olivardia a clinical psychologist and lecturer at Harvard Medical School, adolescent boys are reporting it to health professionals. "There is still a stigma for boys to even be affected by body shaming," he said. "This can make it difficult for boys to process, since they often deny yet experience its negative impact."

For many men I spoke to the impact of body-size bullying trickles into adulthood. When he was younger Gianluca Russo a twenty one year old recent graduate of SUNY in New York was on the receiving end of judgmental comments because of his size. He struggled in sports and theater because of it. He remembers trying out for the school play against a popular classmate and the student telling Russo he wouldn't be able to cut it because he was fat.

"Those moments have influenced every day of my life," Russo said. "As someone who works in fashion, it's been such a tough roadblock to feel comfortable at events and runway shows. After years of being shamed for the way I look, it becomes deeply ingrained in your mind that fat is bad, and that takes so much effort to erase."

Men are also suffering under a culture that prevents us from talking about it openly, lest we be further embarrassed for being weak. "There's a lot of pressure put on boys as they're growing up to be tough, to be a man," says Sam Mudge, twenty four, a student working on a master's in nutrition at Boston University who was mocked in middle school for being skinny. "And usually by that they mean the only emotions you can show are anger and sometimes contempt for those below you. Don't be too nice."

I wish I could tell young men that it gets better. For many it will. People settle into the body type that they're meant to have. Later in life it honestly doesn't matter what you look like with your shirt off. It does though but it doesn't.

As someone who still suffers from eating disorder–related issues to the point of compulsive exercise and self-harm I can also say that it won't get any better until you start talking about it, something that never even occurred to me until about two years ago, when I wrote about suffering from exercise bulimia. In my estimation most young men don't want to hurt one another and might not even understand that they're doing it. As with all bullying putting others down is often just an attempt to make oneself feel better. And a lack of healthy modeled behaviors about how to support one another is preventing many young men from fully grasping the implications of what they might otherwise see as harmless locker room talk or friendly ball-busting.

At the very least people are starting to recognize how stressful the constant pressure to conform can be. Even men's magazines who were arguably a major source of the body image–related anxiety young men have experienced over the past few decades are starting to take stock of their role.

"Men haven't had it nearly as hard as women when it comes to body image, but I think we've only recently started getting to a place where the masculine 'ideal' of what a healthy body looks like is broader and more inclusive than it was just a few years ago," Christopher Gayomali, a senior editor at *GQ* told me. "Now it's less about having four percent body fat and the Brad Pitt 'V' from *Fight Club* and more about feeling healthy and comfortable with what you're looking at in the mirror."

Ryan Sheldon is one adult hoping to present a healthier example for boys. Sheldon is a National Eating Disorders Association (NEDA) ambassador and a "brawn" (plus-size) model who spends much of his time speaking at schools around the country about body image issues. He still remembers being teased mercilessly as a kid and being called "fatty" and having glue poured in his hair by bullies. The abuse was so severe that Sheldon eventually left school entirely.

"I constantly used to think that if you weren't the cultural ideal body image, then you weren't desired," he said. Sheldon would put sheets over his mirrors and avoid the beach or swim with a shirt on. Now he's in front of a camera all the time.

Young men may be looking for outlets to feel safe talking about insecurities like these. Sheldon said he's always heartened when he gives a speech at a school and the boys who are typically the ones cracking jokes find him on Instagram later to tell him how much it meant to hear about others dealing with these issues. "I'm not joking when I tell you this happens after every talk I give at a high school," he says.

Sadly as many of the experts I talked to point out the support systems for men who suffer from body image stress are still woefully lacking particularly compared to those for women even after a couple years later after the last time I wrote this same part. Women frequently engage in conversations about their bodies C. J. Pascoe, a sociologist and author of *Exploring Masculinities: Identity, Inequality, Continuity, and Change* told me. "For young men, this sort of talk involves expressing more vulnerability than is usually considered acceptable," she said. "We often don't recognize disordered eating or body image issues in young men, because they don't talk about it, because we train men not to talk about vulnerability and fear."

Pascoe suggested that school coaches should be primed to look for eating disorders and body issues among their players. Most are not asked to do so or trained in how to respond when they identify insecurities.

I've had my own trouble finding a therapist who specializes in it in the Boston area which is a place not exactly lacking in health care options. But that won't change until more of us start talking. "The best way to push back against body shaming is to be an advocate for body positivity and size acceptance," Claire Mysko CEO of NEDA told me.

"Being an advocate involves maintaining an environment for yourself and others that embraces all body types and views all sizes as acceptable, valuable, and attractive."

Most of the young men I spoke to agree.

"We can fix this issue by showing boys and young men that the traditional image of how a guy is supposed to look doesn't have to be that way," Ashby said. "We don't all have to have Superman's build and have strength be our most defining trait."

This time I'm gonna take the advice to heart. I'm gonna be better. I promise.

THE WORST PEOPLE ALIVE

I DON'T KNOW IF I HAVE MORE OR LESS FAITH IN HUMANITY

Whenever I have occasion to delve into 4chan or alt-right or white supremacist culture for a story I come away from it feeling even more depressed than normal which isn't easy to accomplish because my mental health is already on some pretty thin ice.

The seedy underbelly of internet extremism and the alt-right and white supremacists is clearly a beat that deserves attention particularly as those sorts of ideas continue to penetrate into the mainstream. But that sort of job seems like it must fucking suck shit. What does constantly exposing yourself to the ideas of the worst people alive on a daily basis do to you? Does it destroy your faith in humanity? Does it melt your brain?

I asked some reporters whose work I follow and admire what it feels like to have to look at this absolute shit constantly to make a living.

Our Chief Hell World Correspondents are:

Cristina López G, who covers the alt-right for Media Matters.

Will Sommer, a reporter for the *Daily Beast*, who writes a newsletter focused on conservative media called Right Richter.

Christopher Mathias, who covers hate and extremism for the Huffington Post.

DID YOU CHANCE INTO THIS EXTREMIST/ONLINE CONSPIRACY THEORISTS BEAT OR DID YOU SEE IT DEVELOPING AS A SORT OF UNFORTUNATE BOOM INDUSTRY A FEW YEARS AGO AND DECIDE TO FOCUS ON IT?

LÓPEZ: It was a mix of factors: I was definitely intentional in defining the beat and spending more time on the grossest corners of the internet, but it came as a logical transition from the immigration and Hispanic media, which is what I was covering before. It's not the most uplifting to think of it as a logical transition, but the fact of the matter is that nothing has emboldened the far-right and extremist elements as much as Trump's anti-immigrant rhetoric.

SOMMER: I come from a conservative background in Texas, so more mainstream right wing media stuff (Fox, Rush Limbaugh) was something I was used to keeping up with. I had been following all these characters for a couple years, my girlfriend got sick of me telling her about all the characters, so she told me to do a newsletter about them instead. I started Right Richter in May 2016, but Trump's election and the ensuing various alt-right events and crazy conspiracy theories have really blown this whole scene up.

MATHIAS: I started out covering police stuff, namely the way departments abused stop-and-frisk policies. Then that led into covering police shootings—Ramarley Graham, Eric Garner, Freddie Gray. I covered all those protests, interviewed the families. At some point—in part I think because of how the NYPD surveilled Muslim communities—I started getting interested in Islamophobia. I started covering the anti-Muslim movement in this country, and started covering hate crimes. Then that was a natural segue into covering extremism and Nazis. I covered this neo-Confederate rally in Gettysburg (my hometown), and then I was in Charlottesville later that summer. The last year has been nuts. I think I've been to 7 white supremacist rallies.

WHAT SORT OF TOLL DOES IT TAKE ON YOUR MENTAL HEALTH? I DABBLE IN IT MYSELF, BUT THERE HAVE BEEN TIMES I THOUGHT ABOUT FOCUSING ON IT MORE AND SAID TO MYSELF: NAH, I DON'T NEED THAT SHIT IN MY BRAIN ALL THE TIME.

LÓPEZ: It definitely takes thick skin, but even if you've become an expert in detaching yourself and applying a clinical eye, you can't help but feel the sting every now and then, especially as a queer, immigrant woman. I combat it with a healthy sense of humor, quality filters on Twitter mentions, and enough offline time to counteract the effects of our too-online job.

SOMMER: First off, I want to note that I am lucky in some aspects when it comes to covering this stuff. The fact that I'm straight, white, male, and not Jewish means that I avoid having a lot of the abuse directed at me that other people on this beat face. I think that kind of harassment really increases the mental toll, and I have a lot of respect for people who do this work anyway. Most of my stuff isn't focused on the most extreme neo-Nazi–type sites, which is also nice.

That said! It can get pretty mind-bending/depressing. The worst I had it recently was when I was trying to figure out who was behind QAnon, which sent me into some really jarring places on the internet and had me looking through some bizarre YouTube videos.

MATHIAS: Hard to say to be honest. I'm a pretty happy dude, but of course this beat can be very anxiety-inducing. Mostly because it never stops. I'm on my phone constantly, which isn't healthy. And there's the fear of retaliation by very bad people. I've been doxxed. Nazis talk on podcasts about me and my colleagues getting bricked. There are threats and hate mail. (Note: People on this beat have had it a lot worse than me. And women typically get it the worst.) Also every story is high stakes. If you're calling someone a Nazi, you better be sure. There's a fear of getting something wrong. The flip side to all of this though is that I have a sense of purpose on this beat. Sometimes it feels like I'm doing something important, and that's good.

HAS IT CHANGED YOUR FAITH IN HUMANITY IN ANY WAY? MADE YOU MORE OR LESS CYNICAL ABOUT THINGS?

SOMMER: I think, in terms of conspiracy theories, this whole thing has opened my eyes to how willing people are to believe truly insane stuff.

LÓPEZ: I never had any to begin with—dogs, on the other hand, will never let you down. In all seriousness, what I've become cynical about is social media. I used to think of it as a morally neutral tool with the benefits of interconnectedness outweighing any costs, but the reality is that it's being manipulated by the worst elements, exploiting prejudices and turning them into ideologies, exposing many to hateful ideas and providing economic incentives to push those ideas (*coughs* YouTube Super Chats *coughs*). Now I think of it as a necessary evil we're all unfortunate to be too dependent on.

MATHIAS: I don't know if I have more or less faith in humanity. What I'll say is that it's radicalized me a bit. Part of this beat is seeing how fringe Nazi ideas end up in the mainstream. It's horrifying. And you see the connections between straight-up fascists and those in power. It's so alarming, and it feels like a lot of people—and I guess I'm thinking of white centrist people in the media—aren't addressing this political moment with the language and the urgency and the force that it deserves. It's scary. Keeps me up at night sometimes. You can see how things could get even worse. The other thing I'll say is this: As shitty as the people I've met on this beat can be, I've also met the most dedicated and caring and passionate and intelligent and selfless people working hard for justice, and to stop fascists from terrorizing their communities. It's inspiring.

WAS THERE A PARTICULAR INSTANCE OF SOMETHING YOU SAW THAT SHOOK YOU AT ALL?

MATHIAS: I was in the parking garage in Charlottesville when DeAndre Harris got beat. I remember interviewing a person who had been there when Heather Heyer was killed. It was like an hour after the attack, and their body was shaking, they were so scared and they were crying so hard. That shook me. And then in Portland, when I interviewed the girlfriend of one of the heroes killed on the MAX train—the dudes who stopped white supremacist Jeremy Christian from attacking black teenage girls. The girlfriend had just lost the love of her life less than a week earlier, and she had the grace to sit down with me and tell me about him. I can't describe how sad that interview was. How angry it made me. And then lastly, I was just in Portland for the proto-fascist (Proud Boys and Patriot Prayer) rally there. I've covered a lot of protests, and I've seen aggressive policing, but the Portland PD was nuts. They turned that city into a war zone for no reason. And all the violence was directed at the anti-fascists. They're lucky they didn't kill anyone. It was the first time a protest scared me a bit.

LÓPEZ: While spending a couple hours a day on 4chan, 8chan, and Gab would raise anyone's shock threshold, the amount of misogyny on incel (involuntary celibates) message boards still makes my skin crawl. Another thing that's always shocking every time, no matter how often it happens, is the callousness of extremist shitposting that follows mass shootings—like their empathy is broken.

IS Q REAL? YOU HAVE TO TELL ME IF IT IS.

SOMMER: Haha, sadly, Q is not real.

LÓPEZ: Thanks for this opportunity: I'm Q.

MATHIAS: I am Q.

THE LAST BELIEVERS IN AN
ORDERED UNIVERSE

THEY DIDN'T BELIEVE ME. I PLED WITH THEM

Ben Collins, a self-described reporter on the dystopia beat for NBC News, was meant to chime in with the other group of reporters in the previous thing there you just read but he got caught up reporting on a Pizzagate-style story in which a Portland doughnut shop was being targeted as the latest secret layer of pedophilia in the minds of the brain-worm-infested conspiracy theorists. I separated his out into its own thing even though he missed my deadline which is something I don't think I ever did for him when he was my editor at *Esquire* so hmm makes you think who the real responsible reporter is.

DID YOU CHANCE INTO THIS EXTREMIST/ONLINE CONSPIRACY THEORISTS BEAT OR DID YOU SEE IT DEVELOPING AS A SORT OF UNFORTUNATE BOOM INDUSTRY A FEW YEARS AGO AND DECIDE TO FOCUS ON IT?

My path is a little more direct. I had always been vaguely sucked into conspiracy theories. I grew up in the middle of nowhere with access to a nascent version of the internet and no discernible skills. This was the kind of thing I had time for. I'd downloaded *Loose Change* from Limewire as a kid. A buddy of mine got me a copy of the Warren Commission, quasi-ironically.

I was covering vaguely internetty things for the *Daily Beast* for a while. Weird Facebook groups trolling locals into thinking there would be a Limp Bizkit concert at a gas station in Dayton, Ohio. That sort of thing. It was fun, and I was pretty optimistic about this whole thing as a tool for bringing people together and all of that. Then an old buddy of mine became the center of one of these things.

I went to college with Chris Hurst, whose longtime girlfriend was shot and killed on live TV by a disgruntled coworker. While he was being bombarded with all of this stuff, with the videos and the photos of the actual shooting all over the web, I Googled his name.

In the first couple of pages of results, no matter where you went, you'd mostly see "Christ Hurst crisis actor." There was an autocomplete for "Chris Hurst crisis actor." This was true Wild West stuff, complete goons—not even InfoWars—showing some sheer domination over Google's algorithm. Then I watched their videos on YouTube and went to their Blogspots (it was 2015) and all of that. I just sat there and stewed and got sadder.

I remember pitching a story about it at the morning meeting at the Beast, asking people if they knew what a crisis actor was. Pretty much nobody did, and it occurred to me I didn't even know when I learned the word. It was just always in the ether for me, and I probably would've entertained the idea of it if I stayed living in the woods.

I asked if I could call all the people making these YouTube videos and ask them how they got to believing Chris, who was captain of the intramural Emerson College Wiffle ball team for players who did not get picked at the Emerson Wiffle ball annual combine (which is some unbelievably roastable nonsense), was somehow not the human he said he was. I called a bunch of professors who studied conspiracy theories. Some were political types, others logistical, one philosophical. I still talk to the philosophical one all the time, because he let me see these hapless YouTubers as particularly vulnerable people. This was important, because the only emotions I would've had access to when talking to them was visceral anger and weird despair.

The professor's name is Brian Keeley and he's at Pitzer College, one of the Claremont Colleges. He wrote that these people are the "last believers in an ordered universe," that these folks lean on these things as a crutch to make up for the inherent disorder and chaos that comes with seeing random death and unfair circumstances on the news all day. It helped me deal with it all.

I called the YouTube guys. They didn't believe me. I pled with them. I put the pleading in the piece. They still didn't believe me. The piece ended. That was in 2015. Since then, YouTubers saying garbage like that have discovered you can just do that and nothing else for a living. People who believe that stuff are making decisions at the highest levels of our government. All of those professors who wrote about these conspiracies decades ago, and got called sparingly by reporters, are all on NPR now more frequently than bad jazz interludes.

They have come to dominate the culture. I spent the last few years thinking the rise of these people who are so willing to dehumanize strangers for cash on YouTube was confirmation bias, that I only thought it was bigger because of my beat. I thought I was, if anything, taking it too seriously.

I, uh, pretty speedily recalibrated on election night 2016. Then I realized I had to roll up my sleeves after that guy shot into a pizza shop looking for the child sex basement a month later.

WHAT SORT OF TOLL DOES IT TAKE ON YOUR MENTAL HEALTH? I DABBLE IN IT MYSELF, BUT THERE HAVE BEEN TIMES I THOUGHT ABOUT FOCUSING ON IT MORE AND SAID TO MYSELF, NAH, I DON'T NEED THAT SHIT IN MY BRAIN ALL THE TIME.

I started writing something about this over the weekend, and I was going to tell you how it doesn't faze me as much as it used to, that you frankly get bored by the same picture of a frog above a racial slur, that I've grown out of taking their threats all too seriously.

Then another shooting happened, and a bunch of people made up stuff about the shooter again, and got another innocent guy wrapped up in it again, and you remember how much it wears on you.

You never really get back to equilibrium. You're never really fully, functionally normal. You show up at parties and talk about Paul Joseph Watson as if that's somebody a regular person would be aware of, and they're not, of course they're not, and you just want to hug them and tell them how much you love them and implore them to never look at a computer for the rest of their beautiful, childlike lives. Their lives, I imagine, look like people in a Claritin commercial—running through a field at permanent dawn, picking flowers, and doing absolutely nothing else. It really makes you appreciate everyone else, and grounds you substantially.

There's just a slow creep of insanity through osmosis. You pick up the conspiracy tics that someone, somewhere is out to get you. I have those dreams you wake up in the middle of, that somebody's trying to break in and get back at you for writing about their secret extremist Twitter account or something. And it's just a dumb nightmare, but I wake up and stew on it, knowing there are people who are capable of that, but limited only by their own laziness.

I have, as a coping mechanism, gotten deeply into things that used to occupy the periphery of stuff anyone else would care about. I can identify NBA contract length and money pretty much down to the dollar and year, even for end-of-the-bench guys. My Spotify playlists are immaculate. I go to weirder concerts and bad movies now. It has opened up a lot of my life, simply because I have forced myself to care about other things with the same level of probably too-intense granularity. This is probably deeply obnoxious to everyone else in my life. I am very thankful the people around me have viewed this as a quirk and not a disaster.

HAS IT CHANGED YOUR FAITH IN HUMANITY IN ANY WAY? MADE YOU MORE OR LESS CYNICAL ABOUT THINGS?

I'll refer you back to Brian Keeley here, but there's very little actual malice by the believers of these things.

The people selling the lies? The people who know this stuff isn't true and accuse people of pedophilia as some sort of elaborate revenge fantasy that has come to define and shape their lives? Those people are disgusting, and they've been deeply hurt by something a long time ago that they did not let go of.

But here's Brian on conspiracy as opiate, as coping mechanism:

"Just as with the physical world, where hurricanes, tornadoes, and other 'acts of God' just happen, the same is true of the social world. Some people just do things. They assassinate world leaders, act on poorly thought out ideologies, and leave clues at the scene of the crime. Too strong a belief in the rationality of people in general, or of the world, will lead us to seek purposive explanations where none exists."

The world is big and scary. It's much easier for these people to believe nefarious agents are wreaking havoc than to come to grips with the randomness of their lives. It's religion. Blame the false prophets who are in on it, who have made supplement empires out of the violence. But feel bad for the dupes.

WAS THERE A PARTICULAR INSTANCE OF SOMETHING YOU SAW THAT SHOOK YOU AT ALL?

When I saw that whole family in Q shirts, I realized this is going to be a longstanding thing. I'm not sure how you decouple your parents telling you "don't put tinfoil in the microwave" and "be careful of the donut shop down the street, former First Lady and U.S. Senator Hillary Clinton is kidnapping all of your fellow five-year-olds for rape and murder purposes" in the same breath. You don't unlearn just one of those things. That stuff stays with you, and we're going to face a unique challenge in detoxifying these people from this absolutely abjectly wrong and stupid garbage.

In the meantime, push for more media literacy. Kids need media literacy and civics classes, badly. Worse than they need to learn about calculating diameters or whatever nonsense. This stuff can be taught and it isn't, and it has an enormous, outsized impact on this world. This problem is extremely bad right now, and I'm not sure you're going to fix late adopters to social media, like Boomers who use QAnon as an offseason CSI replacement. But if it's going to get any better, you have to start working to fix it right now.

IS Q REAL? YOU HAVE TO TELL ME IF IT IS.

It's realer than true love.

MAKE YOURSELF AS SMALL AS POSSIBLE

YOU'LL PAY FOR THIS SOMEDAY

Paul Gillespie was editing photos in the newsroom in June of 2018 when he heard the gunshots so he dove under the nearest desk and curled up as small as he could he said. "I was curled up, trying not to breathe, trying not to make a sound, and he shot people all around me," he told the *Baltimore Sun*. A colleague yelled *no!* and he heard a shot and then another colleague said something although he didn't say what that was but it was probably something like *please no* and then he heard another shot.

Making yourself as small as you can is a natural instinct for lots of animals in the wild when they're hiding from predators. It's like trying to disappear for the animals which is what we are ourselves and sometimes I think if you could make yourself so small no one would be able to see you at all that would be a kind of freedom. The guy who talked about hell being other people didn't mean that dealing with their shit was a pain in the ass he meant that we are only conscious we exist because we know we are perceived by others and that our knowledge of ourselves is built upon how they view us. There's a version of us that lives in everyone else who looks at us and that version of us is trapped in there and there's little we can do to free them. At least I think that's what he meant I'm way too dumb to understand philosophy anymore.

Gillespie's colleague Phil Davis a crime reporter for the *Capital Gazette* in Annapolis where the people were being shot to death was hiding under a desk as well and he live-tweeted what he thought might be his last moments alive.

"There is nothing more terrifying than hearing multiple people get shot while you're under your desk and then hear the gunman reload," he posted which is a brave thing to do: to post when you're about to be killed. But it also makes sense because if we want people to know what we're thinking when we're watching TV or eating a nice sandwich we also probably want them to know what we're thinking when we're hiding from a man with a gun.

Five people were killed that day by the man with the gun named Jarrod Ramos who had brought a defamation suit against the paper for reporting on him accurately and later had sent threatening letters and emails to the paper although the people he was actually mad at weren't even there anymore. They say sometimes that we shouldn't repeat the names of shooters on the news or talk about their lives because it might encourage others who want to become famous but to be honest there are so many of them every day now who could ever keep track.

Five people were killed that day by the man with the gun named Jarrod Ramos but that wasn't the only bad thing to happen because the reporters getting massacred also had a negative impact on Tribune Publishing's bottom line. The company which was known as Tronc until recently when they realized that was a stupid fucking name owns a number of newspapers including the *New York Daily News*, the *Chicago Tribune*, the *Hartford Courant*, and the *Baltimore Sun*. They said last year that they were being forced to offer buyouts to a number of employees at their various newspapers because they had had a bad quarter reporting $4.2 million in losses and one of the reasons for that they said in a release was that those reporters had went and got themselves killed.

"Despite the industry headwinds and the after-effects of the *Capital Gazette* tragedy, we performed well in the quarter and continue to establish the infrastructure for long-term success," the company's CEO Justin Dearborn said. "The decline is primarily due to higher newsprint pricing related to the recently rescinded tariffs, as well as the financial impact from the *Capital Gazette* tragedy," he said and he made over $8 million in 2016 so you got to assume he knows what he's talking about when it comes to how to weigh the cost of things.

I watched a video just now of a person driving through the wreckage of fires that ravaged northern California and it showed dozens of abandoned and destroyed cars and a tractor trailer left in the middle of the road and a burned out school bus. That town in particular was called Paradise, California, which is . . . a lot in terms of what the name of a place might be. It doesn't look much different than what the end of the world looks like when you think about what the end of the world might look like. For a lot of people it actually was the end of the world because around a hundred people died in the fires there and elsewhere in California around the same time. Four people were found dead in their cars in Paradise and one was found just outside of their car and I don't want to think about what it is like to die like that.

At a beach in Southern California where another fire was going on people gathered with their horses and other animals to wait out the fire at a safe distance because they didn't know what else to do and one thing people and animals have in common is that they know to run away from fire.

Not too far from that fire a guy whose name I already forget murdered a dozen people inside of a bar where they were listening to country music and having a nice time. It was reported by NBC News that he posted to social media before and during the attack speculating about how people would try to ascertain his mental state and they reported he said that he wasn't insane just bored which is why he had gone and killed everyone.

Something else CNN reported he posted is this: "I hope people call me insane," and then some laughing emojis. "Wouldn't that just be a big ball of irony? Yeah.. I'm insane, but the only thing you people do after these shootings is 'hopes and prayers'. . . or 'keep you in my thoughts'. . . every time . . . and wonder why these keep happening . . ." and that is chilling to read but he's also not wrong about the last part is he?

I don't really know what hell is but I don't think it's a place where bad things happen to people randomly such as natural disasters and death because that's just what the regular world is. I think it's probably more accurate to say it's a place where bad things happen because someone wanted them to happen to you or just let them happen out of negligence and indifference. Where bad things happen and they didn't have to but your life was less important to someone else than what they thought they had to gain.

AT THE END OF THE NIGHT I WANTED A BODY

I GUESS FROM A YOUNGER PERSON'S POINT OF VIEW IT SEEMS FUTILE

It was the end of the night and security had asked a group of men to leave the bar but they didn't want to do that. Around four in the morning someone came back to the bar with a gun and started shooting. When you are drunk and you feel disrespected that is what you do you go back and kill the person the motherfucker will be taught a lesson is what you are thinking at the time.

The security guards at the bar in a southern suburb of Chicago returned fire and Jemel Roberson who was working security that night ended up getting one of the men on the ground and held him there at gunpoint waiting for the police to arrive and take the man in. He had him on the ground there outside the bar with his knee in his back and was saying don't move and things like that a witness told WGTV and then the cops came and now Roberson will never play organ in the church choir again or get to become a police officer himself which is what his friends said he wanted to do one day.

"Everybody was screaming out, 'He was a security guard,' and they basically saw a black man with a gun and killed him," Adam Harris, who was there at the time, told a reporter.

"A Midlothian Officer encountered a subject with a gun and was involved in an Officer involved shooting," the police chief said in a statement in the characteristic disembodied police vernacular where things just sort of happen without any cause. Events are set in motion and officers are involved in shootings and subjects are pronounced deceased.

"One of our beloved Purposed Church musicians who was working part time overnight as security stopped the shooter from shooting more people [and] was shot multiple times by the police and killed," LeAundre Hill the pastor of Purposed Church wrote on Twitter. The night before Roberson had played organ at the funeral for Hill's grandmother.

One of the things the president and the NRA and people who love their guns very much say whenever there is a mass shooting is that we need to harden our schools and our churches and so on ah fuck I'm editing this for the book and there was just another mass shooting in Aurora, Illinois fuck.

Sorry. Hold on. Six people dead and six injured.

One of the things the president and the NRA and people who love their guns very much say ah fuck hold on it's a couple months later and I'm editing this one more time and there's an active shooter in Dallas and looks like he fucked up and got himself killed ok never mind false alarm.

One of the things the president and the NRA and people who love their guns very much say whenever there is a mass shooting is we need to have armed security guards everywhere we go to protect us from people with bad intentions but one thing they don't say is that person had better go ahead and be white. Thankfully the way Roberson was killed by police made the national news because that's what you have to do to be able to pay for funerals now is have your death have a hook that makes it stand out.

Another thing police like to do besides kill people is to put them in jail for the crime of being addicted to drugs. Police like Kevin Simmers a sergeant in Maryland who apparently was very good at doing just that according to the *Atlantic*.

"He relished locking up drug users, no matter how little crack they had on them," the *Atlantic* reported. "If they just had a pipe—fine," Simmers said. "At the end of the night, I wanted to have an arrest. I wanted a body."

One of those bodies ended up being his own daughter Brooke who had become addicted to opioids and had resorted to selling her body to be able to get the opioids she needed. He did everything he could to get his eighteen-year-old daughter clean Simmers said and he put her into multiple rehabs but many of them don't know what they're doing and focus on abstinence-only recovery which a lot of people think is less effective than using low-dose opioids to help with withdrawal symptoms.

Eventually Simmers asked some police friends of his to go and arrest his daughter which they hadn't done before then out of professional courtesy. She spent four months in jail and then when she got out she eventually relapsed. They found her dead one morning in her car "in her own vomit in the backseat, a sweatshirt rolled up like a pillow under her head and a basketball near her feet."

Simmers used to hold contests for a free dinner for whichever officer could lock up the most people in a night but now a few years after his daughter died he has realized the cruelty and pointlessness of the war on drugs.

"Twenty years ago, most people thought arrest and incarceration were the answer to this drug war," he said. "I think most people were wrong—I think I was wrong."

I am glad he is saying that now and it is hard not to feel terrible for him and his family but it would be nice if Republicans and cops could sometimes learn how to experience empathy before something terrible happened to them personally.

Whenever I read stories like these or do or think about literally anything I ask myself what the point of going on is. I don't want to know about this type of shit anymore I say to myself. But you do go on. Most of us do. We figure out a way to go on. It's getting harder to do I think sometimes especially as I get older so I wanted to know how people a generation ahead of me manage to do it. I asked a few of them a simple question: How do you go on? Interpret it anyway you will I said. But how do you go on? Here is some of what they told me:

ROB, 64

Positivity bordering on denial. It can apply to health issues, personal relationships, politics, or just daily life. Kinda like a good Buddhist, subordinating desire and expectations while embracing the present tense with wonderment of your personal experiences. Or ignoring aches and pains, assholes, and other horrible things that require endurance. Positive vibes. Positive vibes. Always. Also, I'd mention distancing myself from people with negative energy.

DAVID, 61

Because it's about more than just me. If I was only concerned with me, I think the temptation to just chuck it all and live in the woods, or worse just end it, might have sometimes become too much to bear. But it isn't about just me. It's about my family. It's about society. It's about people who depend on me—some of them without even knowing it.

LAUREL, 66

How does one go on? Very good existential question. I guess from a younger person's point of view it seems futile, being that so much is lost as one ages. What young people do not understand is all that is gained. It's like being on acid 24/7 as everything gets really intense, because you know it's not forever. I mean, everything is wildly intense . . . even love . . . sex . . . skiing!! Your mind is more focused on the "now"—because what future really is there? AND, there is no pressure to BE . . . because there is no time to BE what you thought you'd be. It's a real head trip and well worth the aches and pains. Yeah, it's better than being young.

BRIAN, 59

Ha! Interesting. Some don't, I suppose. My older brother took his own life two years ago, after struggling for years with depression. I suppose the answer is in that, to some extent. If there are aspects of your life that make you happy, or fulfill you somehow, continuing to exist doesn't seem like such a chore. I have a number of interests and ambitions that sometimes make me feel like I need more time than I imagine I will have. I'd like to continue to improve as a musician. I started running marathons at the age of fifty and have some goals around that. I remarried two years ago. My wife is a wonderful partner and our life together is very serene. There are many places we would like to go together. I sometimes think about famous polymaths like DaVinci and Franklin, and I imagine they felt like one lifetime wasn't enough to learn all the things they wanted to. True, you have to keep going with a body that doesn't look, or feel, or work as good as it used to. Like a lot of people my age I have chronic pain and some health issues.

RAYMOND, 73

That question is more pertinent in the context of retirement. Or, for anyone, after the loss of a loved one. But otherwise "going on" at 70 is like going on at 40 (if one's health is good).

P.S.: Curiosity. How's this going to turn out? I think that's the main motivator. Every night is like the ending of An episode of a soap. "Will Mueller indict Trump? Will Sanders resign? Is the new Octavian album any good?"

DAVID, 63

One just does.

I don't wish death. Sometimes however I do think that all in all it's best I won't be around to see ocean front property in Burlington, Massachusetts. I do feel guilty what I'm leaving for my children though.

WE'RE NOT GONNA DO IT MAN. WE CAN'T. WE QUIT

YOU'RE OUT HERE GETTING LAUGHED AT BY YELLOWCARD FANS. AND FOR WHAT?

Not everything is about the end of the world. Sometimes Hell World is about the relatively minor indignities we're subjected to where we're presented with a choice: figure out how to work through this or piss off back home. It's something that will be familiar to any of us whatever career we end up pursuing but as someone who's spent most of my life performing in bands I can assure you the music industry is its own particularly insidious corner of Hell for the vast majority of the people involved. Even the ones who "make it."

I asked some of my pals who've made it much further than I ever have if they had moments that made them want to give up like most of the rest of us do. I wanted to know if they could pinpoint a specific crossroads or a particularly memorable bowl of shit they had to eat and what if anything convinced them to go on.

RILEY BRECKENRIDGE OF THRICE

Between when we put out *Beggars* in 2009 and *Major/Minor* in 2011 you could kind of tell the writing was on the wall. Spirits weren't particularly high, we were plateauing as a band. Some of the guys seemed like they were kind of burnt out on touring and getting caught up in the cycle of write a record, record a record, get on the road and tour and do it all over again. It can kind of eat you up if you let it.

At the same time Teppei our guitar player's mother was diagnosed with cancer and her health deteriorated very quickly and she ended up passing away. Then my dad got diagnosed with cancer and deteriorated very quickly and passed away. Dustin's father also was diagnosed with cancer and ended up passing away a little bit later. And to top it all off when we were writing *Major/Minor*, which came out in 2011, we had our entire storage space completely emptied out, robbed; multiple drum kits and guitars dudes had been collecting over the years. Everything from instruments to fan art, just old stuff that you can't really replace.

We had a public storage space and our manager went over there one day and the whole thing was empty. He was like, Does this look normal to you? and I was like, Uh, no. Apparently the people next to us were like these crazy drug addicts or something and went on like a meth binge and tore down the drywall in between the two spaces and pulled everything from our space into their space, put the drywall back up, and then started pawning off all of our stuff.

THAT'S FUCKED UP

Yeah! So with stuff like the health problems people were having, the general morale of the band being down and that thing, it was like, man, there are several signs pointing to us that we should not be doing this right now. Somebody or something is telling us to stop. That was definitely the most obvious point where I was like, We need to take a knee and not do this for a while even though I didn't know what else I was going to do. We did end up taking a hiatus like a year later.

DO YOU THINK FANS THINK OF BANDS BEING JUST REGULAR PEOPLE DOING A JOB? OR DO YOU THINK THEY HAVE THIS ROMANTIC IDEA ABOUT IT?

I think there's a decent level of romanticism still there but I think social media has helped make people seem more real. I guess at the same time it's made other people seem like a bigger deal than they are. I guess it depends on how you use it. For us we've always tried to be transparent, but social media has helped us be more open about what we believe in, what we're going through, and what matters to us outside of guys being in a band. Then there are other people who use it like . . . there were only 250 people at this show last night but I'm gonna act like there were 2,000 and post pictures of myself partying with famous people. I'm trying to create this aura of fame when it's not really there yet.

OVER ALL DOES BEING IN A BAND SUCK OR DO YOU FEEL LUCKY TO DO IT?

I think . . . it's a hard question to answer. It depends on where you're at in your life. When I was young and I didn't have a girlfriend, didn't have kids, and a lot of responsibility, it was easier getting in a van and just saying Fuck it I'm gonna do this, and if it sucks it sucks, but I'd rather be doing this than working at a coffee shop or interning somewhere. Now as a father and a married man it sucks being away from my family. That's the part that sucks. But the positive side is I'm out here with my friends playing music, getting to see the world, and I'm making money doing it that I can support my family with. And when I get to come home I'm 100 percent home. I'm not at a job from 9 to 5 and seeing my kids late at night or something. That's not something I would get from any other job. I'd much rather be doing this than some other shit I did during the hiatus, the 9 to 5 kind of stuff my heart wasn't in.

DAN CAMPBELL OF THE WONDER YEARS

It was 2010 and we'd been saving up all of our money, personal money from working jobs, and band money from touring. We had saved up like $12,000. We went on a tour in the U.K. and we were getting ready to fly home. The driver we had was an English guy and he didn't really know how to drive around Germany and his GPS didn't work so he was using an atlas and we missed the flights home from Germany. It was like *The Price Is Right* or whatever, I was watching the money drop. We had to spend $3,000 on flights home.

So now we have two weeks before our first really big U.S. tour supporting Streetlight Manifesto. It was going to be like: this is the start of a career it's not a hobby anymore. We went to see the guy who sold us our van that didn't work anymore. We got a new one that ran well but it was corroded. The bottom was rusted out and you could see the road. He wanted $3,000. So we went to another place, there was one there and we said we'd take it.

It's a couple days away from the tour now so I go to buy the van and they said bad news we found some rust spots on the bottom and we're gonna sell it to auction. I said No, I need it now. I said I'll give you $6,000 for it as is. They said ok. I took it to a mechanic down the street he said it looked good. I was driving back to the guys and it felt a little weird. We get through a day of it and we take it to the mechanic and only five of the cylinders were firing. So we bought this lemon with no warranty because I didn't know what the fuck I was doing.

The tour started and we had to drive to Baltimore in a car and my dad's SUV. We played the first show, drove straight back over night, and then played the next show in Philly. Then there's a day off. We go back to the first guy and we say here's our last $3,000 give me that rusted out bucket that runs really well. We take it home and stay up all night ripping out the seats, building a loft, put the trailer on it. We get about three miles from the house and it's so rusted the trailer hitch rips out of the van. The trailer hits the street and pops open so we're fucked. We were on our way to Starland in New Jersey. We take all the gear out of the trailer and put it in the van. I go get my dad's SUV again, play that show, drive home again back to Philly, load it all into the van, drive straight to Worcester, play one more show, drive back to Philly over night again.

At this point I had called Dave our agent and said, "We're not gonna do it man. We can't. We quit." That's three vans in a week that we owned that don't work now, we lost all this money on this flight. He convinced us to take out a loan and we bought a van that we still have today.

DID YOU REALLY THINK ABOUT QUITTING?

When I heard the trailer hit the street and I looked back and it had ripped out the bottom of the back of the van I was like, Yup, I'm gonna go be a teacher. This is over.

HAD YOU GUYS BUILT A FOLLOWING AT THIS POINT?

We had put out *The Upsides* on No Sleep, we were just starting to pick up steam kind of. We had never made money of our own. Well, actually after these shows we had done around Christmas that year everyone in the band received $100, which was $100 more than we'd made in the past five years doing it. Obviously we made enough on those tours and in our jobs in kitchens and carwashes and shit to save up enough money to buy a van. But you know it was not looking like a viable future for us. I just thought what fucking terrible luck.

LOTS OF BANDS SAY THAT'S THE TYPE OF STUFF YOU HAVE TO GO THROUGH. THE BANDS THAT SAY THAT ARE PEOPLE WHO ACTUALLY MAKE IT THROUGH THAT STUFF THOUGH. THERE ARE TENS OF THOUSANDS OF BANDS WHO PROBABLY QUIT AT THAT MOMENT.

It definitely tests your mettle. I think the biggest thing is, the things you learn from being in a band are, well, problem solving is close to the top of that list. What are you going to do if you're stranded in Germany? What are you going to do when your battery dies on the van and you're in the middle of the West Texas desert and you have to get to the show the next day? I think without times like that you don't learn those lessons and you break down. But we just kind of leaned on each other a little bit and said ok let's fucking figure it out. We can either quit or figure it out.

Our agent was like, Yes you can, you can do it. This tour is going to be great. Trust me.

SEEMS LIKE YOU MADE THE RIGHT DECISION. I'M GLAD YOU DIDN'T QUIT.

So am I! But I can also totally understand why someone would say, Holy shit fate is telling me to walk away from this.

DRIVING BACK AND FORTH HOME ON TOUR EVERY NIGHT SOUNDS BRUTAL.

Every time I walked back into my dad's house I was like a little more defeated. We broke another one.

DID YOUR PARENTS WANT YOU TO QUIT EVER?

No. The only thing was when I stopped college for a semester they said we don't think you should do that. I said I promise you I'm just taking a semester off to see what happens. And I really did go back and we all finished our degrees.

There are some people we meet in bands whose parents had the means to buy them the van right up front and never had to experience that shit. Our families didn't have that so much. My parents didn't have the ability to help with that.

NATHAN HUSSEY OF ALL GET OUT

The lowest point in the band is also an amazing memory. For the record, I would use the word "low" fairly loosely. We were trying our best to get out in front of people by touring nonstop. One time the best we could do was a chain restaurant. We played a Denny's in Orlando, Florida with O'Brother sometime around 2008 or 2009. We loaded in while the restaurant was still open and watched in humility as they rearranged the booths to form a stage for our bands. We weren't too cool for it, though. We got free food which is still always a big deal 10 years later, and I still hear about it from fans who saw the show.

BRENDAN KELLY OF THE LAWRENCE ARMS

Most musicians don't have the option of deciding to quit touring. The free market economy tends to make that decision for them. So anyone who's ever been in a position where they think "Should I stop doing this" is already breathing pretty rare air and living their dream, even if they dreamed of a bus instead of a van and giant theaters instead of dingy shit holes. That being said, being a touring musician still sucks bad enough a lot of the time that these kinds of thoughts enter every traveling performer's mind at some point. And it's not just the shitty drives and constant disconnect with reality. Consider the following scenarios:

Let's say you're on a successful tour. Let's say, and I'm just pulling this out of my ass, but let's say you're on a six-week tour and a young band called Taking Back Sunday is opening up for your band. Every night, things go pretty much according to plan. Taking Back Sunday plays and gets a decent response, then you play and, as the band everyone is there to see, people go nuts. But, hypothetically, what if one day you went to the Chain Reaction in Orange County and the show was suddenly packed. Four times bigger than any other show on the tour. "Holy shit! The OC must finally love the Lawrence Arms" you might think. Taking Back Sunday plays and people go fucking insane. Recall, the crowd is massive. Spilling out into the parking lot and then into the streets. "Wow. Our show is going to be absolutely bonkers!" you're probably thinking as their set ends. Only, as soon as they're done, suddenly everyone leaves and you're playing to the same 30 weirdos that always come see you in the OC.

No big deal. It's the OC and the OC kinda blows. But then, what if that becomes what happens *every night* for the rest of the tour? What if suddenly you're forced to go on stage and essentially jizz mop the main event for the next 21 days. It's (I'd imagine) pretty humiliating. Probably makes you wonder what the fuck you're doing with your life.

But I like Taking Back Sunday, and as much as that situation sucks, it's not like it's incomprehensible. So what about if you're on tour with a couple of bands that are very of-the-moment, but for whatever reason just aren't for you. Like, you can't comprehend why anyone would like their music. But here's the twist: everyone at all the shows loves them to the point of being in tears. Oh, and those same people? They absolutely *hate* your band. Loudly and demonstrably. You may be the only band on the bill that you think is worth a shit, but you're literally the only three people in the room, every night of the tour, who don't think you just absolutely stink. That is a hard thing to deal with.

What if you play a show in Florida and one guy shows up and halfway through your second song he leaves? What if, at that point, the sound guy makes you keep playing so he can still get paid for the night? Something like that may make you rethink what you're doing out there.

What if you play a festival and you're woefully out of place? What if you get thrown on an emo fest in New Bedford, Massachusetts and everything there is just bangs and sadness, and you stagger your drunk asses onto the stage and when you go into the guitar solo during the first song the crowd begins to laugh, like, so loudly that it's as though it were a comedy show? That will make you wonder if you're just making something that no one on earth would ever want to hear and if you're not only bumming out a room, but also wasting your life.

What if you somehow are a no frills punk band and you get mistakenly placed as a headliner on a festival alongside Dillinger Escape Plan and Converge? Can you imagine sitting through 27 brutal bands for like 9 hours knowing with 100 percent certainty that everyone in attendance is gonna throw stuff at you? It's a good, self-affirming feeling that really stays with you for years.

Now, consider that as this parade of public embarrassments haunts your every waking hour, your friends are at home, getting real jobs, making money, having fun, forgetting who you are and hanging out with one another. You may love the people that you spend 20 hours a day in a rolling tin box with, but eventually, you'll start to get annoyed by their idiosyncrasies and, lemme tell you, they'll begin to HATE yours. Your girlfriend, she's at home, hanging out with your friends, living a life that you're not part of, and you're out here getting laughed at by Yellowcard fans. And for what? A bottle of Tito's, a few hundred bucks and the opportunity to share a Motel 6 bed with another guy who was too tired to shower off their flop sweat after yet another horrible embarrassment of a show? In fucking suburban Buffalo no less?

Everyone questions their life choices at some point, but when you're in a touring band you get the opportunity to do that almost every single day. It's a real dream job in that regard.

KEITH BUCKLEY OF EVERY TIME I DIE

I was standing in the small shower of a German hotel room. The shower was small because the room was. The door to the shower was completely transparent for some reason so I could see the single bed under a window that overlooked a bunch of grey wet bricks that came down and in from a few different directions and if anyone had been sitting on the bed they could have seen me but I was alone and I had been for a while. I guessed they felt too awkward to talk to me just yet and I didn't blame them. It was May of 2012 and at that moment I was being held captive by shame from the night before that twelve hours later still radiated an absurd amount of heat and made me want to peel off my own skin and just start fucking running and screaming like that scene in *Punch Drunk Love* except underneath my skin was just more garish skin and there was nowhere to run because everywhere I went would be in flames. I remember understanding clearly in that shower that the world I had spent years assembling around myself wasn't mine anymore, but not in the cool way that you might create something lovely like a child and send it off to school knowing it has its own calling now or how you shoot an arrow from a bow because that is *in* the world and this *was* the world. "Mutiny" is probably the best word.

Then suddenly I had a thought, which was this: "If I smash my head against the tiles hard enough and long enough they'll find me and the tour will have to be canceled." And so I started to do that. The first thump was thick and it vibrated the deep underside of my skull at the crown and tickled my hair follicles but when I did it again all nerves attended to the point of impact and I knew here that it was going to take some inhuman conviction to finish the task. So, I went back to the night before. I wore that skin and sat in the fire feeling it all and hearing every cruel word and felt a hand or fist I still don't know against my jaw and looked into everyone's face as I lost my footing and when the shame appeared I was pleased to find it was still gruesome enough to keep me inspired and so I kept at it. But at around maybe the fifth stupid, hollow thud my brain made some desperate, hail mary sort of blind lunge at self preservation and responded with a thought of its own which was this: "If your band members come in here and find you bleeding with your dick out it's going to be even more embarrassing than what happened last night. Just quit instead you fucking coward." And it was right and I had every reason to do so and so I stopped trying to split my skull open and got out of the shower somewhere in Germany and promised myself that I would quit after the show that night. But I didn't. And I haven't yet. At the time it was because, as I have said, I was a coward. But since then I've learned that the death of one kind of world is just the birth of another kind of world and it turns out that the middle of that fire in the middle of that street running through a creepy foreign city was exactly where the entire violent, bloody and miraculous process took place. What are the odds? Now my wife and I have a healthy daughter and a modest home and I've made really good friends which I owe to the music we make and to take all of this for granted would be infinitely dumber than trying to crack my own head like an egg. I'm also not good at anything else and I'm barely even good at this, so.

GEOFF RICKLEY OF THURSDAY

We were on tour in Canada and had a day off, in a suburb between cities, so we made a big production of going out to breakfast, all together.

I had about seven pancakes and three coffees and I started to feel like I might have to run back to the room to go to the bathroom. But when I got back there something felt wrong. There was a dull, persistent pain somewhere around my lower back or lower stomach area and when the rest of my band came back they were all joking that I was going to be the first touring musician to die from gas pains and kept fucking around that they'd be cursed with the dead farting singer. But the pain got worse and worse and worse until I was rolling around on the ground totally unable to speak.

By the time I couldn't form words anymore, our tour manager grabbed my face and got my attention. "Do you think you want to go to the hospital?"

Thankfully I was able to get out a "Yes."

So they loaded me in a cab and sent me to the hospital. I still remember that the cab driver was listening to a cassette about The Healing Power of Laughter. The voice on the tape instructed us to take a deep breath and push out a full-throated yet sincere laugh. I tried. A mangled sound came out of my mouth. It was full-throated yet sincere. The cab driver stopped laughing but the tape kept on telling us how good we felt.

The next I knew I was on a table and a doctor was telling me it might hurt for a second. When he pushed the plunger on the syringe my central nervous system slipped out of my skin into a warm bathtub against the ceiling. The room lit up around us like it was filled with Christmas lights and the doctor asked me "Does that feel better?"

I watched his words kick up sparkling white swirls through the water of the snow globe that we suddenly found ourselves inside of.

"If the kidney stone was any bigger, we'd have to operate. One centimeter is the cut off. Yours is only 9 millimeters, so we'll let you pass it." He was showing me a sonogram while rubbing something cold on my stomach.

Andrew, our keyboardist, squeezed my leg. I was so happy to see him! I loved him!!! I loved my band!!! I loved the Canadian doctor, the miracle of modern science and all of socialized medicine. The world was a beautiful place and I loved it and I suddenly had to piss.

"Ok, you might pass the stone, now. We gave you some fluids and the pressure is probably building. If you can, catch the stone in this paper cup and we can test it."

I floated into the bathroom and stood at a urinal feeling my whole body inflate like a balloon. Suddenly a small, bone-tinted pebble ricocheted off the urinal and across the room.

I was supposed to catch that . . . I thought before a stream of blood starting shooting out from the tip of my dick. It was pure body horror. I couldn't stop laughing. My dick belonged in *Fangoria* magazine.

I told Andrew that the National Health gets a bad rap: no wait, no fuss, no red tape. The doctor laughed and showed me to the waiting room. Easily 300 people. He told me I was screaming and couldn't even tell them my name. It's policy to admit without intake in such cases. Then he gave me enough painkillers to make the rest of the tour a really nice time.

PAUL MICHEL OF SPIRIT ANIMAL

Christ this job is mind-numbingly, shoot yourself in the face, soul-sucking, fucking boring. At least in the corporate world I could fill out a TPS report or some shit. In the van my only lifeline is Twitter, which is also a form of hell. Wake up bleary-eyed, maybe hungover, definitely not enough sleep, get in a van full of discarded shit that smells like a mix between a teen boy's bedroom and the McDonald's run you forgot you made the night before, drive for god knows how long (boring), arrive on time only to wait till the headliner is done sound checking (boring), wait till your set time (a mix of boring and stress), play for 30 minutes (fun!), and then drink and wait and drink and wait to load out (boring!!). Is that 30 minutes worth it? Some days.

And let me let you in on a little secret about low/mid level touring: dressing rooms are a rare, seldom realized ideal. So you and the 4–10 other members of the opening bands share a little corner of the club the owners deemed too shitty to monetize. Maybe you get a couch, but everybody's shit is on it so you can't lie down and take that nap you desperately need but couldn't anyway because people are blasting demos on their crappy phone speakers and talking over each other and part of you is like this is the life and another part of you is like fuck this I'm going across the street to that shitty bar and hope they have a drink special and holy shit it's only 3 p.m. But then the bands become your friends, so there's a plus, and sometimes the headliner lets you on the bus to smoke their incredibly strong weed, which is a mixed bag.

Touring, like bartending, breeds misanthropy. Finding alone time is impossible so you have to create a little place in your head that, while not a happy or peaceful place, is at least not invaded by other people. Headphones help.

✗

SHE WAS EVERYTHING THE WORLD IS NOT

DURING THE FIREARMS SEASON

"We are in a state of chaos," eleven-year-old Sandra Parks wrote. "In the city in which I live, I hear and see examples of chaos almost every day. Little children are victims of senseless gun violence," she wrote. "Many people have lost faith in America and its ability to be a living example of Dr. King's dream!"

She was writing an essay for her Milwaukee school's Martin Luther King Jr. essay contest in 2016 and people thought her writing was so moving she won third place throughout the whole district. I don't know if they put her essay on the fridge at home but it's all over the internet now and her family probably wishes it were not.

"Sometimes, I sit back and I have to escape from what I see and hear every day," she wrote.

After the contest Sandra went on Wisconsin public radio and talked about her essay. She chose the topic of violence she said because "all you hear about is somebody dying or somebody getting shot and people do not just think about whose father or son or granddaughter or grandson who it was that was just killed."

On a Monday in November 2018 Sandra was watching television with her sister and a bullet came in from out there on the street and it found Sandra sitting there.

"My sister took it like a soldier," her sister said later according to the *New York Times*. "She just walked in the room and said, 'Mama, I'm shot.'"

I'm not sure if Paul Ryan her senator has weighed in on Sandra's death but shortly after the shooting at Parkland in Florida earlier that year he went down to Florida for the National Republican Congressional Committee winter meeting at the Ritz-Carlton in Key Biscayne which is just the most gorgeous place you should go sometime and he raised some money there and a woman named Maria Thorne a teacher down there confronted him inside to talk about gun violence and he said to her he didn't want to talk politics right now and then she was escorted out of the building by security.

The day after Parkland Ryan went on a radio station in Indiana and told the host that they didn't know all the facts of the case yet and so talking about gun control was premature at that particular juncture.

"We need to pray and our hearts go out to these victims," he said. "And as public policy makers we don't just knee-jerk before we even have all the facts and the data."

In 2016 alone Paul Ryan got $171,977 in donations from gun lobbyists, one fact I have recently learned from Politico. Considering he's been in office twenty years you have to figure that's added up to some real money by now. You could retire off that kind of money. Which I guess he went and did.

Sandra's mother Bernice Parks told a reporter that her daughter "was everything this world is not." She said her daughter was not violent and did not like violence but Paul Ryan does you'd have to assume at this point. Seems like the facts and the data are in on that one particular mystery we've been waiting to get to the bottom of.

I looked at his Twitter after she died and Ryan didn't address young dead Sandra who they said was a good girl and I guess you can't blame him because if a politician memorialized every one of their constituents who got shot they wouldn't have time to do anything else like pass tax cuts for rich people. He did post a video about what he was thankful for leading up to Thanksgiving though and one of those things was deer hunting season starting up in Wisconsin again. He's also thankful he'll be spending more time with his family soon after he retires but he doesn't know if they'll be thankful for that ha ha and then he says he's thankful that the system works.

"I'm thankful for the battle of ideas," he goes on, and it sounds like he says *bettle* which is throwing me off my train of thought here. "You know, things can get a little off track, but our system, our way of resolving our differences and figuring things out is still the best in the world and it will endure," he says.

There's a shot of the sign for Janesville, Wisconsin in the video where he lives and where the oldest operating General Motors plant was from 1919 until 2009 when they shut it down. Around 9,000 jobs vanished but GM said closing the plant would save them around $1 billion and that number is larger than 9,000 I don't think any of us would argue with that. Some of the workers there tried going back to school and training for new jobs and got frustrated by it and some became what they called GM gypsies and commuted like Matt Wopat did four and a half hours to go work at another GM plant as the *Atlantic* reported and some people like Jerad Whiteaker whose father and father-in-law both retired on GM pensions took a buyout giving up his right to work in another plant or to collect a pension so he could get a few thousand dollars and six more months of health insurance for his family who did not want to move away from the area.

A few years ago I wrote a story about how we found my long-lost older sister who they had come and taken away from my mother when she had her due to she was very young and at the end of it I wrote I hope someday she just becomes a regular member of the family and not some curiosity and then a couple months back we were all at my cousin's wedding and I got drunk and told her and her husband and the rest of my family that there are no good Republicans and basically ruined the night so I guess that wish came true. I told my mother after that she might have to choose between me and Fox News some day.

Before Thanksgiving everyone writes stories about how to deal with your family's political differences. One thing I noticed this year at my in-laws is that no one drinks at their holiday events anymore and politics never comes up but when my family gets together everyone gets drunk and shit gets real hectic so maybe it's not politics that's the problem it's alcohol.

Besides the drinking people love Thanksgiving so much because of the food but I do not because of the food and I have a hard time around that much food. I have a hard time around any sort of holiday gathering or party or barbecue or anything like that because I am not able to control myself I'm like a dog when it gets into the garbage but I don't have an owner that can whack me on the nose with a rolled-up newspaper or anything I am my own angry owner so I have to punish myself by going to do some more exercise and then I end up hurting myself all over again because I think I can reverse all the eating I did in one go but that isn't true and I know it isn't true but I still believe it and you can't convince me otherwise.

One thing I did on Thanksgiving was listen to a recording of the Boston Symphony Orchestra from fifty five years ago that day. At one point conductor Erich Leinsdorf walks on stage after a break. "Ladies and gentlemen we have a press report over the wires," he says. "We hope that it is unconfirmed but we have to doubt it," he says. "The president of the United States has been the victim of an assassination," he says. A wave of shock and alarm can be heard washing over the audience. "We will play the funeral march from Beethoven's Third Symphony," he says and then there's another eruption of commotion that almost sound like boos and some of the things I've been reading about it suggest the selection of that piece then and there is what made them accept that it had actually happened and that was the noise they were making like it was painful acceptance but when I first listened it sounded at least in part to me like they were saying come on man that's a little on the nose isn't it?

About ten minutes before the performance started Leinsdorf instructed the librarian William Shisler to go pull the music for the piece NPR said. "Run to the archives, collect all the parts for the second movement of Beethoven's 'Eroica' Symphony—the funeral march—and get them to the players as fast as you can. President Kennedy is dead," he told him and then Shisler had to go one by one to each of the musicians and give them the last-minute change to the program and explain what happened. One by one. To the violins: they got him. To the oboes: yes, he's been killed. To the woodwinds: the president has been shot learn this shit real quick.

Leinsdorf said later that week "that he had chosen Mozart's *Requiem* because, as was the work of President Kennedy, it was left unfinished by premature death."

It's a fascinating document of people learning about news collectively that they might not have heard otherwise for a few hours. Sometimes I wonder what it will be like when we hear about the president we have now dying because of course we will all learn instantly on our phones and I picture acrobats and choreographed drum lines pouring out of nowhere into the street and sailors kissing nurses and shit.

On Thanksgiving in 2012 Paul Ryan took his ten-year-old daughter Liza hunting with him. She'd been coming out with him for years to watch but this was the first year it would have been legal for her to shoot from her own blind.

His daughter hunted with a Remington 700 .243 caliber the *Washington Examiner* reported. "The .243 is one of the most popular calibers for deer hunting because it is accurate at long distances and recoils very little."

Earlier that summer when he still thought he might have a chance at being the vice president Ryan talked about his love of hunting to Politico.

"I hunted more before we had kids, and then after that it dropped off quite a bit. I'll schedule some morning hunts on weekends when I can and then work in the afternoons if I have to or will be with the family. During the firearms season, I'll take a little more time to schedule some trips. I'll hunt with my pistol in the morning from my bow stands, and then rifle hunt in the afternoons with one of our kids. We have some two-man ladder stands, and (the children) really enjoy going with me. I bought our daughter a Winchester Model 70 in .243 for Christmas so she can start hunting with me. Wisconsin lowered the hunting age, and she's excited. The kids love hunting and being with me in the stand. We have a great time."

MY HEART BASICALLY ENLARGED

I DON'T WANT TO GO BACK TO THE HOSPITAL

Hedda Elizabeth Britt loves to post to Facebook. There's one on her page on an alarming report about the looming climate change disaster. There's one about the thirteen-year-old girl who wrote an essay about gun violence being shot dead. There's a goofy meme of a cat trying to steal a turkey off the counter she posted on Thanksgiving. And a few days earlier she posted a letter she received from the Spectrum Health Richard DeVos Heart and Lung Transplant Clinic. Britt is a single mother of one from Grand Rapids, Michigan, home of the billionaire DeVos family who are the funders of the clinic in question among many other philanthropic causes in the area. They wrote to her to say she was being denied her request to receive a heart transplant.

"The decision made by the committee is that you are not a candidate at this time for a heart transplant due to needing more secure financial plan for immunosuppressive medication coverage," read the letter which the committee tasked an RN to deliver on their behalf.

"The Committee is recommending a fundraising effort of $10,000," it said and while it's certainly not the worst thing going on here one might like to think the letter telling you you're on your own from your doctors wouldn't have a bunch of typos in it.

"We thank you for the opportunity to participate in your care. If you have any questions, please do not hesitate to contact me."

People are denied medical treatment and transplants in particular all the time and the idea that individuals in America have to resort to crowdfunding their medical care isn't new. Patients are often advised by the social workers helping them to manage their care that they might want to look into raising money from friends and family. But there is something particularly galling in seeing it spelled out explicitly like this by health care providers in a letter. Transplant applicants are evaluated for a variety of factors, including age, relative health, and the ability to be responsible stewards of the highly valuable resource of a life-giving organ, but it seems rare that the capitalist dystopia we live in is admitted to so openly. In essence what Spectrum Health was telling Britt was that she was too poor to bother trying to save. Good luck in all your future heart transplant endeavors!

Back around the time the Affordable Care Act was being debated you used to hear a lot about the idea of "death panels" from the likes of Sarah Palin and the rest of the cruelest vilest pieces of shit on earth. That was all a lie there was nothing like that in there despite what Chuck Grassley and Rush Limbaugh and company said. I don't know what you call this sort of decision making but it sounds like a death panel to me although I'm not a doctor or anything so don't take my word for it.

At least four members of the board at Spectrum make over a million dollars a year and Richard Breon the president and CEO makes $2.6 million. Nine others make over six hundred thousand a year.

Thankfully Britt, who likes to post on Facebook about how she doesn't like Donald Trump very much amidst the regular updates on her health troubles decided to post the letter when she did because when I and a few others saw it going around on Twitter we decided to share it in disgust. It has since been shared a few ten thousand times including by Alexandria Ocasio-Cortez. Hoping to take advantage of the attention it was getting her son started a GoFundMe which raised $11,500 in one day alone. One woman who reached out to me on Twitter offered to pay the entire $10,000.

"It's horrible that we must do this for health care," Britt wrote me in a Facebook message. A friend of hers later told me she was overwhelmed and grateful for the support everyone has shown. A few weeks later the fundraiser had brought in over $30,000.

"The fundraising was remarkable," she told me. "I am actually having my surgery Monday. I will be implanted with the lifesaving LVAD and then it will take me several weeks in the hospital to recuperate. But it least I will then be on the transplant list. That is all I really wanted."

I asked Spectrum for comment on the situation in general and this is what they said:

> While we do not comment on specific patient situations to protect their privacy, Spectrum Health cares deeply about every patient that enters its doors and provides each of them the highest quality of care possible. While it is always upsetting when we cannot provide a transplant, we have an obligation to ensure that transplants are successful and that donor organs will remain viable. We thoughtfully review candidates for heart and lung transplant procedures with care and compassion, and these are often highly complex, difficult decisions. While our primary focus is the medical needs of the patient, the fact is that transplants require lifelong care and immunosuppression drugs, and therefore costs are sometimes a regrettable and unavoidable factor in the decision making process. We partner with our patients throughout their care and work closely with them to identify opportunities for financial assistance. Our clinical team has an ongoing dialogue with patients about their eligibility, holding frequent in-person meetings and informing patients in person to ensure they fully understand their specific situation.

Transplants were very important to Richard DeVos, the man for whom the transplant center is named. The father-in-law of Betsy DeVos the U.S. secretary of education had a heart transplant of his own in 1997. He traveled to the U.K. where he paid £60,000 to skip ahead of a number of other people waiting on the transplant list because that is what you get to do when you are rich. That might sound like a lot of money—and it certainly would be to me or Britt or to you—but he was worth around $5 billion at the time so that is essentially zero dollars he had to pay for his new heart and the extra twenty years he got out of it.

"It is disgusting. People are waiting and dying because there are so few organs available," Lynne Lewis, a twenty-nine-year-old woman with a congenital heart disease told the *Scottish Daily Record & Sunday Mail* back then.

"Yet someone can walk in and pay £60,000 for a heart—money talks."

DeVos wrote a few books before he died at ninety-two including *Hope From My Heart: Ten Lessons For Life*, and one called *Compassionate Capitalism: People Helping People Help Themselves*. Speaking of which one of the things Betsy DeVos has been working on is making the lives of victims of sexual assault on campus much harder including allowing the perpetrators to cross-examine the people they assaulted among other things because bitches do be lying sometimes.

"I believe in miracles and I praise the Lord for giving me this," Richard DeVos said after his surgery according to a *Daily Mail* piece from 1999. "It had nothing to do with money."

He had been refused a transplant in the U.S. because of his age.

"How many Britons in their seventies would get accepted on to the transplant waiting list?" the *Daily Mail* asked before finishing with a characteristically tabloid flourish:

"DeVos, told by doctors he had only two or three years to live without a transplant, is said to be living a 'full life' at his mansion in Grand Rapids, Michigan."

Here's the fucked up thing. Well, there are a lot of them here but here's one irony I particularly relish. We know by now that people need to become sick or injured in a sympathetic or compelling enough way to get people to help their tales of woe go viral so by sending the callous letter the people at Spectrum may have saved Britt's life. If it weren't for that casual fuck you go get some money line none of us would have ever heard of her and she likely wouldn't have been able to raise the money she needed to be considered. So . . . thanks, Spectrum? You took care of your patient after all. You didn't intend to but you did anyway.

A doctor with knowledge of the decisions that go on behind the scenes when it comes to making transplant decisions reached out to me to talk about how it all works. It should be clarified she said that this is not a DeVos center-only policy. It happens at hospitals all around the country like the big one in Massachusetts she worked at.

"It's most startling and repulsive at a DeVos-funded place, but transplant committees de facto discriminate based on socioeconomic factors everywhere, refusing to list until you can show an amount of savings, or if you can't show adequate other personal resources," she said.

"It's very hard to get a transplant without a whole middle class set up. You need to show you have social support, stable housing, prolonged abstinence from substances, savings . . . There's a fair amount of discretion on the part of committees to discriminate under the cover of responsible resource stewardship. The language used—'a fundraising effort'—is maybe unique, but the spirit is certainly not."

The principle behind it she explained is to try to never "waste" an organ by giving one to someone who isn't going to be able to get maximum benefit from it.

"But embedded in the notion of 'risk' is that transplant centers are meticulously tracked, rated and accredited based on outcomes. It isn't just a matter of risk to the patient, it's a matter of risk to the center's reputation and transplant program."

In other words a lot of surgeons won't save your life if it looks like it's gonna be hard because they don't want your death on their stat sheet. Go die on your own time.

Linda Jara is a forty-six-year-old former high school teacher from Philadelphia and the recipient of a heart transplant of her own two years ago. I spoke with her about some of the challenges of being offered a transplant in the first place, the crushing financial burdens, and everything that goes into trying to stay alive once you've "won" the medical lottery like she did.

WHAT DID YOU THINK WHEN YOU SAW THE LETTER RECOMMENDING THE WOMAN START A FUNDRAISER?

My heart went out to her. I was a little bit annoyed at some of these people in the comments questioning if it was real.

The big picture is that this woman can't get what she needs to survive. Right before my first surgery my social worker told me: Right now you meet all the finance goals, but you might want to look into fundraising because it gets really expensive. I remember breaking out in tears. I can't get out of the hospital! I'm from Philly, what do you want me to do sell soft pretzels outside the hospital room? I can't leave this place.

A friend started a GoFundMe but then I was recommended this organization Help Hope Live and they were so much better. Help Hope Live creates fliers and stuff and helps you meet your goals. Every year I do a bigger benefit, so I try to do something once a year. It takes so much work to do. I'm thinking of smaller things to do now, maybe a bowling party. My goal was $85,000 so I could afford one year of medication if I didn't have health insurance. Right now I'm at $75,000 and I'm in a good place but I've used $25,000 since my transplant. I get nervous. It's an expensive lifestyle. I was a high school teacher I don't have $25,000 lying around to pay for medical expenses.

I felt bad for her. It's like a never-ending battle, and you're sick and you're trying to do it . . . it's a lot.

WHAT WAS YOUR ACTUAL MEDICAL ISSUE THAT NECESSITATED A TRANSPLANT?

I got sick out of nowhere. I was blindsided by my illness. I was fine at Thanksgiving of 2014, then by Christmas Eve I was in heart failure. January I was in the hospital and by March I had my first open-heart surgery. I was like what the heck happened? Eighteen months later after a couple false alarms the good heart came in. It's so much to learn, it's so overwhelming, and when you get a letter like that, you realize: Oh you're going to have to fundraise to do this? I guess that's 2018 America.

I had an idiopathic dilated cardiomyopathy. My heart basically enlarged.

WHAT IS IT THAT MAKES IT ALL SO EXPENSIVE? IMMUNOSUPPRESSANT DRUGS?

There's about twenty-six different medications that I take. Immunosuppressant are expensive. For nine months after I was on prednisone, the steroid. A lot of people end up with diabetes, so you have to leave the hospital with insulin. With my insurance it was still like $500 for the insulin. You have to leave with all your medications and they have to come right from the hospital in a giant bag.

WHAT HAPPENED AFTER YOU HAD THE TRANSPLANT?

I was in the hospital for a month after the transplant then I got home and I went into a really bad rejection. My insurance didn't want to pay for my drugs. When I was in the hospital they gave me a name brand anti-rejection drug. When I was discharged they give a lot of people the generic. I got out on a Thursday and by Tuesday I had to go back, I ended up in a strong rejection. My body wasn't able to process the generic anti-rejection meds. That cost me another five days in the hospital. They didn't want to pay for the name brand stuff. It's still a never-ending battle with my insurance. They don't want to cover it. They think there are other ones I can take but my doctor said this one is necessary. They had me calling different pharmacies to see if they had various generic drugs. It's like a never-ending saga. In my head, and this is what I felt for that poor woman, we just want to stay alive and there's all these hurdles we have to jump just to stay alive.

When all was said and done I probably spent six months in the hospital. You don't want to go back there, they're not fun places to be.

WHAT WERE SOME OF THE CRITERIA THAT THEY LOOKED AT BEFORE DECIDING YOU WERE A CANDIDATE FOR A TRANSPLANT?

They have to test your arteries, they put the swan catheter in your jugular, I still have scars from that. Then the heart is matched by size and blood type, the size heart that can fit inside your chest cavity. Then they do cardiac MRIs. That's awful, it's about two hours and forty-five minutes inside that machine.

The second part of it is they review your finances and your family support and they review how compliant you are, how are you at being a patient and all of these others things. I remember I would tell people I don't know how some people do this. If I didn't live where my family lived I would've had to move home. You need all this support, twenty-four-hour supervision for three months, you can't drive or do anything. One time I went to my sisters the second time to my parents. It's a lot. I remember after I had my open-heart surgery they asked me to go in and talk to a woman and her family. She was in the ICU, the family had questions, and they wanted to talk to somebody who went through it. I went and the family didn't even show up except for the woman's sister who was like I can't take her in my house I have three kids. They wanted her daughter to take her and she didn't even show up. I said to my coordinator what's going to happen and she said if she doesn't have family support we can't put the LVAD in and she's going to die. I said this is insane there's people if they don't have the finances or family support they're given a death sentence.

THAT IS AWFUL. HOW ARE YOU GETTING BY NOW?

Transplant isn't even a cure. It's just a form of treatment. A lot of people don't realize that. I will never be great or healthy. Hearts are only good on average for ten years. You kind of are given like a death sentence. Lungs are good for 5-7 years. I'm hoping mine lasts for as long as possible because the other thing is not many centers do a third open-heart surgery. There are complications because of the scar tissue.

My surgeon, fortunately he's one of the best surgeons out there—my brother in law is a surgeon and he told me—he does the third. I'm in Philly we've got three centers here. I'm at Temple. Penn kicks out a lot lot people because they want to keep their numbers high so they won't do transplants for people that need a third transplant. Temple takes more high-risk patients, people who are very sick or too old. I talked to people at Temple who said they had to leave Penn because they maxed out their age in their 60s. It's almost like you have to be sick enough but also well enough to have your body go through the procedure.

THAT'S GRIMLY IRONIC

It is. I met people who were 65 who got kicked out of Penn . . . Temple does up to 70. After that I guess they don't want to put a heart in someone who's 70, there are so many people who are waiting to get an organ.

It's hard. With modern medicine and the technology out there, there are a lot of people who are surviving longer. People who can survive once-fatal car accidents and things like that. There's a company that is inventing a 3-D printed heart. When I saw that I said, man I got sick at the wrong time.

ARE YOU ABLE TO WORK AT ALL ANYMORE?

I can't work right now. I attempted to return to work and it was a failed attempt. It just adds to the overall blow of everything. My career is gone and I know I can never teach again. Right now I do a little work, my friend who is an acupuncturist, I do a little work for her. It keeps me busy. I try to get to the gym to do the cardio. I go to yoga. But there's so many appointments. I have to have an endoscope this Thursday. I've been getting sick lately and it could be my anti-rejection meds, they're so hard on the body.

HOW MUCH MONEY WOULD YOU SAY IT'S COST ALL TOGETHER?

I would say between my two surgeries I was billed way over $3 million. One of the things my social worker and I talk about is what kind of job can I return to? I can't work full-time anymore, that's out. What kind of job would provide health insurance to someone who is not working full-time?

DO YOU THINK IT'S CRIMINAL THAT PEOPLE CAN BE DEPRIVED TREATMENT BECAUSE THEY CAN'T AFFORD IT?

It is. I don't know what the answer is, I just know that it scares me to death they want to do away with the ACA and preexisting conditions protection. What happens if I do go back into the work force? Do I have a company that can deny me insurance?

WELL AT THE VERY LEAST YOU GOT TO LIVE LONG ENOUGH TO SEE THE EAGLES WIN THE SUPER BOWL.

Yeah I did! And now they stink! My dad has had season tickets since 1961 so it was exciting for him, he finally got to see them win. I used to go down to the games but now I can't. Your life really changes, the crowds, let alone I'm afraid someone sneezes on me and I'll end up with the flu. I don't want to go back to the hospital.

THE MAN WHO BOWLED A PERFECT GAME ON 9/11

SO OF COURSE EVERYTHING WAS DEAD SILENCE.

Bill Moro remembers 9/11 fondly. He'd gotten up early that morning to go to work at the paper mill like any other day. Tucked into the southwest corner of Massachusetts, not far from the New York and Connecticut borders, the area around Great Barrington, where Bill has lived his entire 67 years on earth, was once one of the centers of paper production in the country but not so much anymore due to they closed all the plants. Bill's plant, now known as Onyx Specialty Papers, the last mill in the area, sits on the Housatonic River, which travels 150 miles south from there and winds its way down into the Long Island Sound. If he'd picked up a copy of the *Berkshire Eagle* that morning Bill would've seen headlines that didn't seem all that out of the ordinary. Pittsfield's Postmaster transferred, read one. Experts say Mideast talks already in doubt another.

And then it was 9/11.

"I was at work when it happened," Bill said. "Of course we didn't have a television there, but we had a radio and a newsflash came across the radio. So of course everything was dead silence."

Bill and his co-workers finished out the day, and not knowing what else to do he said *fuck it, let's go bowling*, and man is he glad he did because it was the best game of his life. He'd never bowled so well in decades of trying. He'd never bowl so well again. Amidst the chaos and fear and uncertainty of the world changing in ways neither he nor the rest of us yet understood, Bill Moro went and bowled a perfect damn game on 9/11.

I first heard about Bill's game this summer when someone on Twitter posted a picture of him. When you bowl a perfect game at the Cove Lanes there in Great Barrington where he lives they go and put your photo on the wall as a way of commemorating a memorable and festive occasion.

I knew instantly I wanted to talk to Bill when I saw the photo but he wasn't so easy to track down. I reached out to the bowling alley and after a couple weeks Juanita O'Rourke one of the owners wrote me back.

"I do believe that the bowler who bowled the 300 on 9/11 no longer bowls at the Cove and has not for many years," she told me. "I do not have contact information for him although I do believe he is local. Hope that gives you something to go on," she wrote. "Sorry I'm not much help."

O'Rourke bought the lanes with two of her nephews in 2003. Both of the nephews had worked there doing odd jobs in exchange for unlimited video games when they were kids, and the timing was perfect for one of them, Michael Hankey, to try something new because he'd lost his job of 10 years at the Rising Mill when new ownership closed it down the year before. Built in 1873, the Rising Mill was once the biggest employer in the area, and was listed on the Register of Historic Places in 1975.

I asked everyone I knew from the Berkshire County region if they knew anyone named Bill Moro. Why, they'd ask. Uh . . . Because I saw he bowled a perfect game on 9/11 and I wanted to interview him about that, I said, which made me feel like a pervert of some kind. Being a reporter is weird.

And then, finally, on 9/11 of this year, I found what I thought might be the number and address for a William Moro in Great Barrington. Could it be him? Would he even still be alive?

It was our man. The man. Bill the man.

His lovely wife answered the phone and didn't seem all that surprised when I explained sheepishly what I was calling about. "Seventeen years ago today he bowled a perfect game down there," she told me with pride. It was as if they'd been waiting for someone to call this entire time.

Bill and I had a great chat, and then tragedy struck anew: the next day my computer crashed. *Motherfucker.*

The interview, along with a ton of other work I'd been doing, disappeared forever. Was I getting too close to the truth?

A couple months later I said screw it and decided I'd call Bill back and do it all over again. We'd had a great chat and I didn't want to let his story go untold. He was happy to oblige me. After all 9/11 was one of the best days of his life.

Bill and I talked about his big game, the changes to Great Barrington and the paper industry, and his opinions on everything from Donald Trump and Bernie Sanders, to, well, let's just say the pins weren't the only thing Bill was surprised to see fall so fast that day.

WALK ME THROUGH THE GAME THAT NIGHT. WHEN WAS IT?

Well, we started at 6:30 in the evening for practice, and then at 7 the league starts. So of course everybody was talking about the events of the day.

AND YOU ALL DECIDED, DESPITE WHAT HAPPENED, YOU MIGHT AS WELL GO BOWLING ANYWAY?

Yeah. They still held the leagues. Everybody else was going to be there and they didn't cancel anything, so all the teams showed up.

HOW REGULARLY HAD YOU BEEN BOWLING?

Once a week. We bowled every Tuesday night.

TELL ME A LITTLE MORE ABOUT THE DAY.

I was at work when it happened. Of course we didn't have a television there, but we had a radio and a newsflash came across the radio. So of course everything was dead silence. We're listening and listening to all the things that are going on. We stayed at work. When I got out of work I went home and watched the news, got home probably 3:30ish, had supper, then I got ready to go bowling. Just had the TV on all the while listening to all the updates, and the reruns, the constant reruns they were showing.

When we got to the lanes of course everybody was talking there and they had TVs on at the bar. It was a lot of conversation about . . . wondering what would happen next.

DO YOU REMEMBER WHAT YOU WERE ALL THINKING? WERE YOU SCARED? DID YOU THINK WE WERE GOING TO GO TO WAR?

Well, we knew it was a terrorist attack, and the investigation was where they came from, how they got in, how they managed to do all that. It was a high alert for everything, railroads, planes. Of course they grounded all the planes. There was no war, we weren't worried about war, but the talk was about getting back at them. Find out who did it and strike back.

WAS THAT YOUR FIRST PERFECT GAME?

Yes! My one and only. It was fantastic. I had been bowling steadily in leagues probably, let's see, I started in leagues when I was around twenty-eight or so. I'm sixty-seven years old now.

WAS IT COMMON FOR OTHER GUYS IN THE LEAGUE TO BOWL PERFECT GAMES?

Well there's a few guys that . . . they have a lot of pictures on the walls down there of people who bowled 300. Once you get one they put your picture up. There's some guys, I've got a couple of nephews, I think one of them has probably 30 perfect games.

WOW, THAT'S CRAZY.

I never bowled a perfect game again. I haven't bowled in probably 12–13 years now.

WHY DID YOU STOP?

Because of the establishment. They weren't taking care of the facilities very well. The league started, well, we think they were screwing around with the money, so our team voted to drop right out. We got tired of it.

YOU DIDN'T GO TO ANOTHER LANE?

The only one nearby is up in Pittsfield, about 14 miles from here. It wasn't worth traveling all the way up there, bowl for two and a half, three hours, then come back late at night.

YEAH THAT DOESN'T MAKE SENSE. YOU RECENTLY RETIRED FROM THE PAPER MILL YOU WORKED AT?

I'm gonna retire next March. I'll have fifty years in. Now it's called Onxy Specialty Papers.

WHAT EXACTLY DO YOU DO?

Personally? I finish and ship rolls. It's a machine, you're operating a machine, and then you're on a clamp truck, where you load trailers. You do office paper work . . . I started in the paper mill when I was 18.

WHAT'S CHANGED ABOUT IT SINCE THEN?

There's a lot. The progress of the equipment, different papers they make, new procedures. A lot of changes in fifty years!

PEOPLE DON'T SEEM TO USE AS MUCH PAPER AS WE USED TO, RIGHT?

Well it depends on the papers now. It's different papers that we make. It's a specialty. It's not writing paper, it's not newspaper, it's papers they use in transmissions, friction papers. One of our biggest items now is a blood paper they use for sampling blood that goes all over the country. We make paper for laminates.

I GUESS PEOPLE DON'T REALLY THINK ABOUT PAPER THAT MUCH.

Exactly!

WERE YOU IN A UNION THERE?

No they never had a union. They had a couple of votes years ago and they never passed, so we've never been unionized.

THEY TREAT YOU OK THOUGH?

Yeah. The pay is good and the benefits are good.

THE REASON WHY I'M INTERESTED IN YOUR STORY IS BECAUSE THERE'S SOMETHING FASCINATING ABOUT GOING BOWLING DIRECTLY AFTER A TERRORIST ATTACK, RIGHT?

Well that was the concept. Rudy Giuliani, at the time, said America's gonna go about their duty, we're not gonna let this divert us in any way. We're America, we're not gonna be scared by this. Everybody should do what they do, and we did. The whole country did. We didn't just stop. We had jobs to go to, functions to go to.

DO YOU REMEMBER WHAT PEOPLE WERE SAYING, ANY CONVERSATIONS?

No, just discussing who did it and why and how they managed to get on board. You can think about it now, but there's all these conspiracy theories they have out there now too. I've been looking at a lot of that online.

YOU FIND IT A LITTLE SUSPICIOUS HOW THE BUILDINGS CAME DOWN, RIGHT?

Oh yeah. When you hear experts say it was a planned demolition, the way they came down. Thermite and different things that were used, and how fast they cleaned up and got rid of evidence. You gotta admit they did a quick job cleaning up that mess to get things back in order. And Building 7, which was not effected at all. That just came down? That was very suspicious to me.

DO YOU BELIEVE ANY OF THESE OTHER CONSPIRACY THEORIES THEY HAVE GOING AROUND NOW?

Well, there's a few. The biggest one they were talking about on the news just recently was about the Kennedy assassination. The anniversary of that. The government hiding things.

WHO DO YOU THINK DID THAT?

Oh, well, from what I understand Johnson had a lot to do with it. He and Kennedy were always feuding. Kennedy said something or did something to Johnson and Johnson said he wasn't going to let him get away with it. They had an interview with Johnson's mistress. She gave a lot of evidence too, so . . .

INTERESTING. THE WORLD IS PRETTY CRAZY.

It is.

YOU'RE NOT A TRUMP GUY THOUGH, RIGHT? WHAT DO YOU THINK ABOUT HIM?

No! I despise the man. He's not doing a good job at all. I don't like his arrogance. He's manipulative. He wants to be like Putin. He wants to be a tyrant. He wants total control, control over the judiciary, over everything. He gives his family, who are not qualified for the positions, he gives them positions.

WERE YOU A CLINTON SUPPORTER?

Well . . . Much of what she did was good, but because of all the allegations and stuff, we were kind of tired of Clinton for a while. Eight years of her husband, then all her positions in the State Department and everything else. I really don't know, just time for new blood.

WHAT ABOUT BERNIE?

Bernie had very good ideas for the people. Universal health care, that's one of the big topics. One thing Trump wanted was to get rid of was Obamacare. He was gonna make it better: repeal and replace, all that. He hasn't done anything for healthcare!

YOU PREFER CANDIDATES THAT CARE ABOUT WORKING PEOPLE.

Absolutely. The rich are getting richer. The tax plan just showed that. That was supposed to be trickle down. Look what's happening with GM now. Closing plants, thousands of people are going to be out of work. It's just not working.

WHAT'S GREAT BARRINGTON, MASSACHUSETTS, LIKE? KIND OF ARTSY AND CUTE?

Yeah it's a tourist place now. Antique stores, just a lot of shops. A quaint little town.

HAS IT CHANGED SINCE YOU WERE A KID?

Yes it has. It's gotten . . . it's changed a lot for the wealthy people. You've got tourists that come in from the cities, so that changes prices and attitudes. Some of the out-of-towners have gotten involved in restructuring the view of the town. They redid the whole Main Street, which is a mess. It's not very good.

DID THEY PUT A MARIJUANA DISPENSARY OUT THERE? WHAT DO YOU THINK ABOUT THAT?

We have one here. I never had marijuana. I don't do drugs, never did. So I don't . . . I guess it's ok. If alcohol is legal they're just going to have to monitor it the same way they do alcohol.

I THINK I READ SOMEWHERE THAT COVE LANES WAS SUPPOSED TO BE AN INFLUENCE ON THE FARRELLY BROTHERS. YOU KNOW THOSE GUYS?

No I don't know them. I never heard that.

THEY MADE THE MOVIE KING PIN. YOU EVER SEE THAT?

Yes, I've seen that!

DO YOU HAVE A FAVORITE BOWLING MOVIE?

Oh, I don't know that there are many.

WHAT ABOUT THE BIG LEBOWSKI?

Nope.

OH YOU GOTTA WATCH IT. IT'S SO GOOD.

I MADE SOME VERY, VERY BAD DECISIONS

I CANNOT FEEL SORRY FOR HIM I'M SORRY

One of the great things about being the chief of police of Biscayne Park is that they are truly a family there Raimundo Atesiano said at a community meeting in the village just north of Miami in 2013 according to the *Miami Herald*.

"A family who works together and is joined by one common cause which is the protection of life and property for the residents of the village of Biscayne Park," he said pointing his mustache at the crowd very policely and then he brought up detective Raul Fernandez and said that thanks to officers like him they had a 100 percent clearance rate of burglaries that year.

"This is the first time I've ever known that to happen in any department I've ever been in," Atesiano said and everyone clapped because that's good police work you have to agree even for such a small and typically tranquil little village like this one. I don't think anyone is going to look at those numbers and get too pissed off about it.

Shortly before he had gone up there to talk about how good they were at solving crimes Atesiano and the boys had collared a couple of perps which is how cops talk and pinned four burglaries on a local teen, two home burglaries on a man named Clarence Desrouleaux, and five car burglaries on a man named Erasmus Banmah who were not white if you were wondering what particular racial makeup they had. Desrouleaux got deported to Haiti on account of the burgling they had said he was up to.

The weirdest thing happened though because the chief of police went to jail himself due to it turns out he and Fernandez and a few others on the force made all that shit up.

"Atesiano admitted that on one occasion he instructed an officer to falsely arrest and charge an individual for several vehicle burglaries based upon what Atesiano knew were false confessions," a statement from the U.S. Attorney's office in Southern Florida explained.

"According to the documents, Atesiano intentionally encouraged officers to arrest individuals without a legal basis in order to have arrests effectuated for all reported burglaries, which created a fictitious 100 percent clearance rate for that category of crime."

One of the officers explained the marching orders as he understood them after an internal probe was launched in 2014:

> If they have burglaries that are open cases that are not solved yet, if you see anybody black walking through our streets and they have somewhat of a record, arrest them so we can pin them for all the burglaries. They were basically doing this to have a 100 percent clearance rate for the city.

"When I took the job, I was not prepared," Atesiano told the judge at his sentencing hearing. "I made some very, very bad decisions."

He'll go to prison now for three years although he was granted a couple weeks before surrendering to care for his mother who was dying from leukemia which is sad to think about even though he did that other shit.

When we still had dreams we used to live in a shitty little third-floor walkup in Somerville that probably goes for $3,000 a month now and we'd stay up all night and one time my friend was so out of his mind he sat on the stove for a while and didn't realize he had actually turned the burner on and he singed a hole right into his ass cheek and another time he put the CD player in the stove and turned it on and I'm not sure what the thinking behind that was but I'm sure he had his reasons. One time I found a little bag of powder on the door step of the large rowdy Russian boys who lived downstairs and loved EDM although no one knew to call it EDM at that time and I took it and was worried about two things after that which were that I might die off of it and/or they would know it was me and come up and stomp my ass in and things of that nature although neither thing happened.

We'd stand around in the kitchen there smoking cigarettes inside like psychopaths and then the next day we'd crawl back into the light and order takeout and watch TV and since we didn't have cable there was only two things ever on one of which was an infomercial for the Ronco Showtime Rotisserie & BBQ where they'd whip the audience into this uncanny mass hypnosis and have them chant the catch phrase that you probably remember.

Ronco filed for bankruptcy in 2018 but Ron Popeil the man behind the onetime-proud marketing empire sold his stake in the company for around $55 million in 2005 so he's fine you don't have to worry about old Ron Popeil whose cousin is Ashley Tisdale. I'm not sure how that works since he's 83 and she's 33 but they do things a little differently out there in Beverly Hills.

The other thing that was always on was *Law & Order* and I watched so much of that. They wanted you to get really upset when the Internal Affairs guys came in and jammed the detectives up. The rat squad is what they called them but those guys were actually the heroes of the show I realized a few years later and I also realized that Elliot Stabler belongs in prison.

Another popular commercial you probably remember was one known as the "Willie Horton" ad which was produced by supporters of George H. W. Bush for his 1988 presidential campaign against Michael

Dukakis. The ad detailed a series of crimes committed by Horton, a convicted murderer, who went on to rape a woman while on a weekend furlough from prison in Massachusetts where Dukakis was governor at the time. While Bush supported the death penalty for first-degree murderers, the narrator in the ad said, "Dukakis not only opposed the death penalty, he allowed first degree murderers to have weekend passes from prison."

One of those murderers was shown in a menacing-looking black and white mug shot and it was Willie Horton "who murdered a boy in a robbery, stabbing him 19 times."

"Despite a life sentence Horton received ten weekend passes from prison. Horton fled, kidnapped a young couple, stabbing the man and repeatedly raping his girlfriend. Weekend prison passes: Dukakis on crime."

"By the time we're finished, they're going to wonder whether Willie Horton is Dukakis's running mate," Bush's campaign manager Lee Atwater said.

A second ad they showed during the campaign was called the "Revolving Door" ad that talked about how Dukakis vetoed mandatory sentences for drug dealers and vetoed the death penalty both of which seem like pretty good ideas to me but I never got elected president so I don't know. I bought an apple at 7-Eleven for breakfast this morning and didn't wash it before eating it so I don't know anything.

In any case the subtext of the ads weren't very subtle in that the liberal pansy Dukakis was going to let the scary black guys come rape your girlfriend while George Bush would not do that and thankfully we don't hear that sort of thing in political ads any more today.

Weirdly even Roger Stone seemed to think the ad was a bit much he said years later but he lies about a lot of things so who's to say what's real or not.

"I went into the headquarters to see Atwater, at his request," he said in a PBS documentary on Atwater's life. "He locked the office door, and he popped the famous Willie Horton spot onto a television. He said, 'I got a couple boys going to put a couple million dollars up for this independent.' And I said, 'That's a huge mistake. You and George Bush will wear that to your grave. It's a racist ad. You're already wining this issue. It's working for you. You're stepping over a line. You're going to regret it.' And he said, 'Y'all a pussy.'"

Stone was right though because while the people you might expect all praised Bush as a temperate patriotic man who wanted the best for the country when he died in November of 2018 the rest of the people I know were talking about all the other shameful shit he did.

A couple years after the election when he was dying from brain cancer Atwater apologized for producing the most famous racist ad in history.

"In 1988, fighting Dukakis, I said that I 'would strip the bark off the little bastard' and 'make Willie Horton his running mate.' I am sorry for both statements: the first for its naked cruelty, the second because it makes me sound racist, which I am not."

February "marks my fortieth birthday, that deadline I set for achieving my life's goals," Atwater told the *New York Times* in 1991. "I lie here in my bedroom, my face swollen from steroids, my body useless and in pain. I will probably never play the guitar or run again; I can only hope to walk."

I feel bad for him for dying like that just like I feel bad for that corrupt cop taking care of his dying mother, but, you know, not as bad as I feel about other people.

Atwater was nominated for a Grammy that year for a record he made with B. B. King which I think we can all agree to say wait what? when we read that sentence.

"The doctors still won't answer that nagging question of mine: How long do I have?" Atwater went on. "Three weeks. Three months. Three years?"

"I try to live as if I have at least three years, but some nights I can't go to sleep, so fearful am I that I will never wake up again."

Another thing Bush did when he was president was to engineer a drug bust in Lafayette Park across from the White House to illustrate a politically expedient point about the war on drugs. He held up a bag of crack and said it had been seized just outside the White House can you believe this shit? But it had actually been purchased in a sting.

William McMullan, one of the special agents on the job, told the *Washington Post* that it "was not easy to get the dealer [Keith Jackson] to come to Lafayette Park because he did not even know where the White House was."

"I don't think any neighborhood is free from selling drugs," Bush said in a testy exchange with reporters on a tree farm near his home in Kennebunkport, Maine, after the stunt. "I mean, the man was caught selling drugs in front of the White House. I think it can happen in any neighborhood, and I think that's what it dramatized."

"I don't understand. I mean, has somebody got some advocates here for this drug guy?" he snapped at the reporters. "I cannot feel sorry for him. I'm sorry, they ought not to be peddling these insidious drugs that ruin the children of this country," he said.

When he was given a sentence of ten years without parole the judge in the case told Jackson that he should ask the president for a commutation.

"He used you, in the sense of making a big drug speech," said Judge Stanley Sporkin, former CIA general counsel appointed to court by President Reagan in 1986. "But he's a decent man, a man of great compassion. Maybe he can find a way to reduce at least some of that sentence."

He didn't do that though.

"This is a major part of Bush's legacy," Joshua Clark Davis, a University of Baltimore assistant professor in history, tweeted in a thread in December laying out much of the details here. "It's what his War on Drugs did to just one person. But it shows the human costs of that war in miniature detail. A high-schooler was lured to the WH to sell crack and spent 7+ years in prison, so that the President could make a point on TV."

In 2016 his son Jeb struck a different tone on drugs when he was running for president. His daughter had been caught up in the spiral of addiction to opiates and crack and gotten into trouble with the law so he had developed empathy for the issue which is the only way you can get a Republican to experience empathy by having something bad happen to someone they care about.

Some of the things Jeb's campaign said they wanted to do were increase federal support for prevention programs and enact tougher sentences on cartels but also to lower mandatory minimums for non-violent drug offenders and expand access to drug courts so offenders could have monitored treatment which sounds like some wimpy Dukakis shit to me.

Michelle and I go to Kennebunkport every summer now to visit old college friends of mine one of whose parents have a house there near the beach and they all rent a cottage for the week but we don't do that we just go for a night or two because we can't really afford it. They all have kids and are doctors and lawyers and things like that and I say how's the legal practice or hospital or university you're a professor at and all your lovely children and nice house you own and they say it's great I saw you had a viral tweet lately.

It's one of my favorite times of the year because I genuinely care about my old friends even though we don't talk all that much and it's been a long time since college but they are good people and they seem to care about me even though I'm not a particularly good person.

The beach there is called Goose Rocks and it is one of my favorite places in the world even though I don't particularly like a lot of the people who go there since it's a pretty Republican town vis-à-vis the Bush connection. Often times when you go there people will suggest going to have a look at the Bush compound as a thing that you can go ahead and do while on vacation but what I usually say to that is no thank you. Last year I screamed at some guys I thought were Republicans while we were sitting around a fire at a fancy restaurant they have there and I said you're fucking racists and things like that and they got up and left and then Michelle told me they were actually agreeing with me but I didn't hear them which sounds like it's a metaphor about bridging the political divide or something but it's not it's just a lesson about not talking about politics while you're drinking.

One thing I do instead of going to look at where the president's nice house is is I walk out into the water at the beach there and keep walking until I can't walk anymore and then I have to start swimming. The water is warmer there than you would expect and I float out as far as I can and let the waves push me around and Michelle gets nervous and asks me not to go out so far where she can't see me and I try to do that but it's one of the only times I am ever really happy floating out there looking back to the shore where some people who love me are standing and talking and laughing and there they are hello everyone I'm here you can't see me so well but I'm here and we're here together and we're still here floating along near where the famous dead president used to live.

PEOPLE TEND TO LIKE IT SHE SAID

FLAMES WERE COMING FROM A HUMAN BEING

Jackie Crow lost one hundred pounds and she's very proud of that fact and why wouldn't she be that's almost an entire adult human being that she doesn't need to carry around with her anymore. If you lived for years with a one-hundred-pound person riding around on your back and then one day they got off like ok I'm done with the piggyback ride now you'd be elated. Imagine how much more lightly you could step.

Jackie Crow lost the weight by working as a delivery driver for Amazon although not really *working* working for Amazon it was working for herself is what they call it and Amazon just happened to tell her where and when to do the work and monitored how efficiently she did the work all the while being able to increase or decrease her opportunities to do the work whenever they decided. Still it's a job right. It's not though but still right.

Three years ago Jackie Crow who is almost fifty years old was diagnosed with rheumatoid arthritis when she weighed three hundred pounds so she needed to make some changes in her life and when the gig with Amazon Flex came along she made the most of it.

"I feel great. I have more energy, I'm active, I don't need a walker anymore," Jackie Crow told KSHB in Kansas City and we know about her story because Amazon the company with almost $180 billion in revenue a year owned by the richest man in the history of the world shared the piece on Twitter and you have to admit it is pretty generous of them to allow Jackie Crow to lose all that weight.

"Amazon Flex allowed this woman to lose 100 lbs in 18 months by creating a workout while delivering packages," Amazon News tweeted.

Imagine if you had $140 billion like Jeff Bezos and then lost $139 billion of it. Imagine how much more lightly you could step.

People think we live in a harrowing dystopia but the world is really a lot dumber than that. This sounds like something out of Philip K. Dick or whatever similar dude you care to think of but as many people pointed out it's literally an episode of *Nathan for You* and I'd say that's fair that's about what we deserve. The real twist of the knife of Hell World is that we get to slowly boil through the invention of all the punishments of techno-futuristic space capitalism without even living long enough to see the cool stuff like Moon Baseball.

"Amazon Flex allows drivers like Crow the flexibility of picking their own work schedules," is what KSHB wrote about the whole situation with Jackie Crow and they also said the flexibility of the job helped her have time for her family and to help with the other job she has at their family pizza shop. You can be so much more flexible when you aren't given set hours at a job and it's nice to be able to come and go and work whenever you want without the responsibility or benefits of a full time job everyone knows that. Jackie Crow also said the extra money she makes helps her pay for her son's college.

"I use it as a way to get my heart rate up," Jackie Crow said over footage of her jogging briskly up the stairs in the news report. "Amazon!" she says outside the door bending down to drop off the package in a voice that sort of breaks my heart a little. Maybe she says it like that usually or maybe she thought she had to put a little extra something on it because the TV cameras were there. It's not easy to bend down like that when you have arthritis you'd have to guess.

"I'm constantly looking at my watch," she says on the TV and that's probably partly for her health but also because Amazon Flex workers are incentivized to do as many deliveries as possible in as short a period of time because they're all competing for a limited number of gigs available in their area on any given day so you have to go so fast.

I called Amazon Flex just now to see about signing up to get some extra work and the woman at the call center told me I could make no less than $18 and up to $25 an hour delivering packages in my area but a report from Bloomberg said it actually ends up being between $5 and $11 an hour when you factor in expenses like gas and tolls and wear and tear on your automobile because you have to use your own car don't be fucking stupid they aren't going to give you a car to use where would they get cars for their business from?

"Package runs are timed, and workers are kicked off the system for missing delivery windows, which creates an incentive to run red lights, double-park and go over the speed limit, drivers say," according to Bloomberg. "After an assignment, Flex workers are sometimes required to bring goods they were unable to deliver back to the warehouse. The trip is unpaid and can take an hour or more but is necessary to stay in good standing with the company."

UPS pays about $36 an hour plus expenses and the American Postal Workers Union says workers make around $75,000 a year. My uncle was a postal worker most of his life and he raised a few kids and owns a home and seems to have had a happy life but now he has Parkinson's disease which is what killed his father my grandfather and will probably kill me? Remind me to look up if that is hereditary.

I asked the Amazon Flex rep what I needed to do to sign up today.

"Do you have a vehicle with four doors? Do you have a driver's license, insurance?" the nice woman from the Amazon Flex call center said. They also require a background check she said.

"Once you get accepted and you have the app downloaded onto your phone, you will be able to pick up delivery shifts and it will let you know on the app, if it's a block between say 12:30-4:30, it has a certain amount of packages you need to pick up and it will let you know how much you will earn for that four hours. You pick them up, everything is self-explanatory in the app, it's step by step, you punch in when you arrive, then you get paid. Pay usually goes out on Tuesday and Fridays. It starts at $18 depending on the size of your vehicle and how many packages you can deliver. It varies from $18-$25."

There are no limits on how much I can work she told me but there are sadly no benefits offered.

"You're considered an independent contractor so it's like you're working for yourself, you're just being able to deliver for Amazon."

Do people actually . . . like the job?

"People tend to like it," she said. "They like the pay. Who doesn't like to get paid?"

One way I've been thinking about trying to lose some weight myself is to not drink 1,000 calories of whiskey every night. I haven't consulted a dietician or anything but that seems like altogether too many calories of whiskey. On nights when I don't drink I really look forward to it since the experience of not drinking is relatively novel to me in the past two years since my body and brain and heart broke.

In June of 1963 Thich Quang Duc a Vietnamese Buddhist monk burned himself alive on the streets of Saigon as a form of protest against the persecution of Buddhists by the South Vietnamese government. The president at the time Ngo Dinh Diem was a Catholic in a country that was around 90 percent Buddhist and as such set policies that were favorable to Catholics in terms of military and government promotions and land distribution and so on basically the same shit that happens everywhere when any asshole gets into power. It's weird how there are only a few variations on the type of powerful asshole we end up getting over and over again.

Some Catholic priests operated their own private armies I guess and Buddhist pagodas were often raided and destroyed and the people were generally fucked with in all the ways you would expect.

One of the reasons he had gone and set himself on fire was because of some violence the month before. People had taken to the streets of the city of Huế waving Buddhist flags on a holy day and this was a crime. On the other hand Diem had encouraged his people to wave Vatican flags during a celebration for his brother who was a Catholic archbishop a few weeks earlier so this really pissed people off. The celebration soon turned into a protest and the government went in with guns and grenades and people drove automobiles into the crowds and next thing nine people were dead.

The photographer Malcolme Brown was on hand for the self-immolation and he went on to win a Pulitzer Prize for his famous photo of Thích Quảng Đức burning himself quietly and silently there in the street in front of the Cambodian embassy and it is a very good photo but you have to admit that it's a little unfair that he was the one who won a prize off of it since he really didn't do that much of the labor involved here did he.

David Halberstam of the *New York Times* was there as well and here is what he wrote about it in his book *The Making of a Quagmire: America And Vietnam During The Kennedy Era*:

> Flames were coming from a human being; his body was slowly withering and shriveling up, his head blackening and charring. In the air was the smell of burning human flesh; human beings burn surprisingly quickly. Behind me I could hear the sobbing of the Vietnamese who were now gathering. I was too shocked to cry, too confused to take notes or ask questions, too bewildered to even think . . . As he burned he never moved a muscle, never uttered a sound, his outward

composure in sharp contrast to the wailing people around him.

Things pretty much went to shit on account of that and the ensuing unrest. In November an army coup backed by the U.S. revolted against Diem. He didn't have much support left at this point and the CIA said lol go for it. Diem and his brother tried to escape through a tunnel in their church but that didn't work vis-à-vis they got shot to death and then not long after that the U.S. would get involved in the war in Vietnam and next thing a couple million people were dead.

The house I grew up in is so old and the walls are so old they sort of warped out over the centuries and the ceilings are so low because people were a lot shorter then is what we were always told. It was built in 1766 by a guy named Nathaniel Bradford who was the great grandson I think of William Bradford the first governor or Plymouth Colony. He fled his country due to religious persecution.

If that makes it sound like it's some fancy preserved historic home or something that people would come all the way over to there to look at it wasn't it was a piece of shit and I think my parents paid like $20,000 for it in the eighties. There was an outhouse still connected to it and the room where my mother smokes her cigarettes and watches Fox News every night now didn't have a floor back then it was dirt. It's nicer now since my stepfather who is my father made it a lot nicer. My bedroom on the second floor had a ceiling so low that if I had wanted to I could have squatted down and jumped really hard and fast and snapped my neck on it but I never ended up doing that.

I was thinking about the photo of Quảng Đức because I read a piece in the *New York Times Magazine*'s "Letter of Recommendation" column about the band Rage Against the Machine and I remembered I had printed out a photo of the cover of their first album which showed him burning to death and that just about blew my mind as a teenager. I thought it was the coolest thing I'd ever seen so I taped it up on my wall. Not cool but you know what I mean. The sincerity of it.

In the piece Jonah Weiner writes that he first learned about Quảng Đức and a host of other protests and instances of government corruption from that album which is also true for me and then he wrote something that I think about sometimes about how we have to convince ourselves at some point as we get older that being pissed off about that sort of thing is somehow the realm of misguided youth like it's immature to walk around fucking rip shit all the time about how people are being taken advantage of by the powerful and always will be.

> There's a cynical conception of 'maturity' that asks us to disavow things we believed in our youth, not because they were shameful but precisely because they were virtuous. In this view, adolescent dalliances with Rage Against the Machine—like dalliances with vegetarianism and Howard Zinn—reflect an idealism we're meant not to carry into adulthood but, rather, sagely slough off. The prerogatives of the machine, to use [Zach] de la Rocha's shorthand, are mistaken for immutable forces of nature; bending in deference to them, we become the compromised adults our younger selves knew better than to trust.

Around that time I went to my first-ever real concert which was Lollapalooza 1993 and it was held at an Air Force field or something in Rhode Island. The first band that day was Rage Against the Machine and as you can probably guess they just about broke all of our brains. Another thing that happened that day is my girlfriend at the time fainted in the crowd and we had to leave early so I don't remember if I got to see Alice in Chains. That might have been Lollapalooza 1994 actually but in any case she was my first love and she fainted a lot back then and I think I sort of thought of her as a delicate swooning character out of a Brontë sisters novel but now that I think of it again she was probably just starving herself all the time and passing out due to that but no one really knew how to talk about or worry about that since it was the nineties. One time she gave me a Mazzy Star CD single of "Fade Into You" which is still just about the best song I've ever heard.

We didn't drink much back then none of us really did in my group. We'd go skateboarding behind the supermarket although I fucking sucked at it so I'd usually just videotape things and make goofy skits and shit like that. I don't know if I'd want to watch any of those videos right now but my mother has been asking me to come get my sentimental shit out of that room with the low ceilings for like fifteen years and I always say I don't care throw it out throw out the pictures of my old friends and girlfriends like the one who fainted a lot and old papers I wrote and letters people sent me. I say *whatever ma* to my mother like I'm still the exact same age as when I accumulated all that shit but I secretly hope she doesn't throw it out just between you and me.

The thing about not drinking is it makes you realize how long a day is. A day is so much longer than you really think it is when you're there for all of it but life is very short and it goes by so quickly you barely even notice.

They say when John F. Kennedy saw the picture of Quảng Đức the one thing he said was Jesus Christ which is about what you would think someone would say especially a Catholic like he was and I was for most of my life. I guess I still am by default. I'm not sure if you can get that stuff off of you once you've been steeped in it long enough.

One time when I was a young boy I'm not sure how old I got my hands on a copy of Dante's *Inferno* and that fucked me up pretty good I'm not going to lie about that. Some other time I drew a picture of my church burning down and the priest Father Mike I think his name was was also there in the picture I drew was that his name Mom and then I had to go talk to some professionals or something I don't really remember. It turns out I had probably just been fucked up by hearing about how much I was going to suffer some day in a pool of fire when I was a little boy. Imagine if you lived your entire life believing that a deity was watching your every move and tabulating every misstep you made and that if you fucked up enough times you'd be tortured to death forever and then you managed to shed some of the weight of that. Imagine how much more lightly you could step.

WE MET BY THE MOON ON A SILVERY LAKE

IT'S MEANT FOR ONE SPECIFIC PERSON WHO WILL LIKELY NEVER SEE IT

People tend to say the comments section on YouTube videos are one of the nastiest corners of the internet and that's saying a lot because there are enough nasty corners on there you'd have to invent an uncanny geometric shape that doesn't seem natural to hold them all. That's not a shape you'd say but it is some nerd would insist. Hmm you'd say all right man I'm not the shape expert. Fuck you motherfucker he'd say and then it's a whole thing and that's how the internet goes.

It's true that the comments section on YouTube videos are nasty because people are nasty and the internet is a performance-enhancing drug for our nastiness but there is another thing that is true about the comments section on YouTube videos and it is that they're also one of the most nakedly human and vulnerable spaces we have left and when you come across sincerity online it's shocking it's like finding a burnt onion ring in the bottom of your order of fries. What the fuck is that oh I see I don't want that that doesn't belong here but you eat it anyway and it was pretty good.

People talk about lately how whatever it is they start watching on YouTube the recommended videos always end up bringing them to some corrosive white nationalist garbage like Jordan Peterson or Ben Shapiro videos or videos where *Sound of Music*-looking ass teens play video games like *I.Q. Genius* where the goal is to measure as many scalps with a caliper as you can before the time runs out but that doesn't happen to me for some reason. YouTube knows my Brain Force is too resistant and cannot be overpowered is probably what it is. In any case the gremlins that pull the steampunk levers in my own personal YouTube algorithm seem to have decided of late that no matter what video I begin watching I then want to hear a song from *Siamese Dream* by the Smashing Pumpkins next and they are correct about that.

I thought I'd let the YouTube algorithm take me on its data point journey and see what humanity people were experiencing for a little while. Here are some of the comments on the songs it showed me.

Smashing Pumpkins, "Mayonaise"

- "I didn't understand it at the age I was, but my dad once scrolled past it on the radio and frantically tried to find it again. As it played, I could visibly see his eyes wet and shining, talking about he and his friends taking a drive in an open convertible years ago. This song makes me remember that memory like it was my own."

- "Met a pretty french girl while in Montreal and asked her on a date . . . we went to the Pumpkins show at the Metropolis. That was over 25 years ago, since then we wed, had 2 kids and we still get euphoric ever time we hear this song. Stop, listen and enjoy it while you can, trust me, im now 51 and time flies by faster than you think."

- "i got twenty-one days for drug possession charges last summer, i lost my job, my girlfriend left, and all i had left was my empty apartment and my record player. this album was one of the few that wasn't popped and scratched to hell, and upon making it to this song i realized my life isnt over. even if i truly thought it was, i found a way to pull myself out, just like this song said i would. now i've got a new job and a new life ahead of me. it's not over."

- · · "my wife surprised me at our wedding with this song as our first dance. one of those moments I always visualized with a great song like this. to have it happen was something else."

It's been twenty-five years since this album came out. I would have been sixteen at the time which is an impossible age to imagine being it seems like it was yesterday but it was not it was twenty five years ago. I tried to visualize what I would have been doing when we were first listening to this album just now I know we went to see them play it at the Lollapalooza I mentioned earlier and then I went to see the band a few more times later on and they fucking sucked I thought but the image that came to mind which may be a pastiche of other memories is my friend Richie throwing a Frisbee into the wind on the beach in Duxbury. We'd drive along the curving marsh roads past where all the rich people live and I'd think about how nice it would be to live in one of those houses that basically have their toes dangling into the water not for long though lol and I guess I probably imagined that sort of life was an attainable one where you built a home by the water and put up a moat around it and kept people like me away. Richie would throw the Frisbee into the wind and I would throw the Frisbee into the wind and it would seem like it was going to disappear forever out over the ocean but the wind would boomerang it back and you'd either catch it or you wouldn't. Sometimes we'd try to do acrobatic little jumps catching it. He was a lot better at the whole thing than I ever was I will admit but I kept trying it over and over.

I went back to that beach for the first time in years at the end of the summer just over a year ago and it was about to storm and so cold but I had to get into the water anyway. You walk across a long wooden bridge to get to the beach and then you jump in and it fucking sucks so bad it's so cold and there are rocks and seaweed everywhere ah fuck fuck but you're glad you did it afterwards is the point because a life where you can't get into the ocean is no life in my opinion. Every few years I have to return to my ancestral homelands to replenish myself in the sea like getting your driver's license renewed.

Smashing Pumpkins, "Rhinoceros"

- "I remember being about 4 years old when this song came out, standing in a pizza parlor while my dad was ordering pizza and watching this music video play on the TV in total awe."
- "Me, 13 years old, in the back of a bus on a scouting trip returning home from staying on a battleship in charleston, rain is pouring, ad [sic] I have this song on full blast in my hearphones, [sic] dreaming about the girl I met for those 4 days."

I think we're supposed to snicker at these people who leave comments like these on videos for strangers to read and there are probably times when that is the appropriate response but for me it's not this particular day in my life.

People think over-sharing has become an epidemic and it has in some ways but I think what we're thinking about when we think about the ways people are over-sharing online is a manufactured version of who we are the immaculate Instagram life or the irony-poisoned sociopathy of Twitter. But all of these people who leave comments like these on songs that mean a lot to them are the point of music in the first place I think. It's about erecting a sonic space where humans can spill into and find one another inside of the noise. Also it's a good soundtrack for trying to find someone to touch your gross ass but that's secondary to the point I'm trying to make right now so don't think about that too much.

Built to Spill, "Carry the Zero"

- "Sometimes when I am alone, I think of all the regrets in my life . . . I just wanted to kill myself and disappear . . . Never to exist. But then I listen to this song . . . Maybe I am not the only one suffering . . . Maybe I could stay alive a little more."

- "man, how cant I even explain what this song means, nostalgia is probably the closest we can get to the 'life flashing before your eyes feel' pockets of feelings, time, space, and the people around you. theres just no mistake; I know exactly where I was, what I was doing, and how I was feeling when I was deep into this album alongside pavement."

- "I hate flying, I'm deathly scared of it but its [sic] life. Sometimes you have to travel. Still to this day, I crank up this song as soon as the plane starts to jet down the runway. By the time this song is over, usually the plane has leveled out toward our destination and I've relaxed a bit."

I think one of the things that makes me susceptible to the humanity of comments like this is the hopefulness of them in the midst of insurmountable odds. The futility of leaving a comment on a music video that is meant for one specific person who will likely never see it but nonetheless doing it in front of tens of thousands of strangers. Or writing a book chapter like that. I used to worry about embarrassing myself by being vulnerable but I don't worry about that any more.

Elliott Smith, "Needle in the Hay"

- "Can't believe it's 2016. We're still here, together, in our own little midnights, missing you. I hope so hard you're free now."

- "I used to drive into Portland and walk down to 6th and Powell to buy cocaine and heroin, I know those stairs. This song brings up contradictory emotions for me; the horror and the thrill. Its a very strange nostalgia of being so glad to not be there anymore but remembering how fun it could be. RIP Elliot. Lost four of my own, 2 to overdose and 2 to suicide. And I really didn't have any to spare. Robby, Jeff, J.R. and York. I am honored to have know you, and I hold the memories of you in my heart."

- "I feel alone, don't know why I'm in this depression, I feel I have what I want, I try to fit in, I do everything to get noticed but just get pushed away I'm am alone"

I think people think talking to someone who isn't there is supposed to be a sign of insanity but it feels like the most natural thing in the world to me. The only difference between leaving a comment for someone you miss on the internet and saying a silent little prayer in your heart that they'll come back to you for example whispering I miss you when it's dark and quiet is that there's at least a one in a million chance they might actually see the internet comment. None of us are going to ever win the lottery but we still play anyway right because you never know. You do know but you never do.

Elliott Smith, "Miss Misery"

- "this always reminds me of my sister. She and i are very close. I moved away from home because I didn't want my family to see me battle alcoholism and drug addiction. Im slowly getting better but I miss my sister, I cant wait to come home once I am healed and clean."

- "This comment section is full of such a beautiful array of life. I wish we could all sit down in a room and talk about the places we've been, the things we've seen, what has lead [sic] us to go out our way to listen to this meaningful melody. There is so much to learn, in such little time. So enjoy the little time you have here. Don't fill yourself with petty hate. What if you die tomorrow? What was the last thing you said to your friends and family? What was the thing that you said you always wanted to do, but for some reason never did? Would you be worried about your ego? all these materialistic items you buy? When you're lying there on your deathbed."

Band of Horses, "The Funeral"

- "My best friend died in my arms in Afghanistan I used this song on a little video of him and played it at his funeral he made me promise. Goodbye Mikey. Till that morning my brother. I love you see you on the other side"

- "The girl I love brought me here. And guess what, she doesnt love me back"

- "One of my best guy friends in high school died suddenly at 15, about 8 years ago from a brain hemorrhage. It really shocked me and my whole grade. I still remember his funeral that we all attended and seeing his mum cry up the front as she spoke. I miss his laugh, and his ability to make us all happy as we tried to navigate our teen years through school. He was in drama class with me, and he had dreams of being a movie director making comedies. He never got to do that, or have a girlfriend, fall in love, get married and have kids. But I might be able to, and I ask myself why some people can have those things and others cant. Anyways this song made me think of him and this thing called life. We only have a short time here, so we have to make it count"

Explosions in the Sky, "Your Hand In Mine"

- "Ive never wanted anything more than sofia to appear down the aisle at 2.27 of this song, she was my best friend, lover, soul mate but most of all she was my angel, i find it hard to breath without her, she is someone that can't and won't ever be replaced, she was, still is and will forever be the love of my life"

- "My football career just ended a week ago. Can't help but tear up when I listen to this now. At least I went out on top."

- "Find that scared little boy or girl that lives inside your heart and hold them close. Look that child in the eyes and tell them that it's going to be alright. We've made it this far and we'll make it through more. It's what we do. We survive."

- "It's been years, but a man I loved more than anything sent me this song. For a long time after he left me for another person I couldn't even stomach this song without breaking down. It's been a long struggle but finally . . . I can listen to it without overwhelming knots forming in my core. The person who sent me this may have broken me beyond repair . . . but hey, the song is nice."

Camera Obscura, "French Navy"

- "My brother who passed away a year tomoz heard this song on come dine with me he looked it up and he had it on non stop in his flat he loved it I sat at his grave last week and I played it for him I miss him so much love this song whenever I'm down I listen to this"

- "She was so young. Only two years older than me. I am really sad. My thoughts and prayers go out to her family and friends."

Wait hold on.

Sometimes you read the comments and you find a new reason to be sad about a song you've always loved. I didn't realize Carey Lander from Camera Obscura had died. I loved this band so much. She died of bone cancer in 2013 I just read. I did not know that. Why didn't anyone tell me that?

"It's probably too late to help me, but it would be great if we could find something in the future that means children don't have to undergo such awful treatment and have a better chance of survival," Lander wrote on a fundraiser she posted shortly before she died.

That's another thing we can do now I guess. Go and read the comments on medical care fundraisers after the people behind them are gone. Here's one I just read:

"As Carey's parents we have been deeply moved by all the gifts and messages on this page. They have brought real comfort to us. Please keep spreading the word and keep giving, so we can carry through her resolve that no other families experience this heartache and sadness."

THEY WANT TO KNOW IF YOU HAVE YOUR PAIN COMING

YOU LIFT ONE FOOT UP AND GET OUT OF THE WAY OF THE DEATH SPILL SO NONE OF IT GETS ON YOU

"I woke up . . . and it's kind of hard man talking about this, how they violated me," Torrence Jackson said from jail. "I woke up fourteen, twelve hours later . . . I woke up in a room, I asked what happened . . . I go the bathroom and I see got blood in my drawers. I'm bugging, I'm distraught."

They took Jackson to court and released him after that he said and he soon realized he had a broken hand and ruptured interior in his anus. What had happened as an investigation of records by Syracuse. com reported is that the Syracuse police, a city judge, and St. Joseph's Hospital Health Center all conspired together to violate him in more ways than one.

On a Monday in October of 2017 Jackson was pulled over after failing to signal correctly in his car which is what the cops say that you did when they are already planning on fucking with you. He was well-known to local police for a lengthy list of arrests some of which weren't so great such as armed robbery and others that shouldn't even count as a crimes such as drug possession and in any case none of which have anything to do with the way he was treated this particular time.

I shouldn't mention his prior encounters with the law should I isn't that what tabloids and local TV news does whenever something bad happens to well let's be honest a black guy such as their rights have been violated or they've been murdered by police because then it softens up the delicate sensibilities of the reader or the viewer who is presumed to be white because white is the default thing a person can be right at least based on my experience as a white guy the unique protagonist of reality.

It's like when you hear that someone died and you ask the person telling you how it happened what oh man what happened you say and they say it was whatever it was and you're hoping it was something they did to bring death upon themselves because that way you feel less bad like they had it coming. You hope it wasn't that an air conditioner fell out of the sky and crushed their head for example because that could happen to any of us at any time no matter how virtuous a life we live. You hope it's something like they smoked for forty years because then you can go well I don't smoke so I'm not gonna die and you distance yourself from the little oil spill of death that has entered the room once the conversation started you sort of lift one foot up and get out of the way of the death spill so none of it gets on you. Like not long ago I read the news that Colin Kroll the thirty-four-year-old founder of the popular HQ Trivia thing died of an apparent drug overdose and lots of people online were saying how sad it was he was so young and so on and so forth and then I saw a guy post something like how is dying of a drug overdose a tragedy and I guess by that what he means is that once you do drugs you relinquish your subscription to normal human empathy. You either get to do drugs or have strangers be sad when you die is what I'm saying.

That's what the typical rap sheet disclaimer paragraph in a crime story does. No angel this guy Torrence Jackson in other words. When it's a white person they tell you what they majored in in college or what the name of their horse was when they grew up on the farm twenty years ago even when you chop up your family and put them all in an oil drum they say you were a family man and show pictures of you smiling but when it's a black person or a white person who's addicted to drugs and does petty crimes which is almost the same thing in the local news humanity calculus they tell you what crimes they had done before and then you go this guy seems like a real piece of work and you adjust your sadness dial like you're turning down the heat on the stove top coil where you boil your upset.

So the cops pull him over and like I said he was known to police which means a lot of things but also in this specific instance means he was literally known to one of the police that pulled him over who didn't like him very much at all and the cops said he had a baggie of marijuana on him and there was cocaine residue in the car. One time like fifteen years ago we were driving to New York City for a show in this beat-up four-speed Toyota my grandmother passed down to me when she couldn't drive anymore and me and my drummer were doing coke on the way down and I somehow spilled the baggie all over the place and it got into the stick shift well and mixed in with all this tobacco residue and I dunno granola bar crumbs and dog shit and whatever else a dirty person has in their car and I tried to salvage as much of it as I could but even I wasn't gross enough to do more than a bump or two of the tobacco granola dirt. I have some self-respect.

"While stopped, Officer Anthony Fiorini wrote in a police report, he saw Jackson raise his buttocks off the seat so far that his head was sticking out the window," Syracuse.com reported. "That is consistent with someone hiding drugs in his rectum, Fiorini said."

So there's another thing to keep in mind if you ever get pulled over don't shift around in your seat too weird.

Jackson denied that he had any drugs hidden in his rectum but the cops said he was taunting them about it and maybe he was and maybe he wasn't maybe it was a means to fuck with the cops because they'd been fucking with him or maybe he was on drugs and not in the right state of mind and saying shit he didn't really mean. Then again people on drugs as you'll remember from a couple paragraphs ago have it coming. Whatever it is they signed up for it when they did the drugs.

The cops put Jackson in a spit mask and say he was being combative maybe he was maybe he wasn't I don't know and I also don't know what I'd do if I were being arrested while on drugs something that has never happened to me despite having done drugs approximately a thousand times in my life due to I'm a white guy. One time I got pulled over in that same grandmother car just after leaving the dude's house and I was shitting my pants but they let me go. A few years later I'd gotten so many parking tickets on the car that it wasn't worth paying them off to save it so we just sent it to get junked.

The cops wanted to search Jackson's rectum for the drugs and Jackson was refusing and some of the doctors had refused to do it against his will because doctors are not cops they are the opposite of cops their job is to help people. They are cops when it comes to getting their money though aren't they. So the real cop went and got a search warrant at a judge's house late at night and the judge signed it. Thinking about being a judge sitting at home in my library or kid-fucking dungeon the two things most judges have at home and then a cop shows up and says hey we need to search a guy's ass for weed and after having spent all that time in law school then in practice and then on the bench you summon all of your decades of jurisprudence knowledge and you say ok go look up the guy's ass.

Typically by the way in this type of scenario police will wait for you to go to the bathroom to see if the drugs they say you have up there come out or maybe they'll give you a laxative to speed things along but they couldn't wait in this instance.

Some of the doctors were like fuck this we're not about it but the hospital's lawyer soon got involved and told the medical staff they needed to comply with the warrant and one thing gave way to another and Jackson was sedated and while unconscious they inserted a colonoscope into his asshole to see if they could find the dime bag or gram or two of coke or whatever it was. There were something like ten cops there and multiple doctors and nurses and a lawyer and all of that just to snatch this dude's hypothetical bag. Oh wait I forgot to mention that they had already done an x-ray which showed he had nothing inside his rectum or anywhere else but you never know you gotta go and see things for yourself sometimes up close.

Welp they didn't find any drugs and they dropped the drug charges and gave him a traffic violation and he left the next day.

"I felt tampered with" is what Jackson said when he woke up and he didn't realize how badly because then the hospital sent him a bill for $4,500 for the procedure that was performed against his will while he was unconscious at the behest of the cops.

Later on the mayor's office said one of the things they have to take into consideration is the well-being of the suspect because what if the imaginary bag of drugs had exploded?

I went back to the Pain Center yesterday the one I mentioned previously and I filled out the forms they make you fill out every time on that clipboard there Welcome to Pain Management it says which would've been another good name for this book.

It's essentially page after page of a questionnaire asking you about whether or not you've ever gotten into trouble for having drugs or if you've ever misused your drugs or had encounters with the law due to drugs or if people have ever told you you have an issue with drugs and for most of the answers I answer no because it's the truth and mostly what they're interested in are opioids anyway but the real thing they're trying to figure out here is whether or not you have your pain coming. They are gonna treat you either way but if you've already used up your physician empathy points and went and fucked around with medications then they're not going to treat you as well or as effectively as they might have otherwise. When they see you've been addicted to things in the past the doctors just like the cops and the TV news and the readers and the viewers who delight in distancing ourselves from other people who are more deserving of pain than we are think that it's a just penance.

Another thing they have you do is try to describe not just your degree of pain but also the specific qualities of pain. They ask like is it burning stabbing piercing throbbing dull aching and I don't know how to answer those things because I never graduated from the Pain Sommelier Academy. I am not equipped with the vocabulary to tease out the subtle notes of pain inside of my own body and I don't think we've all really gotten together and come to a consensus on what the specific difference between any of those terms are have we or did I just miss it? We're speaking in a language that we don't understand and that no one else understands and the person who's trying to interpret it the doctor might as well be imagining a monkey playing the cymbals in his brain while you're talking which is what they do because your doctor never listens to you anyway.

One thing the doctor said they could do to figure out what's going on with me is poke needles into the nerves in my back and the front side of my body at the same time and try to see which ones light up or something when they sent a little charge through my body. I think. It's a very painful procedure he said but I didn't really listen to what else it entailed because you never listen to your doctor anyway.

Every time I talk to a doctor it's like I just walked into a room and met nineteen different people at a cocktail reception or something and you know there is no way you are going to remember all of their names or where they're from or what they do but the people are actually things that are wrong with you. So you try your best to pick out one of them that will stick.

Experiencing pain sometimes is like suspecting there's a dead mouse in your walls like you can vaguely smell it so you go poking your snout around by the sink and under the stove or wherever and you know you know you know it's there somewhere but you can't find it or tell anyone else where to go to pull it out. You know it's in the kitchen say but that's as close as you can get to narrowing things down and then you just have to wait for decomposition to take over eventually and in the long run none of it will be there and it will have never been there.

YOU START TO LOSE TRACK OF HOW MANY YOU'VE KILLED

CAN'T THINK OF A GOOD SUBHED HERE GOTTA GO

Kirstjen Nielsen said she would have to get back to them with the numbers she didn't know at that particular point in time how many people had died in the custody of the Department of Homeland Security which is to say how many people had died in her custody. You might understand the head of a large government agency not being able to get too granular about all the minute details of everything they oversee on the spot like how much money they spent on blankets that quarter say or how many calories the children they're holding are being fed a day. Someone knows that sure but maybe not the boss but the number of people that have died on her watch seems like a reasonable one to have access to offhand. How many people have died on your watch for example I bet you know.

Well she didn't have the numbers handy despite the fact that a young girl named Jakelin Caal Maquin had just died on her watch something that would probably make me go were I the head of Homeland Security for example Jesus Christ how many people have died with me at the wheel then I'd rip someone a new one.

The girl was seven years old a birthday she had just celebrated on the long trip from Guatemala with her father. She had gotten her first pair of shoes for the trip her family said after she died in America the famous country.

Some reporters found her family back where they had traveled from in a "tiny wooden house with a straw roof, dirt floors, a few bed-sheets and a fire pit for cooking, where Jakelin used to sleep with her parents and three siblings" according to the *Guardian*.

The brothers were "barefoot, their feet caked with mud and their clothes in tatters" and there was a heart made out of wood on the wall to mark her death.

It's not clear if Secretary Nielsen had access to any of those details why would she but the House Judiciary Committee were nonetheless just as much in shock at her ignorance as the rest of us.

Representative David Cicilline of Rhode Island was particularly red-assed when she said she didn't know how many people she had gone and had die.

"Madame Secretary, did I understand you correctly to say that as you sit here today, you do not know how many human beings have died while in custody of the department that you lead, and in preparation for today's hearing, you didn't ascertain that number?" he asked using her formal title which is the legislator version of when your parents are very disappointed in you.

"I don't have an exact figure for you," Nielsen said.

"Do you have a rough idea?"

"Sir, what I can tell you is . . ."

"I'm talking about people who have died in your custody. You don't have the number?"

"I will get back to you with the number," she said which is what you say when your boss asks you what the sales projections are for next year or something like that I don't know I've never been able to hold an office job so just imagine whatever it is bosses ask you that isn't super important and you just have to go poke around a second and figure it out.

Over the summer people were all very excited about activists going after Trump administration officials and other prominent Republicans while they tried to eat out at restaurants. A group of DSA members chased Nielsen out of a Mexican restaurant near the White House in June.

Sometimes people come back from war I guess and they get a taste for the local cuisine.

Kirstjen Nielsen is either a particularly stupid person or a particularly evil one and when we're talking about anyone in this administration your guess is as good as mine. Some of them can be both I suppose. Sometimes especially when I'm drinking a lot I get this pressure inside of my skull and I want to run into a wall over and over again to make it stop but I don't ever end up doing that and probably won't but I just remembered that that happens.

Later in the hearing Nielsen was asked why the administration was threatening to shutdown the government over a dispute about Congress paying for a wall that Trump had promised for so long would be paid for by Mexico.

"From Congress, I would ask for wall. We need wall," she said.

We're all still waiting to hear back from DHS on the number of people who've died in their custody this year or last year or the year before that. While deaths along the border or on the journey here aren't super rare deaths once people have been taken in by the U.S. government tend to be or at least seem to be it's hard to say since the most recent data they've released is from 2015 when there were ten.

Whatever the number is this year in case you're reading this Secretary Nielsen you're going to need to add one to it because and I'm not sure if you've seen this yet maybe you were offline for the holiday but a few days after your appearance in front of the House committee on Christmas Eve an eight-year-old boy named Felipe Alonzo-Gomez also from Guatemala died in the custody of U.S. Customs and Border Protection which is to say on your watch Madame Nielsen. They'd taken the boy to the hospital and prescribed him some medicine and then a few hours later he was vomiting and they took him back to the hospital but he died there and is now dead.

On Christmas Eve around the time that eight-year-old boy was dying I was at my parents' house and I was trying to tell my mother about some of the stuff I was proud of this year like the time we all got together and raised over thirty thousand dollars so a woman would be eligible to receive a heart transplant even though the death panel overseeing her care had said hit the bricks lady due to they didn't believe she would be able to afford the necessary post-transplant medicine. One thing I didn't bring up to my mother is another fundraiser I started to build giant escalators that would run over Trump's imaginary border wall because we aren't supposed to talk about politics.

Eventually the fundraiser pulled in over ten thousand dollars which is something I know because GoFundMe sends me an update every single hour with who all has donated and I can't figure out how to turn it off. The idea of course is a response to the GoFundtheWall nonsense that raised over twenty million dollars for the famous wall we all know and love. The guy who started that thing is a triple amputee veteran which I feel terrible about but he also seems like a real piece of shit con artist who has had multiple Facebook pages he ran called like Patriotic Eagle Jizz taken down for being so bad at lying said NBC News and that is saying something because you can post literally any old shit on there.

The escalators are a metaphor I pointed out on the thing in part because the last thing I need is ICE coming to raid my house or whatever thinking I'm really trying to smuggle people over the border with giant escalators. I mean I would if that were plausible but it's not and it's not going to happen. You would think people would understand it's meant as a joke but people are very very dumb I can't really overstate that. The money is actually going to RAICES the Refugee and Immigrant Center for Education and Legal Services. Here's what they said they can use the money for:

> Donations will help us hire lawyers to defend unaccompanied children who have no guarantee of counsel otherwise, like those in Tornillo; they'll help pay for know your rights trainings in detention centers so people can navigate the asylum process; they help our general mission of providing free and low-cost counsel to migrants in detention centers generally; they help fund the refugee resettlement program, like enrolling kids in schools; they help hire support and advocacy staff to make videos highlighting what migrants go through to raise awareness; they help fund missions to Tijuana to help those in the migrant caravan, like the LGBTQ contingent we're providing housing and legal services to.

A lot of people left nice messages on the page like this one which I laughed at because it's a Mitch Hedberg reference:

$10.00 from Rachel Maher An escalator can never break: it can only become stairs. You should never see an Escalator Temporarily Out Of Order sign, just Escalator Temporarily Stairs. Sorry for the convenience.

But lot of them were like this though:

Comment From Donna

And idiots are actually donating

Comment From Pat

LOL - I think you're throwing your money away if you're donating to this!

Comment From Peter

So u are embezzling!! WTG

Comment From Terri

This account has been reported to GFM as fraudulent.

Comment From Michael

STUPID.. STUPID... It has to be a stupid idea from stupid people

Comment From Will

Ignorance is bliss

Comment From Kaibo

This is a fucking scam. Stop donating to this bullshit

A lot of websites interviewed me about it like Rolling Stone, and Mashable, and Inverse which is nice because it helped raise money and also I like to get attention.

"I didn't think 2018 could get any more 2018-er yet here we are at the last minute with something that perfectly encapsulates this combination of cruelty and stupidity that characterizes this entire year and everything to do with Trump and the wall," I told Mashable. "It just seems like a perfect metaphor for where we are right now."

"These sad people just want to belong to something and throwing their money at this weird racism wall makes them feel like they're buying a membership to part of something bigger than themselves," I said all of which is true but none of it is as true as what I told the *Washington Times* a very bad conservative website.

"Usually it's impossible to parody the delusions of the Trumpist cult but something about the idea of thousands of MAGA nanas with terminal Facebook brain wasting the last of their Christmas gift money and red faced dads taking out a second mortgage on their hot tub dealerships to own the libs and support Mr. Trump's imaginary racism wall seemed too good to pass up," I said.

"It's the perfect encapsulation of the intersection of loneliness and cruelty that binds all these weirdos together," I said.

We talked about a lot of things at Christmas Eve at my parents house and one thing I learned was that my parents and my mother's friend who was there and my uncle had all taken LSD which is something I have never tried since I never really did any psychedelics. My mother said she was dosed by my father though so I don't think that really counts. Well it counts as having done it but not as having wanted to do it which is a big difference. My stepfather who is my father told me another thing which was about a time when we were driving from where we lived with my grandparents in Hanover, Massachusetts to go to Maine and I was about four or so I think and they saw my father-father standing on the side of the road as we drove away like Sideshow Bob or some shit and then he went and burned down the house. When they got to Maine my great uncle who was a World War II pilot handed my stepfather a shotgun just in case and he was like what the fuck do I do with this?

My uncle has developed Parkinson's disease I believe I mentioned which I always thought was going to get me because his father my grandfather died from complications from it but then he told me the other night it's not hereditary and I guess he probably would have looked into that. Losing your hair is though he said which was a pretty good own on me if I'm being fair. Not sure which I'd rather come down with to be honest.

He also told me that one of the biggest heartbreaks of his life was when he had to stop playing soccer probably around when he was my age because his knee gave out. You do something you love for like thirty years and then one day your body just says fuck you pal and then you can't do it anymore.

My uncle was in the merchant marine and now he works for the post office and he tells me about the places he's been throughout the world and I'm always interested and sometimes my mother or aunt yells at him to shut up because he gets off on these weird tangents like a spaced out sixties type of guy but I don't mind. He really likes Carlos Santana I know that. I went to see him play with Journey once in Mexico and it was a whole fucking thing and I wrote about it at the time but long story short my phone ran out of battery was the main thing and I learned some life lessons about patience by which I mean I just bitched about everything in a more resigned tone.

After the LSD chat we all went inside and sang carols around the piano. The one I always sing with my mother and it's a special moment for us every year is "I'll Be Home For Christmas" and sure enough I am home for Christmas every time but some day either I won't be or she won't be there for me to return home to and then what will we do probably still sing it and everyone will be real raw about it.

Michelle and I didn't get a Christmas tree for the first time in as long as I can remember this year and that was mostly fine by both of us for some reason. It could have been worse though at least we didn't throw a fully decorated tree into a dumpster on December 22 like some people I saw did on Twitter.

I'd make a Hemingway saddest story ever joke here about an unused item but I wish people would sometimes know about a different Hemingway story oh and while I'm thinking of it please learn another poem besides "This Is Just to Say" by William Carlos Williams you know the one about the fucking plums in the fucking icebox.

One poem I used to love by Williams was "A Love Song" which goes like this and side note make sure I can reprint this hey OR Books can I reprint this here? No it's ok to leave this part in. Yes I'm sure.

Love Song
William Carlos Williams, 1883–1963
I lie here thinking of you:—
the stain of love

is upon the world!
Yellow, yellow, yellow
it eats into the leaves,
smears with saffron
the horned branches that lean
heavily
against a smooth purple sky!
There is no light
only a honey-thick stain
that drips from leaf to leaf
and limb to limb
spoiling the colors
of the whole world—
you far off there under
the wine-red selvage of the west!

I painted a stanza from it above the window in the shitty Allston apartment I lived in when I was young with eight other people and the maggots in the pantry and the brown water pooled in the shower you had to stand in to get clean and I thought that was some real poetic seeming shit at the time.

I went on a radio show in the U.K. the other day to talk about the wall fundraising thing and I forget what I said but it was basically something like this:

First off there are a couple of things you have to understand about America and the most important is that we are a deeply stupid country.

Secondly and this is probably a bit more alien to people in the U.K. is that we've come to rely on fundraisers as a solution to everything from funding our own medical bills to stupid stunts like this one people have gotten behind to fund the wall. That's in large part because all of our money goes to tax cuts for millionaires and for the pursuit of endless empire around the world something you guys can probably also appreciate har har I said and the host was like you're spot on there mate or whatever. He was really mad about America's eternal wars and I could not argue with him about that.

I can't overstate how saddening and weird it is so to see so many people willing to throw away their own hard-earned money at this empty obelisk of xenophobia I said. I'm usually not one to say this is what you waste your money on but in this case that seems fitting.

From the very beginning of the Trump campaign the wall has been this amorphous thing constantly changing shape both always arriving and defined by its absence I didn't get to say because it sounds pretentious. It's an ancient obelisk to racism unearthed on an archaeological dig in a Borges fable where those who gaze upon it see themselves reflected back in it. I didn't say that part either.

It's the perfect emblem of Trump's entire mythos since it's a belief in something that isn't there. It's throwing good money after bad and hoping to come out on the other side made whole. It's a desperate cry for help from the people involved hoping to belong to anything even if the group they're buying into is defined entirely by its racism.

America is a prison. When you're in prison you have to join gangs you might not necessarily have joined otherwise so you won't be alone and vulnerable and that's what Trump has given all these perverts a chance to feel like they belong.

Another thing from Hemingway I think about a lot and posted about back in June back when we were talking about the baby prisons we have now was the scene from *For Whom the Bell Tolls* when they gather up all the fascists in the town square and march them off the cliff. It's really hard for the people to do at first because even when you're in a war even when you spend so much time hating the other side it's not as easy to execute people as it might have been in your imagination before you actually have to go ahead and carry it out. I suppose directing people to their deaths gets easier after time and with practice though doesn't it. Once you've got a few under your belt maybe you start to lose track of how many you've killed.

I FEEL LIKE I'M LOST HE SAID.
I DON'T FIT IN HERE AT ALL

IT'S A CATALOG OF EMPATHY IS WHAT I'M SAYING

Jorge Garcia hugged his wife and children goodbye. He cried and they cried and the immigration officials standing watch nearby cried just kidding they were probably swelling with pride at a job well done and then the thirty-nine-year-old landscaper got on the airplane to leave Michigan the *Detroit Free Press* reported. He'd lived there most of his life but it was time to return to Mexico a place he hadn't been in almost thirty years. The officials escorted him through security and probably saw the signs people were holding that said Stop Separating Families and things of that nature but it's unclear if they had any reaction to them probably not you'd have to assume.

Garcia had never been in any sort of trouble with the law or anything like that but he had to be deported those are the rules and you have to follow the rules. He and his family had spent over one hundred thousands dollars over the years on attorney fees trying to sort out his immigration situation the newspaper said but while that bought him some time it ultimately didn't matter and now he is Mexican and not American anymore like he wants to be and was. The police can come and basically what they can do is press a button and you aren't who you were five minutes ago you're a whole other person.

"It's a nightmare coming to life," his wife Cindy told the newspaper. She is retired and on disability after working at a truck plant and is worried about how she will support their children. "You have no choice but to face it head-on, and accept what is being thrown at you. Because there is nothing else that you can do."

In February 2018 seventeen people were killed at Stoneman Douglas High School which was probably the most famous of all the mass shootings we had that year and there was a lot you could say about the state of the country and our eternal worship of violence when you heard the news about that but another thing you could say which is what the president went and said was what you would have personally done yourself if you were on hand for a shooting like that.

What he said was that the police at the scene were cowards more or less and that he would have stopped it if he were there.

"I really believe I'd run in there even if I didn't have a weapon," is what the president said about that particular shooting.

There's not really much that's funny about kids being mowed down in their school but the idea of Donald Trump performing any sort of physical activity never mind turning into Jason Bourne is funny. I like to think sometimes about Trump lacing up a pair of Bob Cousy-ass Converse way tighter than necessary and stretching his hamstrings for like fifteen minutes then throwing old boxing gym medicine balls at the shooter from behind a trophy case until he gets winded after twenty seconds.

One of the things gun people say about why we need guns is that we might need to overthrow the tyrannical government some day so we need to be armed as well just in case but we lived through eight years of everyone on the right saying Obama was the actual antichrist coming to turn us all gay and Muslim and now we have had two years of a president who the other side all agree is What If Hitler But Lazy and no one has really done shit about it vis-à-vis overthrowing the government so I don't think that outcome is ever really going to happen. Feels like maybe it would have by now?

I am not advocating overthrowing the government by violent means at this time I should point out but at least I could vaguely respect someone who tried to do it. You'd get annihilated in five seconds but at least you wouldn't be shooting at schoolkids you would be picking a significantly more difficult task to accomplish than shooting kids which is apparently very easy for people to do.

Conservatism is a lack of empathy it is nothing else is what I think. No conservative you know cares about anyone but themselves and maybe their families if we're being generous and they will not change until they personally experience a particular hardship of their own and then they go like ah I see why this is bad now. One thing that is funny though is watching people who've boiled their brains on a non-stop diet of Fox News become increasingly isolated and alienated from everyone who ever loved them because they can't stop mainlining Tucker Carlson.

All of the shit that the left wants makes thematic sense as a bundle deal right? Healthcare and a larger share of wealth for workers and less money spent on bombs. You could look at all of that and figure it came out of the same ideology is what I'm saying it's a catalog of empathy is what I'm saying. But the right has the weirdest potluck beliefs. Welcome to the right: here's your copy of the Bible and a lifetime subscription to *Guns & Ammo* for some reason. You respect golf now. Go fuck yourself.

I bet Donald Trump thought it would be great to have everyone on TV talking about him nonstop every day. I bet that was his dream and I guess there is some justice in the world because the way that wish turned out was a real cursed monkey's paw scenario if I've ever seen one.

In May a box of ammunition fell from a military helicopter and landed on an elementary school in El Paso which would sound pretty on the nose for the grand American experiment before you even know that the school the bullets landed on was called Parkland. Sometimes I think the sociopathic killer operating the simulation we all suffer in has a sense of humor and stirs cute little coincidences like that into the pain stew to amuse himself.

One way of being separated from your family is to be deported by the government and another way is when one of them is killed is what the president said one day in June when he dragged a bunch of bereaved people on stage for a ghoulish photo op about how immigrants are all violent murderers and rapists.

Some of the families really leaned into it like one woman named Laura Wilkerson whose son was killed in 2010 by an undocumented person. "None of our kids had a minute to say goodbye. We weren't lucky enough to be separated for five days or ten days," she said. "We were separated permanently," she said.

When you lose a family member to a senseless murder or accident people will often take any form of emotional support they can even if it's from the worst person alive using them as a political wedge to make other people's lives worse.

Those families on stage all sounded like Trump supporters using the same framing of immigrants as he does and so I want to be very mad at them but if you lost a loved one imagine what this would be like: the president is saying your dead child's name! It would be easy to give over to that temptation. The president is saying my child's name. My child is important now. My pain has been seen. Everyone in the country knows my loss now.

Eight out of the eleven people whose families Trump brought on stage were killed in a car accident to be clear. No less tragic to the family for having lost them but not exactly in fitting with the immigrants are gang members who will rape and kill at will narrative that was being sold.

All of that is very sad and frustrating but I didn't even get to the weird part yet which is that as these people were on stage crying and venting their anger and wishing more than anything their dead loved ones would come back and hug them one more time they stood there holding giant photos of the deceased and on each photo if you looked close you could make out the unmistakable squiggle of Donald Trump's signature where he signed the dead people's portraits.

A couple weeks after he was deported the *Free Press* caught up with Jorge Garcia in his new home that is not his home outside of Mexico City. He stays with his aunt there now and mostly sits in his room not sleeping and missing his family he said.

"I feel like I'm lost," he said. "I don't fit in here, at all."

Cindy said she was having trouble as well but at least she has the children with her. "He has no one," she said. "He's in a country he doesn't know. He is living with a family he has not seen for years. He's not getting much sleep. He wakes up every day at three in the morning . . . it's going to eventually catch up to him."

I don't know if deporting Garcia to Mexico was worth it for the people who carried it out but one thing I do know is that everyone who works for ICE will have spent their careers destroying the lives of others for nothing. No ill will be cured and no problem solved and undocumented people will continue to live and thrive here and their tormentors' lives will be wasted on a brutal and racist pursuit of nothing.

Garcia said he says a Hail Mary and Our Father prayer every night before bed which I do myself occasionally when the old brain water gets sour and I can't sleep due to the Catholicism they implanted in me when I was young. I don't know what sorts of prayers immigration officials say if they say any at all or what goes on in their brain when it's dark. I try to have empathy for everyone but sometimes I can't do it.

I'M BEGGING YOU, DO NOT HELP ME

I'LL COME BACK FROM THE DEAD TO FIGHT THEM BECAUSE IT'S SO EXPENSIVE

I guess they thought I was going to kill myself. I was sitting in my doctor's office complaining about abdominal pain and the conversation drifted to how I'd been feeling emotionally. Did you ever have thoughts about suicide the doctor asked.

Who doesn't am I right haha I said.

The doctor said she'd be right back and it dawned on me a second later what was about to happen.

Ah. Shit.

The next thing I knew an ambulance and the police were there. Very good response time you have to respect that. But come on man I said. There was no way I was getting in that ambulance. I really cannot afford it. And besides if I was genuinely suicidal would I really be worried about paying a bill?

Later on after the dust had settled and I spent a little while sitting in the hospital convincing a series of very concerned doctors that I was only ambiently suicidal and not actually going to do it or am I haha got away with the perfect crime and you'll never catch me now I asked a bunch of people about some of the crazy things they do to avoid taking an ambulance because they're worried they won't be able to afford it. I heard stories about people who had their credit permanently destroyed after a handful of ambulance rides being transferred between hospitals not fully aware of what was happening and not really in a position to object. People spoke of walking to the hospital and almost passing out along the way with severe burns or lacerations. More than a few told me about having to get into arguments with the EMTs telling them in no uncertain terms that no they did not have to go with them. Others weren't so adamant and regretted taking the ride when police or emergency personnel were more insistent.

"I wouldn't take an ambulance now unless it was life-threatening," Mike Taggart told me. A couple of years ago he was walking through a mall in Cambridge, Massachusetts when suddenly his head started ringing. Someone had thrown something off the balcony above and hit him in the head which promptly started bleeding via being a head which is usually softer than a thrown thing.

"Someone called 911, and when they came, they were like, 'You need to go to the hospital, and we have an ambulance,'" he said. "In my ignorance, I was like, 'Ok.'"

The hospital they took him to was less than a mile away but when the bill showed up it was almost $2,000. "I wasn't thinking straight at the time," he said which checks out on account of the having his dome knocked in. "I had insurance, but the deductible was huge."

"I always joke to my friends that if they find me dying, and they call me an ambulance, I'll come back from the dead to fight them because it's so expensive," Adam Lundgren told me. "But that joke comes from a real place of fear of being stuck with a bill I can't pay."

He'd heard enough horror stories from friends about the costs of an ambulance over the years that when he fell down some stairs and broke his arm he said screw it and drove himself to the hospital in pain. "I'd absolutely do it again, too," he said. "It sucks, but I feel like it's necessary."

One friend of mine who actually works in a hospital on the administrative side had a sudden stomach flu and asked for an ambulance. It arrived and took him a few doors down to the emergency room and it only cost $1,000. Another who is a nurse was billed $3,300 for a few miles ride and paid $1,000 out of pocket.

"I drove myself to the emergency room hemorrhaging from a surgical complication because I knew the ambulance ride wasn't covered by my insurance," said a third.

"Last year I was unconsciously put into one so I never paid the bill. The way I see it, I was kidnapped," said a fourth.

Nick Johnson was on the train in Boston when it got into a crash six years ago. He hit his head on the ground and the first responders instructed him to go to the hospital so he did along with five other people.

"Five months later, I got a $900 bill that my insurance wouldn't cover and that decimated my savings," he said. "This for an accident that happened on public transportation and an ambulance that was shared with others." Uber share for ambulance something to look into maybe?

"I've maintained a healthy fear of ambulances ever since. I had a really bad illness last year that caused me to be briefly hospitalized. My folks told me to call 911, but scared of the cost, I walked the five to ten minutes to the hospital."

Jon Payne blacked out after over-exerting himself at the gym a couple of years ago. An employee found him sprawled flat on his back in the bathroom. "He gave me a bottle of water and told me an ambulance was on the way. I immediately thought about the cost," he said. He has insurance, but it's subject to a high deductible.

"I was like, 'Yeah, no, fuck that. I'm fine.' I got my bearings back a few minutes later, and I left right at the same moment the ambulance was pulling up and the guys were getting the stretcher out. I walked right passed them like a slick bank robber."

Imagine that? Slinking away from the people sent to help you.

Paul Adler developed epilepsy at age twenty-six. His first seizure a few years back happened while he was at work in New York and his boss called an ambulance while he was out of it. The bill for the ride was around $1,200. Thankfully he had insurance at the time but since then when he hasn't or has taken on new jobs and been in between insurance he makes a point to ask his co-workers not to call him an ambulance in the event something happens.

"I've requested that they wait until I regain consciousness and cognizance so I could get myself to a hospital in an Uber or taxi instead of shelling out another $1,200 for a ride," he told me.

Please, everyone, I'm begging you, do not help me.

It reminds me of the shitty old Reagan joke about the scariest words you can ever hear except in this case it's "We're the government, and we're here to save your life."

One complicating factor here is that the people who come to help you aren't always the government. In every city and state throughout the country you'll find a wide variety of services from taxpayer-funded fire departments with EMS personnel to hospital-based services to private companies to a combination of all three and more. When it comes time to pay the bill as in all of the confounding complicated corners of our byzantine health-care system the buck often gets passed around. Knowing that some high-end insurance companies will pay the full rate while others will not or that the people being helped might not be able to afford any of it many emergency responders will charge as much as possible hoping the ones who pay full freight subsidize the rest of us.

Our municipalities know all of this too. Getting people to take fewer ambulances is something that cities around the country like Washington D.C. have been attempting to facilitate. In others like Phoenix medical taxi vouchers are offered as a means to dissuade people who might otherwise have to rely on ambulances for non-emergency medical transportation. The reasons why are pretty obvious: it frees up limited resources for more serious emergencies and it's an acknowledgement that people are increasingly unable to pay for ambulance bills that can range anywhere from a few hundred dollars to multiple thousands of dollars.

Much of the cost has to do with the fact that ambulance companies and insurers often can't agree on what a fair price should be and therefore ambulance companies may not contract with insurance companies so they can charge more as out-of-network providers. Complicating things further is that the mercurial nature of this billing can open the door for fraud and abuse. In 2017 Medstar Ambulance, Inc. in Massachusetts was ordered by the U.S. Attorney's Office to pay $12.7 million in fines for inflating Medicare claims for ambulance transports.

The federal government obviously has a lot more resources to invest into making sure they're not being erroneously billed unlike most of us who would rather pretend medical bills don't exist until the last minute just like we do with our medical problems. Most of us don't have the wherewithal to protect ourselves after the fact which is why the difficult choice has to be made on the fly. But perhaps that's an idea I just stumbled on here. What if we provided the government with sufficient funds through a series of fees spread around to everyone that are then collected and distributed to administer necessary services for its citizens as needed?

In the U.K. emergency services and almost all other health-care concerns are provided free at the point-of-service. It's not a perfect system as it can lead to abuse but it's far better than the nightmare life-or-death game show we have here. Truly the American spirit of self-reliance at work: pull yourself up by the gurney straps.

In the meantime as ever in our hopelessly broken system of health care that may be our best hope when it comes to emergencies. Look out for yourself because no one else is going to. Even the people there to save the day.

SOMEONE GOT SCARED AND THEY WERE SCARED

THE SWAT TEAM CAME TO SAVE HIM FROM HIMSELF

Keaton wanted to be an elementary school math teacher his family said in his obituary. He loved reading and played multiple instruments and he worked two jobs in the Twin Cities area where he lived one job at Fleet Farm which is a retail store and one job at McDonald's the famous restaurant because two jobs is what a person needs to survive now. People tell me a lot online that a job at McDonald's isn't supposed to provide a full-time living for people because it's for teenagers and that it wouldn't be fair to McDonald's to have to pay so much to people for flipping burgers the one thing people at McDonald's do.

Keaton who also loved Pokémon was having a hard time I guess and he was thinking about hurting himself so someone called the police because they were scared and when the police arrived Keaton went outside and then the police also got scared because that is the one thing police do at work all day they get scared. They tried to talk to him and then tasered him and when that didn't work Keaton was all of a sudden dead after an officer-involved shooting which is the euphemism for when a gun goes off on its own and kills a person through the magic of the passive voice. Keaton was twenty-two and now he'll always be twenty-two when his family thinks about him forever.

A couple weeks before that a woman in Cobb County, Georgia had the police called on her after she reportedly was threatening suicide the *Atlanta Journal Constitution* reported. Talathia Brooks came to the door when the police arrived and they got on their bullhorns and were asking her to come out and things like that and then they say she came back to the door with a gun. "She did make a very distinctive, overt action toward them with that weapon," Dana Pierce a police sergeant said, "and that's why they felt as though they were at risk of serious body injury or death" and then she was dead.

I know we're not supposed to like Louis C.K. anymore and I don't don't worry I am very comfortable no longer enjoying his work but sometimes at night when I can't sleep I have to watch shows like *Parks and Recreation* over and over again even though it's a psyop to make libertarian epic bacon guys and centrist politicians likable. One bit I remember whenever I read a cop quote is from when Louis was a cop on the show and he was talking about how he liked Leslie and he was like *Ms. Knope was attractive to me. As a man I was attracted to her in her demeanor. I was attracted to her in a sexual manner that was appropriate* because it's funny to talk like a cop when it doesn't involve cop things. It's weird to me how that cop voice is such a passive one but everything they do is reactionary and filled with escalating action.

They tried to save Talathia Brooks after they shot her which is what the police often do and that seems so fucking weird to me firing bullets at someone then trying to bring them back to life. Sometimes they don't try to save the people they shoot though and that is even worse.

A couple years before that a man in Roy, Utah, named Jose Calzada called a suicide hotline saying he wanted to kill himself and then whatever happens after that call is made happened and the SWAT team was at his house and a standoff ensued the *Standard-Examiner* reported. A few hours later they stormed the house and found him in his garage with a gun pointed into his mouth and they ordered him to drop the gun he had pointed at himself and when he moved they shot him to death twenty-two times. The shooting was found to be justified by the police investigation naturally but his family is suing saying he had fallen asleep and was woken up when the SWAT team came to save him from himself.

There are a lot of these stories how many more do you want to read because I kind of don't want to write about too many more. I just remembered a note I took the other night when I was wasted. Sometimes I get ideas for things to write here when I'm drinking but I can't write when I'm drinking. The note I wrote down says "snap neck like pregnant lady light over microwave just never fixed" and I don't really remember what the premise of the pregnant lady thing was exactly but I think it was about being compelled to experience weird sorts of pain like how there's always that joke in sitcoms or whatever about how pregnant women want to eat pickles and ice cream and shit like that. I spend a lot of time on my back porch and I think about whether or not my neck would snap if I fell off of it since it's just the second floor or if I would just sort of fuck up my shoulder pretty bad and never be able to play tennis again. I don't play tennis but you know what I mean. A year or two ago I used to imagine the entire porch collapsing and falling through it and that would fucking suck but sometimes I wished it would happen because I didn't want to think about some stuff anymore. Anyway I'm not going to do that don't call the cops on me.

The other thing is about this pull down light string that dangles over our fridge and microwave corner in our kitchen and if you pull on it and hold it down the light will come on but the second you let it go it snaps back up and the light goes off and it's been that way for at least five years I don't know why we haven't fixed that yet or if it's a metaphor for anything but it could be if you wanted it to anything can be there are no rules. The light goes out if you don't hold on. If you let go for one second the thing you wanted will spark out of existence and then it's gone.

In 2018 police shot and killed at least sixty-four people with mental health disabilities according to the ACLU. "This January, Alejandro Valdez was suicidal and threatening to kill himself. The police shot and killed him. In February Orbel Nazarians was suicidal and threatening himself with a knife. The police shot and killed him. In March, Jihad Merrick was suicidal and pointing a gun at his head. The police shot and killed him. In April, Benjamin Evans was making suicidal comments. Police shot and killed him."

Here's another one from this year about a man in Minneapolis whose friend called a hotline saying she was worried about him. "He calls me all the time saying he wants to die, and I don't know how to deal with it," the friend said. Travis Jordan who was thirty-six and now will always be thirty six came outside and he had a gun the police say. He was from Honolulu and was a sommelier and liked surfing and worked as a mixologist.

"The 311 caller said Jordan had been taking alcohol to deal with depression and anxiety," the *Southwest Journal* reported. "On Nov. 9, Jordan sent the caller a music video about suicide and cried on the phone, saying he didn't want to live and didn't want to think about his future anymore. He'd shown interest in obtaining a gun in the past, the caller said."

His friend was trying to help and obviously all these peoples' friends were trying to help and maybe even the police thought they were trying to help. It's hard to tell how often this specific scenario plays out—the data on police shootings has always been woefully inadequate although that is changing as newspapers and other organizations have begun to dig deeper in the post-Ferguson period where we collectively woke up a little bit but only a little. Of the four hundred fatal police shootings in 2015 one quarter of them involved victims that had been dealing with mental health issues the *Washington Post* found.

"About half the shootings occurred after family members, neighbors or strangers sought help from police because someone was suicidal, behaving erratically or threatening violence," they reported.

In 2014 the Treatment Advocacy Center analyzed public shooting data spanning nearly forty years and found that "at least half of the people shot and killed by police each year in this country have mental health problems."

The *Portland Press Herald* found that almost half of the people shot in Maine in 2000 and 2001 suffered from a mental illness. In 2014 San Francisco public radio station KQED found that nearly 60 percent of the people killed by police between 2005 and 2013 in their city had an illness that "was a contributing factor in the incident."

"There are common elements in many of these instances when a fragile situation turns life-threatening for a person in crisis," they wrote. "That person often has a weapon, police issue commands, the person becomes more agitated, police respond with force."

I don't really know what the answer for this is besides abolishing the police which doesn't seem like it's going to happen anytime soon but a good place to start might be divorcing from the assumed job responsibilities of the armed crime stoppers the added role of also serving as mental health crisis prevention experts? Or barring that because obviously there's no money for that—we need to refund it to the people who own the McDonald's we all work at as our second job—we could send the firefighters or an EMT. Maybe the people whose first instinct is to intimidate and take command of a potentially deadly encounter shouldn't be sent to save us from ourselves by shooting us when we're fucked up? Just spit-balling crazy stuff here man don't listen to me.

One cool thing I just read is that Eugene, Oregon, has a program called CAHOOTS specifically to prevent putting people who are in distress like homeless people or people going through a mental health crisis into deadly situations with police. They employ teams of counselors and EMTs and that is good but the even better part is that they are not armed and not allowed to detain people against their will.

"There's a growing awareness that alternatives to law enforcement are needed, that alternatives to emergency medical services are needed," Brenton Gicker who works for CAHOOTS told KVAL in Eugene a couple years ago. "There's a lot of people having problems related to psychiatric problems and addiction-based problems and poverty problems, that end up getting addressed by the police but may be appropriately addressed by another resource."

I kind of got sidetracked there the whole reason I started writing about this in the first place is because as an added Hell World bonus we now have the option of pressing a button on social media and having the police deliver bullets to the home of someone we are concerned about. As a *New York Times* piece outlined Facebook has been trying to improve upon the way they handle posts that may be interpreted as coming from people in danger of harming themselves.

Self harm is a category that Facebook has emphasized of late Mark Zuckerberg who cares about us wrote in explaining their efforts.

"After someone tragically live-streamed their suicide, we trained our systems to flag content that suggested a risk—in this case so we could get the person help. We built a team of thousands of people around the world so we could respond to these flags usually within minutes. In the last year, we've helped first responders quickly reach around 3,500 people globally who needed help," Mark Zuckerberg who cares about us wrote. Remember when he seemed like he was teasing a run for the presidency lol. Now that I think of it caring about us doesn't seem to be a requirement for the job I guess.

Naturally Facebook doesn't have enough employees to monitor everyone's posts where would they get the money to hire more people so they have tried to improve upon their machines' ability to predict your suicide before it happens.

That's easier said than done they explained in another post.

One of the biggest challenges the team faced was that so many phrases that might indicate suicidal intent—'kill,' 'die,' 'goodbye'—are commonly used in other contexts. A human being might recognize that 'I have so much homework I want to kill myself' is not a genuine cry of distress, but how do you teach a computer that kind of contextual understanding?

Bla bla bla computer talk nerd stuff turns out that Facebook not only has all the data on your preferences like your likes and dislikes and your political opinions and the sports teams and musicians you love and so on they also have an algorithm working on figuring out how likely you are to kill yourself.

Despite their attempts at machine learning which they admit will be imperfect the important thing is that they can't do it without our help in flagging posts from people that we are worried about. And then some other stuff happens. They don't want to share too many details about their proprietary mental health service and suicide aptitude score system because they're a private business and they don't have to come on man.

Whether a post is reported by a concerned friend or family member or identified via machine learning, the next steps in the process remain the same. A trained member of Facebook's

Community Operations team reviews it to determine if the person is at risk—and if so, the original poster is shown support options, such as prompts to reach out to a friend and help-line phone numbers. In serious cases, when it's determined that there may be imminent danger of self-harm, Facebook may contact local authorities. Since these efforts began last year, we've worked with first responders on over 1,000 wellness checks based on reports we've received from our proactive detection efforts.

Here's one question I have aside from all the other questions I have which are a lot but here is one hard one: Honestly if you had to choose whose hands to place your life in who would you prefer Facebook or the cops? I'm not sure I know the answer myself. They both say they're here to help us but it doesn't seem like they know what that means.

THE GOAL IS TO KEEP YOU TRAPPED HERE FOREVER UNTIL THEY CAN BLEED YOU DRY

I CAN'T EXCUSE MY BEHAVIOR EVEN IF IT WAS NEVER A PROBLEM BEFORE

I'm not particularly fond of the cops. Not sure if there has been any confusion about that specific point around here. Sometimes people will ask me they'll go Luke what do you make of the cops thumbs up or thumbs down and I'll say to them I'll go Not a big fan of the cops mate.

That particular stance is due to the whole thing where the police were established as a means for capitalists in burgeoning cities to protect their profits and property at the expense of the poor, minorities, and immigrants in the north and as a slave-catching and freed-black-people-terrorizing group in the south which is surprisingly just about what they still are to this very day!

Here's one thing I didn't realize until just recently did you know the first police force as we think of it in America wasn't established until 1838 in Boston and then 1845 in New York? Prior to that policing was a lot less formal and either done by voluntary community watches or private for-profit policing according to a fascinating history of the fucking cops I read by Dr. Gary Potter of the Eastern Kentucky University.

"The night watch was not a particularly effective crime control device," he wrote. "Watchmen often slept or drank on duty. While the watch was theoretically voluntary, many 'volunteers' were simply attempting to evade military service, were conscript forced into service by their town, or were performing watch duties as a form of punishment," he wrote which doesn't sound too far off from the reasons people become cops now lol sorry to any cops reading this.

Here's another passage I quite liked:

> More than crime, modern police forces in the United States emerged as a response to "disorder." What constitutes social and public order depends largely on who is defining those terms, and in the cities of nineteenth-century America they were defined by the mercantile interests, who through taxes and political influence supported the development of bureaucratic policing institutions. These economic interests had a greater interest in social control than crime control. Private and for-profit policing was too disorganized and too crime-specific in form to fulfill these needs. The emerging commercial elites needed a mechanism to ensure a stable and orderly work force, a stable and orderly environment for the conduct of business, and the maintenance of what they referred to as the "collective good." These mercantile interests also wanted to divest themselves of the cost of protecting their own enterprises, transferring those costs from the private sector to the state.

I was thinking about this after a conversation I had with a friend who has been navigating his way through the system after getting done up for a DUI. He had come to some obvious-seeming realizations about the nature of control that the criminal justice system subjects us to and the dehumanizing feeling of being ensnared by the law.

Here's a weird thing though: as someone who despises the carceral state and the war on drugs and all of the other sundry abuses of power

I also happen to think people shouldn't be driving wasted and should suffer consequences for doing so and I'm not really sure how to square that. Is policing the streets from drunk drivers the one good thing cops do? Can I put emojis in this thing? Not sure how to do that so just imagine a chin-stroking emoji here.

Weirdly despite having broken the law too many times to count in terms of drug purchases and having driven a fair number of times when I probably should not have I've had very few encounters with the police in my lifetime. Much of that is owed to my privilege as a white man from a stable background of course. Some of it is just dumb luck. But I was fascinated hearing about all the extra shit that someone who does get arrested for a DUI or for possession has to go through so I asked my friend and a couple of other people—a woman arrested for coke possession (at Coachella lol), and a black man arrested for possession and for a DUI—to explain what it's like. Is it good? Probably not but let's find out buddy.

BLACK MAN, 39, CALIFORNIA
YOU WERE ARRESTED FOR POSSESSION? WHAT HAPPENED THERE?

Yeah when I was younger. I had a white female officer in San Francisco slam my face into the hood of her cop car because she didn't like my tone. She ended up arresting my Korean friend for an ounce of pot, but the DA threw it out. She knew he would but arrested us just to ruin our afternoons and make us deal with the system as a punishment for not being friendly enough with her. We were twenty-year-old college students in San Francisco who wouldn't play along with her and her partner's Officer Friendly bit. So she got mad, and when that didn't work to properly scare us, she flexed all her power, physical and systemic.

WHEN WAS YOUR DUI?

In LA in 2016 I got a DUI after a car wreck. It was caused by a rich prick white guy in a black BMW. He drove me off the freeway after he lost control of his car on a curve and I avoided him and hit a tree. When the CHP arrived I blew a .10. The legal limit in California is .08. It was after a bar trivia night. Obviously it was my fault. Clearly. But when the CHP and EMTs arrived the cops wouldn't let the EMTs come over and treat me until I agreed to a breathalyzer. I had slammed into a tree at sixty or seventy miles per hour. Never touched the brakes. I had five broken ribs and a ruptured spleen I later learned. At the time I just felt like I was dying. I told the CHP I couldn't breathe and it felt like I had a rib in my lung or heart. The cop said blow and we'll get you help. Afraid I'd die before help would be offered, I blew, knowing my lawyer friends would've advised against that. I blew and got a DUI. It's kinda bullshit to quibble but if I could have done what I knew white friends had done and waited until we got to the hospital, I doubt my BAC would have been so high. But that's an aside. Once I blew, the cop let the EMTs treat me. Another cop who saw what was left of my truck said I must have a guardian angel. An EMT said the same.

SO THEN YOU HAD TO GO TO COURT?

It lasted for eight visits over twenty months due to paperwork mistakes on the court's behalf. My black judge also didn't like my tone, my constant problem with the law, so he sentenced me to eighteen extra days of community service.

I asked my lawyer to attend court with me, since they kept fucking up my paperwork, and when he heard what I'd been assigned without him present, he said that's bullshit and made sure to attend my next court date. He got my community service reduced to three days after I'd performed six. Cut in half just because I had a lawyer. It was always the same black judge. He didn't even talk to me in court when my lawyer was there, and that's after he'd fucked with me on previous court visits when I was alone. I also saw, during my many visits, how he treated other POC versus white kids with DUIs. How much community service he assigned wasn't the same. Some were so rich they could pay to avoid such service. It felt like he was punishing us for being dumb enough to not avoid obvious classist/racist traps that ensnared us in the system, like getting a DUI. It seemed like he felt like being a dick and assigning extra service days was tough love. That was his idea of justice: extra punishment for us.

THE THING MY BUDDY WHO GOT JAMMED UP FOR A DUI RECENTLY WAS SAYING WAS HOW MUCH FEES AND PAPERWORK AND ALL THIS SHIT THEY MAKE YOU GO THROUGH THAT MOST PEOPLE PROBABLY DON'T THINK ABOUT ADD UP BIG TIME. WAS THAT THE CASE FOR YOU?

For sure. Constant fees. Court fees. Rescheduling fees. Payment adjustment request fees. Waiting in line to pay yet another fee so I could go back to court to hear about new fees. It's all people talked about: missed work, babysitter money, partner missing work. Well, that and the Lakers.

DID YOU HAVE TO SEE A PAROLE OFFICER OR ATTEND MEETINGS?

I attended weekly meetings for an alcohol program that took sixteen weeks. They were three hours per meeting at night. Plus court mandated AA meetings, another sixteen. Luckily those were only an hour on average.

WAS THERE ANY FLEXIBILITY IN TERMS OF ACCOMMODATING PEOPLE WITH WORK SCHEDULES OR KIDS OR WHATEVER?

Nope, and if you missed more than one alcohol meeting you had to start over and pay $400 to rejoin the program.

DO YOU THINK YOU'RE AN ALCOHOLIC OR WAS IT A CASE OF YOU HAD A COUPLE BEERS AND WERE PROBABLY TECHNICALLY DRUNK BUT IT'S THE TYPE OF THING ALMOST EVERYONE DOES?

I come from a drinking culture in a small college town. I know alcoholics and drunk driving. I also worked construction and saw how men got popped. This was me not waiting long enough to drive home and maybe should have ordered fries at bar trivia. That said, I have driven home when I definitely shouldn't, and this was not that.

HOW IS EVERYONE IN LA NOT JUST CONSTANTLY GETTING DUIS?

Uber and Lyft have been game changers. By the way my alcohol class was heavily POC, but it is LA, so that may mean nothing.

DID YOU LEARN ANYTHING IN THE CLASSES OR COME TO THINK ABOUT ANYTHING DIFFERENTLY OR CHANGE YOUR BEHAVIOR?

The classes were helpful, ultimately. It was like forced group therapy. It helped me see people that I knew in new ways, and to see myself in new ways, like, how I can't excuse my behavior even if it was never a problem before. The fact I was in that alcohol class was undeniable proof I had some kind of problem, so it was beneficial. I haven't ever got behind the wheel intoxicated since then. And I have had to be more honest with myself about the fact that I may be able to perform inebriated in a way that would avoid detection, but if some rando comes in and jacks me up, then I'm fucked. I could have killed people, and that would have been on me. So I have to be better able to account for the influence of randos. I can't be above the law because I could avoid detection.

It was humbling, and an awareness that I'm in a community, always. No man is an island, that sort of thing. It's not always the lions in the jungle that fuck you up, sometimes it's the mice. So, I can't drink and drive, not because of avoiding cops and getting away with it, but because I owe it to my community not to risk their lives due to my ego that says I'm fine.

WHITE WOMAN, 29, CALIFORNIA
HOW DID YOU GET ARRESTED?

It's so embarrassing. I was at Coachella. Did you know they have plain-clothes cops just chilling around like concert-goers? Well, I did not. So now I'm in a class twice a week where I have to sit with meth addicts and whatnot while an old woman disjointedly talks to us about not getting AIDs and Trump for an hour. But it's cheap, quick, and it'll be gone from my record.

WHAT HAPPENED, YOU DID A BUMP OUT IN THE CROWD OR SOMETHING?

They saw me taking something out of my shoe and rushed me. Like three people in regular clothes all at once ran up to me. I almost ran away thinking they were just robbing me or something. Fuck, that place is hell. Anyway, they are so aggressive with this that they even set up a little police station next to the entrance so they process you and then drive you back into the festival in a golf cart. The mugshots from all their busts must be great. Everyone is in festival gear.

AND THEN DID YOU HAVE TO GO TO REAL JAIL OR JUST GET A SUMMONS OR SOMETHING?

I never had to go to real jail. After they tested my coke right there in front of me in a tent, they did my fingerprints and mug shot and then drove me back to the show. I met up with the group again and everyone bought me beers.

HOW DID YOU FEEL? WERE YOU EMBARRASSED? DID YOU HAVE TO COME DOWN?

My group made it worse by seeing DJ Khaled. Arguably worse than getting busted.

The cops gave me my weed pen back, so that made it better. It's so wild to me that they did that. Coming from [another state], wow I'd have been in real jail real quick.

WERE YOU WORRIED AT FIRST YOU WERE IN DEEP SHIT?

Yeah, I thought I was in real trouble at first. But then I remembered that a lot of my friends have way worse shit like DUIs and they are fine. I mean, I wasn't putting anyone else in danger or anything. And the cop told me coke possession is just a misdemeanor so that helped, too.

WERE THE COPS SHITTY OR REASONABLE?

The cops were so shitty. Just openly mocking me for tearing up. Like, "Haha why are you so upset? Haha you're crying?" I wasn't even really crying! Just some anger and embarrassment tears with no boo-hooing or anything. But I guess you have to be extra shitty to be on that kind of beat. Who dreams of being that kind of cop? Just busting people on private property who are contained and partying in a designated area for partying? I get cops being shitty about DUIs and whatnot, but this is another level of being a shitty narc.

OBVIOUSLY I DON'T SUPPORT ARRESTING PEOPLE FOR DRUGS BUT I'D IMAGINE IT'S A LIABILITY THING OR SOMETHING. OVERDOSES AND SUCH.

Well, I get the liability angle. But I also don't. Like, I've been to so many festivals and have never heard of this. Not at ACL, not at Bonnaroo, not at Sasquatch.

HOW MUCH DID THEY TAKE FROM YOU?

I don't know for sure, actually. Not much. More than a gram, less than two grams maybe?

DID YOU HAVE TO GET A LAWYER AND EVERYTHING?

I got a kind of pre-trial situation. I agreed to take these classes instead. PC-1000 is the program. If I fail to do all my classes by the deadline or if I get kicked out of the program, then I agreed to automatically plead guilty and then I'd actually get sentenced.

My lawyer says the cops at Coachella are so, so bad. He routinely gets cases dismissed because the cops are so aggressive and dumb. They honestly often use "being at a concert" as probable cause, which is ridiculous and not legal. My lawyer gets a slew of Coachella cases every year, he says. He has a flat rate for it and everything. Fifteen hundred dollars flat rate for everything.

Not bad.

Yeah, the program has some fees too. I think I'll end up spending about $500 on it.

WHAT IS THE PROGRAM LIKE? HOW LONG DOES IT LAST?

One hour. I go twice a week just to speed through it. Your time is determined by the number of classes, not months. The length is determined by the court so everyone's is different. I've had two instructors. The first one was good. An ex addict and ex con—he really tried to help the people who needed it without condescending or punishing. The lady we have now is in her eighties, can barely hear what people say to her, and mostly wants to rant about hating Trump. But she also likes to talk about AIDS because she thinks people don't take it seriously these days.

THEY DON'T! AND WHAT IS THE FORMAT? LIKE A LECTURE OR DO YOU ALL SHARE?

It's open. The teacher asks us to check in and then after that she gives us a topic. Usually "just talk about current events." It's the most tedious and useless hour of my day. Although I have learned a lot about how gangs work in jails, which is interesting. I also have to go to eight AA classes. I haven't done those yet.

To be honest I feel like an asshole in these classes. I come in from work in office clothes and I've never had an addiction, really. Maybe Adderall for a year in college. But the rest of the people in my class, they've got real life problems.

DO YOU THINK BEING A YOUNG WHITE WOMAN HELPED YOU GET OFF RELATIVELY EASY?

Probably in some way. But in this case it's not immediately obvious where that came into play for a few reasons: 1) everyone at the Coachella cop tent that I saw was put back into the festival, 2) I never saw the judge and they never saw me unless my mug shot was shown during the hearing that my lawyer attended on my behalf, and 3) there's only one other white woman in the class. So, clearly, this PC-1000 program is giving a lot of people a second chance who aren't just young white people.

HAVE YOU PARTIED AGAIN SINCE THEN?

For sure. The program drug tests but that's why I stick to things that disappear quickly. No weed, for example. Coke is water soluble and so, unlike weed, doesn't stick around in your fatty tissue. I only have drug classes Mondays and Fridays. And I can miss a few as long as I don't miss two weeks' worth in a row. So I can time it out if I need.

WHITE MAN, 42, MASSACHUSETTS
I TAKE IT YOU DID NOT COME AWAY FROM THE EXPERIENCE WITH A GREAT IMPRESSION.

I was always vaguely aware that the justice system was a device to control society, but I was never fully aware of just what a money-making scheme it is and how once you enter it its sole design is to ensnare you and keep you trapped there for as long as possible. Throughout this entire process my one thought has been, Jesus fucking Christ imagine if I didn't have the support of my friends and family, a flexible, steady job, money in the bank, the ability to live in the city. I mean, this process is hard enough for a person with all that. Without those things it would be so easy to get overwhelmed and swept away to spend the rest of your life in a cage.

All of which made me realize for the very first time that almost every aspect of the state is designed to control its citizens. It is never about justice or reform. It is always about money and control, but because those in power are mostly exempt from its tyranny, it is depicted as a benevolent creature. Politicians and police and judges and parole officers and social workers are all out there keeping society safe is the bullshit they tell us. Once you experience it for yourself it's too late because now you're on the wrong side of it all and any complaint you might muster is viewed as suspect because shouldn't you have known better than to do whatever you did to put you on the wrong side of things? Isn't it really on you that you're getting ground to dust?

Don't get me wrong, I know I fucked up and broke the law, and I owe a debt to society. But this is not about paying a debt to society and it never was.

WHAT ARE THE HURDLES PEOPLE HAVE TO JUMP AFTER GETTING ARRESTED FOR A DUI?

On your day in court you have to have enough money for a lawyer, because if not you will be fucked even harder, so you sure better have a fucking lawyer boy. Three thousand dollars. My lawyer showed up to the court house, knew the DA, sat in the court room for thirty minutes having done zero prep work or anything other than utilize his connections developed over the years of working in the field, and the case was continued without finding, preventing me from having a conviction on my record. First hurdle passed.

YOU GOT PAROLE?

On TV parole officers are always checking up on the criminals they're assigned, making sure they're not up to no good or else Lennie Briscoe will pay them a visit to see where they were on the night in question.

I'm sure those parole officers exist, but that's not what this is. This is I sit down with a woman who I will never see again as she outlines the conditions of my parole. Which are: fill out a piece of paper stating my name and address, who I live with, whether I'm employed, if I've been arrested again, and then mail it in—because you cannot fill it out online because that might decrease the likelihood of you getting it in on time—by the fifteenth of the month every month for a year. I also had to sign up for and take the mandatory driver alcohol education classes, my license was suspended for forty days, and I can't leave the state until my parole is over without written permission. That will likely take up to two weeks to obtain, so you better hope you don't have to travel for work or no out-of-state emergencies pop up in the next year, because if so you'll likely have to risk violating parole and hoping you don't get caught.

THE FEES REALLY START TO ADD UP, RIGHT?

Yeah, most importantly it's "Pay us your money, bitch." And pay it on time or else you are in violation of your parole which will mean another court date and associated fees, another lawyer's fee if you can afford it, or the possibility of jail time if you cannot.

All of the fees, roughly a few thousand dollars, cannot be paid in full, and must be paid monthly, because again this increases the likelihood of a missed payment thereby sending you back into the jaws of the system. Also, if you don't want to mail a paper check in every month and risk it not getting to the court house on time then there is an additional fee for paying online.

GETTING TO THE CLASSES WITHOUT BEING ABLE TO DRIVE CAN BE AN ISSUE TOO?

If your license has been suspended good luck getting to the place to do so and to the job that you need in order to pay all the money you owe in order to stay in good standing and not getting shot back to the beginning and starting this process all over. You better hope you have the luxury of an understanding job, the resources to pay for transit, or someone to drive your ass around.

Before you can start your alcohol class you need to go for an evaluation. What that means is you have to sit down with a social worker type who works for the state and not you but is disguised as a health care professional. You should probably not let that fool you because at the end of the evaluation they will make a recommendation to the court re: how to deal with your criminal ass. So you fill out the paperwork on your history of drug use, alcohol abuse, criminal acts, depression and mental health, but you might not want to fill it out too completely for obvious reasons. After you fill that out, you make an appointment to see said social worker. When you get there you need to bring a money order because you can't use a credit card to pay for some reason and you can't use a credit card to buy a money order either, so you'd better have access to $200 because you're going to need that to keep this court-ordered appointment or else—you guessed it—you violated parole and will be returned to the beginning of this Kafkaesque process.

THIS IS REALLY MAKING ME NOT WANT TO DRIVE DRUNK, MAYBE THE SYSTEM WORKS! WHAT'S THE INTERVIEW CONSIST OF?

I'd already sat for an interview with a substance abuse professional in this same building you have to go to who worked with me to find a treatment plan that I've been adhering to and is working and has kept me sober for the last couple of months. But this other person works for the court so you have to do it all over again and sit there while they tell you that you're a pretty sorry human and they're going to recommend you take the two-hour class for sixteen weeks for $800.

The classes only meet evenings so if you work nights that's too bad you're going to have to make it work and you can't miss more than two classes during the sixteen weeks or you've violated parole. The only night I can attend this class conflicts with the support group I'm currently attending on my own volition and has helped tremendously with my mental state and efforts to stay sober but that doesn't really matter to them because you don't have to pay the state to go to that group. Treatment or reform isn't the goal of the system, that would be crazy. The goal is to keep you trapped here forever until they can bleed you dry.

HE'S NOT HURTING THE PEOPLE HE NEEDS TO BE HURTING

IF GOD SHOULD CONDEMN US THE WAY WE DO ONE ANOTHER WHAT HOPE WOULD THERE BE FOR ANY OF US

The first night Anthony Gay spent in the hole he probably didn't imagine there would be seven thousand nine hundred ninety-nine more of them to come. He'd recently arrived at a new correctional facility in Illinois having been transferred along with a man he'd had a fight with at the last one. Then they fought again at the new prison so it was off into the hole. Gay was scared and lonely in solitary confinement which is the name for the place where we pay the state to torture people and then don't think about it while we watch *Mrs. Maisel*. Gay recalled a time when he was younger and he'd taken a bunch of pills and had to be rushed to the hospital.

"Everyone was so concerned about me . . . It felt nice to have people care for me," he said according to the *Chicago Tribune*.

He got an idea.

Over the years as he was transferred around to other even more strict facilities Gay's mental health continued to deteriorate so he'd lash out at guards and get into fights with other inmates and continue to chip away at any hope he ever had of getting out early for good behavior. A few years stretched into twenty.

"Researchers have found little to suggest that extreme isolation is good for the psyche," a piece from PBS's *Frontline* a couple years ago reported which is surprising I would have thought it would make people feel great about themselves.

It's tricky to study the effects of isolation outside of prison settings because it's not exactly ethical to torture people for science it's only ethical to torture people for justice which is the name we give to revenge when we pay the state to do it and then don't think about it while we watch *Mrs. Maisel*.

A lot of the studies on isolation focus on the elderly which is another kind of prison.

One study on isolation *Frontline* mentions was done in the fifties on monkeys. A psychologist at the University of Wisconsin built a chamber he dubbed "the pit of despair" hey remember the *Princess Bride* that was a good movie. Aaaassss yooooooooou wiiiissshhhh. When I was in high school around the age Anthony Gay was getting ready to go to jail my friend and I acted out the battle of wits scene at a school talent show. I just had to correct a typo there I wrote battle of whites before which also would have worked. I was the Man in Black and we did the whole thing I could probably recite it all now. *Both* cups were poisoned lol owned. The year before we dressed up in our Boy Scout uniforms and set up a tent blindfolded on stage and now my buddy is a lawyer and I'm whatever this is.

Remember the scene in the Pit of Despair?

RUGEN: It took me half a lifetime to invent it. I'm sure you've discovered my deep and abiding interest in pain. At present I'm writing the definitive work on the subject. So I want you to be totally honest with me on how The Machine makes you feel.

The thing they put the monkeys in made it so they couldn't climb up the sides of the walls and they didn't have much space to move around.

After a day or two the researcher found "most subjects typically assume a hunched position in a corner of the bottom of the apparatus. One might presume at this point that they find their situation to be hopeless."

The ones he kept in isolation for longer eventually became "profoundly disturbed, given to staring blankly and rocking in place for long periods, circling their cages repetitively, and mutilating themselves." Some of them adjusted after getting out but others never did they weren't inside the hole anymore but the hole was inside them.

For most of the past century some version of solitary confinement has been used throughout the country but more sparingly than it is now, a day here or there, the American Psychological Association says. That's changed in recent decades. Prisoners might spend years at a time in the hole isolated for twenty-three hours a day. Some have spent decades inside. Yale Law School's Liman Program and the Association of State Correctional Administrators released a study in 2015 that said there were at least 100,000 people being held in administrative segregation at the time which is what they call the hole in the biz. Administrative segregation sounds like something Donald Trump is gonna come out for on TV any day now. But that number may have been a little high it's really hard to say because as Solitary Watch points out there are so many prisons under so many jurisdictions throughout the country and so little oversight over how this sort of information is gathered that it can be hard to say what's real or not.

You may or may not be surprised to hear that solitary confinement in America is also used on teenagers and for them much like for people with mental health issues it can be particularly harmful.

In any case it seems fairly safe to assume that people who didn't have mental health issues before going into solitary might come out of it with some but I didn't do a study on that so who can say for sure. Wait hold on a sec fine I'll look one up.

"A robust scientific literature has established the negative psychological effects of solitary confinement. The empirical findings are supported by a theoretical framework that underscores the importance of social contact to psychological as well as physical well-being," according to a study in the *Annual Review of Criminology* titled Restricting the Use of Solitary Confinement.

> In essence, human beings have a basic need to establish and maintain connections to others and the deprivation of opportunities to do so has a range of deleterious consequences. These scientific conclusions, as well as concerns about the high cost and lack of any demonstrated penological purpose that solitary confinement reliably serves, have led to an emerging consensus among correctional as well as professional, mental health, legal, and human rights organizations to drastically limit the practice.

In other words not only does solitary confinement severely fuck with the inmates' mental health it doesn't seem to have any sort of beneficial effect on prison behavior overall. You have to wonder if maybe the pain is the point then.

Here's another nerd:

"The placement of seriously mentally ill offenders in segregation exacerbates their pre-existing mental illness as well as causing the development of new forms of psychiatric pathology," Dr. Pablo Stewart a federal monitor wrote in a report in 2018 to the Illinois Department of Corrections castigating them for their treatment of mentally ill prisoners.

So there you go there's some people smarter than me saying the thing I said so now it's real.

Anthony Gay certainly had mental health issues and those compounded themselves with every trip back to the hole where eventually he realized the key to getting out if only for a short while: he needed to harm himself in more and more dramatic ways. That way he might qualify for a small heaping of sympathy.

He'd try to hang himself or slice open his neck arms legs and genitals. I saw a picture in the newspaper where his forearms were so scarred they looked like the branches of a great tree uprooted and suspended in the air with all of its roots dangling below. The type of tree if it were on your street you'd consider it a great loss if it ever blew over in a storm one day. The type of tree you talk about to people it's that imposing. How many trees do you ever talk to someone about?

He'd gotten the idea from seeing a cellmate of his being rushed to medical care after harming himself.

"Nurses come at the speed of light. Mental health and security," he said according to the *Chicago Tribune*. "They come running, and . . . it hit me. These people really love this dude, they really care. I wanted that kind of attention."

Have you ever been so despondent you thought the only way to get anyone to notice you was demonstrating your pain in dramatic fashion? Me too but not like this. My way is to write a newsletter.

At one point Gay sliced off a piece of his testicles and hung them on the door as an offering to the gods of basic human mercy you might call it.

The state and the prison cops didn't like this sort of shit of course so one cool trick the state attorney did as the *Tribune* reported was to charge him every time he would fuck up and act out but then space out the new charges against him in such a way that the statute of limitations was just about to pass each time. As a result Gay would be held in prison longer and longer and keep going back to the hole which is the type of thing you must have to dream about making happen when you show up on your first day of law school.

Then again Anthony Gay was acting up in prison and causing a fuss so maybe he deserved it and after all very dangerous people like this need to pay their debt to society right but the thing that sent nineteen-year-old Anthony Gay to prison in the first place which I forgot to mention earlier was that he got in a fight with a dude when he was a teen and took the guy's hat and one dollar off of him.

Eventually Gay's case came to the attention of prisoner advocate groups and one of them pointed out how they had been fucking with his sentences to the state attorney at the time whose name is Seth Uphoff. In 2012 Uphoff agreed to have Gay re-sentenced a prospect that gave him a glimpse of some light at the end of the tunnel so he managed to stop harming himself and now he's finally out and suing the state for the torture they had done to him.

Uphoff lost his next election bid against a guy who had the endorsement of the correction officers' union.

I just read a story on Solitary Watch that came from testimonies compiled by the Correctional Association of New York, "a nonprofit organization that monitors conditions in the state's prisons and advocates for a more humane and effective criminal justice system." Here is part of what one of the anonymous prisoners being held in solidarity said of the experience:

> I am enduring. What choice does one have? It is either endure or be broken: mentally, spiritually, physically, or otherwise. Though many will swiftly judge me due to the circumstances that brought me to prison, I am truly sorry for what happened. It is not who I am nor is it who I was. I was a young

irresponsible kid who did something foolish over almost two decades ago. It is not an excuse, but it is the reality. If God should condemn us the way we do one another, what hope would there be for any of us?

Can't do the time don't do the crime that's what I always say right. Sorry this one is getting a little heavy here's a funny tweet to break the tension from Keegan Hamilton one of the producers of the Vice series *Chapo* who was at the trial of the notorious drug kingpin.

"Most exciting moment was before the trial got underway this morning. The lights briefly went out, it was pitch black inside the courtroom. When the lights came back on, somebody shouted, 'He's gone!' Chapo hadn't moved. Everybody laughed, except maybe the US Marshals."

If there's one thing cops love doing more than torturing people or killing them or getting a hundred and fifty thousand dollars in overtime shifts it's crying about how hard and unfair their lives are which I was reminded of in a series of stories that all came out at the same time about the injustice of inmates eating food.

Four major outlets including *USA Today*, the *Washington Post*, the *Atlanta Journal Constitution* and NBC News all reported that inmates at Coleman federal prison in Florida had been served a slightly better than usual allotment of food over the holidays all while the prison's correctional officers were going without pay during the government shutdown. Each version of the story was as bad as the next but in terms of really smuggling weight the *Post's* was something else.

"'I been eatin' like a boss': Federal prisoners served steak by unpaid guards during shutdown" the headline read over a picture of a perfectly plated gourmet restaurant steak that I am going to guess looked nothing like the prison cafeteria food they actually got. Hard to figure out what sort of image the piece was trying to convey with that quote. They eventually changed the photo on the story probably because everyone yelled at them about it.

"This is like kicking someone when they are down," Joe Rojas a crying cop union head said to any publication that would print it and a lot of them did.

"You're giving a gift to somebody who committed a crime, but yet you won't pay the people who are supervising them," Sandy Parr, the food service foreman at well who the fuck cares where Sandy Parr works actually.

A lot of journalists go into the profession because they want to make the world better or to expose injustice and corruption and some of them go into it because they wanted to be cops but are too scared.

Incidentally a recent study from the Centers for Disease Control and Prevention found that "inmates are 6.4 times more likely to suffer from a food-related illness than the general population."

Inmates around the country have taken to suing their captors for the low quality of food. Here's the *Atlantic* on that:

> In May of 2017 for instance a class-action suit was filed against the Oregon Department of Corrections on behalf of current and former inmates alleging that the state-run food service is so subpar it amounts to cruel and unusual punishment. In recent years there have been news reports of inmates served rotten chicken tacos, rancid beef, and cake that had been nibbled on by rodents. Meanwhile in 2018 a Michigan judge dismissed a suit brought by an inmate who said he'd been repeatedly served moldy bread and spoiled hamburger meat. According to U.S. District Judge Gordon Quist, the complaint was without merit: in his view, the Eighth Amendment does not entitle prisoners to "tasty or aesthetically pleasing"

food, only to a diet that allows them to "maintain normal health" according to Michigan Live.

I don't know if that sounds right to me but I think we can all agree that U.S. District Judge Gordon Quist does however maintain the rights under the Constitution to go ahead and fuck himself.

Oh wait hold on I remember one even more infuriating thing from the NBC News version of this story.

"Adding to the staffers' bitter feelings, the working inmates were still drawing government paychecks for their prison jobs, which include painting buildings, cooking meals and mowing lawns," they wrote.

That wage is somewhere between $0.23 and $1.40 an hour according to the Prison Policy Initiative.

I'm so fucking mad my face is real hot right now I gotta walk it off hold on I'll be back in a bit hold on.

In Marianna, a Florida Panhandle town that was ravaged by Hurricane Michael last year things were not going so well for correctional facility workers or anyone there really due to the way the storm destroyed everything including the prison which is one of the biggest employers in town. Also the federal government shut down. A few hundred of the town's seven thousand residents relied on work at the medium-security prison there and so they were forced to start commuting hundreds of miles to where they relocated the inmates. The cops were having trouble paying their bills and worried about when the faucet will be turned back on according to the *New York Times.*

Few of the people the reporter went there to talk to were critical of Mr. Trump and seemed in favor of the wall via the area here is deeply Republican. One woman blamed the president though. She was another prison employee named Crystal Minton who the reporter found clearing remnants of the storm off of the roof of a friend's house.

She was putting off her transfer to the prison in Mississippi she had been reassigned to in the meantime because she is a single mother caring for disabled parents the *Times* said. She has seven-year-old twins.

Maybe Trump is to blame after all she said.

"I voted for him, and he's the one who's doing this," she said. "I thought he was going to do good things. He's not hurting the people he needs to be hurting."

I'm not a political scientist but if you asked me to summarize what it means to be a Republican in America that sounds about right to me. Some people deserve to be hurt and some do not and it's the government's job to do it to them.

RUGEN: As you know, the concept of the suction pump is centuries old. Well, really, that's all this is. Except that instead of sucking water, I'm sucking life. I've just sucked one year of your life away. I might one day go as high as five, but I really don't know what that would do to you. So, let's just start with what we have. What did this do to you? Tell me. And remember, this is for posterity, so be honest—how do you feel?

PEOPLE LIKE THAT THINK FAIRNESS IS A SYNONYM FOR JUSTICE

IT'S A CRUEL JEST TO SAY TO A BOOTLESS MAN THAT HE OUGHT TO LIFT HIMSELF BY HIS OWN BOOTSTRAPS

In January four people were found guilty of the crime of littering and trespassing in the Cabeza Prieta National Wildlife Refuge in Arizona and they faced up to six months in prison for their crimes which are serious crimes for sure due to we all would like to see such natural areas kept pristine and clear of refuse. But the problem is we don't all seem to be able to agree what the definition of trash is some of us think it's Hispanic people.

The four individuals were volunteers from a humanitarian aid group called No More Deaths and the reason they drove their car to a place where the rules say you can't drive your car and littered the eyesore water bottles all over the place is that this is an area where people making the arduous and dangerous journey to cross the border between Mexico and the United States have often died in the past and they didn't want anyone else to have to go and die like that.

They also left some cans of beans behind.

"The Defendants did not get an access permit, they did not remain on the designated roads, and they left water, food, and crates in the Refuge. All of this, in addition to violating the law, erodes the national decision to maintain the Refuge in its pristine nature," the judge Bernardo Velasco wrote in his decision according to the *Arizona Republic*.

"This verdict challenges not only No More Deaths volunteers, but people of conscience throughout the country," said Catherine Gaffney, speaking on behalf of No More Deaths and also on behalf of myself and yourself presumably.

"If giving water to someone dying of thirst is illegal, what humanity is left in the law of this country?"

That's a good question Catherine Gaffney.

Five other people affiliated with the group were set to go on trial in the next couple of months for similar crimes because there comes a point in the swift descent into fascism where it's no longer satisfactory for the state to merely injure an undesirable class of people eventually they have to start making an example of the ones who are trying to help them lest the rest of us go and get any wild ideas about what sort of humanity we have left.

He said a lot about justice but here is one thing Dr. Martin Luther King Jr. said about what justice is.

> I submit that an individual who breaks a law that conscience tells him is unjust, and who willingly accepts the penalty of imprisonment in order to arouse the conscience of the community over its injustice, is in reality expressing the highest respect for law.

When we talk about borders we typically mean the geographic kind and when we talk about walls we typically mean the tangible constructed kind but the clearest border and the most impenetrable wall on earth continues to be the one erected around the Babylonian towers of the wealth hoarders. The world's twenty-six richest people now control about the same amount of wealth as the 3.8 billion who make up the poorest half of people around the world Oxfam said in a report released in January. That gap is widening they said as the roughly two thousand billionaires around the world increased the size of their gold coin swimming pools by $2.5 billion dollars a day. In the United States they estimate thirty people control as much wealth as the poorer half of the population.

"The way our economies are organized means wealth is increasingly and unfairly concentrated among a privileged few while millions of people are barely subsisting," Oxfam's Matthew Spencer said regarding the report. "Women are dying for lack of decent maternity care and children are being denied an education that could be their route out of poverty. No one should be condemned to an earlier grave or a life of illiteracy simply because they were born poor."

Maybe they didn't want it hard enough? Maybe they were just lazy unlike the big rich boys we all love? Not sure if they checked into that in the report it doesn't say. "It doesn't have to be this way," Spencer went on. "There is enough wealth in the world to provide everyone with a fair chance in life. Governments should act to ensure that taxes raised from wealth and businesses paying their fair share are used to fund free, good-quality public services that can save and transform people's lives."

Sounds to me like he's just jealous he isn't a billionaire. I know I'm also not one but I could be someday so just to be safe I'm gonna side with them until all my hard work eventually pays off.

It's Martin Luther King Jr. day as I'm writing this which is the day we all come together to point out that if he were alive he would 100 percent support whatever it is that we happen to already believe ourselves and that he also probably would be our close personal friend. Mike Pence said Trump is basically MLK in his efforts to build the border wall.

You can say anything out there now man it's wild.

I just watched an interview King gave in 1967 to NBC and the interviewer asked him what it was about the negro uniquely among other groups of "immigrants" to America that has prevented them from assimilating and he explained it like so:

White America must see that no other ethnic group has been a slave on American soil. That is one thing that other immigrants haven't had to face. The other thing is that the color became a stigma. American society made the Negro's color a stigma.

America freed the slaves in 1863 through the Emancipation Proclamation of Abraham Lincoln, but gave them no land, or nothing in reality, as a matter of fact, to get started on. At the same time America was giving away millions of acres of land in the West and Midwest, which means there was a willingness to give the peasants from Europe an economic base. Yet it refused to give its black peasants from Africa, who came here involuntarily in chains and worked free for 244 years, any kind of economic base. So emancipation for the Negro was really freedom to hunger, it was freedom to the winds and rains of heaven, freedom without food to eat or land to cultivate. Therefore, it was freedom and famine at the same time. And when white Americans tell the Negro to lift himself by his own bootstraps, they don't look over the legacy of slavery and segregation.

Now I believe we ought to do all we can and seek to lift ourselves by our own bootstraps, but it's a cruel jest to say to a bootless man that he ought to lift himself by his own bootstraps. And many Negroes, by the thousands and millions, have been left bootless as a result of all of these years of oppression and as a result of a society that deliberately made his color a stigma and something worthless and degrading.

That all may be true but I feel like maybe if he were alive and he read an op-ed in the *Boston Globe* from that week by Jeff Jacoby declaring that racism isn't a big deal anymore he may have rethought his stance.

It's easy to conclude that racism is America's most serious problem if you turn on the news and listen to the whining libs Jacoby wrote. In reality racism isn't a big problem it's just a minor problem now. It's like when you have a serious cold and then a few days later it's mostly gone but you've got a bit of a cough still basically.

To prove that point Jacoby looked at surveys of white Americans over the years who said they wouldn't flee if a black family moved in next door to them anymore like they used to and that they had black friends themselves now (you wouldn't know them, uh, they live in another town), and that they're ok with interracial marriage. Pretty compelling case but one thing he didn't do was ask any black people what they thought. He did quote Jonah Goldberg from the *National Review* though so close enough.

I'm not sure if Jacoby read his own paper's recent spotlight investigation into race in the city but among some other great reporting there one thing it found was that the median net worth of African American families in good old Beantown (Go Patriots!) was $8. No that's not a typo although so many people thought it was they had to run a follow up story reassuring readers that it wasn't.

The median net worth for white households in Boston was almost $250,000 and the median net worth for Dominican ones was $0. Those sound like impossible numbers but the way it works is when you add up everything you own all your assets like your house and your car and your savings and all of that and you subtract debt and loans and credit card bills and so on your net worth could actually be negative. Making this all worse of course is that through redlining and predatory lending and discriminatory housing policy and all sorts of other very normal stuff we've continued to legislate economic instability into the lives of black people throughout the country.

On the other hand a lot of us know a black guy we might say hello to now and maybe we wouldn't even get all that pissed off if one of our children dated a black fella so you have to admit all this talk about racism all the time is a bit much.

Another place racism didn't actually exist if you look at the facts was at the March for Life rally in Washington D.C. Turns out those big rowdy Catholic school boys were actually the real victims if you think about it due to they didn't start it it was some yelling black guys and an elderly Native American man who drummed in their faces too solemnly.

People poured over every angle of the videos that emerged of the incident and that was great news for them because when you have so many different angles to look at something you can always find whatever it is you want to see. This is called waiting for all the facts to come in before rushing to judgment which is something the left and the media love to do we love to judge things as they appear to us morally and not wait for the other side to mount a defense on a technicality.

I wrote about the fact-waiting phenomenon and fairness around the time of the killing of Mike Brown by police officers in Ferguson.

"Waiting for all the facts to come in" is a common trope whenever there's a racially charged, or politically tendentious story in the news that captures all of our attention I wrote.

In theory, it's an appeal to some unreachable, platonic model of journalistic balance, the type of "some say, others say" equivocating that comprises most of the work done by our milquetoast national media. This myth presumes that the truth in any story must fall in the exact center of some probability distribution equation between either extreme. It assumes that both extremes hold equal validity, when that is almost never true.

The "waiting for the facts" refrain is most often bellowed from the wrongest people imaginable: 9/11-truthers, vaccine-deniers, climate-change skeptics, police-abuse apologists, homophobes, "race-realists." It's as if in every conceivable argument the truth will eventually out if we just hold on a little while longer, and see how things shake out.

Of course, it doesn't actually mean they want a thorough accounting of the details. Instead it means to wait for a preferred version of the facts to arrive, which are due presently.

In the case of Blue Lives Matters supporters with cop-kissing brains waiting for the facts means forestalling judgment until enough exculpatory evidence can be ginned-up. It means holding out long enough for the police to get their stories straight, to concoct a narrative in which people like Mike Brown are violent criminals. It means laying down covering fire long enough that the character assassins can get the target in their sights. It means anticipating phony injury reports being disseminated, for the likes of George Zimmerman to get their ducks in order, to bolster their defense. It means leaving the story's carcass out in the sun long enough for the vultures to pick it clean.

"Waiting for the facts" means waiting to develop a cover story. It means waiting for the story to blow over. It means waiting until "But that was seven months ago! Get over it!" becomes a legitimate excuse.

In Jeff Jacoby's *Boston Globe* piece about how racism is over he relied on a lot of facts something I am sure he was no doubt very proud of. The worst people alive are very committed to presenting facts but here are some other facts:

While people of color make up about 30 percent of the United States' population, they account for 60 percent of those imprisoned according to the Sentencing Project.

According to the Bureau of Justice Statistics, one in three black men can expect to go to prison in their lifetime.

In the seven-year period leading up to 2012 a black man was killed by a white police officer almost two times a week.

The problem with waiting for the facts is it's a form of control, of maintaining the populace's passivity in the face of curdling fury and well-earned anger. It's similar to the type of reasoning you hear from the right whenever there's a school shooting or a mass-killing. "Let's not politicize this," they say. "This is not the right time."

It's a means of punting and of forestalling the discussion that needs to happen.

The whole retreating to our respective corners fall-out of the March for Life rally video and the smirking MAGA teen was preordained from the moment it happened. No matter what the instance of racism is the right is going to go into the replay booth to buy time looking for the blade of grass that moved to convince the refs their original call was incorrect. Then the refs who are people like Jake Tapper are going to appeal to the letter of the rulebook out of a perverted sense of fairness.

People like that think fairness is a synonym for justice but it's not fairness is an impediment to justice a lot of the time. Fairness might be applying the law as it's written about where and when people can drive onto a wildlife refuge to leave water behind but it's not justice. Fairness might be treating people of different races equally in our personal interactions while ignoring systemic racism but it's not justice. Fairness might be letting people who've amassed large fortunes keep their money because they worked for it after all but it's not justice. Justice isn't fair it's just.

THERE REALLY IS A BEAUTY IN THE DESOLATION OF THAT

IT'S SOMETHING YOU CAN'T PHOTOGRAPH YOU JUST KIND OF FEEL IT WHEN YOU'RE THERE

Wildfires and tsunamis and other devastating natural disasters killed over ten thousand people in 2018 around the world and that seems bad is that bad I don't know. I do know what the World Economic Forum thinks however and turns out as they explained in a report from early January that extreme weather and failed climate change mitigation are the two most threatening global risks for 2019. Big year for those two items they said. Keep an eye on those.

While I was writing that sentence there was a weird sort of moaning sound coming from the other room and I've been like what the fuck is that weird sort of moaning sound coming from the other room this whole time and I just went and looked and it's the Keurig machine I definitely shouldn't have—but it was a gift!—and it's probably crying out for me to put it out of its misery because it feels bad about existing. But guess what bitch so do I so get in line.

Maybe that coffee decision will be made for me before too long actually because I just read a story from *Science Advances* that said 60 percent of coffee species in the wild could go extinct in the next few decades due to climate change. Ah you thought the climate apocalypse was bad but wait until you see me without my cup of joe haha.

Something called the CDP a U.K.-based nonprofit put out a report of their own this year where they asked a bunch of the largest companies around the world to outline their environmental impact. Doesn't look great! they said but there's always a silver lining.

As Bloomberg reported on the responses Bank of America is worried flooded homes will lead to defaults on mortgages, Walt Disney is worried it will be too hot and muggy in Florida for people to want to visit anymore and AT&T thinks hurricanes and fires could fuck up cell towers. Admittedly the worst part of no water is the elimination of human life on earth as we know it but there are other potential drawbacks too that maybe we aren't thinking of like how no water means no Coca-Cola as the company worries could happen.

For their part Visa nodded to the potential calamity of global warming by saying it could bring about global pandemics and armed conflict and also on top of that people would probably stop traveling so much and using their Visa card to purchase the flights which would hit them right in the ass.

"Any such decline in cross-border activity could impact the number of cross-border transactions we process and our foreign currency exchange activities, and in turn reduce our revenues," Visa said.

But it's not all bad news for the brands that we know and love. Some of them have already thought about how the apocalypse could actually bolster their bottom line like Merck & Co. who reported that "as the climate changes, there will be expanded markets for products for tropical and weather related diseases including waterborne illness."

I just looked up some waterborne illnesses and some of them sound horrifying like harmful algal blooms and primary amebic meningoencephalitis but on the other hand some of them are pretty funny sounding like hot tub rash.

Apple said that demand for the iPhone will remain stable in the IRL Mad Max because even in an emergency your phone "can serve as a flashlight or a siren; they can provide first aid instructions; they can act as a radio; and they can be charged for many days via car batteries or even hand cranks."

Google said that demand for Google Earth might increase because people around the world might want to use it to observe everywhere else being swallowed by the sea.

I sometime think it's unfair to the next generation to describe the conditions we live in as Hell World because it's only going to get worse every day from here on out unless something is done about climate change. Pre-Hell World maybe. While it's heartening to see some younger politicians like Alexandra Ocasio-Cortez treat it as the dire threat it actually is many in the Democratic field of hopefuls for president seem to be expressing the typical half measures which is dumb but nowhere near as dumb as what our large wet boy has had to say about it.

"Be careful and try staying in your house," Trump tweeted during a snowstorm this year. "Large parts of the Country are suffering from tremendous amounts of snow and near record setting cold. Amazing how big this system is. Wouldn't be bad to have a little of that good old fashioned Global Warming right now!"

I'm going to get the Keurig and fill a warm bath and put us both out of our misery as soon as I finish writing this.

Among many of the other unnecessary and cruel consequences of the still-ongoing government shutdown is the state of disrepair and squalor many of our national parks have fallen into and that is really curious to me because who are these people who are rushing into national parks like it's a prison riot to cut down trees and piss on the birds and empty out garbage bags into the river and steal steaming pies off the windows of kindly matrons now that the dreaded park rangers are finally off duty?

One such park that felt the absence of federal workers was St. Marks Wildlife Refuge in Tallahassee whose name you probably don't recognize but is the place that served as the bucolic muse for *Annihilation* the stunning book by Jeff VanderMeer, also made into the 2018 Alex Garland film starring Natalie Portman which was severely overlooked and you should go read the book and watch the movie now not at the same time though that would be weird.

Sometimes people will ask me they'll say Luke what is a good book and I will say *Annhilation* by Jeff VanderMeer and also *Cherry* by Nico Walker and then I'll hope they haven't already read those because I'm out of recommendations after that my brain isn't very good anymore.

I interviewed VanderMeer because he was seeing the effects the shutdown had on his beloved wildlife refuge and had been encouraging people to purchase an *Annihilation*-themed T-shirt to support the park.

I'VE READ THE BOOKS AND LOVED THEM SO I SORT OF GET THE CONNECTION BUT FOR PEOPLE WHO HAVEN'T, EXPLAIN WHAT THIS PLACE MEANS TO YOU.

Not to back up too far but I grew up overseas, my family traveled a lot, and I didn't really have a place that I thought of as a place that I was part of. Then we moved to Florida and eventually I moved up to Tallahassee in 1992. I discovered the St. Marks Wildlife Refuge and all the wilderness of north Florida and it's the longest I've been in one place. I feel very much attuned to the landscape, it really speaks to me. And St. Mark's Wildlife Refuge is . . . are you recording or writing it down?

I'M RECORDING.

Ok cool I didn't want to be going too fast. I'm caffeinated.

I USUALLY TYPE AS I GO BUT I'M FEELING A LITTLE HUNGOVER THIS MORNING SO . . .

I understand! Yeah so over time I grew to love this place and in particular St. Marks because it is one of the most unique places on the planet honestly. It has such a diversity of landscapes going from exactly the terrains described in *Annihilation*, which is these pine forests to these black water swamps and then out to basically marshland and brackish water and these lakes full of alligators and then the sea. It has species you can't find anywhere else. It's home to this pine salamander they're trying to save, it's endangered elsewhere because of development. It just has an amazing biodiversity. In fact north Florida in general, the last report I read, is among the top twenty most biodiverse places in the country. And that's gradually becoming in the world unfortunately because of development elsewhere. So north Florida has so far managed not to lose much if that makes any sense.

I THINK WHEN PEOPLE THINK ABOUT FLORIDA WE THINK OF THE BEACHES AND MAYBE SWAMPS AND SUCH BUT THIS ISN'T WHAT YOU NORMALLY THINK OF WHEN YOU THINK OF FLORIDA, RIGHT?

Exactly and that's because there's this huge difference between north Florida and south Florida. I think a lot of people think about south Florida and Miami and palm trees, and we do have some palm trees up here, but our terrain is more, in a way, interesting than that because it has those aspects but it also has aspects of what you might think of as Georgia, then also has the coastline. It's very unique. And then in the refuge you have places with reeds and things that almost remind you of the Pampas of Argentina or something. It's quite fascinating. And in the winter with the thistles and things there are parts of the park where you might think you're in Scotland. It's very strange.

DID YOUR INSPIRATION FOR THE WEIRDNESS IN THE BOOK COME FROM THIS SENSE OF PLACE? DOES IT FEEL EERIE, LIKE A PLACE THAT DOESN'T BELONG?

Yeah it does feel like a place out of time. It also feels very prehistoric when you're way out in the marsh flats. There are little islands and trees among the reeds and the mud. There's something really prehistorical about it. There really is a beauty in the desolation of that. It can be very silent, it can have the light in it that's like a Turner painting or something. It's something you can't photograph, you just kind of feel it when you're there. Part of it is the stillness and the wind and everything too. But the direct inspiration for the entire path that the expedition takes in *Annihilation* with some minor tweaks and supernatural elements so to speak, is the thirteen-mile hiking trail that I do out there taking me through all those terrains.

HOW DID YOUR ATTENTION TURN TO THE SHUTDOWN? ARE YOU IN TOUCH WITH THE PARK THERE? DID THEY REACH OUT TO YOU?

Basically what happened is over time *Annihilation* came to their attention and I was going into the store there and the nature center there anyway. I can't remember what the first contact was, but we had been in contact in general because they were thrilled about the book kind of giving a shout out to St. Marks. They were looking for an item to add to their store and they suggested this Area X T-shirt. To be honest a lot of people suggested a lot of products related to *Annihilation* and I always take it with a grain of salt in part because I want things to look a certain way connected to the series. They showed me this design and I was like holy crap the design is amazing, the cause is great, wonderful. And because of the T-shirt I've grown to know the people connected to the Friends of the St. Mark's Wildlife Refuge better which has been wonderful because they're all really committed to environmental causes. They're really fun interesting people. And most of them are not paid employees they're volunteers. They're manning the shop as volunteers because they believe in the place. That's why it's doubly troubling when something like this comes along and you realize with federal funding cuts and everything literally what they're making at the store, which is

volunteer-run, is helping fund endangered species programs. So it's
really vital.

WE'VE SEEN STORIES ABOUT PARKS GETTING OVERRUN WITH TRASH . . . IS THAT HAPPENING THERE?

Well there are two things. One is it's a little more remote than some of
those parks. I would say there's probably slightly more local traffic to
it. And those local people are very respectful to begin with. But there
has been an uptick in trash, and what's happened is the local chapter
of the Sierra Club, those folks have gone out every week and cleaned
up. I think they've even provided some toilet facilities and things like
that. We have a really strong community here in general and a large
part of that is a respect for the environment and a certain quality of
life. Tallahassee has more tree cover except for two cities in the U.S. It's
something ridiculous like sixty percent tree cover over the whole city.
When you fly in you can't see it basically. That's something that we're
very proud of, we've managed to create an urban landscape that's also
wild. And the St. Mark's Wildlife Refuge is kind of a sign and symbol of
everything that everybody loves around here.

WHAT'S YOUR OPINION WITH WHAT'S GOING ON WITH THE SHUTDOWN IN GENERAL?

It feels like a terrible cynical thing. I believe to some extent Trump
wants this chaos, because, and I don't know if it's even necessarily him
that's the most rigidly ideological about this, but I do believe there are
people in his administration pushing to destroy parts of government
because they believe those parts should not actually exist. Taking the
longer view that's the most troubling part of it. If it was just a petulant
display by the president it would be bad enough, but thinking of it as a
coordinated attack is quite chilling. You see some evidence of that in
the way he opened up some of the wildlife refuges because there were

planned hunts there. Or continuing to delve into oil leases in some of the parks while the shutdown is going on. So it's quite clear where the priorities are. And this is debilitating to everyone. This hurts everyone's quality of life.

It's actually imperative for our own survival with climate change that we keep as much natural space as possible. It's literally a no-brainer in terms of carbon dioxide and also with regards to having clean water and everything else. There's a fundamental dysfunction with this administration where they either don't care because they don't have to suffer the consequences or they literally don't understand how the world works.

It's hard to know what's scarier. So we're reduced to, or made to stand up for our own backyards, literally sometimes, and to really fight to hold onto things. The good thing is that a lot of people are responding to that and don't want to lose what they have, and I think we're seeing a lot of pushback.

YOU WRITE A LOT ABOUT ECOLOGICAL STUFF AND WEIRD THINGS THAT ARE PROBABLY GOING TO HAPPEN IN THE FUTURE. ARE YOU PESSIMISTIC OR OPTIMISTIC? ARE WE GOING TO BE AROUND IN A HUNDRED YEARS OR NOT?

I think the real question is should you stop caring no matter what your answer is to that question. Should you stop fighting? And the answer I have to that is no. We can't really know what all the consequences are going to be. There are so many variables about things that could go wrong or things that could be unexpected about how climate change will play out. Yes it probably will be catastrophic, and we need to be on a wartime footing so to speak to fight climate change. People need to be asked to sacrifice. I think if they're asked the right way and understand the urgency they'll respond to that because I do think it builds a sense of community too. But for my part the answer is I'm going down fighting no matter what. Apathy is really not an answer, especially because there are people who are on the frontlines of climate change experiencing devastation right now. It feels very privileged to just opt out and say, well, it's all going to go down the tubes so why should I care? But to answer your question there's a good possibility if we don't right the course we're going to be in huge trouble.

The *Los Angeles Times* just had an article about what our diets might look like in 2050. It read like something that assumes that our lives are going to be completely the same then as now except we're going to be eating less red meat. There's a real disconnect still about what the real-time on-the-ground conditions could be in 2050.

YEAH IT'S EASY FOR US AS RELATIVELY PRIVILEGED PEOPLE IN AMERICA. IT'S GOING TO DEVASTATE THE MOST IMPOVERISHED AREAS FIRST. YOU KNOW A THING OR TWO ABOUT DYSTOPIAN FICTION BUT I CAN REALLY JUST SEE IT PLAYING OUT EXACTLY LIKE THAT.

Yeah. The problem, especially on the coastlines, is you have very rich communities trying to protect themselves and basically telling the poor, pardon my French, to fuck off. It takes a great deal of denial, like in Miami Beach, to still be building. Or to be building pumps to take water away for flooding that won't be able to deal with the flooding. Even some of the prep doesn't make any sense.

WELL RICH PEOPLE ARE VERY BAD. I HOPE YOU HAVE DONE WELL OFF THE BOOKS THOUGH NO OFFENSE. SO IF PEOPLE BUY THESE T-SHIRTS WHAT IS IT GOING TO GO TOWARD?

It's going to go toward making up at least the 5-10 percent deficit they make from the shop, which because of the lack of funding in some areas is absolutely critical to things like their red cockaded woodpecker program which is something they're experimenting with where they're creating artificial habitats for the woodpeckers because the trees that they love are very rare. Endangered salamanders. Maintenance of the park, which is huge, because there's going to be a lot of maintenance issues after this dies down. They were already making up from a deficit because of the hurricane which caused a lot of unexpected costs with the shutdown of the shop. The other thing is in addition to buying a T-shirt you can still make a charitable donation through that contact point. You're dealing with a volunteer, someone who is spending their time trying to keep things going even through the shutdown. And it is making a huge difference.

DO BIG FANS GO DOWN THERE AND GO TO THE LIGHTHOUSE FROM THE BOOKS? IT IS LIKE A DESTINATION?

It's so surreal to me. It's just a place that I've hiked in for ages. But yeah there are people who go down there just to visit the lighthouse. In fact there's a platform for viewing the lighthouse, and someone actually wrote the words from the tower tunnel on the platform. It's faded a bit but you'll see from time to time on the platform lines from the book. At first I didn't even remember that they were lines from the book. The platform is the appropriate place for it by the way because it's in no way historical like the lighthouse, it's new. What's funny is they mostly use non-permanent magic marker which I appreciate.

I even get people who email to say they got married in a lighthouse because of *Annihilation* which is quite interesting.

THAT'S A LITTLE WEIRD BUT ALL RIGHT.

It is a little weird but sure.

THERE WERE A FEW PEOPLE THAT DIDN'T SUPPORT ME BUT THEY KEPT IT HIDDEN

AFTER A WHILE YOU HAVE TO LET THAT PRIDE GO

In the fifth week of the government shutdown which was a record vis-à-vis government shutdowns something we can all be proud of the Trump administration continued to downplay any effects it was having on the lives of furloughed workers because they would have to do that how else would they justify it to themselves and to their base. They'd have to make up all sorts of fantastical scenarios to be able to look at literal bread lines in the nation's capital and still think to themselves this is fine this is not that big of a deal all things considered we're getting away with it.

In Chicago TSA workers were stopping at area food pantries in order to be able to eat. They would show up in their TSA uniforms on the way to work so the people with the food would see that they're legit. It's like showing your desperation passport. I'm hungry the government uniform they have on says and the people there understand that to be true intuitively because people like that the ones who help people have to see things for how they are they don't have the luxury of engaging in flights of ideological fancy such as people like the president can.

It's hard to ask for help at first a lot of the workers said people like Darrell English vice president of Midway Airport Local 777 a TSA union.

"After a while you have to let that pride go," English told the *Tribune*. He's worked for the TSA for fourteen years which is to say he's worked for the government for fourteen years which is to say he's worked for you and I for fourteen years. The TSA still sucks though lol but not so much I want them to go hungry.

"You are talking to two senior management employees here," a Commerce Department worker at a pop-up food bank near D.C. told the *Washington Post*. Her husband works for the National Parks Service.

"This is pretty humiliating," she said.

Donald Trump doesn't give half of a shit or a fuck about that because he wants the wall very badly. We all know the wall is his thing and we all know he really does not like immigrants but even knowing that it's weird to think about how much he has committed to it right? He doesn't particularly seem like the type of person to commit to anything especially if it's hard but nonetheless he really really does not want Mexicans and Central Americans coming into the country. It's wild man. He lives for that shit. Imagine that being your thing? I'm into writing and exercising and drinking a gallon of brain poison so those are my things but his thing is having Mexican people walk in a different direction.

You may or may not be surprised to hear Trump's particular deal wasn't even the worst brand of horse shit coming out of the administration about the shutdown. Commerce secretary Wilbur Ross said in January he "doesn't really understand why" government workers have started going to food banks. Ross is eighty-one years old and doesn't look a day over five thousand and he's got at least $700 million dollars he can line his coffin with so we have to listen to what he thinks because that's how the news works.

"The thirty days of pay that some people will be out, there's no real reason why they shouldn't be able to get a loan against it," Ross said on

CNBC reminding us of the classic scenario we all know where banks will hand out loans to people who are out of work and barely making enough money to get by as it is.

This may or may not be related I don't know but a report from the Federal Reserve Board last year found that four in ten Americans couldn't cover an unexpected expense of $400 in the case of an emergency.

Ross also said airport workers who weren't showing up to work for free are pieces of shit.

"It's kind of disappointing that air traffic controllers are calling in sick in pretty large numbers," he said.

Many of them can't afford to do work for free he was told.

"Well, remember this, they are eventually going to be paid," Ross said. And even if they aren't, it's not like it's going to be a big hit on the economy over all.

"You're talking about 800,000 workers and while I feel sorry for the individuals that have hardship cases, 800,000 workers, if they never got their pay, which is not the case, they will eventually get it, but if they never got it, you're talking about a third of a percent on GDP so it's not like it's a gigantic number overall," he said.

Very good news for the GDP. Workers might not be so lucky. While an IOU may work for a multi-millionaire I'll pay you *eventually* doesn't tend to work when it comes to rent and groceries for working families.

White House economic adviser Kevin Hassett did Ross one better when he suggested furloughed workers were "better off" over the Christmas holiday because they were getting time off without having to use up vacation days.

"And then they come back and then they get their back pay, then they're, in some sense they're better off," Hassett said.

I don't know what Hassett's net worth is but he was an economic adviser to John McCain and George W. Bush and Mitt Romney and now Donald Trump so I think we can safely assume he's doing all right. Another job I saw he has when I looked it up was something called State Farm James Q. Wilson Chair in American Politics and Culture and Director of Research for Domestic Policy at the American Enterprise Institute and any time you have a job title that takes more than a couple words to describe that means you're rich.

Trump was asked to respond to Ross's weird comments and he came in and straightened out the whole situation with mind logic.

"Local people know who they are when they go for groceries and everything else, and I think what Wilbur was probably trying to say is that they will work along—I know banks are working along, if you have mortgages, the mortgagees, the mortgage—the folks collecting the interest and all of those things, they work along," he said.

"And that's what happens in a time like this, they know the people, they've been dealing with them for years, and they work along, the grocery store. And I think that's probably what Wilbur Ross meant, but I haven't seen his statement. But he's done a great job, I will tell you that."

Shortly after Ross spoke Larry Kudlow, director of the National Economic Council praised unpaid government workers as noble "volunteers" laboring for their love of the president and country.

When asked how coming to work without pay for fear of being fired counted as volunteering Kudlow who is a millionaire in his own right bristled as the question.

"With the respect to people who do have financial hardships . . . they are coming to work," he said. "They honor us by their service . . ." he said. "They do it because of their love for the country and the office of the presidency and presumably because their allegiance to President Trump . . ."

Other Republicans committed to the spin that unpaid workers remained supportive of Trump their own pay be damned. On Fox News Rep. Mark Green of Tennessee relayed a very real story about a TSA worker exhorting the Republicans for their efforts. "Build the wall," the worker told him. Did that actually happen? No one can say anything with 100 percent certainty but I can and I will tell you right now that is the realest thing that has ever happened. That TSA worker's name? Albert Einstein.

Oh shit hold on another thing that was dumb and bad happened which was on Monday of that same week Lara Trump the president's daughter-in-law waded into the shutdown controversy saying that going over a month without pay was a "little bit of pain."

"Listen, it's not fair to you and we all get that," she said. "But this is so much bigger than any one person. It is a little bit of pain but it's going to be for the future of our country. And their children and their grandchildren and generations after them will thank them for their sacrifice right now."

Responding to Ross's comments Nancy Pelosi asked, "Is this the 'let them eat cake' kind of attitude?"

Cake would be a generous offering from this administration. Let them eat shit is a lot closer to what they want.

Want to see something else very bad? I know that you do.

Casey Smitherman a superintendent of schools in Indiana was arrested and charged with three felonies and a misdemeanor including official misconduct, insurance fraud, insurance application fraud and identity deception earlier this year according to CBS.

Smitherman's offense against society for which she now owes us all a debt began like this: A fifteen-year-old student she had often taken an interest in including buying him clothes and helping him clean his house and so on due to his living situation wasn't that great didn't show up to school one day. She went to check on him and he appeared to have a serious case of strep throat or some shit so she took him to a clinic and they refused to treat him which is normal and fine and then she took him to another one and lied to them saying he was her son so that he could avail himself of the insurance she had and he did not. She also picked up some Amoxicillin at CVS under her son's name and illegally smuggled it to the sick boy she was worried about.

"As a parent, I know how serious this illness can be if left untreated, and I took him to an emergency clinic," Smitherman said in a statement. "I knew he did not have insurance, and I wanted to do all I could to help him get well."

The amount of her fraud including the clinic visit and prescription was $233.

I saw a video of Smitherman they had on the local TV news there in Indiana and she was crying and saying she was sorry for her mistakes.

"I know this action was wrong. In the moment, my only concern was for this child's health," she said. She said she didn't contact child services because she didn't want to see him placed in foster care so she just went ahead and helped him on her own.

Good news though the DA agreed to let her off easy. As long as she doesn't get into any more trouble for another year the charges will be dropped they said.

And then a couple weeks later she resigned anyway saying in a statement that her "recent lapse in judgment has brought negative attention" to the school and herself as the *Indianapolis Star* reported.

"I am very embarrassed for that, and I apologize to the board, the community and the teachers and students of Elwood Community Schools. I sincerely hope this single lapse in judgment does not tarnish all of the good work I've done for students over the span of my career."

Everyone knows there's a Dril tweet for everything that's just how our brains are wired now but for me there's one tweet that has become so reliable an illustration of how the centrist Democrat mind works that it's long since become hacky to even use it. Those of you with Twitter Brain Damage will know it as maplecocaine.jpg and it goes like this:

"Conservatives: Lets round up Muslims and put them in camps

Liberals: Hire [clap] More [clap] Women [clap] Guards [clap]

The most recent instance of this was a week or two ago when someone went to the *Washington Post* and pitched an idea to the editor and the editor said sure that sounds good to me let's see it and then they wrote a piece about how, yes, Mike Pence's wife Karen better known as Mother was in fact working at an elementary school that explicitly bars LGBTQ employees and students but isn't it nice that as a woman she's able to go back to work?

I bring that up because I was wrestling with the concept behind the joke when the news dropped that the Supreme Court would allow Trump's ban on transgender people serving in the military to go forward. This is obviously offensive to any person of decent conscience of course and I am fully supportive of inclusion and acceptance, but wait, I thought, why should I care about this particular issue, isn't it something like saying:

Make [clap] the [clap] servants [clap] of bloody [clap] American empire [clap] more inclusive [clap]

After some reading around I came across a piece by writer Laurie Charles that addressed this head on.

"There is no better PR for the modern imperialist adventure than a bit of 'pinkwashing'—the act of a company or government institution presenting itself as LGBTQ-friendly in order to downplay or distract from oppression it causes," she wrote on Foreign Policy In Focus.

"Wealthy nations with a big financial stake in the military industrial complex depend on pinkwashing to justify violence they inflict abroad as well as on their own citizens."

Sort of like when the NFL pretends to care about breast cancer and domestic violence for a month by putting on pink socks or whatever.

"Anti-imperialists are right to deride such violent propaganda, and ultimately allowing trans people to simply to be tokenized by the military industrial complex will never be a pathway to liberation. However, it would be a terrible mistake to think that transgender representation in the military has no impact on our rights in wider society," she went on.

Essentially the idea is that by letting the government experiment with such exclusionary practices in an area that is clearly given so much prominence the end result is expanding those harmful ideas outward into other parts of society. Much as we might wish it were not the military is still a pretty big deal vis-à-vis American norms.

Indeed as I was writing this lawmakers in Utah were trying to legislate the official existence of trans people out of existence by making it illegal to change a person's given biological sex on a birth certificate according to the *Salt Lake Tribune*.

Transgender service members have been speaking out against the illogic and cruelty of the ban that week and hoping to talk to one I came across the story of Riley Dosh, who is as she says the first openly transgender graduate of West Point to be discharged from the military.

Dosh was honorably discharged after she graduated in 2017 and denied a commission she had very much wanted since she was young. She was caught between enrolling during the Obama era and graduating after Trump had taken office and set his sights on rolling back his predecessor's policies. I spoke with Riley about her experience coming out while at the prestigious military academy and how Trump's tweet-fart-born policy has affected her life and the lives of her fellow transgender military hopefuls.

WHAT WAS YOUR REACTION TO NEWS FROM THE SUPREME COURT TODAY?

Well I didn't think I'd have to be rehashing arguments for why trans people should be in the military but here I am. I knew the Supreme Court was going to say something about it. I thought they would either take it up or return it to lower courts and at least put an injunction on the policy instead of allowing it to go forward.

ARE YOU AT ALL SURPRISED?

I am a little bit. I would say I'm surprised. This is something that has been reviewed for years now and the last administration saw no problem with allowing trans people in the military and suddenly we're back to this. This policy is literally based on Trump tweeting at 7 a.m. in the morning. People are trying to create a policy around the erratic decision.

THE IDEA THAT THE HEALTH CARE IS TOO EXPENSIVE TO SUPPORT TRANS PEOPLE IN THE MILITARY THAT TRUMP AND OTHERS HAVE PUT FORWARD IS BULLSHIT, RIGHT?

Yes, cost was one of the reasons Trump cited. That number is actually small. The Rand Corporation, by no means a liberal think tank, published a number between $2–8 million, often cited around $5 million, which in comparison Trump's border wall would cover the costs of 15,000 trans service members for the next 46,000 years. The difference in a million and a billion is lost on a lot of people. The cost here is literally a rounding error in the military's health care budget.

THERE ARE SOME EXCEPTIONS CARVED OUT IN THE RULING WHICH ARE CONFUSING, BUT IT'S ESSENTIALLY A BAN ISN'T IT?

They want to try to grandfather people out, and they're not going to allow people to join or reenlist. If they get this little bit here they'll continue pushing the policy even if the courts say they can't. They'll keep tweaking it a bit to say that they can't enlist.

WHY EVEN BOTHER WITH THE EXCEPTIONS THEY MENTIONED? TO MAKE IT LOOK LESS HOSTILE?

Exactly it's to make the policy look just different enough from the original ban that it requires a new court case. But it still is going to have a similar effect and it's going to lay down a precedent for them go to back to their original policy.

YOU DECIDED TO COME OUT IN THE MIDDLE OF YOUR TIME AT WEST POINT?

I came out as trans when I was at West Point. I was on track to graduate and I passed my commissioning physical, all the required standards as male. Then the decision to commission me, it was still on the books as requiring a waver, which was described to me as like a waver for a broken arm. A third of my class required wavers. The decision for that was pulled up to the Pentagon level and three weeks before I graduated they decided not to commission me. I was out on the street after graduation in 2017.

DID YOU FEEL BETRAYED?

I think so. I had been repeatedly told it would be a risk but that I shouldn't have anything to worry about. The administration at one point was fully behind me commissioning and the policy was already in place saying yes trans people can be in the military including service academy cadets, but suddenly somebody decided it's going to be too complicated and we're just not going to do it. They just turned their back on me.

MATTIS'S HEART WASN'T REALLY BEHIND THIS I READ.

His standpoint seemed to be he'd not have supported the policy in the first place to allow us to serve, however he recognized that reversing policy that had just been put into place would be more destructive than continuing to allow the policy to go forward. He didn't see it really as a problem so he didn't do much to implement Trump's idea of the policy.

ARE ATTITUDES IN THE MILITARY ON PAR WITH THE GENERAL PUBLIC WHEN IT COMES TO TRANS ISSUES IN YOUR OPINION?

I think they're generally on par with the public. I think a lot of stereotypes of the military come from the veteran base which tends to be older and white and male.

HOW DID PEOPLE TREAT YOU IN THE ACADEMY?

By and large it was good. All my friends and the people around me supported me. There were a few people that didn't support me but they kept it hidden behind anonymous social media. I never found out who they were in particular but beyond that everyone, to me at least, was very accommodating and friendly about the whole ordeal.

SO YOU HAVE TO COME UP WITH DIFFERENT PLANS FOR LIFE ALL OF A SUDDEN?

I did. Everyone who graduates just about goes on to commission and the very small number of us who don't we have to find new career paths. The problem is that West Point does not really line you up with a job in the private sector. In addition to that I was told three weeks before I grad- uated when I was already busy with

finals and other things so I did not have much time to prepare for a complete career switch. I was able to eventually find a new job and I'm happily employed now.

WHAT DO YOU DO?

I'm a data analyst consultant.

IS BEING IN THE MILITARY SOMETHING YOU ALWAYS WANTED TO DO?

Ever since I was thirteen years old I wanted to go to West Point and join the military.

IT'S NOT EASY TO GET IN RIGHT? WERE YOU A GOOD STUDENT AND ATHLETE AND ALL THAT?

Not at all. It took a very long nomination process. I did cross country and track and I was also on the math team and consistently on the honor role. Most people who go to West Point are pretty model high school students.

DO YOU THINK IN GENERAL THINGS ARE GETTING BETTER FOR ACCEPTANCE?

It's kind of hard to judge because you're viewing it from the lens of being in the moment kind of thing. Especially today with the emerging news it seems very negative. However, despite that, by and large public opinions of trans people have absolutely improved. The attitudes toward trans people from just five years ago are very different than they are today. How we listen to these trans people and they're able to come out and express themselves has absolutely changed for the better. So while we're fighting for things and having a hard time doing it, we weren't even able to fight for those things five years ago.

HOW DO YOU IDENTIFY POLITICALLY? ANY CANDIDATES YOU THINK MIGHT BE BETTER FOR TRANS ISSUES THAN OTHERS AT THIS POINT?

Politically I'm a liberal. I've heard pros and cons for various politicians. The one thing for me for any politician that gets nominated is they will be a better president, especially on these issues, than Trump. Trump has been devastating to the LGBT community. Any contender will absolutely be better than what he has done so far.

I'M CURIOUS ABOUT JOINING THE MILITARY. ARE YOU PATRIOTIC AND BELIEVE IN AMERICA AND ALL THAT STUFF?

The thing is that I very much do love America, however I will say that is not a requirement to join the military. There are cisgender people who join entirely for free college or join the National Guard a for a little extra money every month and that is totally ok. The idea you hear is that trans people are just joining the military to get cheaper health care. Most of the ones I know want to join to be in the military, but even if they weren't doing it for patriotic reasons, that would still be ok there's nothing wrong with that.

TOTALLY WASN'T MAKING THAT TRYING-TO-GET-FREE-HEALTH-CARE ARGUMENT I MEANT MORE LIKE, WELL, IT'S NOT THAT I HATE THE TROOPS PER SE, I JUST REALLY, REALLY DON'T LIKE WHAT WE DO WITH THEM.

Oh I understand. The military of any country is going to have problems due to the fact they are subject to the will of the country, and if the country is doing something that's not great then the impression falls negatively on the military as well. However I will say when I was at West Point one of the biggest topics we talked about was war crimes. They would say these are how these war crimes occurred, how we got into bad situations, and this is how we can prevent that. So while yes there are a lot of bad things that have occurred, there's constant focus on: this is really bad how do we fix it, and how do we not be as damaging to the communities that are in the war zone.

IF THIS ALL GOES AWAY WOULD YOU CONSIDER TRYING TO ENLIST AGAIN?

I am looking at my options for commissioning right now and have been for the past year.

SO YOU HAVEN'T GIVEN UP HOPE YET?

If I do end up going back in it would be the in Reserves, because I have a structured life now. It would be quite a jump to go back to active duty, but I do have hope.

IF THEY'RE BLACK JUST SHOOT THEM

WHAT IS THE INCENTIVE TO GO OUT AND MAKE A SPECIAL EFFORT?

One of the many lightning-fast decisions police have to make in their daily struggle putting their lives on the line to protect our freedoms is what to do when they come across an intoxicated person in a public place such as a parking garage. That was the topic of discussion at a meeting in February of 2017 as Sergeant Gregg Lewis addressed his squad in Portland, Oregon. You have to exercise your judgment Lewis told the boys for example if it's a businessman in a suit being publicly drunk in a rich seeming way you might not want to haul him off to detox because then he might sue you but on the other hand if it's a black homeless person you can just go ahead and shoot them to death because they aren't really people.

A number of officers present that day reported him soon thereafter Oregon Live reported which is somewhat heartening I suppose—not all cops baby! The exact phrasing of what he said in their accounts varied but the takeaway was the same.

"If you come across a guy in a suit and tie that came downtown and had a little too much to drink . . . he's probably not the guy you want to detox straight out of the garage. He will most likely sue you," one officer reported him saying. "If it's a homeless guy, you will probably be safe. I doubt he's going to sue you."

"If you find a homeless black person make sure you shoot and kill him," another recalled.

"If they're black just shoot them," reported yet another.

The remarks came a few days after a seventeen-year-old black boy named Quanice Hayes had been shot to death by police in the city. Hayes was a suspect in an armed robbery and when police found him they told him to crawl toward them on the ground but one of them named Officer Andrew Hearst said the boy seemed like he was reaching into his waistband so he shot him three times with an AR-15 including once in the head. (The AR in AR-15 stands for assault rifle.)

A while later they found a tan-colored toy air gun a few feet away from his body. Hayes and his girlfriend had been playing around with the fake gun in a hotel on Instagram the night before according to a story on Longreads. At one point they tried shooting it at the bathroom mirror but couldn't get the glass to break but police are more precious than even glass so you can never be too safe.

Lewis who had worked on the force since 1991 wasn't fired until a year after the remarks and the reason for his firing wasn't made public until another year after that in January of 2019 none of which we would know about if the police union hadn't filed a grievance on his behalf that could lead to his dismissal being overturned and putting him back in the line of duty.

While a number of the city leadership expressed their dismay and disgust with the situation they nonetheless were set to offer a settlement of $100,020.53 in back pay to Lewis and to erase the fact of his firing retroactively in which case he would be considered retired and receive pension credit for his adjusted service time. That $20.53 is particularly galling in its specificity isn't it. We can offer a hundred grand how does that sound? Fuck you give me every penny.

The city said the risk of going to arbitration in which case Lewis might end up being allowed to go back to work was too great so it would be better to pay him not to be a police officer anymore and just have the whole thing done with and maybe they are right.

The Racism Olympics were a real close contest that month with images surfacing of Virginia governor Ralph Northam posing in either a KKK costume or in black face in a picture from his medical school yearbook at Racism Medical School and Liam Neeson confessing out of nowhere that he once harbored a fantasy about killing a black guy to extract a sort of cosmically balancing racist revenge on a man who had once raped a friend. But when it comes to the real uncut stuff you can never really beat the cops like this one guy named Gary Steele a police officer in Detroit. Steele pulled over a black woman on a Tuesday night in February and found she had an expired registration so he had her car towed as local news station WXYZ-TV reported.

Steele offered her a ride home on what was a freezing night but the woman who was a twenty-four-year-old named Ariel Moore refused. Steele did what anyone else might do in that situation he fired up his Snapchat and mocked her as she walked away. "Bye Felicia," he can be heard saying on the video which he also went ahead and decorated with some lovely stickers saying "Celebrating Black history month" and "What black girl magic looks like."

In a total shocker it turns out Steele was charged with domestic violence in 2008 for assaulting his girlfriend and shooting a gun near her head not because he did this Snapchat business just because he's a cop and cops loves to do domestic violence. A while back the National Center for Women and Policing pointed to a pair of studies that found a marked increase in instances of domestic violence in the families of police officers.

Two studies have found that at least 40 percent of police officer families experience domestic violence, in contrast to 10 percent of families in the general population. A third study of older and more experienced officers found a rate of 24 percent, indicating that domestic violence is 2-4 times more common among police families than American families in general.

The studies they pointed to are somewhat outdated by now but on the other hand those numbers might even be low for all we know because it seems likely we wouldn't even have records of a significant number of such cases. Police violence barely gets tabulated nationally when they murder someone never mind something so minor as knocking their old lady around.

As the *Atlantic* noted in a 2014 piece on the topic, "Research is so scant and inadequate that a precise accounting of the problem's scope is impossible."

And even if the domestic violence does go into the books it tends not to result in much in the way of punishment.

"[M]ost departments across the country typically handle cases of police family violence informally, often without an official report, investigation, or even check of the victim's safety," they wrote, adding that "even officers who are found guilty of domestic violence are unlikely to be fired, arrested, or referred for prosecution."

Something else cops love to do besides beating their families and getting away with it is stealing money from people over nothing. This year *Greenville News* in South Carolina ran a multi-part investigation into the routine practice of civil forfeiture through which police departments in the state enrich themselves by seizing money and property from people suspected of, not even convicted of, committing crimes.

The investigation found that in a fifth of forfeiture cases in South Carolina, no one is convicted of a crime. In 19 percent of cases, there is no criminal arrest. Law enforcement seizes property from black people 71 percent of the time, with the overwhelming majority of cases involving younger black men.

Some of the police they spoke with said the process was fair because the people could always go in front of a judge to get their property back and spend the money they no longer have on a lawyer. But as they also found in the study in 75 percent of the cases the police end up keeping all of the shit they take and in 19 percent people only get part of it back. In cases like this it's not like a typical criminal trial instead the burden of proof is on the suspect to prove that they didn't acquire the $500 in cash in their glove box or whatever from criminal activity. The amount of money seized they found tends to be smallish amounts like that because well like they said in the Portland drunk hypothetical rich guys tend to be able to sue you and poor ones can't.

Some of the other police they talked to cried about how hard it would be for them to do their jobs if they didn't get to steal money all the time.

Clemson Police Chief Jimmy Dixon said if police didn't get to collect forfeiture money it would hamper the department's ability to conduct long-term drug surveillance.

"It could potentially shut down our K-9 unit," he said. "Overall, our ability to conduct undercover narcotics operations could be stifled."

Lt. Jake Mahoney with the Aiken Police Department said they'd have to divert money from the budget to cover drug enforcement.

Greenwood Police Chief Gerald Brooks said it would "sharply curtail our drug enforcement activities."

The best response however came from a fella named Jarrod Bruder who is the head of the South Carolina Sheriff's Association. He said the quiet part out loud.

Without being able to keep the money they take "what is the incentive to go out and make a special effort?" he asked. "What is the incentive for interdiction?"

I just saw a story where Howard Schultz the billionaire former Starbucks head said the word billionaire is offensive and that billionaires should be referred to as "people of means" or "people of wealth" instead.

The day he said that would have been Trayvon Martin's twenty-fourth birthday and a little something I unfortunately always think of every year on this day due to I have brain troubles is just how much Ben Shapiro the famous respectable conservative intellectual was happy that he was killed.

Shapiro has tweeted about Trayvon many dozens of times over the years but this one in particular tends to stick with me from 2016 where he posted that "Trayvon Martin would have turned 21 today if he hadn't taken a man's head and beaten it on the pavement before being shot."

There's also this one from the same day where he posted that "Trayvon Martin was 5'11" and 158 lbs," which I want to say is funny because it shows how a 5'11" 158 lb. teenager would of course seem like a towering giant to Shapiro but that type of spite doesn't particularly make me feel much better at the moment.

An interesting if depressing thing to look at is Shapiro's history of tweeting about this topic. The first time he did it was on April 1 of 2012 a couple months after Trayvon's death. For dozens of tweets for over a year Shapiro got almost no engagement on any of them. Most of Shapiro's Trayvon content would go by almost entirely unremarked upon, often getting zero likes or replies for a while after that. The first that seems to get any sort of modest response is this one from 2013:

How about honoring Trayvon Martin by standing up for less banging of heads on sidewalks?

Then things dip back down again until a couple years later.

> To earn love from the black community, Hillary makes a pil-
> grimage to the shrine of St. Trayvon of the Blessed Hoodie

He didn't stop riffing on the murder all that time mind you he kept at it but no one seemed to care as much as he did until later on. That's how the greats get ahead by the way whether it's an undersized white guy like Julian Edelman who just works harder than everyone else until he becomes Super Bowl MVP or an undersized white guy like Ben Shapiro who punches in to his job at the Racism Store every day and puts his head down and gets the work done.

Around 2016 something happened that seems to have increased the potential audience for racist tweets though and Shapiro started doing real numbers. All of a sudden out of nowhere sharing and trafficking in barely concealed racism started to become socially acceptable and even downright beneficial for people. We may never fully understand what that shift was.

FOR A SELECT FEW THERE ARE NO CONSEQUENCES

I UNDERSTAND THE ANGER AND DISAPPOINTMENT THAT MANY OF YOU FEEL

Andy Rubin created the Android software that's the thing we all know about ol' Android Andy as everyone calls him but another thing we know about him now is that after an investigation into a sexual misconduct allegation in which he is said to have coerced an employee into a sexual act in 2013 he was asked for his resignation by Google CEO Larry Page. Google is actually called Alphabet now but I'm not going to call it that it's like when they keep renaming the sports stadium or concert venue in your city after a different bank every other year and someone tells you that they're going there to see a show or whatever and you're like what the fuck is that is that new and then they say the old name from a few years ago and you're like oh that place. Then you think well I better switch to this other bank for all my banking needs due to it sounds like it's affiliated with cool stuff.

Rubin leaving the company sounds pretty bad like it would come with all sorts of negative consequences you would think but as the *New York Times* reported despite his departure from the company he was awarded a $90 million severance package at the time which we didn't know about for four years because Google had managed to keep the whole thing quiet. They even praised him on the way out the door. The payments were reportedly broken up into installments of $2 million a month the last of which was paid out toward the end of 2018.

Shortly after that all became public in November of 2018 thousands of Google employees around the world walked off the job to protest among other things the way sexual harassment allegations were being handled within the company. Richard DeVaul the director of Google X had also resigned that month when it was reported he had sexually harassed a job applicant.

"I know firsthand that our human resources and employee relations processes aim to protect the company, not the employees," Colin McMillen who works at the Google offices in Cambridge, Massachusetts, and walked out told me around then. "I know second-hand multiple stories of people taking credible allegations of harassment or worse to HR and getting unhelpful solutions."

"A slap on the wrist for any credibly accused harasser is totally unacceptable and unjust, no matter how much money they bring in or what amazing products they helped build," another employee from the Cambridge office who asked to remain anonymous said. "The lowest-paid worker must be given the same respect in a dispute as the most successful executive," they said.

At the time chief executive Sundar Pichai sent out an email apologizing for the way the company had handled such allegations in the past and said that forty-eight people and thirteen managers had been fired over the past two years which is good news I guess but you sort of wish all that harassin' hadn't happened for so long.

"I understand the anger and disappointment that many of you feel," he wrote in the email to employees. "I feel it as well, and I am fully committed to making progress on an issue that has persisted for far too long in our society, and, yes, here at Google, too."

All of which sounds very nice and understanding but whoops it turns out Google has been asking the government to narrow legal protections for workers organizing online all along something that would curtail for example their ability to arrange actions like the walkout.

In 2014 the National Labor Relations Board expanded employees' rights to use work email to organize. In the meantime Google's attorneys have been asking them to cut that shit out Bloomberg reported in January because it's unfair for workers to use the email they have beneficently been provided in order to try to make their conditions somewhat better.

Sometimes I can't tell if Google and companies like them are evil or not because on the one hand they do a lot of evil shit but on the other hand they say things that sound good in press releases and company memos so you have to guess the truth of the matter is located somewhere exactly in the middle of those two poles if you're a blue check mark media guy with a brain like a sinking rowboat like me.

Elsewhere in the *New York Times* report on Google the climate of sexual relationships between other employees was detailed including one affair between David Drummond the chief legal officer and Jennifer Blakely a senior contract manager. When the two revealed they had a child together to human resources Blakely said her career stalled out while Drummond's accelerated.

"For a select few, there are no consequences," she told the *New York Times*. "Google felt like I was the liability."

That's often true at a lot of companies ah fuck hold on I am super late to a meeting I was supposed to go to at eleven but I thought it was at noon fuck hold on.

Sorry about that. They want me to do an emo podcast or something. Not my problem. After the coffee meeting I went to the store to get some laxatives because I wasn't feeling that regular due to not drinking I guess? There are a lot of mysteries revealed and withheld by the human body every day and it's a journey and you love to be on it. The digestive system is like . . . a beautiful woman to me.

Where was I anyway oh right. As was seen in Brett Kavanaugh's Supreme Court nomination and with much of the discussion surrounding sexual assault and misconduct allegations brought to light by the #metoo movement at large there persists a dogged undercurrent of fear about how such accusations can ruin the lives of men. Won't someone think of the poor men. But much like everything else when it comes to powerful men it turns out having your life ruined in such a fashion can be a pretty lucrative proposition because for every Louis C.K. who claims he "lost $35 million in an hour" after the news about him jacking off all over the place came out there are men whose downfall comes with a significant financial parachute.

In September of 2018 when Les Moonves stepped down after further sexual harassment allegations had been brought against him there were conflicting reports about what if any payout the CBS chief executive would be owed. At the time CBS said it would place the $120 million he might have otherwise expected aside until an outside investigation into the matter was complete. Once it was they determined that Moonves had obstructed the investigation and among other things that he had had an employee who was "on call" to perform oral sex on his old gross dick the company decided that he was not eligible for the money after all. Moonves being a decent man said all right fair enough I'll take the L here I'm already rich just kidding he's going to arbitration to get it because he still thinks he's owed the cash.

You ever walk around just looking at guys thinking this fucking guy then you see another guy and you think this fucking guy.

In 2016 after he resigned from his position as the CEO of Fox due to his facing numerous sexual harassment allegations of his own Roger Ailes walked out the door with a reported $40 million package according to the *Guardian* but he's dead now lol you old dead piece of shit.

Another big time Fox News perv Bill O'Reilly reportedly paid out tens of millions of dollars to settle allegations brought against him a while ago but in a weird twist he landed on his feet financially as well. Even after Fox had been made aware of the payouts and allegations his $25-million-a-year contract was renewed. What a world man. You can do whatever.

While he was eventually forced out after it turned out he had harassed too many women to feasibly ignore anymore O'Reilly was set up to receive all or a significant portion of his contract upon his departure the *New York Times* reported.

On the plus side Matt Lauer's contract was canceled after he was fired from NBC and casino executive and prolific creep Steve Wynn reportedly lost hundreds of millions in potential severance following his resignation from Wynn Resorts Ltd. the *Wall Street Journal* said so there is occasionally justice in the world but not as often as you might like there to be.

One thing that people love to talk about vis-à-vis the universe balancing out on the side of the good guys (me and you) is when some random dude catches a break like in July of last year when a young Alabama man named Walter Carr was held up as an exemplar of the indomitable spirit of American perseverance.

Carr is a twenty-year-old college student and he was set to start a new job on a Saturday morning with the moving company Bellhops. At the last minute his car broke down and he wasn't able to find a ride from friends to get there so he decided to walk instead. He began the roughly twenty-mile walk from his home at midnight hoping to get there by 8 a.m. the next day to meet the rest of the movers according to ABC News. He brought along a knife to protect himself against any stray dogs.

Along the way around 4 a.m. in the morning Carr was stopped by local police officers if you know what I mean who out of the kindness of their hearts if you know what I mean asked him where he was headed. When he explained the situation and after his story checked out they decided to give him a ride the rest of the way even going so far as to take him to breakfast.

"He was very polite. It was 'yes sir' and 'no sir,'" one of the officers later said. I bet he was!

When he arrived at the moving job a few hours later complete with a police escort they explained the situation to Jenny Lamey the woman who had hired the movers. Inspired by Carr's work ethic and apparent decency she shared the story on Facebook where it soon went viral and before long the story eventually came to the attention of Bellhops CEO Luke Marklin who arranged to meet Carr a few days later for a big surprise.

"This is how you pay it forward . . . treat your employees with respect and incentivize them and bet you'll get a much better worker for it," wrote one commenter on Twitter when the story came out. "It is awesome to see a young man not make an excuse like it's too far to go to work, and then see him rewarded for it. Wish the young man and the company all the best in the future," wrote another.

"He's such a humble, kindhearted person," Lamey said. "He's really incredible. He said it was the way he was raised."

"We set a really high bar for heart and grit and . . . you just blew it away," Marklin told Carr when they eventually met and then Marklin gave him his own used 2014 Ford Escape as Alabama.com reported. Barely used!

On top of that a GoFundMe set up by Lamey to help Carr with his car troubles eventually raised over $90,000.

"Nothing is impossible unless you say it's impossible," Lamey told the *Post*.

Nothing except for paying workers an actual salary with benefits which you may not be surprised to hear Bellhops does not actually do. Essentially Uber for movers—Marklin came to the company from Uber—Bellhops relies on the labor of young college students like Carr who take jobs on a gig-by-gig basis. The company operates in dozens of cities around the country and has raised tens of millions of dollars in rounds of funding since it was founded in 2011 but it still pays movers between $13-16 an hour.

"It's a transitional job," CEO Cameron Doody told BuzzFeed News in a story from 2015 about how they do things. "It's not a career," he said which is what people always say about jobs that don't pay very well or offer benefits or anything like that. Working at McDonald's isn't supposed to be a career people say. Fuck you they say.

Alabama by the way is only one of five states that has traditionally never spent any state money on public transportation that a guy like Carr might have been able to use to get to his job that's not a job.

Naturally Bellhops were very proud of themselves for helping the one guy there and reveled in all the attention. You can't buy this kind of publicity.

"I want people to know this—no matter what the challenge is, you can break through the challenge," Carr said. He also wants to become a Marine some day he said and you can imagine how much the Facebook page-lookin mole people liked that extra flourish.

To some Carr's story was yet another example that if you work hard enough and keep a positive attitude good things will come to you. To others it was a glaring indictment of the brutal and indifferent hell of the nightmare capitalist wasteland we all suffer in.

It's also a reminder that much like when it comes to getting sick or injured in America which needs to be done in a tragic but endearing enough way to go viral so people will pay your medical bills all you have to do to make it in this beautiful country is have your life fall apart in such a way that the news wants to write about it then hope the benign feudal lords will see fit to offer you a token reward as an aspirational example to the rest of us so we shut the fuck up.

I don't know what you think when you hear a story like that or one when like a girl scout or whoever raises $600 selling lemonade so her mommy can stop having to go to the "ompcolojist" all the time but it's impossible for me to feel much relief or happiness for anyone because the existence of the story in the first place by its very nature highlights how many people don't get to win the feel good lottery. It's like when you're watching a big Hollywood action film like *Avengers* or *Transformers* or whatever and the camera follows one guy who keeps dodging robot missiles and you're like thank god they made it! but meanwhile every skyscraper in the city just got demolished by a space monster's giant ass and tens of thousands of people are dying in the rubble but still the one guy made it. Every fucking movie is a holocaust it's fucking crazy but then the hero pulls the main lady close at the end and they don't fuck because it's PG but everyone goes home happy and stops thinking about the piles of crushed bodies in the background because the camera didn't focus on them it was busy showing something else.

THEY'RE JUST COVERING IT UP. THIS KEEPS HAPPENING

THEY'RE NOT ABLE TO SEE A LOGICAL WAY OUT

The doctor on the phone in the recording is distraught. "We've just had another doctor jump and hit . . . suicide from Mount Sinai," the woman says. "And they're just covering it up. This keeps happening."

She goes on: They're working twenty-eight-hour shifts. She's scared for herself and she's scared for her patients' safety. They're being told to go back and do their work.

You can hear her voice in *Do No Harm* the documentary from Emmy-winning filmmaker Robyn Symon and you can see the body of Dr. Deelshad Joomun where she landed laying there under a yellow tarp on the ground below. She had jumped in her white lab coat.

In the span of two years three physicians and one medical student died by suicide at Mount Sinai St. Luke's Hospital in New York City a grouping of deaths that garnered a lot of sensationalized media coverage. But the hospital's attempt to brush things under the rug pointed to what has become a trend regarding the issue of physician suicide across the country: most people—medical professionals, institutions and the public at large—are complicit in pretending there's nothing to see here.

Last fall Symon lead a group of physicians and activists on a march to Mount Sinai in part as a memorial for Joomun and the other estimated four hundred physicians a year lost to suicide as well as to put pressure on Congress to pass legislation that would restrict the number of hours that residents—medical trainees on whom much of the work at hospitals is pushed onto—are allowed to work. As of now it can be more than eighty hours a week including twenty-eight-hour shifts.

"We're marching to protest the inhumane working conditions within hospitals, which include long work hours," Symon told me that week. "The Institute of Medicine and many sleep experts have said after sixteen hours the brain is just not functioning normally. Every other profession has work hour protections. Doctors are dealing with human lives. Why would you want them to stay up all night? It's a very dangerous situation."

Symon and others who study the epidemic of doctor suicides like Pamela Wible a physician in Eugene, Oregon, who runs a suicide hot-line for medical professionals say that these types of work conditions play a role in the disproportionate number of suicides among doctors. The most recent study by the CDC attempted to analyze suicide rates by occupational groups but the report was retracted due to inaccuracies. Regardless the disproportionately high rate of doctor suicides cannot be disputed.

"Mostly due to exploiting cheap labor, medical trainees have not been protected by many of the labor laws that the rest of the country enjoys. They are in an educational system that is rampant with human rights violations, and, as a result, some don't make it out of their training because they take their [own] life," Wible told me. "They're not able to see a logical way out, they're $300,000 in debt from loans, all these people are dying around them, and they have guilt for any mistakes they may have made after working twenty-eight hour shifts. It's just a perfect storm."

"All of these forces are converging on these young idealistic humanitarians who go into medicine. I think they don't quite understand what they're getting into, what their working conditions will ultimately be," Wible said.

While numbers vary the American Foundation for Suicide Prevention says male physicians are 1.4 times more likely than men in general to commit suicide and women physicians are 2.27 times more likely. Suicide is the second leading cause of death among medical residents after cancer and the leading cause among male residents. Although to be honest those numbers are likely a lot lower than the reality of the situation.

"That number is so unreported," Symon said of the commonly referenced four hundred physician suicides a year.

"Doctors are very good at making their own death look like an accident, accidental overdose or car accident. And the institutions and the families themselves, because of the shame surrounding suicide, are prone to brush things under the rug, hide it or leave it sort of nebulous what the cause was. It's hard to know the exact number of deaths among medical students. It's at least twice the national average," Symon said.

Wible told me two doctors she dated while she was in medical school later went on to kill themselves. She started to take the issue of physician suicides more seriously once three of them in her relatively small city of Eugene, Oregon, with a population of 160,000 killed themselves within a span of about a year.

"It's really a town where everyone is happy. I was thinking, 'If there are three in Eugene in a year, how many are there in Chicago, Philadelphia, New York?'" she said.

She began compiling a list of physician suicides on her website not long thereafter in 2012. Since then, she's collected information on over one thousand a number she says is very low since the data is largely sent in by family members of the doctors who've died.

Symon said every doctor she spoke to over the course of making her documentary admitted to knowing one colleague who had been lost to suicide and many knew more than that. She doesn't know how to fix it and I don't do you but as with many problems like this it's a lot harder to fix something when people don't feel comfortable admitting it exists.

"Talking about it, opening a dialogue about this epidemic that's been hidden for decades, really a century it's been going on for and known within the medical community," she said. "The first step is talking about it. They were trained to put your head down, go about your work, be tough, show no weakness, you're the healer. This is what they've been bred to do."

MISERY IS A THIN BLANKET BUT IT'S BETTER THAN BEING COMPLETELY EXPOSED

YOU SEE IT FOR WHAT IT REALLY IS AND IT LOOKS LIKE OBLIVION

Within the next thirty years sea levels rising are projected to put 311,000 coastal homes in the contiguous U.S. at risk of regular flooding a study from the Union of Concerned Scientists from 2018 says. They also get into the numbers in terms of property value saying things like the collective market value of the homes in question is $117.5 billion but I don't know what that means that doesn't particularly mean anything to me. I don't really have the ability to hold the concept of thousands of homes underwater and how much they would have cost if they weren't underwater in my mind at the same time. Did you ever drop your phone or something into the water and you think ah fuck that phone was worth $800 but it isn't anymore is it so it's pointless to think about things that used to be true.

"By the end of the century, 2.4 million homes and 107,000 commercial properties currently worth more than $1 trillion altogether could be at risk," they said and they also said the state that will get it the worst is Florida.

Miami and the Florida Keys and the Tampa–St. Petersburg area are the cities particularly at risk they said. One time Michelle and I went to Miami and we did not particularly like it we felt like loafing malformed land beasts or cast-outs from a medieval village like the guy who would be so ugly they would chase him off and make him go live on a hill alone. I went to a gym there and it was a normal gym nothing weird or anything and then later I read that someone came in there with a gun and killed some people. On Miami Beach we sat under a shared towel they made us buy at the little beach kiosk for twenty dollars and refused to buy a second one out of principal and we watched a couple who looked like they film all their workouts like *did you get it did you get it are you filming* throw food to the swarming seagulls and hated them quietly amongst ourselves and they also filmed that for Instagram I'm guessing. The birds all swarmed and shit everywhere and cried while I went swimming but Michelle didn't which isn't particularly remarkable since I generally go swimming and she generally doesn't but we both have our own specific shit going on so that is how that works. Sometimes we both do and it's very nice.

One time in St. Petersburg we went to the wedding of some old friends and I got the type of sunburn on the beach that you take a picture of thinking everyone has got to see this sunburn and then you don't ever get around to showing anyone because who cares and then it fades away. The night after the wedding everyone was feeling pretty good about themselves so we went out into the dark waves and then a small shark swam up and everyone freaked out like get the fuck out of the water someone yelled. I sang a song during the ceremony which is something my close friends used to have me do and in this case it was a Bright Eyes song called "The First Day of My Life."

A couple of times we went to the Florida Keys which is the Massachusetts of Florida and so it is the place we belong. We have done all the things you are supposed to do there such as go have your allergies fuck you up at Hemingway's cat shit home and eat conch fritters and key lime pie and get recreational alcohol poisoning on boats of various sizes. We both really liked that show *Bloodline* set in the Keys so one time we tried to go see as many of the locations from it and I wrote about it and I wrote things like this about the experience:

It was a slow, plodding trip, making our way out toward Boca Chica Key, where Osborn wanted to show us a sandbar perfect for swimming, just off the coast of a busy Naval Air Station. We passed by the local jail, with beautiful views overlooking the water. "Waterfront property," he joked. "Even going to jail's not bad here."

Along the floor of the shallows, sea-sponges were in abundance. Around 100 years ago, they were the most valuable fishery in all of Florida, with around 600,000 pounds produced annually. Today it's a tenth of that. The Japanese were one of the chief markets, utilizing them for a number of medical uses, including their natural ability to soak up blood.

Turning up around the Keys, northwest, he brought the boat to a stall. "Look there," he said. A dark shape bobbed just beneath the surface, in waters clear enough to see through, but roiling enough to obscure the visage. We trailed the fish for a while, heading it off to get a better look. My wife and I leaned in closer, and before he could even explain what it was, I felt it announce itself. "That's a 350-pound bull shark," Osborn said. Having never seen a dangerous shark in the wild before, its liquid, primal energy was visceral. I am not cut out for life on the water, I thought.

Although we traveled a few miles away in the opposite direction from the shark, our swim on the sandbar was fraught with anxiety. Another stop, to snorkel in the shallows near a mangrove outcropping, was similarly nerve wracking. Along these outgrowths you might find mud piles four or five feet high, and see little caves in the mud with antenna sticking out. That's partly how they find their lobsters here. The gnarled branches of the saltwater trees, jutting out of the water, growing over one another, brought to mind a scene from *Bloodline*. This would be a good place to lose a body, I thought. A heron burst forth from the bushes as I swam determinedly back to the boat. Overhead fighter jets roared in the sky, coming and going from the nearby naval base, their lethal power a mirror image of the shark whose presence I couldn't shake.

Here's me back again this isn't a quote from the other piece. After that we went to a couple of dive bars and talked to locals about what they thought about the show and most of them said it wasn't realistic because nothing on TV is ever real right and they'd say that's not what it's like on this Key they'd say it's actually worse on another one because the other place is always worse than the one you live in. Wherever people live there is always a bad place nearby that has to be used by point of comparison due to it lets us feel better about our own particular set of shit. Most people don't spend a lot of time all that worried about people from places they don't come into contact with and never will although if you can get them really riled up about that that could be an effective strategy for such things as fascism. The famous thing everyone says about horror movies is that the monster is always scarier when you don't get a close look at it you have to fill in the gaps with your imagination and it's really hard to think of something as a monster when you see it at the grocery store buying toothpaste and diapers. I got a really good look at that bull shark though and it was still really fucking scary though so maybe the saying isn't true.

I read a story on Business Insider about a condo on Miami Beach which is a two-story penthouse that is on sale for $68 million dollars. That would shatter the price for a home there they say and it looks very nice but the catch is that it will probably be underwater at some point. Not the condo itself because it's very high up at the top of a tall building but everything else below it. I guess maybe you could get back and forth to it with a boat or a helicopter.

People don't seem to think the end of the world is actually around the corner people like the president and probably all of the people you have muted on Facebook and I don't really understand why they are so resistant to the idea. I guess it's hard to imagine the world ending just like it's hard to imagine yourself dying.

They say that the scientists are just talking about climate change for the money and I guess that's possible since climate scientists are famously wealthy as we all know but then again so are oil companies and their lobbyists and the politicians they buy off so you gotta hear both sides in my opinion.

There's a short story that has stayed with me for a long time called "The Ceiling" by Kevin Brockmeier for which he won the O. Henry Award in 2002 which was something that seemed like an enormous deal to me at the time I'm not sure where people stand vis-à-vis that being a thing or not anymore since I've let the part of me that cared about literature atrophy since then.

In the story the narrator notices a dark shape across the light of the moon one night and day by day it gets bigger and bigger and at first they aren't sure if it's expanding in space or getting closer. Some of the people in the town say it's not actually there and that people are just seeing things. Soon they realize the birds and insects have all disappeared and no one knows where they've gone and things start to get tense but by and large people go on with their lives going to work and getting their hair cut and carrying on extramarital affairs the three things people do.

"By the time the object had fallen as low as the tree spires, we had noticed the acceleration in the wind," it reads.

In the thin strip of space between the ceiling and the pavement, it narrowed and kindled and collected speed. We could hear it buffeting the walls of our houses at night, and it produced a constant low sigh in the darkness of movie halls. People emerging from their doorways could be seen to brace themselves against the charge and pressure of it. It was as if our entire town were an alley between tall buildings.

Eventually the ceiling as they call it gets low enough that towers begin to crumble and then low enough that people can touch it and then low enough that they can perceive the shape their breath takes when it presses against them like a window on a cold day.

The rest of the town seemed to follow in a matter of days, falling to the ground beneath the weight of the ceiling. Billboards and streetlamps, chimneys and statues. Church steeples, derricks, and telephone poles. Klaxon rods and restaurant signs. Apartment buildings and energy pylons. Trees released a steady sprinkle of leaves and pine cones, then came timbering to the earth—those that were broad and healthy cleaving straight down the heartwood, those that were thin and pliant bending until they cracked. Maintenance workers installed panels of light along the sidewalk, routing the electricity through underground cables. The ceiling itself proved unassailable. It bruised fists and knuckles. It stripped the teeth from power saws. It broke drill bits. It extinguished flames.

One afternoon the television antenna tumbled from my roof-top, landing on the hedges in a zigzag of wire. A chunk of plaster fell across the kitchen table as I was eating dinner that night. I heard a board split in the living room wall the next morning, and then another in the hallway, and then another in the bedroom. It sounded like gunshots detonating in a closed room. Melissa and Joshua were already waiting on the front lawn when I got there. A boy was standing on a heap of rubble across the street playing Atlas, his upraked shoulders supporting the world. A man on a stepladder was pasting a sign to the ceiling: SHOP AT CARSON'S. Melissa pulled her jacket tighter. Joshua took my sleeve. A trough spread open beneath the shingles of our roof, and we watched our house collapse into a mass of brick and mortar.

The story is really about a marriage collapsing though and the ceiling is a metaphor by the way in case that isn't obvious.

You see a lot of people on the news all the time saying things like the Green New Deal are fantasies and unrealistic and unafforda-ble. I watched an interview with Howard Schultz the billionaire with a humiliation fetish who will never be president and he said he was concerned about climate change but that the Green New Deal was immoral. I don't know what he means by that or what anyone means when they talk about the price of reversing climate change. The idea of trying to address it through sensible economic policies and not huge and costly leaps of imagination and the expenditure of vast sums of money is hard for me to understand because what will money even mean once it's over. It makes no sense it's like a person with terminal cancer saying they'd rather not pay for risky surgery today because they still have to save up their frequent flier miles but what does flying even mean when you're dead the concept of flight doesn't even exist anymore.

I used to hear people say that alcoholism is a progressive disease and not entirely register what that meant but now I take it to mean it's something that keeps getting worse and worse the longer you pretend it's not there.

It's mid February when I'm editing this part of the book hey guys and lately I've stopped doing things like drinking every single day which is what I had been doing for a couple of years there in case that whole "drinking way too much" theme hasn't really stood out in the book. I guess the reason for that is I stopped wanting to be dead all the time(?). Or maybe I stopped wanting to be dead all the time because I stopped drinking all the time who's to say which came first. I haven't quit entirely although maybe that will come at some point but going down to two or three nights a week has been sort of a revelation. I had forgotten what it's like to go to bed sober longing for restful sleep instead of muttering fuck you into the void as it tackles me into unconsciousness. I had forgotten how to read a book for an hour and drift off to sleep then wake up without cursing my return. I used to read so much before bed and then one day I didn't read anymore. I'm reading a book right now called *The Cabin at the End of the World* by Paul Tremblay and it's good and tense but it bothers me how often he diverts from the main narrative which is pretty rich coming from me the guy who wrote all of this.

There's a common saying about drinking which is that when you do it you're borrowing happiness from tomorrow and that made sense to me for a long time because drinking was something that made me happy in the short term then miserable the next day but after a while the happiness wasn't the point anymore it was the misery I was after.

Borrowing misery from yesterday. Misery is a thin blanket but it's better than being completely exposed.

I sort of miss that aspirational annihilation lately. I feel like I robbed myself of something comforting like when you're in an emotionally abusive relationship that you know logically you don't deserve but then when it's over you still end up missing them and someone says you're better off now and you are like yeah you're right but you're just saying that so they'll shut up. When you're drinking to lean into depression it is harmful obviously but at least it feels like you've got a tangible end goal you're working toward. The thing is you need to keep at it and if you get some space from it you see it for what it really is and it looks like oblivion.

So fine I don't want to die all that much at this particular moment no guarantees and I also don't want the earth to die but I know both things are going to happen I guess we just gotta figure out how much we want to prolong the inevitable and what we're willing to sacrifice in the process.

THAT IS SO MUCH WORSE THAN YOU WERE PROBABLY ALREADY IMAGINING RIGHT?

YOU GET THE MONEY AND YOU HORDE THE MONEY

In June of 2018 the Department of Homeland Security Inspector General conducted an unannounced tour of Essex County Correctional Facility in Newark which is funny because this time it was DHS scaring cops by showing up without warning. Ah fuck the cops are here. No one likes to see the cops fuck with anyone unless it's a group of more powerful cops fucking with smaller-time cops then that is always very good. Surprise bitch the cops are here.

What did they find well it wasn't great what they found there let me say that right upfront. If you somehow thought what they had found there was going to turn out to be normal and good then you're probably reading the wrong book buddy because a report they released in February 2019 revealed sickening health and safety violations and a failure to report misconduct by guards among other things.

From 2015 to 2018 ICE paid three counties in New Jersey alone including Essex, Bergen, and Hudson Counties over $150 million according to WNYC. In Essex County they were holding around eight hundred such immigrants at the time of the inspection.

While protests have risen in New Jersey and around the country about such practices local politicians are often loathe to abandon the significant revenue stream the contracts provide saying things like it would result in a need to raise local taxes. People don't want to pay higher taxes is something they say. Most people would rather have the immigrant torture mills run in their backyards without thinking about it they don't actually come out and say but that's the idea anyway.

The facility in question like many around the country contracts with ICE to house undocumented immigrants who are awaiting hearings on their immigration status or waiting to be deported and otherwise being made to eat shit both figuratively and literally.

The DHS report detailed a "host of food safety problems that could endanger the health of detainees."

Among the issues they found were raw or expired meat, "open packages of raw chicken leaking blood all over refrigeration units," and "slimy, foul-smelling lunch meat, which appeared to be spoiled."

"Although this mishandling of meats can spread salmonella, listeria, and E. coli, leading to serious foodborne illness, we observed facility staff serving this potentially spoiled meat to detainees," the report found.

In interviews with detainees DHS heard of frequent complaints of vomiting and diarrhea. "For dinner, we were served meatballs that smell like fecal matter. The food was rotten," one reported in a grievance. "The food that we received has been complete garbage, it's becoming impossible to eat it. It gets worse every day. It literally looks like it came from the garbage dumpster; I have a stomach infection because of it and the nurse herself told me it was caused by the food," said another.

Elsewhere they found unsanitary conditions in the living and shower facilities which were often moldy and littered with peeling paint.

"During our inspection, we found ongoing leaks in every housing unit holding detainees. We observed two of the leaks dripping directly onto detainee beds," they reported. "We also witnessed trash cans placed around the facility to catch water leaking from the ceiling. These leaks can cause mold and mildew growth, which can spread throughout the facility leading to serious health issues for detainees, including allergic reactions and persistent illnesses."

One more thing is that the facility lacked outdoor recreation space which is required under ICE contracts and when a place like this isn't even living up to the famous hospitality standards of ICE you know something has gone really wrong.

On top of the multitude of health violations the facility also failed to report a significant security incident in which a corrections officer left behind his loaded gun in the bathroom. Maybe he was dealing with a particularly serious bout of diarrhea from eating in the cafeteria and lost track of space and time as a long stretch on the shitter can often do to a person. Have you tried taking a shit without having your phone on you lately it's wild. You just . . . sit there and think about the shit coming out.

A detainee working on a cleaning shift found the cop's gun and reported it before anyone used it thankfully. I don't know what might have happened due to I've never been to prison but it seems like having a loaded gun going around in one might be a disruption vis-à-vis morale. The guard was suspended for ninety days which really ended up being forty-five and the detainee was told not to tell anyone and then they all never reported it to ICE so they wouldn't get in trouble and risk having the money spigot turned off. The only people who hate the idea of snitching on their colleagues more than criminals are the cops.

The Economic Policy Institute released a report of their own about a different type of prison with horrific conditions which is known as the American economy. Among the things they found were "rising wage inequality and sluggish hourly wage growth for the vast majority of workers" despite steady productivity growth. It's hard to say where all of the value from the productivity growth is going if wage inequality is increasing maybe it's just disappearing.

"Although the unemployment rate continued to fall and participation in the labor market continued to grow over the last year, most workers are experiencing moderate wage growth and even workers who have seen more significant gains are just making up ground lost during the Great Recession and slow recovery rather than getting ahead," the report said.

They also found that from 2000 to 2018, "wage growth was strongest for the highest-wage workers, continuing the trend in rising wage inequality over the last four decades."

Here's an interesting complicating factor in the data as pointed out by the *Washington Post*. Due to how rich people are afforded all manner of allowances that people like us would never have even thought about the real wage growth disparity number is probably a lot worse than the report says because "for confidentiality reasons" wages are only recorded up to a certain point.

> "All workers who report weekly earnings *above* $2,884.61 (annual earnings for full-year workers above $150,000) are recorded as having weekly earnings of *exactly* $2,884.61, to preserve the anonymity of respondents," [Elise] Gould writes. That top-code threshold hasn't been updated since 1998. As a result, the survey is becoming less useful for tracking top incomes at a time when public concern over inequality is growing.

In other words when it comes to tracking wages for the richest among us they just put an arbitrary cap on it and say eh close enough.

You know who is pretty rich it's the Walton family who own Walmart and they had their best quarter in a decade leading to a $3.3 billion gain in the family fortune at the beginning of 2019. Shares in Walmart rose 2.2 percent according to Bloomberg and so that means the family controls $175.2 billion now a number that's gone up $14 billion since 2019 began which was fifty-two days ago as of this writing. That's $269.2 million a day which isn't bad all things considered.

Here's a really dumb take from the editor of a very dumb magazine called *Quillette* which you do not need to worry about if you post on Twitter fewer than thirty times a day.

"I would say that most of the time, inequality and poverty in advanced economies cannot be solved via the simple redistribution of wealth," Claire Lehmann tweeted in February. "If you've ever worked, lived or spent actual time with people trapped in the underclass, the problem is not *lack of money*."

"I've known people who have held down jobs and who are generally fine until the fortnightly paycheck comes, then it's a 3-day bender until they end up passed out somewhere or arrested. The cycle continues. This is not a problem caused by a lack of money," she wrote and I agree with her that addicts deserve to live in squalor and die without being able to afford treatment I think we can all agree on that. They can't be trusted with the money because who knows what they might do with it.

One thing I don't understand is why people on the right are always so quick to worry about what poor people might do were they to come into money. You've probably heard even otherwise "liberal" people you know decline to give money to a homeless person because they don't know what they are going to do with it right. I'd rather buy him a sandwich your friends says and then they don't.

Why don't those same people ever seem to worry about what the very wealthy are doing with their money? What are the Waltons doing with the $269.2 million the kindly stock market put into their rattling change coffee cup? I'd be really interested in hearing the answer to that. Probably not spending $269.2 million at the liquor store I think it's safe to assume because rich people don't do that they have a different addiction which is called having money that's the normal kind of addiction and it's also sometimes called success. You get the money and you horde the money and you look at the number as it gets bigger and bigger so big that you have a guy come in and tell you what the number is because at that point you're so rich you don't even need to read numbers you just listen to them and then at the end of the day you know it's there. Ah, the large number you think to yourself.

There are all kinds of ways that addiction can destroy a person's humanity and break them down into a hollow shell whose only goal each day is satiating the need for the substance be it alcohol or drugs or whatever else and that is not good we all know that but at least those sorts of addicts are actually using the thing they crave which you have to respect in a way. The drugs are not going to waste they are being consumed I can safely report that. I can probably count on one hand the number of times I went out and got drugs myself and then held onto them for safe keeping later. A money addict on the other hand just gets the money from their money dealer and sets it aside and after a while forgets it's there because they don't actually get high on possessing and having the money their real addiction is just taking it to make sure no one else can. No one could ever spend as much money as the Waltons have in a lifetime but to be able to prevent other people from having it? Now that is something you could really get off on.

✌

WE PRETEND WE DON'T SEE EACH OTHER

IF I CRY—SOMETIMES I CRY, BECAUSE I'M PRETTY SICK—THEY WILL JUST TRY TO MAKE ME FEEL BETTER

Here is how it will go starting today. You will continue your life apace cresting on the occasional minor victories and accomplishments and suffering through the humiliations and indignities and losses and at one point the latter will begin to outnumber the former and that is in the best case scenario where you get to be the type of miraculous person whose pain is largely back-ended in life and doesn't arrive early like a surprise guest who got the date of your party wrong. The door bell rings and Jeff is outside what the heck Jeff my friend what brings you over on this specific day and Jeff says he thought the party was today but it wasn't it's not until a later date but nonetheless Jeff is here now.

Long into the middle thickness of your life you will continue to accumulate friends and family members and acquaintances and then there will come a tipping point and you will stop doing that and the doors of your train will close like there's no more room and so people have to be left behind on the platform there as you speed off. Then later on still the number of people who you know and have access to will begin to steadily decrease and keep decreasing and maybe you will sense when this switch flips and maybe you will not. At some point the people who die on you will stop feeling like they're dying at a reasonable and fair death-age and they will start dying at a cruel and unimaginable age which is the age you are. You will see a family member at a funeral who you haven't seen since the last funeral and you will shoot the shit a little bit there with them and then when it's time to go you will say welp see you at the next one and you'll think I should make an effort to see my cousins more but you won't and then one day it will be too late.

You know how when you want a vampire to bite you so you can live forever and the vampire is like no way dude I won't do that to you you don't understand what it's like to live for centuries and to see everyone you ever loved die and everyone is like this is the most romantic shit I've ever seen? That type of thing happens all the time in real life it turns out and we consider it a happy ending like when you see a story about a 110-year-old dude and you're like wow that dude was born before cars were invented and lived to see fuck robots. That's the best-case scenario you get to live a life long enough where someone can say some shit like that about you.

I don't think about that one TV show *Mad Men* that often but I just thought about a line from it that I like which came when Ida Blankenship the secretary died and Bert Cooper was eulogizing her and he said "She was born in 1898 in a barn. She died on the thirty-seventh floor of a skyscraper. She's an astronaut." Later on in the show Cooper died while watching a man walk on the moon for the first time and that is called literature.

So you get lonely is what I'm saying and sure maybe you have kids but they're old themselves now and have their own kids and sure the grand-kids love you if you're lucky and maybe come and sit in your house and you get to look at them and impart life lessons on them but they don't listen to you they're screwing around on their phones trying to do socialism.

There have been studies that suggest loneliness is as deadly as smoking fifteen cigarettes a day or alcoholism both of which are things

I do ah fuck and loneliness affects elderly people frequently due to all of that weird shit I said up above. Young people report being lonely a lot too like in this study that said Generation Z is the loneliest generation so one solution here might be to get young people to spend more time with their grandparents (?) but that seems like it might be difficult to do since no one has ever been able to monetize that sort of thing until now.

I just read about a thing in the *Wall Street Journal* called Papa which is essentially Uber for grandkids or grandkids on demand—grandkids on demand? we talking about my phone calls with my mother over here haha—and it works just about exactly like you would imagine which is that you pay $17 an hour to have a college kid come over and recognize your humanity and then the company gives the kid a cut of $10 and they also learn life lessons I guess? The article also talked about how they have robots now that old people can talk to when they feel lonely but it doesn't mention whether or not they can fuck the robots.

Papa is only available in Florida as of now but obviously they would like to expand due to being a tech company and if you're not constantly expanding you might as well put your entire company in the toilet because it is shit.

Here's a couple paragraphs from a story on Papa from the *Washington Post*:

> Barbara Carroll-Marks, 66, a retired systems analyst and author in Pompano Beach, says the interactions she has with her Papa Pals are a stark contrast to her experiences with other paid care providers, who didn't seem like they wanted to be there.

> "I loved them from the first day I got them," she said. Marks, who has Parkinson's Disease, alternates between the same three Pals, and they come almost every day, often for 6 to 9

hours. It reminds her of being with her own grandchildren, she said.

"If I cry—sometimes I cry, because I'm pretty sick—they will just try to make me feel better," she said. "The other day I was crying and Rachael, one of my girls, rubbed my back, and it was such a compassionate thing to do."

"We are specifically a service that links two generations," the founder Andrew Parker told the *Post*. "Our emphasis is this is a really fun day for a senior. Someone who might say, 'I don't want to bother my daughter or son but I want someone who can be with me for a day so I don't have to annoy my kids.'"

And here's the thing about me at this particular moment I don't know if this is necessarily an aggregate ill? Is it? I cannot tell honestly. Obviously the gig economy aspect and the idea of elderly people being too afraid to ask their families to come confront their mortifying decrepitude are bad but maybe our tech capitalist nightmare inadvertently does something good from time to time? Given enough time a million tech dudes typing code into a million MacBooks could accidentally invent compassion as the famous saying goes.

Every time I go swimming which as we know is a whole fucking thing for me I get in the hot tub they have there next to the pool like some kind of fucking asshole and I just sit there breathing through my mouth with my big dumb fucking head poking out of the water like a carrot bobbing in a roiling stew. There are kids everywhere bombing around and screaming and their screams reverberate off the tile of the giant room. There's a window above the hot tub which doesn't even feel good I don't know why I go in there I get nothing out of it and the window looks out onto a flagpole they have out back behind the YMCA and the American flag flaps in the wind and all the elderly men and women come and sit there next to me and everyone is silent and we pretend we don't see each other we pretend we aren't sitting there in the same bath tub soaking up each other's piss as it leaks out of our bodies and eventually it gets too lonely for me to be in there so I get up and jump into the pool where I can pretend like I'm going somewhere.

NOT TO BE TOO CLICHÉ BUT LIFE CAN STILL BE BEAUTIFUL

I WANTED TO SHOW PEOPLE I WAS STILL ME BUT ALSO SHOW MYSELF I WAS STILL ME

I don't know if I'm supposed to start this one with the falling off the roof or the feeling trapped inside of the magnetic coffin. One is my story and one is someone else's and one certainly has a more drastic denouement but comparing them isn't the point. It is but it isn't.

I came across Dain Dillingham a fine writer and an even finer young man one day when I was crying on Twitter like I often do about my injuries. I had been inside the MRI machine that day and it is so bad I can't explain how bad it is to be in there for me. Some people say it is soothing and they fall asleep in there but some people are fucking psychopaths so who's to say what's right. For me it doesn't get much worse or at least it hasn't yet. You're shoved into the space oven and you cannot move and the ceiling is on your face and the walls are pushing in against your arms and then you listen to the worst ambient drum and bass concert you've ever been to for a half hour. And this is the best-case scenario. Do you know how hard it is to even get the insurance company to let them turn the MRI on for you? They're like your dad with the heat when you were growing up. Turn that down we're not made of money. They are though. Not your dad the insurance companies. Maybe your dad is too in which case may I have some of the money?

Dain replied to my tweet as other people did with stories of being in the MRI and his was obviously let's say more notable than mine to be fair because everyone has their things right.

"First MRI after being paralyzed from the chest down they hand me a buzzer and say 'Press this if something feels wrong' & then I have to tell them 'Yo my HANDS DON'T WORK' so they paused, thought and said, 'Just yell and we should be able to hear you.' Man what," he replied.

Ah.

Dain and I chatted and he seemed funny so I went to read some of his stories he posted to Medium and the weirdest thing I've ever done in my life happened next I found myself reading someone else's stories on Medium.

"Often when I meet new people and tell them the story of how I got here, after the condolences and 'I'm so sorry's' the question that usually comes is 'will you walk again?'" he wrote in one. "And I think I understand why that is. Most people view walking as the most important thing. The thing you think 'I couldn't live without.'"

People want Dain to get better sometimes he thinks because they want to know that they might be able to get better someday were it to happen to them which of course it won't but just in case right. It's like how when someone dies you ask how they died and the person tells you and you go oh ok that could never happen to me I'm not going to die from that I'm good for now.

"So I understand now that people want to know if I'll walk again in hopes of reminding, or perhaps assuring themselves, that broken things can be fixed again," he wrote.

I talked to Dain on the phone from Seattle where he lives now about the injury he suffered and how he's made his way back to writing and I don't want to say it was inspiring because he doesn't always like that sort of framing of people with disabilities but I will say I really genuinely enjoyed our conversation and I'm not sure I can remember the last time that happened to me. Hopefully this will be the last time on Hell World I enjoy talking to someone because I don't want to lose my edge.

YOU TWEETED AT ME THE OTHER DAY AND WE CHATTED A LITTLE BIT IN THE DMS AND THEN I WENT TO YOUR MEDIUM AND READ SOME OF YOUR STUFF AND I REALLY LIKED IT. I STARTED TO THINK LIKE I TOLD YOU HOW I'M ALWAYS WHINING ABOUT MY INJURIES AND HERE'S A GUY WHO HAS GONE THROUGH SOMETHING A LOT MORE SERIOUS AND I FELT LIKE I SHOULD SHUT THE FUCK UP.

The one thing I try to tell people usually off the bat is, well, ok, first off, here's what I went through: five and a half years ago in the summer of 2013 I had an accidental fall. I was celebrating my birthday with some friends. We were on an apartment rooftop hanging out late at night. I took a step backwards not realizing where I was at and I fell about ten feet straight onto my neck. I shattered my c5 vertebrae and I was paralyzed from the neck down immediately. My brother and friends were able to call 911 and I was real close to one of the best spinal cord hospitals here in Seattle. I was really fortunate to get there within minutes and I was in surgery by the next morning. It was my twenty-eighth birthday. Needless to say it was a big change hearing the doctors say you're paralyzed from the chest down. Back then I wasn't even strong enough to lift my arms.

Usually what I tell people is that my experience is toward the extreme end of trauma and health in general but when I write about myself I don't ever want anybody else to feel like what they're going through is minimized because of mine. We all have our hurdles. You could look at yourself and be like I can still walk I just have a bad back but a bad back can still be a huge hurtle for a lot of things.

MAN DID YOU ALWAYS HAVE SUCH A GENEROUS SPIRIT? WERE YOU ALWAYS LIKE THIS OR WERE YOU AN ASSHOLE WHEN YOU WERE YOUNGER BE HONEST?

Haha, no I think I was pretty generous. I was talking to some friends about this the other day, some other people from the Midwest. I don't know if some of it comes from a type of Midwest stoicism approach to life. You just grow up taking things as they come and have a keep-plugging-away mentality. I credit a lot to growing up with my mom, a single mom who raised my brother and I. My dad was in and out of our life, and he passed away pretty young from cancer. He had struggled with drugs on and off. I think him dying young actually was my first kind of trauma. Dealing with that and having a mom who was always honest with me about his struggles we would have open conversations around mental health. She's had depression in her family, we've had drug addiction and alcoholism in our family. She was somebody that was always like very honest about the hard and tough things of life but was also this person that was like life can still be good. Not to be too cliché but life can still be beautiful. Nobody wants to have to learn from the hard shit but it's just part of it. The thing in our family is it just is what it is and you kind of keep moving.

WHAT DID YOUR MOM DO?

My mom spent almost thirty years of her life counseling sexual assault survivors. Her work in general revolved around a lot of trauma and pro-cessing that. I think growing up being around that and knowing what her work was and seeing her doing that helped. She did a lot imple-menting education in our schools for sexual harassment. I think I just grew up around trauma. I have thought at times that this happening to me, in a lot of ways, I think I was prepared for it, however unknowingly. I was maybe braced against it better than some other people would be.

YOU WERE AN ATHLETE AND GETTING USED TO NOT HAVING ACCESS TO THAT PART OF YOURSELF ANYMORE WAS PARTICULARLY DIFFICULT OF COURSE.

It was hard. I was an all-state athlete in high school in Kansas and I played basketball in college. Before my injury I was working as a win-emaker. My older brother was working out here in the wine industry and got me a job in it. I was somebody who used my body every day so to suddenly have that kind of taken away from me was hard for a lot of reasons. Obviously the sheer physicality of it. Also your identity gets wrapped up in a lot of those things. You try to figure out who you are after a lot of this other stuff gets taken away.

What happened to your back?

I THINK JUST YEARS OF LIFTING WEIGHTS WEIRD CAUGHT UP WITH ME BUT WHATEVER I FEEL GUILTY EVEN BRINGING THAT UP.

Nah. Something I deal with too has just been that loss of independence and doing the things you used to do without even thinking about them. Whether it was getting in a car and going on a road trip, now you're like I can't do that or it takes a lot of planning. Asking for help. I had to become somebody like that. Maybe it's going to the grocery store and needing something off the top shelf or getting dressed. If you're just stuck home with a bad back and you gotta ask somebody to get groceries for you or something that kind of thing can be real hard. And there's definitely an element of masculinity around it, that a man should be able to do things for himself. You start feeling like, Who am I? What am I?

YOU HAVE USE OF BOTH YOUR ARMS AGAIN NOW?

My diagnoses is incomplete quadriplegic. Usually that just means you have some kind of feeling below your level of injury. I have some feeling. It's not the kind of feeling a regular person has. I don't feel temperature. Hot and cold I don't feel below my nipples basically. That was a problem once. I burned myself real bad with a heating pad. I have this huge scar across my stomach. Things like that were hard to get used to. You have to listen to your body in a different way. I don't have the same signals as I used to. I can use my arms basically but my triceps don't really work. I can lift my arms and do stuff like that but when your triceps don't work they don't extend the same way. My left hand doesn't move much. My right hand I've regained some strength.

AND THAT'S HOW YOU WRITE?

I type everything on my phone with my right thumb. I've regained the ability to write with pen and paper also which was nice it was something I missed. I tried voice programs but they're just kind of weird. It's weird, you know how it is, just one of those writing process things. Everyone has their own way. The talking I just couldn't really get the same rhythm to it. But that was huge for me to be able to get that because those first two weeks especially I literally couldn't even lift my arm. People were feeding me. My brother would check my phone for me. When I finally got the ability to be able to lift my arm and kind of aim my thumb toward the phone to tap a few things out . . . I remember the first Facebook post I wrote. It was maybe 250 words or something and it must've taken me almost an hour to type it, but it was huge for me to be able to do that. Ok. You can communicate again.

I was fortunate to not have any head trauma or brain injury. If you lose your body you're at least still able to retain who you are so to speak. I was still able to be me. I could still have my sense of humor and ability to reflect on everything.

BEING ABLE TO GET BACK ON TWITTER . . . IS THAT A BLESSING OR CURSE?

I know right! It's so crazy. I thought about this a lot though. In this day and age having access to social media and being disabled—and I think other people too, not just disabled—having the ability to reach out and be a part of the community is good. I think about people injured twenty-five to thirty years and the level of isolation they must have felt.

One thing that happened is almost 100 percent of my friends' houses became inaccessible to me. They live in old houses without elevators or they have too many steps. So how do you continue seeing your friends? Maybe you're not working, so how do you be social? I was a sociable guy and I am still. I love being in crowds and hanging out. That went down drastically and you really feel the effects of isolation. Being able to get on Facebook or Twitter and connect with disabled communities on Facebook helped.

Also just checking in with your friends helps. Social media can be double-edged because on the flip side you see a lot of your friends doing things you used to do or making strides in their career or family life that I feel way behind on because of this injury. I think people feel that anyway and social media can give those feelings no matter what the fuck you're going through. But being able to have that and saying I couldn't leave the house today it was nice to be able to talk to some people and interact . . .

I REALLY LIKED THE THINGS OF YOURS I READ. IS WRITING SOMETHING YOU'VE ALWAYS BEEN DOING THROUGHOUT YOUR LIFE?

Thank you. I definitely wrote before, but it wasn't something I took as seriously. I always had a notebook full of poems growing up that I would write in. I'm of the generation where we had Instant Messenger and Facebook came out my freshman year of college, and I was always the guy that had funny posts and would write a little more. Then after my injury I wrote something that kind of went semi-viral and all of a sudden I had like 5,000 people following me on Facebook and it was cool because when I try to think of positives with the injury I do think it gave me a chance to have a bigger platform to reach people with a message of positivity. I say honesty I guess, not necessarily positivity. I try to be positive, but honest more than anything, talking about the hard days and the good stuff.

Writing was something to help me process all the shit I was going through. I've always been pretty introspective, especially after my dad passed away. I turned inwards with a lot of the processing I was doing. I was still outgoing and popular but some of that harder stuff I think I kept on the inside for years and years. I think going through this injury and this life change I was like I needed to write because I don't know how else to work through some of that grief and trauma.

I READ SOMETHING YOU WROTE ABOUT LOOKING INTO YOUR FAMILY'S HISTORY AND BEING DESCENDED FROM SLAVES AND ONE OF THEM BEING LYNCHED FOR SOMETHING HE PROBABLY DIDN'T DO? IS THAT SOMETHING YOU KNEW ABOUT GROWING UP?

We've always known that. My dad was black, my mom is white. Dad is a Dillingham. So we knew that side. Speaking of Facebook, when it first came out I remember you could search people's name. I was like lemme put in Dillingham. I remember connecting with a lot of white Dillinghams. I connected with one and she said her mom is a big genealogy person and she tracked Dillinghams that came over from England, some of the first colonists over here in the 1600s. The family split and one group went to the south one went to the northeast. Long story short, we're descended from them.

My friend wrote this book, *The Man From the Train*, and it ended up having the lynching of a Dillingham from an area I know my family was in. I was like holy shit. Unfortunately my dad was not very close with his side of the family so there's a lot I don't know about that side of the family and it's something I'd like to learn more on.

IN ONE OF YOUR PIECES YOU TALK ABOUT FEELING A SORT OF PRESSURE FROM PEOPLE TO IMPROVE FOR THEIR SAKE? AS IF THEY NEED TO SEE YOU WALK AGAIN TO SOOTHE THEIR OWN FEARS?

People want to see me get better to restore their own hope. Yeah I do feel that. The one thing I get a lot is people being like, *God has a plan for you,* that whole thing. We did not grow up very religious. I'm not very religious but I believe in a higher power. I've got some God faith in me. But it's really hard to hear that from people when they're kind of like *God is teaching you a lesson.* I like to think God didn't need to break my neck just to teach me about being a humble person.

I have felt that from people in the past, people who want to see me walk again, or see me get better. I was fortunate to receive these kind of compliments, they were like *You're the last person this should have happened to. You don't deserve this.* So I think my injury shook a lot of people's faith in a lot of ways. It brought up a lot of questions about why do these things happen to people. I think people want to see, not necessarily a miracle, but they do want to see me walk again because it can restore something they might have lost or answer a question they might have had. I do feel that pressure a little bit. I feel it for myself. There's some days where I wake up, I have a person who helps me get dressed, but I wake up and have these muscle spasms that I get in bed and they can lock up my arms and legs. I'm used to them now. You wake up every morning you're just lying in bed stuck in bed. Some mornings I don't think about it, but some mornings I'm like *Yeah, why the fuck did this happen?* Is there anything that's going to happen in life that will make me think *Oh this was worth it,* or *That's why this happened?* Is there something that's going to give me that kind of understanding or purpose? I look for that too.

EVERYONE, ALL OF US, WE'RE ALL, AT THE END OF THE DAY, LIKE, WHY THE FUCK ARE WE HERE? WHY DOES ANYTHING HAPPEN?

Yeah totally. You don't have to be a disabled person to wonder what your purpose is in life. *What am I doing? Should I be doing more?* Those are existential questions we all face, but for someone with a more prominent physical disability those are little more obvious.

SOMETIMES I GET THE IMPRESSION FROM READING AND LISTENING TO PEOPLE WITH DISABILITIES THAT PEOPLE ALMOST TREAT THEM LIKE THEY'RE THE FUCKING TROOPS OR SOMETHING? THANK YOU FOR YOUR SERVICE, SIR. DOES THAT ANALOGY MAKE SENSE TO YOU?

The way people are like *Oh you're an inspiration*? Yeah . . . it's another double-edged sword. A lot of people say I'm an inspiration and on the one hand you're like, when something like this happens to you you only get two options either you just lie down and die or you keep going every day as best you can. I think in general people are capable of more than they give themselves credit for. A lot of times people will be like *I could never do that* and it's like, well, yeah you could. You just do. What are you going to do kill yourself because you can't walk? Unfortunately there do seem to be these portrayals in media that disability is this end of the world thing. But if some people are disabled and do want to end their own life I think that's a whole other discussion.

But the inspiration thing. When I write or talk to people I say if I'm an inspiration to you I hope it's because you see my vulnerability and willingness to be honest about the things I'm going through. I don't want to be an inspiration for . . . What happens a lot of time is people do this thing where they're like *You make me thankful because you make me realize my life could be worse*. Which is kind of a shitty thing. I'm glad I made your day better. I get where you're coming from you're not trying to shit on my life, but . . .

AM I DOING THAT?

No. I don't want you to feel like that.

NO! YOU CAN TELL ME.

No! It's hard to explain. You didn't do it don't worry. There's just times when people straight up say that. *You make me grateful.* But it's hard. When I write I do write with a sense of: I'm thankful for what I have. Even though I've lost a lot of things I try to be thankful for what I have. I've got the ability to write and communicate. I think it's good for people to remember to be thankful for the things they have and not take them for granted but I don't enjoy my life being used as a comparison. It's tough. It's a thin line.

I THINK YOU PROBABLY KNOW FROM READING MY STUFF THAT YOU COULD TELL ME TO FUCK OFF IF YOU NEED TO.

Yes, you strike me as the type of person I could be a straight shooter with. I don't know if this is a Midwest thing but I really do see people's best intentions. I know that when people say things like *God has a plan* nobody is setting out to say some shitty things to me. I get that comes from a well-meaning place. I know that intentions aren't everything though so I get why that can really bother some disabled people. There are some days when it's thrown me off.

The thing that's hardest about physical disability is people feeling entitled to know what happened to you. It's happened on the bus or at the park. It's sunny and I'm chilling and someone comes up and just wants to know what happened to you. I'm a pretty good-looking guy. I maintain my youth. People say you don't look like you belong in a wheelchair. First of all that's a weird thing to say and second of all you just walked five hundred feet across the park and talked to a dude with his headphones in and asked what happened to him. It may feel innocuous to you but it was the greatest trauma of my life and you want to make me relive that right now because you're curious? I'm not a very confrontational person. I have trouble saying no to that question. There are days when it's thrown me off. I was like, hey man, I was having a good day.

Another thing that happens is lot of times it's ostensibly about me but really people want to talk about themselves. I've had people ask me and then be like *Oh well I fell one time and was almost paralyzed* and I'm like, yeah but you weren't. My family always laughs. We seem to bring everybody's stories out of them. If there's a person at the grocery story or on the bus who wants to tell a crazy story they're going to tell it to us.

I think I consider it more of a gift in life than a curse. I've heard a lot of great stories, but some days you're just like I'm trying to go to the store right now. I'm not here to have this existential life discussion with you.

WHAT DO YOU LISTEN TO ON YOUR HEADPHONES?

I listen to a ton of podcasts. All the sports ones. I listen to Bill Simmons. True crime. I listen to audio books. I'm a big history buff so I listen to all of the things on history I can get my hands on. Military history. Religious history. Greek mythology. All that kind of stuff. I'm not a very big fiction person I'm more into non-fiction.

WHAT SORT OF BANDS DO YOU LIKE?

I've been bad about listening to music the last couple of years. I got to this point and I don't know if it was because of podcasts, where I stopped finding music to be very engaging if that makes sense. I was more like I'd rather listen to something where it feels like I'm learning a little bit. Not that listening to a sports podcast counts as learning. Just that engagement factor. I can't sit down and listen to an album.

I KNOW WHAT YOU MEAN. A COUPLE YEARS AGO I HAD THIS SHIFT WHERE LISTENING TO MUSIC ALL ALONE MADE ME FEEL EVEN MORE ALONE BUT HEARING PEOPLE TALK I FELT LIKE I WAS WITH SOMEONE.

Yeah it's interesting. I will almost always go to sleep listening to an audio book or podcast. The voices kind of put me out. When I was listening to music I was listening to hip-hop and indie shit. The National is one of my favorite bands I love them. I probably shouldn't listen to them though. When you're depressed they have that way of making depression feel good. It's something I've thought about over the last year.

Have you ever thought about doing a podcast?

NO! I NEVER WANTED TO DO ONE. I'M JUST A WRITER. I GUESS I'M A MUSICIAN, TOO, BUT I'M A WRITER I DON'T WANT TO FIGURE OUT A WHOLE OTHER THING. THIS IS MY PODCAST.

People say it to me too and I'm like I dunno it's a different beast. The one thing that does make me want to start it is writing is more difficult for me these days. I miss being able to sit down at a keyboard and type a hundred words a minute. There are times when typing is physically tiring for me. I think maybe I could cover more if I did a podcast. Bob and weave a little more aimlessly.

YOU HAVE A VERY PLEASANT VOICE AND YOU'RE A GOOD CONVERSATIONALIST SO THERE YOU GO.

Well thanks, if I ever start one I'll call you up.

YES I'LL OWE YOU THE INTERVIEW BACK. ONE MORE THING. YOU SAID THERE WERE CERTAIN TROPES IN WRITING ABOUT DISABILITIES YOU TRY TO AVOID?

I think we talked about it a little bit. Probably the inspiration thing is what I try to avoid. And the thing about look how hard his shit is you all should be grateful for what you have. I don't like to do that. Or look at how hard his shit is you shouldn't be complaining about anything. Fuck that dude, that shit is real to you. Yeah I don't walk but there's someone out there who has two kids and a crazy schedule and can't get where she needs to go. She gets to complain too. All the hurdles that we face they feel very real to us and I don't think it's fair or right or even productive to be like your life isn't as hard as this other person so what am I complaining about?

I was thinking a lot about what has helped me process the trauma and I think being honest about the hurdles I have is just like being real about stuff. Life is hard for me in this way but it's good for me in these others. Just that ability to still . . . I'm just glad to still be feeling. I've never gotten numb to the whole thing which is what I would worry about more than anything.

I remember when I was first in the hospital. I use an electric chair mostly. I was learning to drive it, you gotta learn to drive it. I was with my physical trainer and we got to elevator and she was like see if you can press the buttons. I was trying for two minutes. I was like, I can't press an elevator button. It hit me like a ton of bricks. When I was in the hospital I had a pretty good sense of humor about everything. Part of it was everyone around me was pretty down and I was feeling like I gotta pick everybody up. Not only that I wanted to show people I was still me but to show myself I was still me. I'm the youngest and the youngest tends to be like the peacemaker.

But I couldn't press these buttons, man, it just hit me really hard in the moment. I started crying pretty good. I just cried and I didn't say anything. Finally I gathered myself a little bit. I said I'm sorry. My therapist said, she said, you know I'd be more worried about you if you didn't cry. That kind of hit me that has always stuck with me. The things we go through, the feeling can be really heavy and so hard. But I'm so glad to have them. Sometimes I feel hurt about what I'm going through but I'm glad I still feel the ups and downs. I think that everybody should feel your ups and downs. You're allowed to do that. Try not to stay down for too long though.

MAN I'M SORRY, BUT YOU ARE AN INSPIRATION.

Haha.

I DON'T MEAN IT LIKE THAT!

Yeah, yeah. I mean I wrote this piece the other day and I was remembering how I like to go to church for Christmas Eve. You go to church and at the end you hold the candle light up and sing. I remember the first time going after my injury I was nervous I wouldn't be able to hold the candle up. I tied this metaphor into holding the candle to holding my life light up and being nervous I wouldn't be able to be a light for people anymore. We may say the word inspiration but most of us do want to be a light for people, your partner, kids, somebody . . . or for yourself. You want to be a light. I feel writing has been really rewarding for me to get messages from people who say I was having a tough time and I read your words and they helped me. That stuff feels good. I do want to shift people's perspective sometimes. Maybe there is a different way they can reframe their circumstance. That is something I want to do. I know there's a lot of disability advocates that get down on the inspiration porn of disability and I 100 percent see that stuff. I don't like to push back on that but sometimes I'm like you know what shit's allowed to be inspiration sometimes. It just is.

DON'T WORRY I DIDN'T LEARN ANY LESSONS.

Haha you know my number man. If you're ever having a hard time about how to make it through you can always call.

YOU SHOULD STILL BE HERE

I'M SORRY I MISS YOU PLEASE COME BACK

A young woman is crying on a voicemail recording. "You left and I didn't say goodbye. I'm so sorry," she says sniffling and barely composed. "You should still be here. You. Should. Still. Be. Here." A plaintive piano composition plays under her words and the pain in her voice is visceral. "You died from pneumonia not your cancer. You're supposed to be here." Then her tone changes. "You left me without ever saying goodbye. And for that I'm bitter as hell. So screw you."

"I would say: Jesus Christ I wish you were gay," a second voice comes in. "I wish you were gay, and I wish you could see how perfect we would've been together. I wish you thought I was as amazing as I think you are... But most of all I wish we hadn't drifted away from each other. I wish we hadn't stopped being friends after college, because I love you, but you're not her anymore. You're a different person. And I miss you."

The messages come in the second episode of *The One Who Got Away* a participatory podcast from English artist and designer Oliver Blank. The idea behind it is simple: We all have someone who got away whether it's a lost love or a deceased family member or a friend we've had a falling out with. What would you say to that person if you had one more chance?

Blank remembers the first time the question occurred to him. The wall was all that was left standing he said. It was a few years after Katrina had devastated New Orleans but it wasn't uncommon to find abandoned ruins in the Bywater neighborhood near where he was living at the time. Written across the wall in an elegant white graffiti script were the words "What would you say to the one that got away?" The contrast of the artfully composed expression and the decay of the building stuck with him. "It was like someone stood there and really made an effort to make it beautiful," he said.

In 2012 Blank was collaborating on a project with artist Candy Chang called "Before I Die" in which people wrote the one thing they absolutely needed to do on chalkboards that they would assemble from kits provided by the artists. At the same time he had undertaken a number of participatory art pieces himself. One commonality among much of his work was his fascination with telephones. In one called "Music for Forgotten Places" he'd compose music for abandoned buildings in cities around the country then leave a note for people who came across them with a number to call in and listen to while standing there. A second called Waiting set up a phone number outside spaces like abandoned shopping malls with signs that instructed them to call into another number which held a never-ending loop of infinite hold muzak.

"I really love working with telephones because you get the whole experience before the call even starts," he said. "People think: Am I going to call it? I usually don't call anyone anymore. You dial the number, there's anticipation, you hear it ringing, then there's the intimacy of pressing the object to your face and hearing music or a voice in your ear. It's got all of this intimacy and emotion and yet it's still quite solitary. You can do it in public and have this intimate emotional experience."

In 2014 he was approached by The Art Assignment a PBS Digital program—hosted by Sarah Urist Green and her husband John Green the author of *The Fault in Our Stars*—in which viewers are given an artistic project to complete on their own. Did he have any ideas for prompts they asked. Looking back through his notebook Blank came across something he'd scribbled down about the graffiti. What if they set up a voicemail line in which people could call in and lay themselves bare anonymously? Green loved it but Blank wasn't sure how it would work. He expected only a handful of calls thinking he'd make a nice little piece of sound art out of it and then move on from there. But with a big boost from Green who shared the number to his millions of followers on Twitter a deluge was summoned.

Blank's first idea for using the material was to set up a never-ending radio station in which the calls which were now numbering in the thousands would play successively over and over. At the time the technical logistics eluded him. He finally came to the idea of a podcast.

"It took four years for me to get it together," he said. "In that time I went through so much: divorce, depression, a couple of different jobs. Every time I was checking in on the phone number to hear the calls coming in, I'm seeing these calls line up and . . . the weight of them. I was feeling like the custodian of these messages of loss. It's really heavy stuff. I'd listen to an hour of calls and get super sad and withdraw from the project. It took me four years before I finally said I have to do this before this becomes the most self-referential project ever."

The calls themselves might range from ten seconds—a mercifully short one in the first episode has a woman simply repeating "Why? Why? Why did you leave me?" over and over—to lengthy ones in which people hang up then think of something else to say and call back in with more.

"When you left I was relieved," a voice says, conflicted. "I miss you. That feels wrong because you treated me like shit. I miss you, but I hope to god I never see you again."

At first owing to Green's audience many of them tended to be from younger women and teenagers sharing stories of high school love or of being torn away from friends when their families moved and they were forced to change schools. Over time the demographics broadened with callers into their fifties and sixties sharing their perspective on decades of regret.

Some are off the cuff and raw and in the others you can tell that people took the time to write them out. That was something he didn't like at first but the subtle emotional shifts in those cases eventually won him over. A caller might begin composed and determined then suddenly lurch into territory that was likely unexpected to even themselves.

In a call Blank received which he shared with me a young woman begins speaking casually in the tone any of us might use checking in with a sibling we haven't spoken to in a week or two. She tells someone named James she'd been reminded of him when she found some things in the bathroom with his name on it. She has an old picture she keeps above her bed, she says. She's fifteen in the photo; James is eight.

Before long she begins to cry. "I just want to say I love you and I'm sorry for not being there for most of your childhood," she says. "I'm really sorry you only lived with our family for 11 months."

"That gets to something," Blank said of the call. "It's really difficult for people to share, it's difficult to listen to, but that point where we get to something underneath. Why is this person really on your mind? That tipping point of release of emotion where someone begins to recognize *this is really what was going on with me*. I don't think she called with that initial sentiment in mind."

Not all the calls are completely harrowing. A recurring theme is about pets who've gone missing. Another motif are calls tinged by loss but coming from a better place of acceptance and usually from older women. "There's this kind of warm knowing where the person has reached the point where they have come to terms with the one who got away. It's a different kind of call entirely. You feel comforted. They're setting it out: 'I feel like I lost something, yes I loved you, and yet I'm at a point in my life where I placed that loss into the tapestry of my life and I'm at peace with it.'" Older men, on the other hand are often remorseful and sound more broken.

Sometimes a person might be speaking to themselves. *I am my own one who got away.* There was a turning point in their life where they might have taken a big leap such as moving across the country or taking a new job opportunity that scared them or going back to school but for whatever reason they couldn't bring themselves to do it. *I don't know if I made the right decisions in life*, they say. *I was scared of what might happen. Of what I might learn about myself.*

"That's one of the most difficult ones: feeling disconnected from yourself, like your life got away from you," Blank said.

If it all sounds hopelessly bleak it often is. But there's a beneficial side, both for the callers and for listeners. While some calls are imbued with the hope that their one who got away might hear the message others sound as if they've finally unloaded something heavy they've been carrying for however long. "I believe it's cathartic," Blank said. "I think you can hear that, an emotional narrative arc in some of the calls. A kind of letting go. They said the thing they really needed to say. They finally let it out."

To get to that moment of release there's a particular contour in a call that Blank finds especially emotionally resonant. After starting by addressing the one who got away in the third person something shifts and they begin speaking to them directly as if they were there on the line themselves.

"I think that's the magical thing that happens. People forget that they're on a phone line and they're speaking to silence. They feel like they have a direct connection to that person. The things they have to release, they really do come out in the call.

♥

IT'S GOING TO BE A LONG RECOVERY

I'M FOR FINDING REALISTIC MEANS TO HELP RESTORE THE OPPORTUNITIES FOR UPWARD MOBILITY IN THIS COUNTRY

"I am finally home," Carrie Ann Lucas posted to her Facebook page on February 6 along with a smiling emoji that said she was feeling thankful. "Coming home forty eight hours after major surgery and after being in bed for thirteen days is not the brightest idea I've ever had, but I am thankful to be home. It's going to be a long recovery, but I can do it from my own home where I get better care," she wrote and then on the post there are fifty comments with people saying like so glad you're home and hang in there and hoping for a speedy recovery and things like that that any of us would post if it were someone we knew. She didn't write the next post on her page on February 24 though because she had died that day and her family had to post for her now and one thing they said is that her insurance company killed her.

Lucas managed to do a lot in her forty seven years having been a teacher and a lawyer and an ordained minister and an advocate for people with disabilities with groups like ADAPT and Not Dead Yet. Among her most passionate causes was working to expand rights and protections for parents with disabilities after having been discriminated against herself in her efforts to adopt children in the past although she eventually adopted four of her own. She was one of the people leading the push to see a law passed in Colorado to prevent the disability of a parent from being an excuse to remove a child from a home.

In 2017 Lucas was among a number of protestors who occupied Colorado senator Cory Gardner's office for a couple of days asking him to save the Affordable Care Act. When police came to remove them Lucas refused to tell them how to operate her wheelchair saying "I'd rather go to jail than die without Medicaid" as reported by *Denverite*. Eventually she was arrested anyway which she live-streamed to Facebook. Gardner's office said at the time that "the police were forced to remove them due to several factors, including serious concerns for their health and safety," which is probably true Gardner probably didn't want to see anyone get hurt or die in his office. Like all Republicans he prefers sick and poor people to go and be sick and poor and die on their own time somewhere where they don't have to look at it or know about it.

Around the same time protestors from ADAPT and other groups were occupying the offices of lawmakers around the country including in Columbus, Ohio at Senator Rob Portman's office which I reported on for *Esquire*. The protestors there weren't treated anywhere near as well as the ones in Colorado and the police reacted with violence which is the natural instinct for a police officer when confronted with any problem.

"If you were to conceive of a metaphor for what the impending Republican healthcare plan could do to people with disabilities who rely on Medicaid, you could do a lot worse than the image of the state mercilessly dumping people out of their wheelchairs onto the ground," I wrote.

It was considered a pretty big victory when Republicans failed to repeal the ACA owed in no small part to people like Lucas and other protestors who were willing to put their bodies on the line but it wasn't exactly a happy ending was it because insurance companies still exist and they still have the discretion to sentence people to death to save money.

"Carrie had a severe neuromuscular disease, a rare form of muscular dystrophy. She relied on a power wheelchair, and had used a ventilator for years. However, her death was premature and caused by inappropriate and brutal cost containment procedures of an insurance company," Lucas' family wrote on Facebook.

"In January of 2018 she got a cold which turned into a trachea and lung infection. Her insurance company UnitedHealthcare refused to pay for the one specific inhaled antibiotic that she really needed. She had to take a less effective drug and had a bad reaction to that drug. This created a cascade of problems, loss of function (including her speech). United Healthcare's attempt to save $2,000 cost over $1 million in health care costs over the past year. This includes numerous hospitalizations, always involving the Intensive Care Unit which is par for the course for ventilator users."

"Insurance companies and government programs must not be allowed to deny people what they need," they wrote.

"Just last month she was having to ration her insulin for her type 1 diabetes because of the same insurance company and how impossible it is to work between private insurance and Medicare and Medicaid. This is a great example of why people with disabilities should not be forced into insurance or health plans and why we need Medicaid as the primary health delivery system for this country."

Lucas very much did not want to die although she knew that that type of thought for people with serious disabilities can happen from time to time when things are particularly tough. That's something she said when she was speaking out against a proposed law in Colorado in 2015 that would have given dying patients the right to get a doctor's assistance in ending their lives. That is a pretty controversial subject I'm not going to lie and the rare one where people on either side of the argument have very valid concerns and I am not entirely sure what I think about that. *The Coloradoan* reported on the hearings for the bill which ultimately did not pass:

> Lucas uses a wheelchair and ventilator because of a neuromuscular disease. She told lawmakers that she worries the proposal would make it easy for a disabled person who is depressed to get medication from a doctor. Without her ventilator, Lucas told lawmakers, she would have only hours to live. And, she said, if she were to get depressed, she thinks she could go to a doctor who doesn't know her well to get the drugs.

> "And they probably would give me that lethal prescription instead of referring me to mental-health treatment that I would so desperately need..."

Does your doctor know you very well? I always get star struck when my actual doctor makes a surprise drop in once a year like I just got invited back stage and fuckin David Bowie walks in and I forget how to talk or who I even am and then they breeze out before you even get to say what you'd been planning to tell them. Your specific appointment with the doctor always feels like a warmup to something more important they have to go do afterwards.

Sometime in March of 2019 Ivanka Trump who is the one we were meant to believe is the good Trump weighed in on the prospects of the Green New Deal and we had to hear about it due to she is the president's daughter and presidents' daughters have traditionally been on TV opining about the relative merits of prospective legislation that's just how things have always been done.

I wrote about it in what was a pretty good piece I think if for no other reason than I got the *Boston Globe* to print the word "paypigs."

Commenting on the GND's call for universal healthcare, a job guarantee, and free higher education Ivanka said "I don't think most Americans, in their heart, want to be given something. I've spent a lot of time traveling around this country over the last four years. People want to work for what they get."

It's wild writing for the *Globe* again a few years after I stopped because they refused to give me a free login to read the site despite having been a contributor there for like ten years lol and then I talked shit about it on Twitter like I tend to do and things went south but anyway the reason is they still have a comments section which feels like such an anachronism like a holdover from an era of internet that was still just as bad but more *locally* bad if that makes sense. The commenters there don't seem to have moved on from the things they were chap-assed about in the good old days which is people abusing welfare and food stamps and not working hard enough like they do.

"Cake would be too euphemistic a characterization for what the first daughter thinks the rest of us should go and eat," I wrote.

"The thing is, there are far too many of us who are tying the bibs around our necks as we step up to ask for a second helping. Americans, a country comprised entirely of temporarily embarrassed millionaires, love nothing more than the taste of crap," which is a bit of a compromise because I wanted it to be shit and then they changed it to junk and I said what about [expletive] even that would be better than junk and then they landed on crap and that is how the news sausage is made my friends. Anyway I tried to anticipate the mind geniuses in the comments in my piece.

"I can already sense a lot of you lining up in the online comments section to tell me as much in so many words. I'm just jealous, you'll say. But I'm no more jealous of the billionaires of the world than I would be a fish with four heads downstream from a nuclear reactor. I'm angry about the fact that either exist. Maybe having four heads would seem cool for a while but nonetheless it's an abomination to nature and conscience and a testament to our collective civic and governmental maleficence."

I thought that was a pretty good analogy buddy. Was it good you tell me. Tell me if I'm good or not that's why I'm writing this book in the first place.

"We already have a guaranteed jobs program. It's called 'federal employees.' Just try to fire one of them for something like watching porn at work all day..." one person commented.

"I can't stand Trump and am no fan of Ivanka but I don't see how her comments are way off base and offensive. I am ABSOLUTELY against the government 'guaranteeing jobs' and who is going to pay for the 'free education?' The economics of these policies don't add up. I'm for finding realistic means to help restore the opportunities for upward mobility in this country," added another and that commenter's name was Nancy Fucking Pelosi not really but it's basically her take on the healthcare question isn't it?

"Thirty trillion dollars. Now, how do you pay for that?" Pelosi asked of the cost of single-payer healthcare in an interview with *Rolling Stone* around that time.

"All I want is the goal of every American having access to health care," she said. "You don't get there by dismantling the Affordable Care Act," she said and *having access* to something is another way of saying people shouldn't have it.

That same week Rep. Pramila Jayapal introduced a Medicare for all bill that stood in stark contrast to the typical incrementalist horse shit Democrats are famous for. Is horseshit one word or two?

"This Medicare for all bill really makes it clear what we mean by Medicare for all," Jayapal said. "We mean a system where there are no private insurance companies that provide these core comprehensive benefits."

To the question of how it would be paid for Jayapal pointed out there's never a question about funding the military or tax cuts so shut da fuck up (more or less) which is the only correct answer when anyone ever tries to use cost for an excuse about why better things can never happen.

People get confused sometimes about why the left is always so much more critical of centrist Democrats than the right. *We need to stay together we can't be divided while Trump is in office!* they say and it's always an attempt to forestall progress actually being made. *We can't do this now it's not the right time* they say by which they mean I don't want to do this ever and I just want you to shut up for now.

It's right and good and just that Democrats be made to eat plate after plate of shit from the left because for one thing look how quickly the Overton window has shifted with the emergence of a mere handful of leftist politicians now. Turns out we could've been trying this whole time!

Or think of criticizing Democrats this way: When you're playing basketball and the other team scores a basket you don't get pissed off at the guy do you he's just doing what he's supposed to do. You don't say what the fuck are you doing man? But if a guy on your own team took the basketball and shoved it up his shirt and pulled down his shorts and started doing cartwheels with his dick and balls out toward your own goal you might rightfully feel justified in screaming at him to get his shit together or he's off the team. You might take that guy aside and say buddy are you sure you understand what you're supposed to be doing here?

I just showed my old college pal the inside of my spine and it felt weird. I sent him a CD of my MRI in the mail which are two things I imagined I would never do again having a CD and mailing something and then he called me up to talk about it and he told me the discs in my spine didn't look great but to keep up what I'm doing in terms of staying active and exercising and stretching and all that shit and then a minute later we joked about Bob Kraft being a horny old man and talked about jerking off and man being a dude is confusing.

The weirdest part to me is this is a guy whose balls I used to throw things at in college. We'd play a game where two dudes sat across from each other with their legs spread and you had to lob like a baseball or a landline telephone or a thing of washing detergent and try to hit them just so in the scrotum until one person gave up and now he's a prominent spinal surgeon. And then he told me he's been reading *Hell World* and how great it is and things like that and I was thinking like dude you repair people's spines for a living and I don't use commas in articles about how the news made me depressed I don't think it's actually comparable. He can look inside a person's body and tell them what's going on in there like when you cut down a tree and count the rings and can see how long it's been alive and how much longer it has to go.

THIS MIGHT BE MY LAST NIGHT I CLOSE MY EYES

I'M NOT TAKING IT OUT FOR ANYBODY

Police in Bolivar Missouri say they got a 911 call that someone could smell marijuana so they mounted up and headed down to Citizens Memorial Hospital and got to work like police do everywhere putting their lives on the line to protect us. Inside they found Nolan Sousley a man with stage 4 pancreatic cancer who had stopped his chemotherapy treatment because it was no longer working. So the cops rifled through his shit trying to find the weed that wasn't there.

Sousley posted a video of the encounter to his Facebook group page Nolan's Tribe of Warriors Against Cancer in March where it was viewed over 500,000 times.

"I was set for the best night's sleep last night," Sousley explained in a video the next day.

"I had just gotten comfortable...then this all happened . . . This is the one night I was gonna get a good night's sleep. You know why? Because I was in a place where if I closed my eyes and I went to sleep and I died while I was asleep they could maybe bring me back to life. That's how I look at going to sleep every night. This might be my last night I close my eyes . . . That's how I have to look at life right now."

The ordeal itself was longer but the video from his hospital bed stretches on for six minutes that feel like an eternity as one cop ransacks Sousley's belongings and another stands there looking embarrassed and fidgeting with his plastic gloves. There's usually one cop that feels like shit about being involved in this sort of thing isn't there. Not enough to not be there in the first place but still.

"I just want to go home doc. I want her to take this off me and I want to go home," Sousley says when his doctor arrives to see what the hell is going on.

"We got a call saying there's marijuana in the room," one of the cops says. "I smelled marijuana whenever I walked in the room," someone else in the background says who looks like a hospital cop which is an even worse type of cop to be because they don't even have power but they want it. Sousley says that's not possible since he doesn't even smoke anything.

"I don't ever use a ground-up plant. It's an oil I use in a capsule, there's no smoking it. I take it like a pill."

His friend Tim Roberts who is there with him tells the cops the stuff he uses is necessary because he's really fucking sick obviously.

"What he's using manages his appetite, his weight loss, his nausea," he says.

Medical marijuana was approved in a Missouri ballot measure in November 2018 but it won't available until at least early 2020 as Sousley mentions to the police. He doesn't have time to wait he says. What would you do he asks the cops. I'm not going to play the what if game one cop says.

The cops tell him they're not going to arrest him they'll only give him a citation if they find marijuana. We're just looking for marijuana the cop says.

Sousley doesn't take opioids he takes THC his friend says. It's my right to live Sousley says and it all sucks the whole thing fucking sucks to look at or even think about but here's the worst part in my opinion which is at the end of the video when the cops haven't found anything and the doctor is trying to get the whole thing to come to a conclusion and the cops still won't leave because there's one bag left that the dying man won't let them stick their snouts into.

"This is my bag of medication and I'm not letting them look through it," Sousley says.

"It has my final day things in there," he says and his voice is cracking now like he wants to cry. "And nobody's gonna dig in it. It's my stuff. It's my final hour stuff in that bag and that is my right. And I'm not taking it out for anybody."

The police told the Springfield News Leader that they never ended up finding any marijuana and the Bolivar Police Chief Mark Webb also said that they had to take their Facebook page down and that some of their employees were in tears due to the calls they were getting so that's how the cops' feelings ending up getting hurt.

The next day Sousley and his family and a friend whose nine year old son uses THC due to he has seizures every day of his life sat down for a video to talk about what happened and why medical marijuana is so important.

"I'm not gonna just sit here on this couch and die I'm gonna stand up for something," Sousley says. "And by god this is what I think I was put here to do . . . Everybody always says 'I'd do anything, I'd do it too, anything to stay alive.' Everybody says it but nobody does anything about it. Well, Nolan Sousley, 5 foot 7, 135 lbs., welterweight, I'm gonna do something about it. I'm going to say something. Why can't I do what I want to do . . . It's my choice," he says.

"My big deal is I choose to live," he says.

"Everything that I do in my life right now I look at it like I'm doing it for the last time," he says.

Naturally thousands of people left messages of support for Sousley and called the cops motherfuckers and things of that nature but not everybody was outraged. Plenty of people said that the cops were just doing their jobs like this one nice person who just messaged me on Twitter.

"It's they're job," she wrote. "They got called to a scene by someone else. The cops didn't go looking for it they were called there. Stop being ignorant."

"People like you disgust me," she wrote.

Here's a question I have what's a bigger nightmare when you're in the hospital and preparing to die the cops showing up or an extremely cursed video doctor robot?

That same week a seventy nine year old man in California named Ernest Quintana was informed that his lungs had gotten too bad and that efforts to extend his life were not going to help anymore so it was time to be put on comfort care but instead of a human being explaining it to him it was a doctor on a video screen wearing headphones like he was logging in to play Fortnite. A terrible robot wheeled into the room and told the man it was time to die.

"This was horrible for me and him," his granddaughter Annalisia Wilharm posted to Facebook. Was it time to take her grandfather home she asked the doctor on the screen and the doctor said "I don't know if he's going to get home" and making matters worse is that the conversation was exceptionally hard to hear as she told the *Mercury News* because the noise of the machine that was helping him breathe was too loud so the doctor robot had to keep repeating himself. You're going to die. What. I said you're going to die. Sorry what. Not in so many words exactly but like that.

"When that robot said that to him, he looked over at me and said, 'Well, I guess I'm going to go quickly,' and put his head down," recalled Wilharm, 33. "It was pitiful."

Her mother Cathie Quintana said the hospital didn't inform other family members about the grim prognosis which they had to learn through her daughter.

"It was handled with no compassion at all by this robot, there was no bedside manner, no nothing," Cathie Quintana said. "It needed to be a person, for God's sake. My mom and myself should have been there. We want to never have this happen to anyone again."

"This is a highly unusual circumstance," Michelle Gaskill-Hames the senior vice president and area manager for Kaiser Permanente Greater Southern Alameda County told the *Mercury News*. "We regret falling short in meeting the patient's and family's expectations in this situation and we will use this as an opportunity to review how to improve patient experience with tele-video capabilities."

She also pointed out it's not a robot so don't call it a robot although that's how InTouch Health the company who makes it refers to it. Go look it up on YouTube go look at this absolute fucking horror nightmare fuel. Please proceed to the self checkout aisle to be informed about how much longer you have to live citizen.

Naturally like in the other story people are upset about this but not everybody is. Not one guy at the top of the comments.

"Once the socialists take over and give everyone 'free' healthcare even talking to a robot doctor, let alone a real one, will probably be a luxury," a person named Snowbird wrote and I wonder what it's like to be a person like that who is constantly paranoid about an always soon to be arriving hypothetical dystopia because what do they think the world we have now actually is?

The reason that robot exists is the same reason robots and computerized customer service exists anywhere and that is because someone decided it would save them money in the long run. Whether it's ringing in a roll of toilet paper at CVS or building a car or explaining that you are about to die it's just cheaper to not have an actual person there doing it.

The people who profit off of this are ones like the disgusting health care villains I wrote about in my column in the *Boston Globe* that week. Here's a bit of it below concerning a man named Shane Boyle who died $50 short of his GoFundMe to cover the price of his insulin:

> I don't know if you feel any portion of blame for Boyle's death, but you should, much like I do. Because every day that goes by without the passage of universal health care for every American is an abrogation of duty and an absolute failure of responsibility. You and I may not bear as much blame as drug makers like Eli Lilly (who announced just this week that they will finally be offering a generic version of insulin for a 50 percent discount after sustained criticism from patients and lawmakers alike for years), but still, at least some of that is on you and me and the representatives we elected.

> (Incidentally, diabetes meds have been around since the 1920s, but the price of insulin has gone from $20 per vial in 1996 to around $275 today. I'm not sure how much money Boyle made but David Ricks, the CEO of Eli Lilly makes about $16 million a year, which is very nice for him.)

> Not to single out Mr. Ricks. He's hardly alone among the gilded class of health care and medical execs gorging at the trough of misery and pain like ravenous vampire hogs. Here's another one that just came across my feed at random, a guy named Daniel Loepp who you've never heard of and is the president and CEO of Blue Cross Blue Shield of Michigan. He must be very good at his job since he made $19.2 million in 2018, up from from $13.42

million in 2017, which, for rough comparison, is more than, say, Kyrie Irving makes a year. Then again people like Loepp are a bit better on the defensive end, swatting away requests for coverage left and right. Elsewhere in the upper echelons of health care. By comparison, Michael Neidorff, CEO of insurance company Centene, made $25.26 million in 2017, according to Crain's Detroit. Joseph Zubretsky of Molina Healthcare made $19.74 million. David Cordani of Cigna made $17.55 million. Bruce Broussard of Humana made $14.87 million.

Shane Patrick Boyle of Houston didn't get the final $50 he needed to live, but the memorial page set up for him and his mother after their deaths ended up raising $5,150 of the $5,000 goal, which is great news until you remember the fact that they died.

What would you do to save your own life? How much money would you raise? Would you use marijuana to manage your pain and risk arrest? Would you smash the fucking face in of a robot doctor that lurched into your room to tell you it was over? Hopefully you never have to find out but if we're being honest you will probably get your answer by the time this is all over.

THEY SAY IF WE'RE FATTER WE CAN ACCEPT MORE POLLUTANTS

THE RIVER SMELLED LIKE LICORICE

In March the West Virginia House of Delegates passed a rules bill that failed to make the state's water any safer. After almost a year of hearings on a rules change proposed by the state's Department of Environmental Protection that would have used federal guidelines handed down by the Environmental Protection Agency to more strictly enforce the amount of pollutants and carcinogens that are dumped into the rivers and waterways the Republican-controlled legislature punted. You will not be shocked to learn there had been a strong lobbying push lead by the West Virginia Manufacturers Association aka the people doing the polluting in question.

All of that is very predictable of course but you might actually be surprised to hear the line of argument used by the WVMA. In essence it was that since West Virginians are so fat and drink so little water and eat such little fish compared to the rest of the country that it would be unfair to the polluters to hold them to the same standards used in other skinnier and thirstier fish-eating states.

"There's a bit of circular logic there," Angie Rosser the Executive Director of the West Virginia Rivers Coalition told me.

"We're saying we can allow more pollutants because we don't eat as as much fish, but we don't eat as much fish because there's so much pollution."

The WVMA also argued wrongly that people who are heavier can handle a bit more pollution in their diet and no I'm not kidding.

The WVMA likes to present themselves as a group of local manufacturers concerned about the well-being of the state but among their two hundred odd members are corporations like Dow Chemical, DuPont, Proctor & Gamble, Mylan Pharmaceuticals, Marathon Petroleum Company and other massive international polluters.

In 2017 DuPont agreed to pay $670 million in a class action lawsuit after a cancer-causing chemical used in the production of teflon was found to have contaminated waterways throughout the region and into Kentucky and Ohio. Also in 2017 West Virginia State University sued Dow Chemical and Bayer who they said "through both direct actions and negligence allowed the plant to leak the chemicals 1,4-dioxane; 1,2-dichloroethane; and chloroform into the ground and water around the school."

The EPA classifies all three as likely carcinogens.

In 2014 runoff from a Freedom Industries lol plant that produced a chemical that treats coal leaked into the Elk River leaving some 300,000 residents around Charleston without potable water. Residents at the time said it made the river smell like licorice according to *Scientific American*.

Incidentally the WVMA also operate a Political Action Committee that you can donate to.

"The West Virginians for Manufacturing Jobs Political Action Committee assists the WVMA's ability to support pro-industry candidates, and can directly correlate to success on Election Day and legislative success!" they say. "With the help of you and your colleagues, the WVMJ PAC will elevate the position of WVMA leadership in shaping policy-making decisions for West Virginia."

That certainly seems to have worked this time around!

I asked the WVMA to explain if they stood by their argument that West Virginians are too fat and don't drink enough water.

"During several legislative committee meetings concerning Senate Bill 163, we have openly shared this approach to criteria re-evaluation," Rebecca McPhail explained in an email. "Unfortunately, some are trying to develop a narrative out of context that does not represent the work we are presently undertaking."

Then she wrote some other shit including the words "trophic level of fish consumed" "cancer slope factors" and "ultimate criterion" all of which basically translated into our companies didn't want to spend a single dime more than they absolutely have to preventing people from getting sick.

I called Angie Rosser of the West Virginia Rivers Coalition after that because I felt like my mind was polluted with corporate horseshit. She was surprised that I called at all saying she's always "intrigued when people from other parts of the country pay attention to what happens here, which is what we need."

CAN YOU EXPLAIN THE OVERVIEW OF WHAT JUST HAPPENED ON THIS VOTE FROM YOUR GROUP'S POINT OF VIEW?

Under the Clean Water Act the state is required in effect to put limits on the amount of pollution allowed in our waters in a way that protects the designated uses of those waters. The "human health criteria" is what was at stake for us this past year. Human health criteria covers a group of pollutants that are most harmful to human health. It covers the toxins and cancer-causing chemicals we have to keep at certain levels so they don't cause diseases in the water we drink and the fish we eat or in direct contact through swimming or boating.

Our standards for human health criteria were largely put in place in mid-1980s. A few have been updated since then, but by and large they are over thirty years old. In 2015 the EPA came out with new recommended updates. They recommended all the states take a look at these and adopt them. They were based on the best available science. The science has since changed and new studies have been done. We understand more about the risks involved and the appropriate exposure levels now.

Every three years states are required to go through a review of water standards. That's what our state DEP was doing, they were looking at EPA's recommendations. They decided of the ninety four updates recommended West Virginia would adopt sixty. There was one change they made from the EPA recommendations, where they used a state specific fish consumption rate.

In 2008 the West Virginia DEP commissioned a study about the West Virginia fish consumption rate related to a mercury issue. They were convinced at the request of the West Virginia Manufacturers Association to apply that 2008 study. The rate was found to be half of the national average so they changed our numbers from what the EPA recommended. Instead of using 28 grams per day of fish consumption they brought it down to 9.9 grams.

IS THEIR ARGUMENT THAT PEOPLE EAT LESS FISH IN WEST VIRGINIA?

Yes that was what this one study said. We said the study didn't take into account any of the social factors of why people aren't eating fish here. One of the reasons we contend—and I know which is why I don't—is that we have fish contamination advisories on every waterway in the state. Growing up here we all go fishing but we're told don't you dare eat them. There's some circular logic there to me. We're saying we can allow more pollution because we don't eat as

as much fish but we don't eat as much fish because there's so much
pollution.

I SAW THAT THE WVMA ARGUED THAT WEST VIRGINIANS WERE TOO FAT AND DIDN'T DRINK ENOUGH WATER SO THAT IN EFFECT IT WAS OK TO HAVE HIGHER LEVELS OF CONTAMINATION?

The overall criteria is determined by different data inputs, three of
those are fish consumption, body weight, and water consumption.

WHERE WAS IT THEY ACTUALLY MADE THAT ARGUMENT, IN A HEARING?

It came up in a couple places. One is the WVMA, they've been the
lead opposition of this and represent a lot of the chemical manufacturing companies which are the main industries that discharge these
kinds of toxins and carcinogens. In their comments on the proposed
rule change not only did they recommend we use the West Virginia
fish consumption rate, but also suggested we use the average body
weight for men in West Virginia, which is substantially higher than
the national average body weight that the EPA used. The DEP denied
that request. They went with the national average. They didn't find it
legitimate enough, and just going with a male bodyweight doesn't protect kids you know. That was what the industry were pushing for. To
account for bigger body mass, again that would result in allowing for
more pollution. The typical logic behind that is if we're fatter or heavier
we can accept more pollutants.

ISN'T THE OPPOSITE ACTUALLY TRUE? THAT CARCINOGENS ARE BETTER STORED IN FAT CELLS?

Correct. I'm not a public health expert but we talked to them and they
say exactly that. And people who are obese have other diseases as well
that compromise their health. The idea that because you have more fat

you can take more toxins isn't true. Your health is also being compromised by other ailments.

SO WHAT HAPPENS NOW?

Ultimately the legislature passed the bill without the updates, so we're at the status quo with our standards being terribly outdated, leaving public health at risk, and we're relying on science conducted prior to 1985.

But the whole argument brought by the industry is that they need more time to study, so the industry is coming up with their own findings because they don't trust the findings of the government.

Between now and October DEP is supposed to be getting this information from the industry and any other stakeholder groups, and propose a new rule in the spring of 2020 that will go for another round of public comments and get before the legislature again in 2021. In essence it's a two year delay to study this some more. The industry is going to have a lot of sway in this. What we didn't hear specifically, only in generalizations, is that certain chemical manufacturers are going to have a hard time complying with these new standards. But when the rep from Dow Chemical was on the witness stand and questioned by the legislature she said she couldn't answer any questions, she wasn't allowed to, that they had to be submitted in writing. I don't know if that ever even happened.

It's hard, we're supporting the science, but it seems at the end of the day these general statements that it's going to create job losses for West Virginia because these companies are going to pay more to comply won. But we don't even know how much they'd have to pay. That doesn't seem to matter to these legislators who say the industry says just trust us. The industry says this isn't great for us, just trust us on that.

ISN'T THAT JUST A MICROCOSM OF AMERICAN LAWMAKING IN GENERAL?

Yeah, and it's counter to science-based facts on this. On the state and national level it seems science gets pushed aside over political and financial gain. When it comes to protecting public health risks that is a dangerous way to operate. What's disheartening to me is that we've got one of the highest cancer rates in the country and I can't believe we're not being protective of our residents instead of just dragging this out and coming up with economic reasons why it's not worth protecting our residents or why they don't believe in the science.

THE LEGISLATURE IS REPUBLICAN CONTROLLED RIGHT?

Both the Senate and House are Republican controlled and we have an interesting governor who is now Republican but was elected as Democrat then announced he was changing. That created some political chaos.

[side note from me Luke here: his name is Jim Justice lol and he's the richest man in West Virginia and of course he's a coal baron and of course he inherited the business from his father]

WHAT ARE SOME OF THE COMMON POLLUTANTS WE'RE TALKING ABOUT HERE?

Cyanide and DDT are a couple people would recognize, but there are a lot you can't even pronounce. When you start reading about their health effects, over half of them are known or suspected carcinogens. People bring this up too, and it's true, we only regulate sixty of these when there are tens of thousands we don't regulate and don't know much about, and that's been coming to light in West Virginia. Dupont had a chemical that was part of the Teflon making industry. There was a big settlement for $670 million around all of the problems they've caused with people's health over the years. We had a big chemical leak in Charleston that poisoned the drinking water a couple years ago. It was a coal chemical that's not regulated, it's not on the list of standards. It's hard for me to reassure people because there's a lot you don't know about what you don't know. The chemical that poisoned the water in 2014 smelled like licorice. It caused rashes. People were aware just by the odor that it was in the water. I often think about the things that don't have an odor or immediate effects like we're discovering long term.

AND THE COAL INDUSTRY REMAINS A CONTROVERSIAL ISSUE THERE AS WELL RIGHT?

They recently lowered the coal severance tax. They bussed a bunch of coal miners in to be in the gallery the day that vote was taken. Lowering that tax will cost the state sixty million dollars a year and then we say we don't have any money to help with other needs. The proponents of that bill say it might save one hundred to five hundred jobs. The state is losing a lot of money for one job. That to me just illustrated where we are politically and just kind of this political-paralysis when it comes to doing anything that might draw opposition from the industry. The coal industry is still culturally and politically a big force but when you look at the economics . . .

IS IT SAFE TO SAY THAT THESE BIG CHEMICAL COMPANIES ARE DONATING TO POLITICIANS' CAMPAIGNS?

Yeah . . . I haven't taken a real close look at that myself, there's a whole other conversation happening every year in our legislature about disclosure laws. They attached a bill this year to raise the caps on campaign donations . . . I'm not real schooled on our disclosure laws and how PACs are formed. Anecdotally I've heard about a lot of donations coming through these PACs, but it's hard to tell who's behind them. It's very common. Last year one of the exciting moments that got some attention nationally was when a citizen during a public hearing on a water issues got up there and started listing all of the campaign donors to the committee chair and literally got dragged out of the hearing. Her name is Lissa Lucas. So there is that assumption and expectation. Oil and gas is another big lobby in our state and it is becoming bigger, and they also got their severance taxes decreased. It's pretty blatant. People can draw their own conclusions from that. There's a sense of pride in some legislators on how much they can help the industry grow and ease their environmental requirements and responsibilities.

HE STAYED THERE FOR A FEW HOURS DEAD ON THE TARGET FLOOR

THE MALLS ARE THE SOON-TO-BE GHOST TOWNS, WELL, SO LONG, FAREWELL, GOODBYE

Whenever I have to go to Target it makes me wish I were dead but I've never spent much time thinking about what it would be like were I to actually collapse and then die in the middle of the store mostly because at that point the aftermath would not be my problem.

It turns out it might not be that much different than business as usual if an incident at Target in Milwaukee is any indication because they had a guy go ahead and die there in April of 2019. They called the emergency services who came and tried to revive him and all which is very nice and good but he died so then they went ahead and just sort of left the store open and let people keep shopping for pet food and diapers and Aquaman on Blu-Ray and cookware like a lovely Select by Calphalon 12" Hard-Anodized Non-Stick Jumbo Fryer with Cover and other essentials.

"There was a man on the ground with CPR very actively being performed on him by firefighters and EMTs," a local woman named Ruth McGeehan told TMJ4 Milwaukee. It was weird she said but she kept shopping figuring it would all sort itself out but it didn't because her sister showed up about thirty minutes later to do some shopping of her own and she said the guy was dead right there under a tarp and he stayed there for a few hours dead on the Target floor.

"I wish I hadn't been given the option to walk into the store," McGeehan told the station. "I would have been totally fine if they were closed and gone somewhere else to do my shopping," and I am sure that is true but that is the reason they couldn't close isn't it is because think of the couple of thousand dollars they might have lost out on if they did. The boys upstairs would have had someone's ass off of that you can bet.

I don't know where you want to die but I spent a lot of time in the hospital this year having various doctor appointments and that tends to make a person think about death. A lot of times when people are close to death they say they want to go home to die and to not die in the hospital due to how grim it is there and that is true but not as grim as a Target with people wheeling their carts around filled with Sara Bareilles CDs and other sundries and their kid is screaming and screaming and you've never heard a kid scream like that but soon you're dead and the screaming stops. All the different kinds of screaming stop.

The Target near where I live in Watertown, MA is in the saddest little skeleton of a mall. It's like a little rescue mall like some rich guy would buy it because he got sad when he saw it and then he would go around pointedly telling everyone it was a rescue mall when they came by so everyone knew he had a charitable soul.

On one end of the mangy mall there's a Best Buy and on the other end there's a Target and in the middle they've got one of those vape shops that also sells like luggage somehow and also the DMV is there and a chain buffet of some kind and a Papa Ginos which is where I had my first job. It wasn't at this one it was in Kingston, MA and the first thing they had me do was wash dishes and then I graduated to the fryer where I would throw any type of shit you can imagine into the oil to see what would happen to it which is it would get a lot smaller. Then I moved on to running the pizza oven and finally they let me deliver pizzas which was considered to be quite the step up in those days.

When I was in college we went to eat at another Papa Ginos near my school and we got a salad and brought it back and stuck it up under the drop tile ceiling in our dorm to see what would happen to it over the course of the semester if we just left it there and it wasn't good. Nothing good happened to it is what I will say. It got bigger. Sometimes things will get bigger and sometimes things will get smaller and that's what is known as chemistry.

The other day I was talking about birds with Michelle and I told her male and female birds both have the same type of genitals which is called a cloaca and they sort of smash them together (?) and she looked at me like she had already dialed 9 . . . 1 . . . like how do you know so much about birds fucking and I said the only science class I ever took in college was ornithology which is the study of birds and then she asked me what else I knew about birds and I said that was it. I forgot it all except for the stuff about bird dicks.

Around the time I would have been studying bird dicks and delivering pizzas which I needed to do to buy CDs and gas for my car so I could deliver pizzas out of it and listen to CDs in it an album called *The Lonesome Crowded West* by Modest Mouse came out and it was ¿cómo se dice? *very good*. The first song on it is called "Teeth Like God's Shoeshine" and the lyrics go like "Here's the man with teeth like God's shoeshine. He sparkles, shimmers, shines. Let's all have another Orange Julius, thick syrup standing in lines. The malls are the soon-to-be ghost towns, well, so long, farewell, goodbye" and boy did I think that was some profound and sad shit to say about a mall at the time but turns out it wasn't especially prescient or profound or anything it was just a true statement about the very obvious state of malls.

Every time I've opened the fridge lately something has smelled a little off. I poked around in there lazily and I couldn't find the source of the smell immediately so I decided the work that it would take to isolate the rot or to deep clean the entire thing top to bottom was much too big a task so I convinced myself instead it doesn't smell that bad and that attitude is also why I'm very bad at making any sort of progress in therapy.

Speaking of making progress one of the things my doctors said recently is that I should probably stop smoking and I think maybe I probably should. I'm not going to yet due to the inability to change thing I just mentioned and also how I love smoking very much but I have been using a Juul a lot more in lieu of a cigarette and I also got some nicotine gum. Today I've been rotating back and forth between them in a disgusting smorgasbord trio of nicotine known as *the smoker's hat trick*.

Everyone knows that smoking will kill you but you sort of think it's not going to make a difference until you're like seventy and you get cancer but no one tells you things that might actually scare a young person such as it makes you look a lot uglier than you might otherwise be a lot sooner or that if you get injured smoking will make it take forever to heal which is probably what is going on with my whole deal. Mostly the nicotine gum is just making my face real hot. I got a hot face from chewing gum.

The trick about getting older and dying is you don't want to become a person who goes to the hospital a lot. Eventually we all will end up there but you want to forestall it for as long as possible. There is a very identifiable person you see at the hospital when you go as much as I do lately where you know they've spent more than their fair share of time there. Regulars like. After you've been to the hospital a certain number of times it changes something about you. You have to be wearing a track suit all the time now for some reason. When you first start going to the hospital a decent amount you start off thinking ah shit I hope I am never like those people over there and then one day you are and you have to start nodding hello to the Hospital People like you just passed a guy on the road with the same kind of Jeep you have. You flash the high beams. Hey man. But instead of speeding by each other you shuffle by real fucking slow.

In the bathroom at the Pain Center where I go to I found a scratch off lottery ticket wedged into the handlebar they have so old people can pull themselves up off the toilet with their arms when their legs don't work no good and I was like ah there is no chance this is a winning lottery ticket someone stashed here in the pain toilet but I checked anyway to make sure on account of you never know. All things considered the idea of someone going to see the doctor about chronic pain and stopping off in the shitter to scratch a lottery ticket did not make me feel particularly great I have to be honest with you here. I did not feel too great about it at all. The classic feeling of bad.

Whenever people depict the Grim Reaper in art or stories or whatever it's always a nightmare looking skeleton guy with a big scythe and he goes around harvesting souls with the scythe and he seems pretty into it all things considered but if there really was such a thing I think he would probably be more like the guy collecting all the shopping carts from the parking lot at Target just sort of slogging around miserable wrangling the carts that got blown away in the wind or that someone left out in the middle of nowhere. So the guy grabs it and he's like what the fuck did they do to this one and he sort of leads it back to the rest eventually pushing them all together in a train and he's got one where the wheel won't work right like it doesn't want to go. This fucking blows he says but he's got to do it because it's his job.

My landlady is currently dying at home right beneath the floor I'm laying on to write this. She's real old like old as hell and she's been dying at home down there for a couple of years now which is better than the alternative I guess which is to die all of a sudden out of nowhere somewhere else. You have time to prepare is the idea. Or maybe it's worse I don't know because you have to watch it coming. We used to see her bopping around all the time or like down in the basement doing laundry and stuff and she even drove her car around up until about a year ago but now she just basically sits down there with her nurse and blasts the TV so loud. The nurse makes Caribbean food a lot and I can smell it and I think man it would be nice to get my hands on some of that but probably not worth it if it meant I was going to die soon.

Sometimes the nurse takes her for a walk down the street and I just saw them doing that when I was taking out the trash bins and my landlady said she says to me she goes all these years I wanted to thank you for taking out the trash. The point isn't that I'm a good boy or anything because that's a pretty minuscule task for a person to do around a house but rather that that could very well be the last thing she ever says to me and then I'll have to think about that moment for a long time.

A couple of years ago I made a half assed stab at thinking about maybe trying to quit smoking and I went to see a hypnotist but I didn't really want to quit at the time which is exactly the wrong way to do things. I wrote about it for *The Atlantic* and if you would like to read about what it's like to get hypnotized to stop smoking you may do so now and if that doesn't interest you you are dismissed. The rest of it is below and it is a whole other article from another time and place.

"It's all about choice," said the man with the soothing voice. "If you're here to please someone else, you can stick around and have some fun, but more than likely you're going to go out and smoke after."

I was sitting in the basement of the public library in Arlington, Massachusetts, with a motley group of about twenty, all of us desperate and skeptical, with one big thing in common: We smelled like an ashtray.

In theory we'd come together because we didn't want to smoke cigarettes anymore. "I'm here for health reasons," one woman said. "Cigarettes are too expensive," said an elderly man. "When thinking of my children, sometimes I feel as if I'm taking from them," offered a middle-aged mother.

"I'm going to school for dental hygiene," added another attendee. "We're supposed to promote health, but how can I tell someone else to stop smoking if I am myself?"

These are all good reasons why people might want to quit smoking. For me, it's the same, plus vanity. And, fine, the grim specter of an earlier grave. (You can't look good when you're dead.) But if I really wanted to quit, then why was the only thing I could think about how much I wanted to walk out of there and go smoke a cigarette?

Mark Hall, a professional hypnotherapist and licensed social worker, was well aware of that, of course. He quit smoking many years ago himself—he says he still remembers reaching for a phantom lighter that wasn't in his pocket—and he has been holding sessions like these for more than twenty years, aimed at convincing others that they can do it themselves. Typically his hypnotherapy sessions cost around $150, or $95 with insurance coverage, but this event, sponsored by the Sanborn Foundation for the Treatment and Cure of Cancer, was near my home, and open and free to the public. In other words, there was no reason not to go, except, perhaps, a question that had been frightening me all week as the meeting approached: What if it doesn't work? Or, maybe even worse: What if it actually does? Then what the hell am I going to do? As crazy as it sounds, smoking is such a major part of my daily routine, the prospect of losing it is scary.

"Does anyone here feel like cigarettes are their best friend?" Hall asked, telling us to clap our hands, then to clap them again, this time leading with the opposite hand of what we were used to. It felt weird. The sound in the room changed noticeably as well. The point, Hall said, was that smoking is a habit we all perform as involuntarily, through muscle memory, as the way we choose to clap our hands.

People may undergo hypnosis in order to address all manner of problems—from addictions, like mine, to emotional trauma. There's some evidence that it could be an effective tool in dentistry, treating eating disorders and post-traumatic stress disorder, and helping with pain during childbirth. But despite its prevalence, there's still ample confusion about what it actually is, sometimes even among those who've already committed to it. I certainly had no idea what I was in for as I relaxed into my superlatively uncomfortable chair, ready for, well, something. Or maybe nothing.

Hypnotism is such an amorphous concept that when I asked a couple practitioners what it is, they spent a good portion of the discussion telling me what it is not. Many of us are familiar with the process of hypnosis from the popular brand of hypnotist entertainers, where guests are plucked from nightclub audiences to go embarrass themselves on stage. Or, if not that, then from fictional depictions of a Freudian type smugly waving a stopwatch in front of a patient's face. Those are both big misconceptions, Hall explained while prepping his crowd for the descent into a state of enhanced relaxation.

"My hypnosis is a therapeutical tool, not entertainment," he said, beginning to put us at ease. But, he joked, "If you told someone you'll be here tonight I encourage you to go home and start clucking like a chicken."

The practice as it's followed today generally traces its origins back to the 1840s, when Scottish surgeon James Braid built upon the idea of what he called "nervous sleep," or, more specifically, "the induction of a habit of abstraction or mental concentration, in which, as in reverie or spontaneous abstraction, the powers of the mind are so much engrossed with a single idea or train of thought, as, for the nonce, to render the individual unconscious of, or indifferently conscious to, all other ideas, impressions, or trains of thought."

But conflating hypnosis with sleep (the word is derived from the Greek word for sleep), is inaccurate, according to the hypnotist and author Charles Tebbetts, as relayed by his student C. Roy Hunter in his book *The Art of Hypnosis: Mastering Basic Techniques*. Hypnotism "is actually a natural state of mind and induced normally in everyday living much more often than it is induced artificially. Every time we become engrossed in a novel or a motion picture, we are in a natural hypnotic trance," Tebetts wrote. Hunter writes that it's more accurate to say that all hypnosis is actually self-hypnosis. The hypnotherapist, much like a physical trainer then, is merely helping the subject convince themselves to do something they were already capable of doing, nudging them in the right direction.

While there are a wide variety of approaches and styles of hypnotism employed today—something that further confounds our ability to understand it objectively, or to study it scientifically—one thing that they tend to have in common is an emphasis on relaxation, focus, harnessing a desire to change within the individual, and building linguistic and visual relationships between emotions. As the American Association of Professional Hypnotherapists explains: "Hypnosis is simply a state of relaxed focus. It is a natural state. In fact, each of us enters such a state—sometimes called a trance state—*at least* twice a day: once when we are falling asleep, and once when we are waking up."

Hypnotherapists say they facilitate this process, just without the sleep part. More or less. Again, for every positive study you read about hypnosis, there are numerous, often conflicting other accounts. In a 2000 study for the *International Journal of Clinical and Experimental Hypnosis,* Joseph P. Green and Steven Jay Lynn reviewed 56 studies on the results of hypnosis on smoking cessation. While it was shown to generally be a better option than no treatment at all, many of the studies combined hypnosis with other therapeutic methods, making it difficult to isolate its effects.

Likely few people try to quit smoking through hypnosis alone, and no two practices are exactly the same, which is part of what makes it so difficult to know if it works.

Moshe Torem, a professor of psychiatry at Northeast Ohio Medical University and the president of the American Society of Clinical Hypnosis, one of many such professional groups around the country, explained to me the components of typical hypnotherapist's process.

"Hypnosis is a different state of mind associated with four major characteristics," he said. First is a "highly focused attention on something." It could be an issue you're having, or a problem you want to address. Second is disassociating oneself from the immediate physical environment. "You focus on the beach in Florida in the middle of a Boston winter," he said, anticipating my particular winter-addled frame of mind perfectly. "Instead of traveling there, you go there with your mind, and you're fully focused on the beach."

Probably a nice place to smoke a cigarette.

The third element is suggestibility. The person becomes more responsive to suggestions given to him or her. Fourth is what he calls "involuntariness." That means when you come out of hypnosis, you feel subjectively like you haven't done anything, but that something has been done to you. You may recognize that you're being told to lift your arm, for example, but you feel as if it is being lifted by some external force. Which makes sense, since when I reach for a cigarette, especially when I know I don't need it, I'm being governed by similar subconscious impulses.

The end result, ideally, finds the concepts suggested by the hypnotist—either positive reinforcement for resisting smoking or negative associations with cigarettes—taking root in the subconscious as a sort of bulwark against the impulse to smoke.

This might be a pretty good time to pause and call bullshit, particularly since, during the demonstration in the library, that's exactly what I was thinking myself. Hall himself tried a little of both techniques, telling us that we were ready to stop smoking, that this was something we wanted, but also told us horror stories about smoking. Not of cancer, which can be easy to ignore until it's too late, but of his trips to tobacco farms, where he'd seen all manner of disgusting things—rats and tree frogs and pesticides and pigeon shit falling into a tobacco shredder and so on. You're smoking tree frogs and pesticide, he said. To be honest, that didn't sound much worse than what I always sort of assumed I was smoking.

No way any of this is going to work on me, I thought, as I prepped myself to lilt off into my own special place on the beach, my compatriots drifting away into their own safe places.

"Don't try to be hypnotized," Hall said. "Trying to be hypnotized is like trying to go to sleep."

It's a concept that Torem echoed when we spoke.

"The worst thing you can say is 'Today is the day that I don't want to smoke,'" he explained, likening it to what he called the Rhinoceros Principle, otherwise known as ironic-process theory. Ask someone not to think about a rhinoceros, and what's the first thing he thinks of? The same holds true for saying "don't smoke," according to Torem.

"People don't like to be told "don't,'" he said. "If you say 'don't smoke,' it's the same thing as saying 'smoke.'" The unconscious mind doesn't understand the word 'don't,' he said, echoing a common, albeit undocumented, claim from hypnotists.

And yet, every day, posters, commercials, and cigarette labels tell people not to smoke. I tell myself not to smoke. It doesn't seem to be working fast enough. Although the number of smoking adults in the U.S. dropped from 20.9 percent to 17.8 percent from 2005 to 2013, smoking is still responsible for 480,000 deaths per year in the United States, and six million worldwide, the Centers for Disease Control and Prevention reports. Most of them have been told: Don't.

The numbers on the success rates of hypnotherapy for quitting smoking are fuzzy, which makes sense, since the practice itself is questionably scientific. Hall says it's 50/50 for his clients.

"Hypnosis is not magic for most of us," he says. "Hypnosis is just a tool that helps in making what you're trying to do easier."

It is but one of the tools in a crowded supply closet that those who try to quit might reach for. The U.S. Department of Health and Human Services released a series of Clinical Practice Guidelines in 2008 that outlined a number of effective practices for smoking cessation. Among them, they found, were individual counseling and the use of medications like the nicotine patch and nicotine gum. Even better was combining the two. The HHS doesn't explicitly endorse or condemn hypnotherapy.

That's in part because there isn't enough data. While some studies have shown positive results, they differ too much for anyone to draw a solid conclusion. Few studies that have been done over the years met HHS's inclusion criteria, owing in part to the vast array of methodologies used. "There was no common or standard intervention technique to analyze," the guidelines read. "Moreover, an independent review of nine hypnotherapy trials by the Cochrane Group found insufficient evidence to support hypnosis as a treatment for smoking cessation."

A later meta-study in 2010 from the Cochrane Group also forestalled a judgment on hypnotism's efficacy. "Although it is possible that hypnotherapy could be as effective as counseling treatment there is not enough good evidence to be certain of this."

While his organization hasn't done its own study, Lee Westmaas director of tobacco control research at the American Cancer Society told me, "At this time there's not enough evidence to say that hypnosis works definitively."

"Perhaps for some people it might work," he said and, indeed, I have friends who swear by it. "Possibly there might be a minority of people for whom it works, but if that's the case we don't know who."

"You seem like exactly the type of person hypnosis would not work on," a friend told me when I mentioned I was going to try it, implying I'm too skeptical and set in my ways to be open to something like this. Still, there I was, ready to see what would happen. Hall's voice worked a strange alchemy on me in the library, and I drifted off into what seemed like a state of intense relaxation. I could've fallen asleep easily. I didn't even pull out my phone and refresh Twitter for a whole half hour.

And then, something strange happened. I could feel some deep recess of my subconscious fighting against Hall's words. I thought of scenes from exorcist movies, of demons recoiling from a priest's incantations. "No, no, don't abandon me," it seemed to scream. "I'll be good. I'll be good."

When we came out of the session, he asked us how we each had felt. Some reported feeling a sense of heaviness, others said they felt as if they were floating away. One woman couldn't remember a word he had said the entire time. An older man in a Red Sox jersey said he could hear him but couldn't make out the words. "Me relaxing to that degree made me realize how much my body is fighting to breathe cleanly," the elderly man said. Another woman said she felt as if she wanted to cry. I shared her emotion. It felt as if something was being taken from me.

So did it work? As it is for hypnosis in general, the jury is still out. I left the session feeling noticeably different. I sat in my car outside for a half hour and did not smoke. I went to dinner nearby and sat, and had a drink, and did not smoke. Eventually I caved in to the craving, but I didn't like it. I'm still smoking, I just don't enjoy them anywhere near as much as I used to anymore.

A common idea among hypnotists is that you have to truly want it to work, or it won't. They can't do it for you. At the very least, I can say I'm willing to try again. I don't entirely want to stop smoking just yet. But I want myself to want to.

I HATE WHAT THEY'VE DONE TO ALMOST EVERYONE IN MY FAMILY

PROGRESS IS MADE ONE FUNERAL AT A TIME

Mom don't read this chapter. I love you very much and I will call soon I promise but don't read this one ok because it's about me jacking off just kidding it's about a sore spot for me which is feeling like you've lost a piece of your loved ones to Fox News brain cancer. Or maybe do read it maybe it will be beneficial I don't know I don't know anything aside from this one thing which is that Fox News has stolen something from all of us. Sean Hannity and Bill O'Reilly and the rest have kidnapped and brainwashed many of our otherwise lovely and kind family members and I'll piss on their graves one day with a huge fucking boner that makes it hard for the piss to come out and I'll be like ah fuck and it'll splash out weird. Don't ask me why they're buried next to each other it just makes sense.

I love my mother she is one of the kindest and sweetest people you will ever meet. She is a survivor of domestic abuse and a very strong woman for that and I would be nothing without her. One thing she does or did for a long time is make quilts for children with cancer and also people bring her the t-shirts and sweaters of a loved one who has died and she makes them into a quilt for them so they can wrap themselves up in the memories of the person who is gone. She's a good person and as far as I can tell Not Racist and I have never heard her say anything overtly terrible politically speaking like the type of thing you might hear from white nationalists like Tucker Carlson or Hannity.

But I do know that she has watched those motherfuckers on TV a lot over the years perhaps every day and well you can't be subjected to that sort of thing for too long without it rubbing off on you.

As such my mom and I have agreed to not talk about politics anymore because I always werewolf into the type of pedant who turns Christmas into the 25th of Shit but sometimes she'll say something she thinks is safe and innocuous and my bullet time poster brain will slow down and see intuitively it's some Fox News-inspired talking point and so it makes me not want to talk about anything to avoid any sort of disagreement and then I keep it all inside which is a condition known as being Massachusetts Irish trash which is what we are.

Of course Fox News didn't invent the white supremacy and racism that are at the heart of America and many of our family members would've believed that shit otherwise on their own but Fox has definitely supercharged it or activated something that was dormant and weaponized it. (One other caveat: "My parents watched the bad TV and got racist off it" is clearly a much less serious problem to have than being someone whose life is put at risk by the type of stuff Fox News promotes.)

I mentioned this on Twitter the other day and unsurprisingly a lot of people have had similar experiences in their own families some of which are much worse than mine. I asked a dozen or so of them to share how they lost a family member to Fox News or how their relationships have become strained:

My folks were always reactionary conservatives—they blocked MTV growing up because it was a "perverting influence"—and they grew up to be Trump voters. It has destroyed my ability to trust them and go to them for advice and help, and in doing so, taken out most of the central columns in the essential parent-child dynamic. It makes me angry every day. Words cannot describe how much I wish I had just one intellectually sound, reliable parent at this time in my life, but Fox News got to them first.

I'd probably leave it alone if they hadn't absolutely terrorized me about my "morality" as a child. And I know it does a lot more harm than good, but now I text my dad every time I'm catcalled or sexually harassed/intimidated in public, and I frequently remind my mom that her "protest vote" will likely end with me getting stripped of my health insurance and an attempt at removing my bodily autonomy. I don't know if they even care of have the intellectual capacity to understand other peoples' suffering.

I've spent basically two years reminding them every way in which their little "protest" has caused people harm. I send them videos of obviously fucked up Mexican kids in detention.

I don't know what to do with all this anger and shame except to try to reflect it back with the Archimedes laser of my iron will to be a total cunt 24/7.

My father was always conservative. He wasn't particularly interested in politics until his brother turned him on to Rush Limbaugh and conservative AM talk radio in the mid-nineties. His family was extremely racist going back generations, and I'll go ahead and assume white racism finds a more welcoming home in the Republican Party than the Democratic Party, while I know that example is not absolute. Anyway, I regret ever showing him Fox News. I turned it on as a teenager and showed it to my parents as a goof. I was laughing at how irresponsible Bill O'Reilly acted on air as an anchor. My mother, a centrist Republican, thought it was funny. My dad started watching regularly.

Soon it was the only programming he ingested other than talk radio. He became addicted to the anger. He thought if he was angry at all the "injustices" Fox News presented to him he must be righteous. He grew more irritable. He banned watching any news other than Fox News in his presence and failure to adhere would lead to abusive emotional outbursts. Soon he lost his sense of humor. Everything became about punching down at gays and minorities. Then he started making derisive comments about Democrats during family functions when it was considered inappropriate. He declared his favorite show was "The Five," which then led to it being required viewing at our dinner time. If any real life occurrence interferes with him viewing "The Five" our family would be subjected to hours of screaming and cursing. He then became more paranoid, claiming that power or cable outages were a plot by the Democrats (who secretly control everything).

My mother had enough. Out of the blue, she filed for divorce. He was crushed, couldn't understand why, and took comfort in drinking while watching his friends on TV. She is happier than I have ever seen her and he is sad and angry living in the basement of a rented house, still watching "The Five," Tucker Carlson, Jeanine Pirro, etc.

Rupert Murdoch ruined my family and my country. If a genie gave me wishes I would hope his private plane crashes into the sea and every single person that works for Fox News gets trapped in the building and burns alive.

Growing up, my dad was the one person I knew who taught me to be a critical thinker and educate myself on topics before I spoke about them. Right around the 2008 election he became a Fox News talking point machine, saying some awful shit I never knew he'd believed.

When I'd press him on where he heard it and how he knew it was true he'd just shut down. Nowadays there is just this quiet stalemate where we've agreed to not talk about anything political, but I see him slipping from time to time because he almost can't help himself. Maybe he was always like this, but lacked the exhaust chamber to say out loud what he was thinking. I'll never know. It just sucks because I know the people he hates so much are basically the same people as me.

Yeah he's racist. I wouldn't have thought so back in the day, but I guess it was always there simmering under the surface. Like a lot of people I think old age and his chosen form of media have made him feel more safe about saying stuff out loud.

My only guess is that they no longer recognize the world around them. Instead of just acknowledging that it's just the way things go, they've retreated into this fear of "the other" which almost always turns out to be someone who isn't white.

My dad, an immigrant, has had brain poisoning for years and years through this whole shit. He listened to Limbaugh in the nineties and it only got worse when he got Fox News. He used to think Trump was a dipshit but is now all in on the idiot's cruelty. He and my mom separated last November. There were other reasons but one of the big ones was his Fox addiction. I went down to help him get set up in a new apartment. He cried a lot. We found an apartment and furniture and I got the utilities set up but I did not sign up for cable TV. He did that after I left, before he got a job.

The thing that makes me maddest about this is that it's about money. My dad was diagnosed with prostate cancer a year ago. It's the cancer that doesn't matter if you catch it and he's seventy six so it's probably not what's gonna get him. It did make him start thinking about his mortality though. He's on all the email lists and I guess Mike Huckabee has been selling his email to fucking everybody, including one list I noticed when I was getting his email set up called "Beyond Chemo."

They are selling him his own anger and a bunch of mushroom pills for all the money he doesn't have anymore. He's gonna die destitute because of this shit and people belong in prison for seeing this as a business opportunity.

I met my mom for dinner last night. Somehow it ends up on politics and yeah, my mom's now a big racist, shaking in her boots at the word "socialism." We also agreed to the no politics thing, but she's a big time Facebooker. Inevitably she'll say something dumb from a meme or some shit and I'll just have to go off again.

I don't think she was always like that. I know she was a Bush person, but I don't think she has always had such interpersonally toxic beliefs. It's been at least since 2014, because I remember hearing her say something ignorant about Ferguson and having a physical reaction to it.

My instinct is to challenge her and try to "educate" her but then the response is "you're calling your mother a racist?" and that type of question just makes it hard to say anything, especially to my mother.

In a vacuum, my godfather and godmother are some of most kind people I've ever encountered in my life. So much so that my parents decided to name me after my godfather. I was not very close to my grandparents into my adult life as they died early in my adolescence, but they could easily be replacements and I will absolutely bawl my eyes out when they pass.

Fox News has absolutely turned their brains to mush and anything even remotely political immediately morphs into what I know must be a Fox News talking point. Politics is something that is a large interest to them, so it is very common that they will say something that will make me immediately shut down the conversation and leave so as to not be confrontational. It's a shame because I always love spending time with them, but there is no way the two people that raised me to be the person I am today have such little regard for others as they regurgitate such, in my opinion, absolutely abhorrent views of people of all walks of life. It is truly a tragedy.

I consider myself to be someone with strong conviction in my beliefs, so sharing the namesake Martin with my godfather has literally thrown my life into an existential identity crisis that I barely survived in the last two years. I'm going to therapy to deal with all this and I'm confident I am going to be a stronger person for it.

After Obama was elected I thought my dad had turned a corner when he said he stopped listening to talk radio, especially Rush Limbaugh, on his long work commute, because he said that Limbaugh had gone off the deep end.

I don't watch Fox News because of course it warps the psyche of anyone who does, but it must have changed tone after Trump was elected. My dad slowly became even more xenophobic and angry than he used to be.

My daughter's dedication was this weekend, and both my parents and my wife's parents stayed at our house. Our respective fathers couldn't even have dinner without it becoming the two of them, loudly, indulging in their angry, ever more hateful fantasies of "what's really wrong with America."

The two of us are worried about letting our daughter stay with them for any long length of time, because their toxic anger and resentment is slowly becoming their entire identity.

I just know that I'm with you. I hate what they've done to almost everyone in my family. It's absolute poison and the only thing I think is worse is that there are people who think that destroying the morals and conscience of multiple generations is worth a few more bucks, because I absolutely refuse to believe that people like Hannity don't know what they are doing.

I wish I could do something, but who has the time or energy to combat that? And how the hell do you reteach someone to have empathy?

My pastor says "progress is made one funeral at a time" and it's hard to disagree with him at this point.

I was raised by a strong pro-choice feminist mother, who now tells me "cute stories" that happen on "The Five," the shitty Fox daytime show, loves Trump, and thinks abortion should be illegal after six weeks. Depressing doesn't even cover it. You can't break through that wall of shit.

I grew up in a house where we openly talked politics. Now, it's noticeably absent from our conversations. She actually said that she hopes my daughter, who is four, grows up to be conservative. When I said "absolutely not," she seemed truly baffled. Their brains are rotting on this stuff.

I will say that whenever she spends time with my minority friends she seems to temporarily soften on the racist stuff, then she goes back to Texas and watches a few hours of Fox and it's back to "normal."

I am also an orphan of Fox News. My mom's brain is completely broken from it, and we have less and less to talk about it every time we see each other. I think what really did it for me was after Tamir Rice was murdered I brought it up at breakfast for some insane reason and my mom said "well, he looked fully adult." Prior to that she had said stuff like she thought Obama was a Muslim and other racist Fox News parroting, but when she erased the human worth of a child like that I knew she was truly lost.

I would describe it as I still love my mom but I don't really like her.

I pretty much don't go home anymore, having only been in Phoenix twice over the last three years, only at Christmas, because my family and friends all have broken Fox Brain. But of course I called at Thanksgiving to say hi, which was when my dad called Obama the n-word during the call apropos of nothing.

I'm not totally sure when it started since I haven't lived at home since 2002. It slowly built, but the rift probably started around 2008 when I was volunteering for Obama. It got most heated when my mom went to a Trump rally in Phoenix ahead of the 2016 election.

We've pretty much agreed not to talk politics anymore, but occasionally my mom tells me things like Brett Kavanaugh is innocent because women always lie about getting raped and like you I just stopped calling and answering texts eventually.

I haven't actually talked to my sister about this stuff because she's pretty religious and seemingly a never-Trump Republican, but she was abused by a babysitter as a kid and raped in college and despite living ten miles away from my parents with three grandkids she's cut off all communication with them after my mom pretty much said she didn't believe her.

I can't necessarily say it all stems from Fox News, but it's on in the house pretty much 24/7 and I can't imagine that doesn't play a factor. But I probably had MSNBC brain while I was there, as I had it on eight hours a day at work and then watched Maddow and Hayes when I got home.

I lost an uncle to Fox brain. He was a middle school teacher in a small upstate New York town, was on the board of the teachers union, and a big labor guy. After he retired he started thinking unions were for lazy people and talked a lot about how the government gives free stuff to immigrants who come here illegally. A couple weeks ago we were talking about my student debt and he said if I was an illegal the government would take care of that for me. It fucking sucks.

I asked him why he thinks that's true and told him I thought they just put them in cages, but he just rolled his eyes and started talking about something else. We mostly just don't talk as much anymore because it's not worth it for either of us.

My parents came to visit me in LA recently, from my hometown in Goatfuck, IL. They are the sweetest, warmest, supportive, most generous people on earth—but over the past few years I've picked up on distinct symptoms of Fox News brain poisoning.

During their trip we were just hanging out and chatting when my dad, unprompted, says "They say there's a lot of Mexicans here in Southern California." Uh, yeah, dad. This actually used to be Mexico, so I think some people of Mexican descent may have stuck around. Then my mom chimes in "Oh sure, they just come right over." Come right over?! The implication being they all scaled a wall, not even considering the fact that most families have been here for generations, descended from people who migrated here for a better life just like our own familial ancestors did.

I just bit my tongue, because above all, my family is one that eschews any form of conflict in favor of suppressing all emotion. I later heard my mom droning on to someone about how there are only two genders and just silently stewed.

All this is to say I feel your pain about almost feeling like you've lost a loved one to Fox News poisoning. It's a hard thing when the glowing prism through which we view the ones we love is shattered, and there's no way to put that image of them back together again. It's something I've honestly had trouble dealing with over the past few years.

I might recommend adding Facebook poisoning to the diagnoses as well. In the tiny town in which I grew up, there's no local paper anymore and nothing in the way of culture or things to do period. Sometimes my mom's only glimpses of the outside world come from Facebook and Fox News, and the impact of those poisonous outlets is becoming clearer and clearer.

It happened to my dad and my aunt. Last time I saw my aunt she told me there's an ISIS training camp in upstate New York and it has been there for years. She used to be a new age hippy person. Now she barely leaves her house in the woods in central Massachusetts.

My dad is dead but in the last few years of his life he got totally warped. He went from voting for Gore, then Kerry and fucking hating Bush and the wars to thinking Obama was gonna destroy America. He started working a night shift job and would come home during the day and fall asleep with Fox News blasting. I really think it rotted his brain.

My dad was still pretty nice at the end but it got to us not being able to talk politics at all. I've talked to my mom about it and she agreed. She said his lack of sleep really messed with his brain and made him very paranoid. He was getting into survivalist paranoia when he died. For like months after when we were cleaning out his stuff we would find guns hidden in the house. I only got aware of politics a bit before Obama was elected so we could have interesting conversations, but by like 2009 or 2010 he was pretty changed. My whole family avoids talking politics to my aunt these days. Her and her husband, who was a college professor in physics, don't believe in global warming and all this other shit. They think since I moved to Boston that I'm gonna get murdered or seduced by "evil women."

They're total cranks about that stuff but still very sweet so it's very weird and uncomfortable. My aunt was telling me about the ISIS camp in a very matter of fact way, like she would be describing the weather or the Patriots game.

You're gonna get a lot of stories about people losing family to Fox and the right but for a little counter-programming, we actually got one of my cousins back before it was too late. He listened to InfoWars religiously from 2009-2015 or so and is an avid hunter who lives in the woods and smokes a lot of weed and plays a lot of video games so I thought he was a goner for sure, but thanks to the infinite patience of his little sister, he actually came to his senses and realized what a dangerous crock he had bought into.

I'm sure he's an outlier but not all of them are lost causes just yet.

He could see how disappointed we all were, but having his baby sister tell him every day that she loved him but that he was slowly rotting his own brain seemed to do it. There's part of me that wonders if what sealed it was the fact that InfoWars was going mainstream and it wasn't as cool or exciting to believe in Jade Helm or whatever if those beliefs weren't truly counterculture. He's still got problems, but he drifted away from all that and we gave him plenty of positive reinforcement when he did.

I hope someday the spell breaks, at least for some of these folks. But I'll never forget as a kid thinking that there was no one left on earth who liked Nixon, then one day I ran an errand for my dad and the old guy I met with opened a closet door to reveal a Nixon shrine, so who the hell knows.

My parents haven't been broken by Fox News, but what I find almost as disturbing is how even parents who have never watched a moment of Fox News can parrot their talking points—like mine. My mom is an actual immigrant from Venezuela and she started talking the other day about how refugees are an undue burden on our healthcare system and the reasons it's bad. She's an educated person who has never watched Fox News! But Hannity and Tucker have so permeated the culture that their noxious shit can be found coming out of the mouths of ostensibly "liberal" people. It's terrifying.

Part of it is she's always just been one of those "I did immigration the *right* way" people so it doesn't take much to rub her wrong on that front. But I think she must've read some *Wall Street Journal* or *Washington Post* op-eds that gave her that particular idea.

Here is a text I got from my father this morning, a guy who gets all his news from Hannity. Another case of "so so close to getting it," but still a giant swing and miss.

My simple takeaway is the American people are being fed information, and there really is no way we can absolutely know what the actual truth is.

I saw this article as a call to question, look and never stop seeking the truth. In the age of click bait, producer driven news casts, deep discussions of ideas and knowledge are not mainstream. My point, things may not always be what they appear to be.

There is shit going on in the deep state that is not R or D. Many dirty hands doing dirty shit, and the stuff we hear about has been scrubbed or shaded many times....

Have an awesome day.....

He's genuinely a really decent guy who refuses to acknowledge the harm his political views cause in the world. I have absolutely been calling less, picking up the phone less, wanting to visit with family less, and all of this as his first grandkid was born this year and my new-found identity as a dad has made it even more painful to see the relationship with my own father strain under this tension.

IT JUST SUCKS BECAUSE I KNOW THE PEOPLE HE HATES SO MUCH ARE BASICALLY THE SAME PEOPLE AS ME

IT WAS SOMEWHERE AROUND THE 100TH RESPONSE THAT MY BRAIN TURNED TO MUSH.

Last week which I guess is last chapter in the context of this book, I collected stories from people who, like me, had close relationships that had been strained or ruined by family members who'd become obsessed with Fox News. It was a very big deal! I wrote about it again in *New York Magazine* which is technically where this chapter you're about to read is coming from and the *Guardian* also reprinted it and hundreds of thousands of people read it. AOC and Mark Ruffalo and all sorts of big shots shared it too. Nice job buddy.

No matter where the stories came from they all featured a few familiar beats: A loved one seemed to have changed over time. Maybe that person was already somewhat conservative to start. Maybe they were apolitical. But at one point or another, they sat down in front of Fox News, found some kind of deep, addictive comfort in the anger and paranoia, and became a different person—someone difficult, if not impossible, to spend time with. The fallout led to failed marriages and estranged parental relationships. For at least one person, it marks the final memory he'll ever have of his father: "When I found my dad dead in his armchair, fucking Fox News was on the TV," this reader told me.

"It's likely the last thing he saw. I hate what that channel and conservative talk radio did to my funny, compassionate dad. He spent the last years of his life increasingly angry, bigoted, and paranoid."

Something about the piece struck a chord. It had gone viral, and wave after wave of frustrated and saddened Fox News orphans began to commiserate with me and with each other on Twitter and in my messages. Others wrote of similar phenomenon in Australia with the television channel Sky or in the U.K. with the tabloid *Daily Mail*. I heard from more than a hundred people who felt like they could relate to what they all seemed to think of as a kind of ideological brain poisoning. They chose Fox News over their family, people told me. They chose Fox News over me.

There was the one reader who wrote of his Puerto Rican uncle becoming a Fox News junkie, and turning on his own people, as he put it, in the aftermath of Hurricane Maria. "He was literally sitting in the dark and still defending Trump," he said, which seemed a metaphor almost too on the nose. Hearing stories like that over and over again all weekend wasn't pretty.

As some critics of the piece pointed out, it seems a bit silly, if not stupid, to scapegoat a cable-news network for our family members' interpersonal shortcomings. I get that. I don't have an empirical way to assign blame or figure out causality. Maybe Fox News causes some people to turn toward hard-right conservatism; maybe it's merely a precipitating factor; maybe it's neither, and for most people, change in political attitudes came from elsewhere. In requesting stories about family members and Fox News, I wasn't undertaking a scientific experiment—merely seeking to see if there are other people who had the same experiences I had, and felt the same way I did.

What I learned is that there are. Whatever the actual direction of causality, there are many, many Americans who blame Fox News for changes in their loved ones, and many people out there who feel as though their friends and family members have been lost to a 24/7 stream of right-wing propaganda.

Dozens who responded to my piece talked about the sad lonely twilight of their parents' or grandparents' lives, having been spurned by, or having disowned much of their families over political disagreements. Older people, recent studies have shown, are much more likely to share misleading information online, but the anecdotes I was hearing seemed to indicate this behavior wasn't limited to the internet. Young parents wrote that they don't want to bring their children to visit aging Fox-brainers. "The worst is when my children go to spend time with their grandparents and come home with Fox News talking points coming out of their mouths," one told me. "I have to decontaminate them every time."

I heard from several people that Fox News was a key factor in a divorce. One reader told me about his father, a one-time Trump skeptic turned believer. "He and my mom separated last November. There were other reasons but one of the big ones was his Fox addiction," he wrote. "I went down to help him get set up in a new apartment. He cried a lot. We found an apartment and furniture and I got the utilities set up but I did not sign up for cable TV. He did that after I left, before he got a job."

Another person told me that Rush Limbaugh sent his father on the path to isolation before eventually mainlining Fox News on a regular basis. Eventually, out of the blue, his mother filed for divorce. "He was crushed, couldn't understand why, and took comfort in drinking while watching his friends on TV. She is happier than I have ever seen her and he is sad and angry living in the basement of a rented house, still watching "The Five," Tucker Carlson, Jeanine Pirro, etc."

For some, the Fox-driven political affiliations of family members represent a deep betrayal. A son wrote to me of his widowed father choosing Fox News over the well-being of him and his wife, both of whom are disabled. "He is aware that the GOP wants to take away health care and he still voted for Trump. He still likes Trump."

If I had to pinpoint the most common reaction to all the thousands of replies to the story, I'd say it was one of exasperation—and desperation. I didn't realize so many other people were dealing with this, many said. "Does anyone know an online support group for people going through this to share tips on deprogramming and/or surviving these relationships?" one asked. "If not . . . would anyone be interested in starting one?" It's not the worst idea. The most positive story I heard came from a woman who brought her brother back from the edge with persistent and careful and sustained bridge-building work, showing him the error of his paranoid conspiracy thinking.

One problem is that once someone gets pulled into the Fox News vortex it naturally leads to other scummier enterprises. You might start out signing up for a Fox email list or one from the president then quickly find your email being sold far and wide to increasingly less reputable charlatans. "The thing that makes me maddest about this is that it's about money," one correspondent said. His dad had been diagnosed with prostate cancer a year ago. "I guess Mike Huckabee has been selling his email to fucking everybody, including one list I noticed when I was getting his email set up called Beyond Chemo. They are selling him his own anger and a bunch of mushroom pills for all the money he doesn't have anymore," he said. "He's gonna die destitute because of this shit and people belong in prison for seeing this as a business opportunity."

Those who hadn't yet broken off with family said maintaining the relationship with a person they love is exceptionally difficult, and requires all manner of safeguards. "I've been on eggshells with my dad for half my life now," one wrote. "It really hurts having a father who is kind and smart but has Fox News brain worms. I can only talk to my dad about the weather. Anything else will set him off, even football . . ."

To be fair, there is a rough analog on the other side of the political spectrum, even if it seems, anecdotally, relatively muted. More than a few readers wrote to say this all made them thankful they merely had to contend with Dem-Boomer family who had gone mad for Maddow and Russiagate. "My grandma is a huge Maddow person and operates the same way as Fox News brained people," one wrote me. "The signaling she gets and reiterates from MSNBC happens in the same sort of 'brain rot' way. Like, she heard something on there, or on Facebook, that was about how Trump is about to get impeached—and every day I talk to her and she repeats that."

"I love her, and she's bright and it's obviously less offensive" than Fox News, the reader continued, "but the whole fucking garbage corporate 24 hour news model is insidious and so so fucking bad."

The unfortunate familial balancing act is one I know well from my own family, where an argument, even among people who have explicitly agreed to avoid politics altogether, can erupt at any time. (Many people insisted, like I do myself, that their Trump-kissing parents are the kindest, sweetest people in the world and it makes no sense they would be Fox News viewers.) But it's one thing to have grown up a liberal in a conservative family, and learned how to navigate difficult political conversations your entire life—even if those conversations have only gotten more difficult. But many of the people I heard from talked about a transformation, whether gradual or sudden.

One woman told me about her mother, who has stopped talking to her since becoming convinced Democrats are murdering children. It wasn't always this way, she explained. Her mother had been a Democrat until 2008, and then something switched.

A lot of the stories echoed that turning point. There was something about Obama that seemed to make a lot of previously apolitical or moderate family members lose their minds. Gosh—what could it have possibly been?

This is, I think, where the channel's genius lies. Any salesperson or con artist will tell you that you can't incept a thought in a mark's mind out of nowhere. You have to find the hook that's already there—fear, or desire—and exploit it. When it comes to exacerbating and honing the anxieties of aging Americans you can't do much better (or worse) than race and immigration.

Because the truth is, Fox News didn't invent racism, and many of our family members would've believed in it on their own. This may have been the hardest thing I learned from the stories I heard: Fox didn't necessarily change anyone's mind, so much as it seems to have supercharged and weaponized a politics that was otherwise easy for white Americans to overlook in their loved ones. "Maybe he was always like this, but lacked the exhaust chamber to say out loud what he was thinking. I'll never know," one person told me. "It just sucks because I know the people he hates so much are basically the same people as me."

I WAS DEPRESSED AND I WANTED TO FEEL MORE DEPRESSED SO I WENT TO CHEERS

THE REST OF THE WAY INTO BOSTON FROM WHERE MY BONES LIVE

There were moths in my belly on a Saturday afternoon so I got into my silver 2011 Toyota Corolla with a very normal bumper and a clean back seat and drove down Belmont Street past the lamp store and the amazingly ungentrified storefronts that haven't changed in decades and past the pub where the old townies were singing along to Cheap Trick the other night and then turned left and drove by Mount Auburn Cemetery where we go for walks sometimes in the winter when all the trees and tombs are covered in snow and where Henry Cabot Lodge and Henry Wadsworth Longfellow and Charles Hale and Charles Sumner and Francis Cabot Lowell and Bernard Malamud and Frances Sargent Osgood and Arthur M. Schlesinger Jr. and B. F. Skinner and Hannah Adams' bones all live and then I stopped for gas because the fucking light had come on and I forgot to do it earlier so my momentum was sort of waylaid. How much the guy said and I said twenty bucks please and then he put the gas in the car while I sat there silently and then I drove down to the second worst intersection I know about where Mount Auburn and Memorial Drive and Soldiers Field Road all empty into one another and I can't believe fifty people don't die a day and I got onto Storrow Drive which was backed up on account of the Boston Calling music festival was happening at Harvard Stadium.

Michelle had gone over to the concert earlier with a friend but I didn't want to go this year due to there was nothing there for me. They had Lil Nas X who does that country song people say isn't a country song and Greta Van Fleet who do those Led Zeppelin songs that people say are Led Zeppelin songs. I don't know man I'm just not going to ever go to a concert with a ferris wheel again at this point in my life. The other night I went to see my Twitter pal Mike who invented emo play a show and I didn't know what to talk to him about when we met for the first time beforehand so I talked about sports and getting old because that's what guys talk about and later on he and the band played some songs that have made me cry for about twenty years.

I met Tom Brady a couple times I told Mike before the show and then I did the thing I always do when I meet a musician I admire which is I told myself the whole time I wasn't going to ask for a selfie and then gave in and did it at the last minute anyway. It changes the energy when you are a fan of someone as opposed to just another guy standing there with a guy. I'm sorry I just want the kids at Emo Night to think I'm cool I said and that was the truth.

The rest of the way into Boston from where my bones live follows along the Charles River and since it was one of the three to four days of actual spring weather we ever get the paths were crowded with people jogging and biking and I sped along past Boston University and past Fenway and past the Back Bay where the rich people live although I guess it's probably more accurate to say anywhere in Boston is where the rich people live and I exited down by the Boston Common where the really rich people live and circled around a few times looking for parking and found a space not far from Cheers which is a bar you have probably heard of but which I've never been to which you may or may not be surprised to hear.

The other night on the local news they had the owner Tom Kershaw talking about some charity thing or other and naturally they asked him about Cheers and one thing he said was how people would come in over the years and be so excited to see the exterior of the bar that they recognized from the famous TV show and then they would go inside and be like what the fuck is this because it looked nothing like it did on TV. After years of that he finally tried to make a closer replica of the TV bar upstairs in another room. People want things to be like what they think they are like.

There were groups of tourists outside taking photos of the facade of the bar they remember from the TV show that hasn't been on in thirty years and there was a bouncer asking them not to crowd the entrance. I went downstairs into what is essentially a shitty sports pub like any other and then walked through one of the gift shops and then up some back stairs to another level where there is another gift shop and the bar made to look like the TV bar that still doesn't really look anything like it.

On yet another level upstairs there is a function hall where a wedding reception was being held and dads in pink shirts and pink faces and women in bad dangling pearls who looked like all my aunts when they would get mad at me walked arm in arm to get into the wedding reception past the paper cutouts of George Wendt and John Ratzenberger. Some day that couple will tell the story about their wedding and they'll say oh we had it at the place that one TV show Cheers was based on and the other person will say that's wild.

Have you ever been to Cheers in Boston? It used to be called the Bull & Finch Pub but is now called Cheers like the TV show. There's a guy's bones near my house called Charles Bullfinch who was one of the first American-born professional architects but I'm not sure if there's any relation there.

I used to have classes right down the street from the bar when I was at Emerson and I never went in I think because it always symbolized a sort of resignation to me or maybe it said something about Boston that I was actively trying to pretend wasn't true for a lot of my life. People want the place they live to be like what they think it is supposed to be like. In any case you do not need to go it's essentially any chain pub you would go to off the highway exit by the Target in any town you live in in America except instead of being spacious it is cramped. It is basically a money-printing factory for the owner but this is still Beacon Hill where space is at a premium and which is also where all the Boston Brahmins buried in Mount Auburn Cemetery I mentioned earlier used to live when their bones could still move.

I was trying to remember if I could remember any poems by Longfellow besides the one about Paul Revere we all know and bits of this one called "My Lost Youth" came to mind. He was writing about Portland Maine but that was still part of Massachusetts at the time so it counts. Part of it goes like this: "A boy's will is the wind's will, And the thoughts of youth are long, long thoughts."

One time a couple of years ago I went on a helicopter tour of Paul Revere's ride that started out in Concord or wherever and I would like to be able to say it was pretty cool but I was basically shitting into my pants the entire time. It was one of those tiny piss-dick helicopters with like three seats. It was smaller than a 2011 silver Toyota Corolla and it was flying through the sky. That's where they invented America the pilot would say to me pointing and I would be like ah that's wild.

Here's what happened almost five seconds after I walked into Cheers and I know this is going to sound too good to be true but someone yelled out my name. Luke! the guy said and I don't know if he was trying to do it like they did for the guy on the TV show but I didn't realize it was actually happening so I ignored it. Then the guy came over and turned out it was someone I sort of know and he said I wouldn't expect to see you here and I was like that is a fair assumption. What are you doing here are you writing a review or something he said and I said uh sort of because you can't say the truth to people you don't know that well which is something like I was depressed and I wanted to feel more depressed so I went to Cheers and guess what it worked.

So I drank my Harpoon IPA and ate some baked beans to really lean into the whole thing while "You Dropped a Bomb On Me" by the Gap Band was playing on the radio and the people around me all stared emptily at the bar that was retroactively made to look more like a fictional bar that was based on a real bar none of which are now or were ever even real. There is a picture of Lord Byron on the wall over there near where the young father was squirting ketchup onto his french fries while his children waved their arms around like little bugs turned over onto their backs and I don't know what the fuck Byron has to do with any of this it should be a portrait of Borges.

Jesus Christ hold on I just fucked up the coffee maker somehow it's leaking all over the fucking counter hold on a minute.

Goddamnit.

So the guy says to me he goes my sister was visiting so I brought her here and I said that's wild and then someone messaged me on Twitter to say she had worked at Cheers fifteen years ago and I was like what was that all about and she said most of the customers were European tourists or people from the midwest or Yankees fans who came to see a game at Fenway and this is what they thought Boston was supposed to be like.

"It was my first restaurant job," she said. "You would bust your ass for a full shift and make $100. Like if your section wasn't full all day you didn't make shit."

What else I said and she said "Everyone complained it didn't look like the show."

I drank the fucked up coffee anyway just now even though it was filled with grinds and my stomach doesn't feel very good.

"It's on in Europe, they fucking love it," she said about the show Cheers.

"It was the weirdest restaurant job I've ever had. People would ask 'Instead of lettuce and tomato on my burger can I get a cup of chowder?' like they had never eaten in a restaurant before."

Then another guy messaged me to say he had just been in earlier that same day. He had moved from Chicago to New York recently and was visiting Boston for the first time. "It felt like something that needed to be checked off the list," he said.

"It was kitschy," which was expected, he said, "but well done for a kitschy place. Our bartender was really friendly, which I always appreciate."

Then I asked him if he went over to the Boston Common to see the flags and he said he had and so I went over to look at the flags too but not before the bartender asked me if I wanted to take my mug home for an additional eight dollars and I told him no thank you not at this time.

Around the corner there were 37,000 flags planted in the grass each one of which was meant to represent "every brave Massachusetts service member who gave his or her life defending our country since the Revolutionary War" according to the group the Massachusetts Military Heroes Fund who put them there.

I guess one of those flags in there is supposed to represent Charles Russell Lowell whose bones are near my house. He was the valedictorian of Harvard in 1854 and a railroad executive and a general in the Union army and he was mortally wounded at something called the Battle of Cedar Creek in Virginia in 1864 at the age of twenty nine and I normally don't have a particularly high opinion of troops and especially generals but I guess fighting to stop the institution of slavery is about as good a reason to go to war as I've heard of. Cedar Creek and the Civil War made me think about An Occurrence at Owl Creek Bridge just now remember that shit? How much did that story fuck you up when you read that as a kid like holy shit. Ambrose Bierce was one of the first dudes in the stream of consciousness game so thanks for that buddy.

Over by the flags large groups of tourists were posing for selfies and taking pictures to post to Insta so people would know that they had been there to see a symbol of something. There was a merry-go-round spinning right next to the flags and the kids on it all seemed happy waving their little arms around like bugs riding a horse.

The flags looked beautiful I have to admit but I don't know why we make war memorials look good they should look terrible. Each of those flags is supposed to represent a noble spirit ascending to Valhalla or whatever but it's really 37,000 individual deaths in the wet mud. A war memorial should be a guy with his guts hanging out crying for his mother or a guy without a leg getting denied mental health services at the VA.

Edward Everett Hale's bones aren't near my house but his brother Charles Hale's are. He was a legislator in Massachusetts that did all sorts of shit like the time when he went to Cairo and arrested John Surratt who was an alleged conspirator of John Wilkes Booth. By the time they caught Surratt the statute of limitations on his conspiring had run out so he got away with it but his mother didn't. Mary Surratt ran a boarding house in Washington D.C. that Booth frequented and after Lincoln's assassination she was snatched up and sentenced to be hanged and this is a fun fact she was the first woman ever executed by the federal government! She maintained her innocence and her conviction was controversial and questionable at the time which is how all instances of capital punishment remain to this day so glad to see that some things remain the same.

Among all the things Edward Everett Hale probably imagined for the future of the country he loved one of them was certainly not having a statue of him decked out in a Patrice Bergeron Bruins sweater over by a food cart selling fried dough with a sign that says "Who's Ya Daddy?" and yet that is something that you could see this year if you wanted to.

I was trying to figure out what it was I was supposed to feel while looking at all those thousands of flags that someone got killed to turn into and my answer is I don't know. War is bad doesn't seem like a very novel thought but it makes me exceedingly uncomfortable whenever we honor our brave fallen heroes because every time you do that it just makes it more possible for the next group to sign up to die for what is in all likelihood not going to be such a reasonable cause as fighting to end slavery.

The Army posted a tweet the other day that was something like "what does service mean to you?" which I presume they thought was going to generate a bunch of tales of bravery and sacrifice and shit but the responses were not that at all.

Here are a few:

- I didn't serve but my brother did he never went to war but still shot himself in the head so. he was the sweetest most tender person I'll ever know and the @USArmy ruined him

- My son served and did one tour of OEF, he made it back, re-enlisted, and shot himself in the head. He was 21 years old . . .

- My brothers both served in Desert Storm. I lost my youngest brother when he took his life after not being able to cope with his PTSD. I'm losing my older brother to alcoholism and his battle with lymphoma, triggered by chemicals he was exposed to while over there.

- The Army was part of the reason my ex shook our daughter to death. That was 21 years ago. I will never be OK.

- Well my dad served two tours of Vietnam, was shot down several times, given three medals - and then, funny thing: after he got out, the VA refused to help pay for any of his medical care. He died a few weeks ago. And you sent us - a flag in a plastic bag. REAL heart-warming.

- Depression, anxiety and isolation . . . one suicide attempt and enough anger and frustration to last the rest of my short life (and then some). An "other than honorable" discharge and everyone in my chain-of-command was either releived of duty or transferred after My discharge.

- My grandpa got a serious back injury serving in the navy during the Korean War. He got addicted to pain medication and went crazy thinking aliens were in the yard. He also held a gun to my mom's head. Then he abandoned his wife and six children

- Some days all my dad can do is scream because of his war ptsd from touring pre/post 9/11. Other days he doesn't even recognize who I am, let alone my mom. His therapist said his brain will always be in war mode. Thanks for that.

- Do I get to reply for the dead? They can't type for shit anymore. My husband became an ex because of his PTSD, then he got Agent Orange cancer and died. My cousin died of Iraq chemical cancer, my other cousin is in remission from the same thing atm, and also has PTSD.

- I was forced to resign my commission while serving in Kuwait during the first Gulf War because I am gay. I received an other than honorable discharge despite excellent performance reviews. Not to mention I was exposed to low levels of exploded chemical weapons.

- My friend Jason died in Baghdad. Survived 3 car accidents there & a sniper shot to his vest insert. Died in a building that collapsed from an explosion in 2006. His younger brother was so tore up that he shot himself in the woods in front of his girlfriend & died.

I was trying to figure out why the patriotic people in America love dead troops so much but don't seem to care about the living ones due to we keep trying to send them to get hurt and die in places like Iran (?) and then when they come back we don't take care of them adequately we look the other way like they're an ex from a bad breakup we pass by on the street like oh shit.

I guess it's a lot like how they love the unborn. A dead troop and an unborn baby aren't actual people you have to take care of anymore or yet they're just an idea you can do whatever you want with and what the fuck are they going to say about it anyway their bones aren't even moving.

I HAVE DECIDED THAT SEEING THIS IS WORTH RECORDING

COULDN'T YOU HAVE ANY CHANCE OF SURVIVAL?

There's a place called Pictured Rocks National Lakeshore on Lake Superior known for its multicolored cliffs and caves and arches and rock formations that look like castles. The sandstone cliffs here are something like 500 million years old which is old even for a cliff to be. There aren't many reviews of the park on Yelp but they're all five out of five stars except for one which is four stars by Angela W. of Seattle and underneath her name it says she has no friends which I know means no friends on Yelp but is also a pretty funny thing to see under a picture of a person's smiling face. The rest of them say a lot of nice things about the cliffs and views and such. "The most beautiful hike I have even taken in my life, period," wrote Maya G. from Michigan. "Not strenuous but it does run close to 7 miles. The falls are out of this world and the lookout point will take your breath away. Not to be missed."

In September Tu Thanh Nguyen from Sunnyvale, California, was hiking here and at one point along the way she stopped to take a selfie with the water and the rocks and the sun and the sky as a backdrop behind her to post to her Instagram it's probably safe to assume. Look what a beautiful time I'm having she would show her friends and then she fell into the water 200 feet below and died in the water. We know about how she died because it's a popular kayaking area and some kayakers saw her fall and rowed over to retrieve her body. *Did you see that holy shit ah shit.*

I was just looking for stories about it on Facebook and I saw one from NBC Bay Area where people were commenting on how they'd been there and it's beautiful but very dangerous and one woman named Daniela had a question which was this:

"I don't wanna be morbid. I respect the places and it is a very sad occurrence but I have a question. If you fall that height into the water, couldn't you have any chance of survival? I don't have a very good perspective and I don't mean to be rude or anything."

Kid Rock filmed his video for the song "Born Free" here I should also mention.

In "Understanding a Photograph" John Berger differentiated photography from fine art. Any work of fine art whatever its aesthetic value is reduced into a signifier of its own scarcity. By their placement in museums sculptures and paintings were transformed into property.

"Museums function like homes of the nobility to which the public at certain hours are admitted as visitors," he wrote. "The class nature of the 'nobility' may vary, but as soon as a work is placed in a museum it acquires the mystery of a way of life which excludes the mass."

Photographs being as infinitely reproducible as they are did not suffer this same fate. They have no rarity value he wrote. They are simply a record of a thing seen.

"Photographs bear witness to a human choice being exercised in a given situation. A photograph is a result of the photographer's decision that it is worth recording that this particular event or this particular object has been seen."

Because everything that will ever happen cannot be photographed although we're certainly giving it a shot in the age of the smart phone a photograph's meaning can be divined from the choice to capture the event in question.

"The urgency of this message is not entirely dependent on the urgency of the event but neither can it be entirely independent from it. At its simplest the message, decoded, means: I have decided that seeing this is worth recording."

This is true of both remarkable events and the banal ones. A selfie in front of a fucked up looking background and a selfie in front of a gorgeous one. But Berger argued the true meaning of a photograph— which is largely derived from prior external knowledge of the objects portrayed in any case—isn't about the decision to shoot x instead of y but at x time instead of y time which by necessity leaves many other moments outside of its scope.

The only decision the photographer can take "is as regards the moment he chooses to isolate," he wrote. "Yet this apparent limitation gives the photograph its unique power. What it shows invokes what is not shown. One can look at any photograph to appreciate the truth of this. The immediate relation between what is present and what is absent is particular to each photograph: it may be that of ice to sun, of grief to a tragedy, of a smile to a pleasure, of a body to love, of a winning racehorse to the race it has run."

A photograph invokes not what is shown but what is not seen. The totality of everything else in existence is brought to mind by its absence.

At least that's what I think he was saying, who can ever really tell what these nerds are talking about half the time.

A few months before the nice lady fell into the water and died in the water a man named Prabhu Bhatara was walking home from a wedding in the Nabarangpur district of Odisha in India and he spotted an injured bear. The area doesn't look particularly scenic from what I've seen on news stories about that day but maybe the angle wasn't very good in the video so I am not going to judge. Prabhu poked and prodded at the animal and sensing that it was safe to approach he leaned in close to capture a selfie with it against the advice of his friends. The bear mauled him to death in any case and he died after that which you can watch in a video someone took from a good safe distance. You shouldn't but you could if you wanted to.

In it you can see a group of people not far off screaming out and yelling *jesus fucking christ* and such in Hindi I'm guessing and they don't really do too much to help him from what I can tell which is depressing but who's to say what anyone would do when a bear is mauling your friend. I sometimes think I could fight off a reasonably sized bear or a not exceptionally mean dog but then other times I get squeamish when I'm carving a chicken or something and you have to cut through the hard sinew there on the bottom and I think to myself I don't particularly feel like doing this anymore.

I suppose the thing that we're supposed to think when people die when they're taking selfies is that they are dumbasses and we're supposed to share the stories on Facebook and Twitter with comments such as *what a dumbass* and to be content in the knowledge that none of us would ever die while taking a selfie but a weird sort of thing happens when you turn the front-facing camera on doesn't it? Everything else in the world beyond the scope of the camera sort of disappears and you become hyper-focused on getting the shot. You become momentarily distracted by your own visage and you're fucking with the lighting and poking the screen and the fucking lighting sucks you think and you poke the screen until it doesn't suck.

A lot of people die taking selfies. From 2011 to 2017 there were at least 259 deaths while taking a selfie as a team of researchers based in India found. The mean age of the people who died was twenty-three and 72.5 percent of the people who died were men probably because men think that death is something that only happens to other people.

The most famous country to die in while taking a selfie was India followed by Russia then the U.S. then Pakistan. All of those are countries with nuclear weapons although I don't think that's related and they don't say anything about nuclear weapons in the study.

Sometimes the people who die while taking a selfie are doing something risky but other times they are murdered. In the first recorded instance in searches online for "selfie death" sixteen-year-old Mohammad Chaar was killed in a car bombing in Beirut just moments after posing in a picture with his friends.

Drowning and transport incidents such as taking a selfie in front of an approaching train and falling were the top three ways people died while taking selfies. "Also, most of the selfie-related deaths because of firearms occurred in the United States," the researchers noted but they probably didn't need to say that because no shit buddy.

"Taking selfies is considered to be a mode of self-expression in today's generation like looking in a mirror," they wrote. "Selfies are well popular among Facebook, Twitter, Instagram, and Pinterest users. It is rewarding for individuals seeing the number of likes and positive comments and this further influences them to post unique pictures which may also involve indulging in risky behavior to click selfies."

When I read that part I thought about Berger talking about museums being a "mystery of a way of life which excludes the mass," and isn't that what we're doing when we take selfies at exotic places in that we're excluding the mass who are not there. We're implying the absence of everyone else in the world but ourselves which is bullshit because at these popular attractions there are usually like fifty other people there taking the same shot but never mind because the important thing is it appears as if we are uniquely here in this place among everyone else to exist at this unique moment. And then people back home see the photo and ideally they want to have sex with us I think is the process at work there.

The researchers concluded that more attention should be paid to particularly dangerous areas where people are drawn to take selfies. "'No selfie zones' areas should be declared across tourist areas, especially places such as water bodies, mountain peaks, and over tall buildings to decrease the incidence of selfie-related deaths," they wrote. Places like the Pictured Rocks National Lakeshore I guess although I don't think you could do that for places such as The Spot Where That One Hurt Bear is Chilling Out Presently but I understand what they mean.

It's unclear what became of any of the selfies of the people who died while taking them. I wonder if any of them managed to capture the moment of their own death and the realization on their face of what was to come. The moment they transferred from the realm of the present to the absent. I wonder sometimes too if when we die we're given a camera roll to scroll through like the iPhone does for you where it arranges every captured moment of your life into location and time and the people you were there with.

I wonder if before I die I can get one last look at all my moments before I turn into nothing and whose faces would I see the most. I wonder if I would be happy with the way I look as my history flashes before my eyes or if I would say here let me see that no no delete this one I don't want this one playing in my fucking brain just as I'm about to atomize into a billion particles of absence I look fat in that one.